Lexical Commentary on the Pastoral Epistles

First Timothy

Rick Brannan

Appian Way Press

Cover photo "Codex Monacensis folio 148 verso with fragment of Matthew 21 (with a commentary)" from Wikimedia Commons:
https://commons.wikimedia.org/wiki/File:Monacensis_f.148v.jpg

Cover design by Eli Evans

Published by Appian Way Press
Web: http://AppianWayPress.com
Email: info@AppianWayPress.com

Contents

Preface

I have long had an interest in the Pastoral Epistles. In 2003, I began studying them in earnest by working through their vocabulary, outlining them, and generally digging as deep as I could.

As I worked through the vocabulary I consulted the standard lexicons. I began looking up cited examples of words occurring outside of the Greek New Testament. It didn't take me long to stand in awe of the writings of early Christian writers such as Clement of Rome, Ignatius, and Polycarp.

My eyes were opened to a new world, but it was unfortunately a world that only seems to live as seldomly-consulted citations in commentaries and lexicons. But there is explanatory power in these references. So I began on a project to explore the vocabulary of the Pastoral Epistles, consulting these very works that seem to be discounted by most. This volume on First Timothy is the result of that effort.

This work proceeded in fits and spurts for a few years, between 2003–2006. During that time, when I had material to review, I would invite a group to my house for dinner and discussion. It was really dinner and then thrash-whatever-Rick-had-written time, but it was helpful and shaped much of the form of this material. I'm grateful to Eli Evans, Vincent Setterholm, Bob Pritchett, Dale Pritchett, and Bob Friske for the hours upon hours of teaching, reproof, and correction they freely gave.

I'm also grateful to my wife, Amy, who patiently put up with me getting up early in the mornings off and on over the past 10 years to work on "wrapping up the First Timothy thing." I couldn't have done it without you.

Rick Brannan
April 2016

Series Introduction

The notion of "word studies" is viewed derisively in some circles. This is not without some merit, for so-called "word studies" are often built on poor foundations, drawing conclusions that are far afield from the texts on which they are based.

Yet examining the meanings of words, in context, is an important part of proper exegesis. This is acknowledged by those who write on the subject. Gordon Fee notes:

> In any piece of literature, words are the basic building blocks for conveying meaning. In exegesis it is especially important to remember that words function in a context. Therefore, although any given word may have a broad or narrow range of meaning, the aim of word study in exegesis is to try to understand as precisely as possible what the author was trying to convey by his use of this word in this context. Thus, for example, you cannot legitimately do a word study of σάρξ (flesh); you can only do a word study of σάρξ in 1 Cor. 5:5 or in 2 Cor. 5:16, and so on.[1]

And Donald Hagner:

> One of the most fruitful areas of study for exegesis is the study of the exceptionally rich vocabulary of the NT.[2]

Despite the necessity of word studies and the insight they provide, both Fee and Hagner are also quick to caution their readers of the dangers of word studies. These warnings must be taken to heart in order to responsibly examine the words of the New Testament in the proper context. Only upon so doing will the exegete arrive at conclusions to form the foundation of proper exegesis.

The Unique Vocabulary of the Pastoral Epistles

Of all of the epistles attributed to Paul, the three epistles known as the "Pastoral Epistles"—First Timothy, Second Timothy and Titus—exhibit the largest proportion

---

[1] Gordon D Fee, *New Testament Exegesis: A Handbook for Students and Pastors*, Third Edition. (Louisville: Westminster John Knox Press, 2002), 79.

[2] Donald A. Hagner, *New Testament Exegesis and Research: A Guide for Seminarians* (Fuller Seminary Press, 1999), 10.

of unfamiliar and infrequent words. Indeed, the Pastoral Epistles contain more *hapax legomena*[3] (proportionately) than the other Pauline epistles.

To responsibly exegete the text of the Pastoral Epistles, one must become familiar with the vocabulary. However, particularly with words that do not frequently occur in the New Testament, the examination of word meanings involves more than simply looking up words in a lexicon and choosing a gloss that seems appropriate.

The Scope of this Series

This series evaluates the vocabulary of the Pastoral Epistles in light of associated or historically proximate writings. Material that uses similar language or parallel concepts is evaluated in the hopes that such material will shed light on meanings of words and phrases in the Pastoral Epistles.

This series is not a work of exposition. It seeks to be informative, not innovative; relying on testimony of similar writings from the same general time frame or similar perspective to help establish how a particular word would have been understood in its context. This understanding is then intended to inform one's exegetical process.

Many commentaries and other works of exegesis frequently use material from secondary sources to provide background information or examples of word usage, duly noting references to such works in footnotes or endnotes. This work seeks to provide full quotations (in translation) of these works. Instead of relegating these citations to the doom of footnotes that are seldom if ever used, the cited text itself is brought into the argument for the reader to evaluate. As such, this work also serves as a functional introduction to one use of secondary sources and, for some, quite possibly as an introduction to the material itself.[4]

This work does not purport to be exhaustive in examination of such sources. However, the sources highlighted provide insight to the discussion at hand. This leads to an informed understanding of the text, which should be the goal of any such study.

---

[3] A technical term meaning words that only occur once in a given corpus (here the New Testament).

[4] For brief background on some of the secondary sources cited, please consult the *Works Cited* section below.

Works Cited from Outside the Protestant Canon

A fair portion of the cited works in this series may be unfamiliar to the reader. These works are valuable for study as they provide some historical and cultural insight. Most importantly, they provide a witness to usage of the Greek language using concepts and terminology similar to those encountered in the New Testament.

Greek Old Testament (Septuagint)

The ancient work commonly known as the Septuagint is a translation of the Hebrew Bible into Greek. It also includes non-canonical material not found in Hebrew Bible. The Greek Old Testament is valuable because it is an early witness to the text of the Hebrew Bible, and also because it is an early witness to Greek words, structures, and use. The non-canonical material is commonly called the "deuterocanon" by those in the Catholic tradition and "apocrypha" by those outside of that tradition.[5]

Deuterocanon/Apocrypha

The deuterocanon is comprised of the material from the Septuagint and Vulgate[6] that is not reflected in the Hebrew Old Testament or Greek New Testament. It is primarily of a Jewish nature, though the material is not considered canonical. Many times, this material is described as "intertestamental" and placed between the Old Testament and the New Testament in printed editions of the English Bible. The Catholic church labels this material "deuterocanonical," or part of the "second canon." The material dates from about 300 BC to perhaps 70 AD.[7]

The material is primarily historical in nature, though there are some expansions of canonical material. For example, some expansion of Esther occurs in the "Additions to Esther" (a single narrative in the LXX, typically separated from the canonical portions of Esther in English versions).

---

[5] The distinction is not so simple; there are writings such as Fourth Maccabees that both Catholic and Protestant tradition would call apocryphal (or even pseudepigraphal) and not deuterocanonical. Essentially, the deuterocanon is a fairly defined set; the apocrypha is a wider and less defined grouping that typically includes all deuterocanonical writings.

[6] The Septuagint is the Greek version of the Old Testament, the Vulgate is the Latin version of the Bible.

[7] ABD 1:292.

English translations of this material are taken from the *Lexham English Septuagint*,[8] which is a translation of H.B. Swete's edtion of the Septuagint.[9]

Old Testament Pseudepigrapha

The term "pseudepigrapha" is a compound word comprised of the two Greek words meaning "false writings." A pseudepigraphal book is one that is falsely attributed. These were typically attributed to notable figures of the Old Testament (e.g. *Testament of Judah, Martyrdom of Isaiah*) and in many instances provide additional speculative information concerning the lives of the person honored in the title.

Many of these documents were written in Greek, between 250 BC and 200 AD.[10] This material is primarily Jewish in nature though some of it is was rewritten from a Christian perspective.

There is no formal corpus for the Old Testament Pseudepigrapha, it is a loose collection of documents. Different editions include the works the editors see fit to include.

English translations of this material are taken from Charlesworth's *Old Testament Pseudepigrapha*.[11] The translations contained in Charlesworth are largely based on eclectic editions. Where possible, the translations have been checked against Penner and Heiser's *Old Testament Greek Pseudepigrapha*.[12]

Apostolic Fathers

The corpus of writings known as the "Apostolic Fathers" is a collection of documents from authors who, for the most part, succeeded the Apostles chronologically. Dated

---

[8] Rick Brannan et al., eds., *The Lexham English Septuagint* (Bellingham, WA: Lexham Press, 2012).

[9] Henry Barclay Swete, *The Old Testament in Greek: According to the Septuagint*, 3 vols. (Cambridge: Cambridge University Press, 1909).

[10] ABD 5:537.

[11] James H. Charlesworth, ed., *The Old Testament Pseudepigrapha, Vol. 1: Apocalyptic Literature and Testaments* (Garden City, N.Y: Doubleday & Company, 1983); James H. Charlesworth, ed., *The Old Testament Pseudepigrapha, Vol. 2: Expansions of the Old Testament and Legends, Wisdom and Philosophical Literature, Prayers, Psalms, and Odes, Fragments of Lost Judeo-Hellenistic Works* (Garden City, N.Y: Doubleday & Company, 1985).

[12] Ken M. Penner and Michael S. Heiser, eds., *Old Testament Greek Pseudepigrapha with Morphology* (Bellingham, WA: Lexham Press, 2008).

ranging from 80 AD through 200 AD, these documents were written in Greek and are explicitly Christian.[13]

English translations of the Apostolic Fathers are taken from *The Apostolic Fathers in English*,[14] which uses Kirsopp Lake's edition of the Greek text as basis.[15]

First Clement: A letter written to the Roman church. It is traditionally held to be written by Clement who was the leader of the church in Rome at the end of the first century, though the document itself makes no authorship claim. It is typically dated in the 90s.

Second Clement: While traditionally attributed to Clement, most today do not hold to Clementine authorship of this document. Less of an epistle and more of a homily, it is notable as an extremely early non-New-Testament example of Christian exegesis. It is typically dated in the 140s.

The Ignatian Letters: This collection of letters was written by Ignatius, the Bishop of Antioch, while he was being transported from Antioch to Rome to stand trial. He would become a martyr in Rome. These letters are mentioned by Polycarp (see below) and date back from the earliest of times. Eusebius places Ignatius' martyrdom in the middle to end of the reign of Trajan (roughly 110–117). The surviving letters of Ignatius are:

- Ignatius to the Ephesians
- Ignatius to the Magnesians
- Ignatius to Polycarp
- Ignatius to the Philadelphians
- Ignatius to the Romans
- Ignatius to the Smyrnaeans
- Ignatius to the Trallians

Polycarp to the Philippians: Polycarp was the Bishop of Smyrna. Tradition holds that he was a disciple of the Apostle John. Polycarp's letter freely quotes Scripture and the teaching of the Apostles. This letter must have been written between 110 (the probable date of Ignatius' correspondence with Polycarp) and 155 (the probable year of Polycarp's martyrdom).

---

[13] For more information on the Apostolic Fathers, see Rick Brannan, "Apostolic Fathers," ed. John D. Barry and Lazarus Wentz, *Lexham Bible Dictionary* (Bellingham, WA: Lexham Press, 2012).

[14] Rick Brannan, *The Apostolic Fathers in English* (Bellingham, WA: Lexham Press, 2012).

[15] Kirsopp Lake, *The Apostolic Fathers*, vol. 24, Loeb Classical Library (Cambridge, MA: Harvard University Press, 1912); Kirsopp Lake, *The Apostolic Fathers*, vol. 25, Loeb Classical Library (Cambridge, MA: Harvard University Press, 1912).

Martyrdom of Polycarp: This is the account of Polycarp's martyrdom, which most likely took place in 155 or 156.

Didache, or the Teaching of the Twelve Apostles: Known simply as the *Didache*, the book is a church manual from the earliest of the Christian era. It is typically dated around the year 100.

Epistle of Barnabas: This document could qualify as pseudepigraphal as its title claims Barnabas is author, but virtually no textual scholars today accept the authorship of Barnabas as possible. Date of composition is uncertain, though many scholars date the work between 118–130.

Epistle to Diognetus: Unique amongst the Apostolic Fathers due to its apologetic nature, this document provides a glimpse into how Greek pagans viewed Christianity, and how Christians portrayed themselves to Greek pagans curious about the new religion of Christianity. The author is unknown. This work is commonly dated between 150–180.

Shepherd of Hermas: This work is comparatively large. It consists of three primary parts ("Visions," "Mandates," and "Similitudes"), each containing several chapters. Scholars offer a date range from 110–140 as a probable window of composition. Based on available manuscript evidence, this writing was popular in the ancient world.

Other Literature Roughly Contemporary with the New Testament

Papyri

In the late 1800s/early 1900s, several archaeological discoveries were made in Egypt. One major find was discovery of an ancient garbage dump near the city of Oxyrhynchus. The dump contained several papyri, including many dating from the 1st century BC and 1st century AD. These papyri are collectively known as the Oxyrhyhchus Papyri and have been in the process of being published since their discovery. Over 70 volumes have been published by the Egypt Exploration Society.

In addition to the Oxyrhynchus Papyri volumes, works by Deissmann[16] and Milligan[17] have been consulted.

The Works of Josephus

Flavius Josephus was a hellenized Jew who lived and wrote during the second half of the first century AD. His corpus of material consists of four primary documents: *The Life of Flavius Josephus, Against Apion, Wars of the Jews,* and *Antiquities of the Jews.* His work is valuable as it preserves history of the period of Jewish wars and destruction of the temple. In addition, the corpus is large and therefore provides a source to compare and contrast the language used in the New Testament with Greek from the same era.

The English translation used is that of Whiston,[18] verified against Neise's Greek edition.[19]

The Works of Philo

Philo was a Jew who lived in Alexandria (Egypt). Scholars estimate he lived from 20–15 BC through 50 AD,[20] during the same time that Jesus Christ lived. As Philo is a true contemporary, then, of the New Testament writers, his extant writings in Greek are valuable to consult as witnesses for word usage along with grammatical and syntactic structures reflective of Hellenistic Greek written in a religious context.

The English translation used is that of Yonge,[21] unless otherwise stated. Greek text is taken from *The Works of Philo: Greek Text with Morphology.*[22]

---

[16] Adolf Deissmann, *Light from the Ancient East: The New Testament Illustrated by Recently Discovered Texts of the Graeco-Roman World,* trans. Lionel Richard Mortimer Strachan (London: Hodder & Stoughton, 1910).

[17] George Milligan, *Selections from the Greek Papyri: Edited with Translations and Notes* (Cambridge: Cambridge University Press, 1910); George Milligan and James Hope Moulton, Vocabulary of the Greek Testament (Peabody, Mass.: Hendrickson Publishers, 1997).

[18] Flavius Josephus, *The Works of Josephus: Complete & Unabridged,* trans. William Whiston, Later Printing edition. (Peabody, Mass: Hendrickson Publishing, 1987).

[19] Flavius Josephus, *The Works of Flavius Josephus: Greek Text with Morphology,* ed. Benedict Niese (Bellingham, WA: Lexham Press, 2008).

[20] ABD 5:333

[21] Philo of Alexandria, *The Works of Philo: Complete and Unabridged,* trans. Charles Duke Yonge (Peabody, MA: Hendrickson Publishers, 1995).

[22] Philo of Alexandria, *The Works of Philo: Greek Text with Morphology,* ed. Peder Borgen, Kåre Fuglseth, and Roald Skarsten (Bellingham, WA: Lexham Press, 2005).

Christian (New Testament) Apocrypha

Much like the pseudepigraphal writings associated with persons known from the Old Testament, there are pseudpigraphal writings associated with persons known from the New Testament. These writings are known as "New Testament Apocrypha" or "Christian Apocrypha." The Christian Apocrypha contains works in various genres also known from the New Testament: Gospels, Acts, Letters, and Apocalypses.

This work does not consult the Christian Apocrypha with frequency. When it does, it usually focuses on word usage found in non-canonical gospels. English translations of this material are taken from *Greek Apocryphal Gospels, Fragments, and Agrapha.*[23]

---

[23] Rick Brannan, *Greek Apocryphal Gospels, Fragments, and Agrapha: Introductions and Translations*, vol. 1, 2 vols. (Bellingham, WA: Lexham Press, 2013).

Conventions

There are several conventions used in the presentation of information in this commentary.

Chapter Structure

Each chapter begins with a title and reference range, such as "The Goal of the Teaching (1Ti 1:5)." Following is the translation of the range cited in the heading. The translation is from the *Lexham English Bible* (LEB)[1] and based on *The Greek New Testament: SBL Edition* (SBLGNT).[2]

Verse divisions provide the next level of structure, allowing easy reference by verse number throughout the whole of the commentary. Following the verse division, the third level of the structure is comprised of phrases or clauses from the verse under discussion, like "but the goal of our instruction" for the first section discussing 1Ti 1:5.

Discussion

Several conventions are used within passage discussion to convey information to the reader.

Dictionary forms: At the start of discussion on a passage, the dictionary (or lemma) form of a Greek word is used instead of the inflected form found in the Greek text. This allows for easy lookup in standard lexica.

Single quotes: Single quotes are used to denote glosses or word sense translations of the dictionary form of a word. These convey a quick idea of the sense of the Greek word with vocabulary not tied to the present passage.

Lexicon citations and word counts: Page number citations to the most relevant lexicon article (usually BDAG, though at times LSJ, M-M, or others) are included as footnotes, typically following the final single-quoted word gloss. These footnotes also

---

[1] Harris, W. Hall, III, Elliot Ritzema, Rick Brannan, Douglas Mangum, John Dunham, Jeffrey A. Reimer, and Micah Wierenga, eds. *The Lexham English Bible*. Bellingham, WA: Lexham Press, 2012.

[2] Holmes, Michael W. *The Greek New Testament: SBL Edition*. Lexham Press; Society of Biblical Literature, 2011–2013.

include word counts within the NT and also within the PE. These allow the reader to quickly get an idea of how common the word is in the NT and, conversely, whether the word is common in the PE or not.

Quotations: Heavy use of quoted material from the NT and from other corpora is a distinctive of this work. The goal of these citations is to show similar use of the word under discussion to build understanding of word usage. To this end, the English text that translates the Greek word or words under discussion is *italicized* if the goal of the citation is as an example of word usage.

ABBREVIATIONS

ABD	*Anchor-Yale Bible Dictionary*
BDF	*A Greek Grammar of the New Testament and Other Early Christian Literature*
BDAG	*A Greek-English Lexicon of the New Testament and Early Christian Literature, 3rd edition*
EDNT	*The Exegetical Dictionary of the New Testament*
ESV	English Standard Version
KJV	King James Version
LAE	*Light from the Ancient East*
LEB	Lexham English Bible
LN	*Greek-English Lexicon of the New Testament based on Semantic Domains*
LSJ	*A Greek-English Lexicon*
MS	manuscript
MSS	manuscripts
NA28	Novum Testamentum Graece, 28th edition
NASB95	New American Standard Version (1995)
NET	New English Translation of the Bible
NIV	New International Version
NKJV	New King James Version
NRSV	New Revised Standard Version
NT	New Testament
PE	Pastoral Epistles
RSV	Revised Standard Version
SBLGNT	The Greek New Testament, SBL Edition
TCGNT	*A Textual Commentary on the Greek New Testament*
TDNT	*Theological Dictionary of the New Testament*
UBS5	United Bible Societies' Greek New Testament, 5th edition

Bibliography

Arichea, Daniel C. ; Hatton. *A Handbook on Paul's Letters to Timothy and to Titus.* New York: United Bible Societies, 1995.

Baldwin, H. Scott. "A Difficult Word: αὐθεντέω in 1 Timothy 2:12." Page 288 in *Women in the Church: An Analysis and Application of 1 Timothy 2:9–15.* Edited by Andreas J. Köstenberger and Thomas R. Schreiner. Second Edition. Grand Rapids: Baker Academic, 2005.

Balz, Horst Robert, and Gerhard Schneider. *Exegetical Dictionary of the New Testament.* Grand Rapids, Mich.: Eerdmans, 1990–.

Bauer, Walter. *A Greek-English Lexicon of the New Testament and Other Early Christian Literature, 3rd Edition.* Edited by Frederick William Danker. 3rd ed. University Of Chicago Press, 2001.

Blass, Friedrich, Albert Debrunner, and Robert Walter Funk. *A Greek Grammar of the New Testament and Other Early Christian Literature.* Chicago: University of Chicago Press, 1961.

Brannan, Rick. "Apostolic Fathers." Edited by John D. Barry and Lazarus Wentz. *Lexham Bible Dictionary.* Bellingham, WA: Lexham Press, 2012.

———. *Greek Apocryphal Gospels, Fragments, and Agrapha: Introductions and Translations.* Vol. 1. 2 vols. Bellingham, WA: Lexham Press, 2013.

———. *The Apostolic Fathers in English.* Bellingham, WA: Lexham Press, 2012.

Brannan, Rick, Ken M. Penner, Israel Loken, Michael Aubrey, and Isaiah Hoogendyk, eds. *The Lexham English Septuagint.* Bellingham, WA: Lexham Press, 2012.

Bullinger, E. W. *The Companion Bible.* Enlarged Type edition. Grand Rapids, Mich.: Kregel Publications, 1999.

Campbell, R. Alastair. *The Elders: Seniority within Earliest Christianity.* London: T&T Clark, 2004.

Charlesworth, James H., ed. *The Old Testament Pseudepigrapha, Vol. 1: Apocalyptic Literature and Testaments.* Garden City, N.Y: Doubleday & Company, 1983.

———, ed. *The Old Testament Pseudepigrapha, Vol. 2: Expansions of the Old Testament and Legends, Wisdom and Philosophical Literature, Prayers, Psalms, and Odes, Fragments of Lost Judeo-Hellenistic Works*. Garden City, N.Y: Doubleday & Company, 1985.

Deissmann, Adolf. *Light from the Ancient East: The New Testament Illustrated by Recently Discovered Texts of the Graeco-Roman World.* Translated by Lionel Richard Mortimer Strachan. London: Hodder & Stoughton, 1910.

Deissmann, Gustav Adolf. *Bible Studies: Contributions, Chiefly from Papyri and Inscriptions, to the History of the Language, the Literature, and the Religion of Hellenistic Judaism and Primitive Christianity*. T. & T. Clark, 1923.

Ehrman, Bart D. *Apostolic Fathers: Volume II. Epistle of Barnabas. Papias and Quadratus. Epistle to Diognetus. The Shepherd of Hermas*. New edition. Loeb Classical Library 25N. Cambridge, Mass: Harvard University Press, 2003.

Ellicott, Charles J. *The Pastoral Epistles of St. Paul : With a Critical and Grammatical Commentary, and a Revised Translation*. Bellingham, WA: Logos Research Systems, Inc., 2008.

Fee, Gordon D. *New Testament Exegesis: A Handbook for Students and Pastors*. Third Edition. Louisville: Westminster John Knox Press, 2002.

Flavius Josephus. *The Works of Flavius Josephus: Greek Text with Morphology*. Edited by Benedict Niese. Bellingham, WA: Lexham Press, 2008.

Friedman, David Noel, ed. *The Anchor Yale Bible Dictionary*. 6 vols. New York: Bantam Doubleday Dell Publishing Group, Inc., 1992.

Gill, David W.J., "A Saviour for the Cities of Crete: The Roman Background to the Epistle to Titus" in Williams, P.J., et. al., *The New Testament in its First Century Setting: Essays on Context and Background in Honour of B.W. Winter on His 65th Birthday*. Grand Rapids: Eerdmans, 2004.

Hagner, Donald A. *New Testament Exegesis and Research: A Guide for Seminarians*. Fuller Seminary Press, 1999.

Harris, W. Hall, III, Elliot Ritzema, Rick Brannan, Douglas Mangum, John Dunham, Jeffrey A. Reimer, and Micah Wierenga, eds. *The Lexham English Bible*. Bellingham, WA: Lexham Press, 2012.

Holmes, Michael W. *The Greek New Testament: SBL Edition*. Lexham Press; Society of Biblical Literature, 2011–2013.

Hort, Fenton John Anthony. *The Christian Ecclesia: A Course of Lectures on the Early History and Early Conceptions of the Ecclesia.* London: Macmillan & Co, 1897.

Johnson, Luke Timothy. *The First and Second Letters to Timothy: A New Translation with Introduction and Commentary.* New Haven; London: Yale University Press, 2008.

Josephus, Flavius. *The Works of Josephus: Complete & Unabridged.* Translated by William Whiston. Later Printing edition. Peabody, Mass: Hendrickson Publishing, 1987.

Kittel, Gerhard, Geoffrey W. Bromiley, and Gerhard Friedrich, eds. *Theological Dictionary of the New Testament.* Grand Rapids, MI: Eerdmans, 1964–.

Klauck, Hans-Josef. *Ancient Letters and the New Testament: A Guide to Context and Exegesis.* Baylor University Press, 2006.

Knight, George W. *The Pastoral Epistles : A Commentary on the Greek Text.* New International Greek Testament Commentary. Grand Rapids, Mich.; Carlisle, England: W.B. Eerdmans; Paternoster Press, 1992.

Lake, Kirsopp. *The Apostolic Fathers.* Vol. 24. Loeb Classical Library. Cambridge, MA: Harvard University Press, 1912.

———. *The Apostolic Fathers.* Vol. 25. Loeb Classical Library. Cambridge, MA: Harvard University Press, 1912.

Liddell, Henry George, Robert Scott, Henry Stuart Jones, and Roderick McKenzie. *A Greek-English Lexicon.* Oxford: Clarendon Press, 1996.

Louw, Johannes P., and Eugene Albert Nida. *Greek-English Lexicon of the New Testament: Based on Semantic Domains.* New York: United Bible Societies, 1996.

Lust, Johan, Erik Eynikel, and Katrin Hauspie. *Greek-English Lexicon of the Septuagint.* Rev Blg. Hendrickson Pub, 2008.

Meecham, H. G. *The Epistle to Diognetus: The Greek Text with Introduction, Translation and Notes.* Manchester: Manchester University Press, 1949.

Metzger, Bruce M., ed. *A Textual Commentary on the Greek New Testament.* 2 Revised. London; New York: United Bible Societies, 1994.

Milligan, George. *Selections from the Greek Papyri: Edited with Translations and Notes.* Cambridge: Cambridge University Press, 1910.

Moo, Douglas J. "1 Timothy 2:11–15: Meaning and Significance." *Trinity J.* 1 (1980): 61–83.

Moulton, James Hope, and George Milligan. *The Vocabulary of the Greek Testament*. London: Hodder and Stoughton, 1930.

Penner, Ken M., and Michael S. Heiser, eds. *Old Testament Greek Pseudepigrapha with Morphology*. Bellingham, WA: Lexham Press, 2008.

Philo of Alexandria. *The Works of Philo: Complete and Unabridged*. Translated by Charles Duke Yonge. Peabody, MA: Hendrickson Publishers, 1995.

———. *The Works of Philo: Greek Text with Morphology*. Edited by Peder Borgen, Kåre Fuglseth, and Roald Skarsten. Bellingham, WA: Lexham Press, 2005.

Swanson, James. *Dictionary of Biblical Languages with Semantic Domains: Greek (New Testament)*. Oak Harbor: Logos Research Systems, Inc., 1997.

Swete, Henry Barclay. *The Old Testament in Greek: According to the Septuagint*. 3 vols. Cambridge: Cambridge University Press, 1909.

Wolters, Al. "A Semantic Study of αὐθέντης and Its Derivatives." *J. Greco-Roman Christ. Jud.* 1 (2000): 145–75.

Zerwick, Maximilian. *Biblical Greek, Illustrated by Examples, English Edition, Adapted from the Fourth Latin Edition*. Translated by Joseph Smith. Rome: Pontifical Biblical Institute, 1963.

FIRST TIMOTHY

Paul's Greeting (1Ti 1:1–2)

Paul, an apostle of Christ Jesus according to the command of God our Savior and of Christ Jesus our hope, to Timothy, my true child in the faith. Grace, mercy, and peace from God the Father and Christ Jesus our Lord. (1Ti 1:1–2)

Verse 1

Paul, an apostle of Christ Jesus

Paul begins his first letter to Timothy by announcing himself as writer and by sending greetings to the recipient. He uses an expanded form of the typical epistolary salutation. These salutations consisted of mention of the sender/author, followed by mention of the recipient, followed by a greeting or salutation of some sort.[1]

Paul states that he is "an apostle." He intends this as a title. This is a claim of authority for the message that follows.

In very general terms, an apostle (ἀπόστολος) is an ambassador, sent with the authority of someone else.[2] When the ambassador speaks, he speaks for the one who sent him. The same is true with Paul. When Paul writes these words, they are as if they have come from the one who sent him. The same language is used outside of the New Testament as well:

> Therefore it is necessary (just as you already do) for you to do nothing without the bishop, but be subject also to the council of elders as to *the apostles of Jesus Christ* our hope. If we live in him, we will be found in him. (Ign., *Trall.* 2.2)

In his letter to the Trallians, Ignatius (the bishop of Antoich) encourages the recipients to be subject to the elders in the same way that they consider themselves subject to the "apostles of Jesus Christ," reinforcing the idea that the authority of the apostles is valid and that it is based on the one who sends them.

---

[1] Hans-Josef Klauck, *Ancient Letters and the New Testament: A Guide to Context and Exegesis* (Baylor University Press, 2006), 17–27.

[2] BDAG, p. 122. Occurs 79x in NT. 5x in PE: 1Ti 1:1; 2:7; 2 Tim. 1:1, 11; Tt 1:1.

according to the command of God our Savior

The word translated "command" (ἐπιταγή) was also used in ancient inscriptions, where it pertains to "oracles or divine commands."[3] Paul reminds those reading the letter that he is acting in submission to the command (ἐπιταγή) of God.

The phrase "God our Savior" occurs infrequently in the New Testament, primarily in the Pastoral Epistles.[4] Similar phrases occur in the LXX though the usage is not always consistent. An example similar to usage in the Pastoral Epistles occurs in Psalm 24:

> This one will receive a blessing from the Lord and mercy from *God, his savior*. (Ps 24:5 [LXX 23:5])[5]

Consider also Third Maccabees:

> Set free the sons of the almighty living God in heaven, who from our ancestors until now produced an unimpeded stability with glory in our state affairs. Now indeed the king chose these things; and those who were unbound immediately praised *their holy, savior God*, having escaped now death. (3Ma 6:28–29)

In this case, God is praised explicitly because He had literally delivered these people from certain immediate death. Without divine intervention, they would have been killed. The term "savior" (σωτήρ)[6] describes what God has just accomplished. However, in the Psalms and the Pastoral Epistles, the whole phrase "God our Savior" is used as a sort of title.

Ascribing the title of savior to deity was not a strange thing to do in ancient Greece. The history of this usage is easily traced back to at least the fourth century B.C. where it was used to render thanks to Zeus for safe travels. The same terminology soon came to be used of other Greek deities.

The term σωτήρ was also used to describe rulers such as the emperor or provincial governors. This is not strange in light of the claim to some sort of deity of many of these rulers. In some locales the subjects of the emperor were known to worship the

---

[3] LSJ, p. 663, ἐπιταγή. Occurs 7x in NT; 3x in PE: 1Ti 1:1; Tt 1:3; 2:15.

[4] The phrase "God our Savior" or similar phrasing is found in 1Ti 1:1; 2:3; 4:10; Tt 1:3; 2:10, 13; 3:4. Note, however, Lk 1:47 and Jude 1:25.

[5] Note "savior" could also be translated as "deliverer." The Hebrew Bible typically has something like "the God of our salvation" in such instances.

[6] LSJ, p. 1751, σωτήρ. Occurs 24x in NT; 10x in PE.

emperor as a god.[7] An inscription dated 48 AD records the town council of Ephesus acclaiming Julius Caesar as "manifest god and common savior of living people."[8] [9]

In the context of 1 Timothy, however, Paul is establishing the importance of the one who called him to the role as apostle. He says that God, the one who saves us, is the one who placed him in the role of apostle. He says that he speaks with the authority of the one who called him. The potential allusion to emperors or governors who style themselves as savior of those they rule is convenient. While the allusion may be intended, this cannot be known for sure.

and of Christ Jesus our hope

The term "Christ Jesus" identifies "our hope" (ἐλπίς):[10] Jesus, the Messiah, the Son of God is the source of hope of salvation. As Paul instructs in his epistle to the Romans, salvation provides the hope of redemption of the body.

> For in this hope [redemption of the body] we were saved. Now hope that is seen is not hope. For who hopes for what he sees? But if we hope for what we do not see, we wait for it with patience. (Ro 8:24–25)

Recalling even the name of Christ, the Messiah, should give cause to recall this hope: Jesus Christ saves sinners.[11] This same hope was appealed to in Ign., *Trall.* 2.2, examined earlier. And similar language occurs in the *Apostolic Constitutions:*[12]

> You have loosed the boundary of death,
> You who are the Maker of life for the dead, *through Jesus Christ, our hope!* (*Const. Apost.* 7.34.8, emphasis added)

He is the foundation of hope, not the object of it. This same Jesus, the Messiah, has in conjunction with God the Father called Paul to the office of apostle.

---

[7] LSJ (p. 1751) notes a citation from *Greek Papyri in the British Museum* (1.177.24), dated in the first century A.D., which uses σωτήρ to refer to a ruler. Other references to inscriptions and papyri show such terminology was not exceptional. Inscriptions dating to the third century B.C. confirm this.

[8] Milligan and Moulton, *Vocabulary of the Greek Testament*, 621.

[9] Author's translation of the inscription: θεὸν ἐπιφανῆ καὶ κοινὸν τοῦ ἀνθρωπίνου βίου σωτῆρα. Note that "manifest" could also perhaps be translated as "incarnate."

[10] BDAG, p. 319, ἐλπίς. Occurs 53x in NT; 4x in PE.

[11] Cf 1Ti 1:15.

[12] Later cited in the *Hellenistic Synagogal Prayers* (*SynPryrs* 3.27).

Verse 2

to Timothy

Paul writes this letter to Timothy, his longtime co-worker and friend. Timothy is frequently mentioned in the New Testament.[13] Though Timothy is the formal addressee of this letter, Timothy is not the only intended reader. The community of believers at Ephesus is the intended audience for these words.

Paul encountered Timothy in Lystra (Ac 16:1–5). He was already a disciple (μαθητής), most likely due to his mother's influence. His father was a Greek (Ελληνος), which could be either "one who participates in Greek culture, but not necessarily an ethnic Greek,"[14] or perhaps a Gentile. Other believers in the area knew of Timothy and thought highly of him.[15] Paul invited Timothy to join him and his ministry. This ministry is clearly outlined in Acts:

> As they went on their way through the cities, they delivered to them for observance the decisions that had been reached by the apostles and elders who were in Jerusalem. So the churches were strengthened in the faith, and they increased in numbers daily. (Ac 16:4–5)

Timothy, then, was most likely a companion of and co-worker with Paul from the early 50's through the time of Paul's death.[16]

my true child in the faith

Timothy had been a companion and co-worker of Paul's for perhaps a decade, yet Paul refers to Timothy as his "true child." The Greek word translated "child" is τέκνον and is used in a number of different contexts in the Greek New Testament.[17] Some instances have to do with a physical relationship between a parent and child (*e.g.* Lk 1:7), but as several other instances presuppose a non-parental relationship (*e.g.* Mt 9:2; 2Jn 4).

---

[13] In epistolary salutations: co-sender in 2Co 1:1; Php 1:1; Col 1:1; 1Th 1:1; 2Th 1:1; Phm 1; recipient in 1Ti 1:2 and 2Ti 1:2.

[14] James Swanson, *Dictionary of Biblical Languages with Semantic Domains: Greek (New Testament)* (Oak Harbor: Logos Research Systems, Inc., 1997).

[15] μαρτυρέω, which means to provide witness or speak well of.

[16] The traditional date of authorship of 1 Thessalonians, in which Timothy is mentioned as a co-sender, is in the early 50's, perhaps even the late 40's. Paul's death is traditionally held to have occurred in the mid 60's.

[17] BDAG, p. 994. Occurs 99x in NT, 9x in PE, 1x in Philemon.

When Paul refers to Timothy as his "true child," he uses the word γνήσιος. This word is not simply the opposite of "false," but carries a rather different meaning: that of legitimate or genuine.[18] One of the earliest Greek papyri known is a marriage contract that uses this word to describe the new relationship of the husband and wife:

> Heraclides takes Demetria of Cos as his *lawful* wife from her father Leptines of Cos and her mother Philotis, ... (Elephantine Papyrus 1, emphasis added)[19]

Paul also used the word γνήσιος in Philippians 4:3:

> Yes, I ask also you, *true* yokefellow, help them, who struggled along with me in the gospel with both Clement and the rest of my fellow workers whose names are in the book of life. (Php 4:3, emphasis added).

The figurative sense of γνήσιος is further expanded:

> In the Hellenic world ancestral connections were highly prized; hence this term referred originally to having connection with the γένος by birth: 'belonging to the race.' Hence literally of children *born in wedlock, legitimate* ... figuratively, of affective relationship, especially as developed through sharing of values or experiences.[20]

With Paul's claim that Timothy is his "true child in the faith," Paul establishes Timothy's authority to act to rectify the situation at the church in Ephesus. This is as if Paul is sending his son in his place (Luke 20:13) in order that his agent (Timothy) will be respected as if he were Paul himself.

Grace, mercy, and peace from God the Father and Christ Jesus our Lord

Of the Pauline greetings, only the Pastoral Epistles[21] contain the threefold greeting of "Grace, mercy, and peace." Other Pauline Epistles contain some variation of "Grace to you and peace."

These are more than simply kind words from Paul as he proceeds to tie them to their source: "God the Father and Christ Jesus our Lord." He sincerely desires for the readers of this letter to experience the grace, mercy and peace that he has experienced as a result of his own salvation.

---

[18] BDAG, p. 202. Occurs 4x in NT: Php 4:3; 2Co 8:8; 1Ti 1:2; Tt 1:4.

[19] Milligan, *Selections from the Greek Papyri*, 2. Elephantine Papyrus 1, circa B.C. 311–310.

[20] BDAG, p. 202.

[21] Here and in 2Ti 1:2. The phrase "grace, mercy, and peace" is used in the Johannine greeting of 2Jn 3. See Wis 3:9; 4:15 and also *1Cl inscriptio*, Ign., *Smyrn. 12.2*, *Mart. Poly. inscriptio*.

Background (1Ti 1:3–4)

Just as I urged you when I traveled to Macedonia, remain in Ephesus, so that you may instruct certain people not to teach other doctrine, and not to pay attention to myths and endless genealogies, which cause useless speculations rather than God's plan that is by faith. (1Ti 1:3–4)

Verse 3

Just as I urged you ... remain in Ephesus

Paul uses the phrase "as I urged you." The word translated "I urged" is the Greek word παρακαλέω.[1] Paul uses similar language with the Ephesians in his earlier letter to the church there:

> Therefore I, the prisoner in the Lord, *exhort* you to live in a manner worthy of the calling with which you were called (Eph. 4:1, emphasis added)

Similar language is used by Ignatius in his letter to the Philadelphians:

> But *I urge* you to do nothing according to selfish ambition but according to the teaching of Christ. (Ign., *Phld.* 8.2, emphasis added)

An exhortation is a call to action. It is usually paired with the action itself. In 1Ti 1:3, the action is to "remain in Ephesus." The word translated 'remain' is the Greek word προσμένω. Here the sense is that of 'to stay with.'[2] When paired with a location, the verb indicates staying in a particular place. Here is an example of a similar structure from the *Sibylline Oracles*:

> A terrible wrath will also come upon Phrygia because of the pain for which Rhea, mother of Zeus, came and *remained* there. (*Sib. Or.* 5.131, emphasis added)

Paul intends for Timothy to stay in Ephesus, and reminds him of this in no uncertain terms.

---

[1] BDAG p. 764. Occurs 109x in NT, 8x in PE.

[2] BDAG, p. 883. Occurs 7x in NT; 2x in PE: 1Ti 1:3; 5:5.

when I traveled to Macedonia

Many translations insert this circumstantial participle between "I urged you" and "remain in Ephesus." Functionally it clues the readers in to a previous conversation between Paul and Timothy about Ephesus. The word translated "when I traveled" is πορεύομαι.[3] It is common in travel narratives found in Luke and Acts. The word also occurs in Hermas' *Shepherd*:

> *While I was traveling* around the countryside, about the time as last year, walking I remembered the vision of last year, and again the spirit took me away and carried me to the same place as last year. (Hermas, *Visions* II, i, 1, emphasis added)

This instance in Hermas and the instance in 1 Timothy are both modified by a prepositional phrase giving the location of travels; in Hermas it is "around the countryside," in 1 Timothy it is "in Macedonia."

so that you may instruct certain people

The word translated "instruct" is παραγγέλλω.[4] This word typically means to 'instruct or command.'[5] It is in the second person singular; meaning Paul is directly addressing the primary reader, Timothy. Josephus uses the same word in much the same way in his *Antiquities of the Jews*:

> I therefore *charge* you, that you do not, for the time to come, seek for any occasion of sedition or disturbance, but that everyone be allowed to follow their own religious customs. (Jos., *Ant.* 19.311, emphasis added).

Here one party is directing another to ensure that a particular instruction is carried out among a larger group of people. The situation is much the same between Paul and Timothy. Paul intends for Timothy to personally deal with these "certain persons" who are causing problems.

not to teach other doctrine

In this one phrase, the primary problem in the Ephesian church is disclosed. There were teachers in Ephesus claiming to be Christian whose teaching was not Christian. Details of the "different doctrine" are not disclosed at this point; the only detail is

---

[3] BDAG, p. 853. Occurs 153x in NT, 2x in PE: 1Ti 1:3; 2 Ti 4;10.

[4] Cf. comments on 1Ti 1:5 and 1Ti 1:18.

[5] BDAG, p. 760. Occurs 32x in NT; 5x in PE: 1Ti 1:3; 4:11; 5:11; 6:13, 17.

the Greek word translated as "different doctrine": ἑτεροδιδασκαλέω.[6] It means to teach otherwise or to teach differently. The word also occurs in Ignatius' letter to Polycarp:

> Those who appear to be trustworthy yet *teach strange doctrines*, do not let them amaze you. Stand firm, like an anvil being struck with a hammer. It is the mark of a great athlete to endure punishment and to achieve victory. But especially for God's sake we must endure all things, so that he may also endure us. (Ign., *Poly.* 1.3, emphasis added)

This word assumes a previous standard (doctrine, in Christian terms) and that the teaching going on is contrary to the established standard. Paul, as the party responsible for establishing the proper standard of doctrine within the Ephesian church, desires the improper teaching to cease. Paul's interest is that Timothy approach the specific parties responsible for promulgating erroneous teaching and ensure that they are either immediately corrected or removed from the fellowship.[7]

This problem of pursuing "different doctrine" was not unique to the Ephesians. Paul wrote to the Galatians concerning this problem as well:

> I am astonished that you are turning away so quickly from the one who called you by the grace of Christ to a different gospel, not that there is a different gospel, except there are some who are disturbing you and wanting to distort the gospel of Christ. But even if we or an angel from heaven should proclaim a gospel to you contrary to what we proclaimed to you, let him be accursed! As we said before, and now I say again, if anyone is proclaiming a gospel to you contrary to what you have received, let him be accursed! (Ga 1:6–9)

As with the Galatian Christians, Paul desires the eradication of doctrine opposed to the gospel. This is one of Timothy's primary responsibilities in his ministry to the Ephesian believers.

Verse 4

and not to pay attention to myths and endless genealogies

What are these myths and endless genealogies?[8] Tt 1:14 classifies myths plaguing the Cretan fellowship as "Jewish" (Ιουδαϊκοῖς), but this classification cannot be blindly

---

[6] BDAG, p. 399. Occurs 2x in NT: 1Ti 1:3; 6:3

[7] Cf. comment on 1Ti 1:20.

[8] Myths are mentioned four times (1Ti 1:4; 4:7; 2Ti 4:4; Tt 1:14) and genealogies are mentioned twice (1Ti 1:4; Tt 3:9).

applied to the style of myth encountered in Ephesus. Ephesus is also known for prevalent worship of the goddess Diana, who was worshiped by pagan Greeks as Artemis (Acts 19:24–29). In addition to worship of Artemis, the cult of emperor worship took hold in Ephesus at an early date and perhaps to a greater degree than in even Rome.[9] Any or all of these sorts of cultic practices could be legitimately classified as myth or fable or legend of some sort, especially when contrasted with the further clarification Paul gives later in the verse. The word translated "myths" (μῦθος) is of no further help, it simply denotes 'a myth, legend, or other fictional sort of story or tale.'[10]

Beyond speculation, not much is known regarding the "endless genealogies." The Greek word γενεαλογία is classically defined as 'tracing a pedigree.'[11] Tracing of the family line, for some reason, had become obsessive. Paul uses the adjective "endless" (ἀπέραντος) to describe this pedigree-tracing.[12] The word only occurs here in the New Testament, but does occur elsewhere. One instance is found in the LXX of Job:

> Behold, the Almighty is great, and we shall not know him. The number of his years is even *infinite.* (Job 36:26, LXX, emphasis added)

It also is used in *First Clement*:

> The ocean (*endless* to humans) and the worlds beyond it are governed by the same commands of the Master. (*1Cl* 20.8, emphasis added)

The logical conclusion is that lineage had, for some reason, become important amongst the Ephesian believers, and that they were spending endless amounts of time tracing lineage.

which cause useless speculations

The "useless speculations" detract from the gospel. The Greek word is ἐκζήτησις, which only occurs here in the New Testament.[13] It is translated "useless speculations" here as it is a plural. The word does not occur in contemporary literature such as the writings of the Apostolic Fathers, or in the Works of Josephus for Philo.

---

[9] Regarding emperor worship in Ephesus circa 90 AD, see *The Face of New Testament Studies: A Survey of Recent Research*, pp. 52–54.

[10] BDAG, p. 660. Occurs 5x in NT: 1Ti 1:4; 4:7; 2Ti 4:4; Tt 1:14; 2Pe 1:16.

[11] LSJ, p. 343, cf. BDAG, p. 192. 2x in NT, both in PE: 1Ti 1:4; Tt 3:9.

[12] BDAG, p. 101. Only here in the NT.

[13] BDAG, p. 303. Only here in the NT.

The non-prefixed form of the word (ζήτησις) does occur in the NT,[14] notably in Tt 3:9, a passage similar to this one:

> But avoid foolish *controversies* and genealogies and contentions and quarrels about the law, for they are useless and fruitless. (Tt 3:9, emphasis added)

In that passage, "foolish" comes from a different Greek word (μωρός), but similar ideas are communicated. These are disputes or controversies that serve no purpose. The same basic idea is present with ἐκζήτησις in 1Ti 1:4. The ἐκ- prefix functions to strengthen the word and confirm that the explorations serve no purpose. This is more than a simple investigation based on the evidence at hand.

These speculations, promoted by the previously mentioned myths and endless genealogies, have consumed the attention of the Ephesian believers. The word translated "cause" is παρέχω, which means 'bring about' in this setting. The word is used similarly in Acts 16:

> As we were going to the place of prayer, we were met by a slave girl who had a spirit of divination and *brought* her owners much gain by fortune-telling. (Ac 16:16, emphasis added)

In this situation, the slave girl produced gain for her owners. The word also occurs in Ignatius' letter to the Ephesians:

> Therefore how was he made known to the ages? A star in heaven shone brighter than the rest of the stars, and its light was inexpressible, and its newness *caused* astonishment. (Ign., *Eph.* 19.2, emphasis added)

Here, the astonishment is a result of the appearance of the star, hence the translation "caused." A similar usage is recorded in the *Shepherd of Hermas*:

> Therefore take the power, which comes from above. The hail is a very small, tiny grain and when it falls upon someone's head, how much pain *it causes*! (Hermas, *Mandates* XI, 20, emphasis added)

Here as well, παρέχω is used to indicate the result of some occasion. This time, it is describing the pain that results from a hailstone, small though it may be, striking a person on the head. In a similar way, "speculations" are caused by the focus on endless myths and genealogies.

---

[14] BDAG, p. 428. 7x in NT, 3x in PE: 1Ti 6:4; 2Ti 2:23; Tt 3:9.

rather than God's plan that is by faith.

The concept of "God's plan" (οἰκονομίαν θεοῦ) deserves examination. The Greek word translated "plan" is οἰκονομία.[15] One lexicon notes that in this context οἰκονομία means 'training in the way of salvation' and recommends this phrase be rendered as 'divine training.'[16] NET translates this phrase as "God's redemptive plan." These meanings are plausible but somewhat removed from the general meaning of οἰκονομία, which is the work or output of an οἰκονόμος. An οἰκονόμος is a household manager, one who allocates the resources of the household according to the owner's wishes and ensures the smooth running of the household. Consider this example from 2Ki 18:

> They shouted to Hezekiah, and Eliakim the son of Hilkiah, the *steward*, Shebnah the scribe, and Jehosaphat the recorder went to him. (2Ki 18:18 [LXX 4Kgdms 18:18], emphasis added)

In the above context, Hezekiah is the king of Judah and Eliakim is his οἰκονόμος. Eliakim was the king's household manager. He is the one who made sure the house of the king ran smoothly. And, in the above context, Eliakim is one of those sent out to meet Sennacherib's army, listen to the words of the leader of the army, and report back to Hezekiah. Eliakim, as steward, had tremendous responsibility before the king.

If the οἰκονόμος is the manager or steward of a household, the οἰκονομία is the work or plan by which the household is run. The phrase οἰκονομίαν θεοῦ, then, refers to the stewardship of God's own house. This is where the ideas of "training in the way of salvation," "divine training" and "God's redemptive plan" come from.

The word οἰκονομία is used in the parable of the dishonest steward as recorded in Luke 16:

> And he called him and said to him, 'What is this that I hear about you? Turn in the account of your *management*, for you can no longer be manager.' And the manager said to himself, 'What shall I do, since my master is taking the *management* away from me? I am not strong enough to dig, and I am ashamed to beg. I have decided what to do, so that when I am removed from *management*, people may receive me into their houses.' (Lk 16:2–4, emphasis added)

In these three verses, the word οἰκονομία occurs three times. In each instance above, οἰκονομία refers to the responsibility of the manager to properly oversee the use of

---

[15] The English words economy and economics (which have to do with the efficient allocation of resources) come from this Greek term.

[16] BDAG, p. 698. Occurs 9x in NT, only here in the PE.

his master's resources. In the example of the dishonest steward, improper oversight of resources (poor stewardship) led to the dismissal of the steward.

Further understanding of οἰκονομία comes from examining its usage in the *Letter to Diognetus*. Speaking of Christians, the author of this letter writes:

> For as I have said this is no earthly discovery handed over to them, nor do they desire to guard a mortal thought so carefully, nor have they been entrusted with *the management* of human mysteries.[17] (*Ep. Diog.* 7.1, emphasis added)

While the object of stewardship (or management) in this example is different than in 1Ti 1:4, the general syntax of the phrase is the same—with οἰκονομία in the accusative and the surrounding nouns in the genitive case. Note Meecham's discussion of the word:

> The word οἰκονομία extends its meaning from 'management of a household' to management or provision in general (cf. [*Ep.Diog.*] 7.1). It came to be used of the various operations of the divine will, particularly of God's 'dispensation' effected in Christ for the salvation of men. [18]

This stewardship from God is qualified as being that which is by faith. God's plan operates on the basis of faith. In other words, faith is the currency that is used in the economy of God.

---

[17] Brannan, *The Apostolic Fathers in English*.

[18] H. G. Meecham, *The Epistle to Diognetus: The Greek Text with Introduction, Translation and Notes* (Manchester: Manchester University Press, 1949), 106. This discussion is in his note for *Ep. Diog.* 4.6, not 7.1.

The Goal of the Teaching (1Ti 1:5)

But the goal of our instruction is love from a pure heart and a good conscience and a faith without hypocrisy (1Ti 1:5)

Verse 5

but the goal of our instruction

The word translated "goal" is τέλος. The basic meaning is that of 'end, finish, or termination;'[1] though τέλος developed many supplemental and context-sensitive meanings over time. In this context, the meaning of 'aim' or 'goal' is appropriate as the context indicates that it is the end of the effort, thus the purpose or reason for expending the effort. The word translated "instruction" is παραγγελία, which is less common in the New Testament. The basic sense of the word is that of a message that essentially commands or orders someone (or a group) to do something.[2] This is commonly known as a charge. Consider *First Clement*:

> Therefore, having received *commands* and being fully convinced by the resurrection of our Lord Jesus Christ, and full of faith in the word of God, they went forth with the full assurance of the Holy Spirit, proclaiming the gospel, that the kingdom of God was about to come. (*1Cl* 42.3, emphasis added)

Here the charge or παραγγελία is received by the apostles and dutifully acted upon.

Paul does not establish a new charge for Timothy, but rather confirms that the charge is a common one.[3] Paul includes Timothy in the fulfillment of the charge that has been laid on him by none other than Christ Jesus. Paul sets Timothy's goal in service to the Ephesian fellowship: to oppose the false teachers, myths, and endless genealogies of verses 3–4.

---

[1] BDAG, p. 998. Occurs 40x in NT, only here in PE.

[2] BDAG, p. 760. Occurs 5x in NT, 2x in PE: 1Ti 1:5, 18. The verb form of this word occurs in 1Ti 1:3. Cf. comments on both 1Ti 1:3 and 1Ti 1:18.

[3] Note that the charge is actually being explained and clarified from 1Ti 1:5 all the way through 1Ti 1:18. The basics of the charge, however, are in 1Ti 1:3–7.

is love from a pure heart

The phrase "a pure heart" is relatively straightforward in its meaning. The word for "pure" (καθαρός) generally means 'clean' though it does have some ceremonial, ritual and religious undertones in its primary senses.[4] This leads to the preference of the translation "pure" instead of simply "clean" in this instance. This is the same language used in Ps 51:10 (LXX 50:12) when David pleads to God for mercy:

> Create in me a *clean* heart, O God, and renew a right spirit in my inward parts. (Ps 51:10 [LXX 50:12], emphasis added)

The word for "heart" (καρδία) eventually becomes shorthand for all that "heart" actually means when it occurs in this sort of context. That is, καρδία refers to the figurative usage and assumes that the heart is the center or seat of 'physical, spiritual and mental life.'[5] Its literal meaning is minimized and the figurative meaning becomes primary. Paul indicates that one's innermost motivation must not be for impure motives, but rather for pure motives. Love is a result of these pure motives.

and a good conscience

Paul next mentions "a good conscience." The word translated "good" (ἀγαθός) is a common word expressing the concept of good or goodness.[6] The word for "conscience" (συνείδησις) has to do with being aware of information concerning something. The primary sense, however, seems to be a bit more refined and carries the connotation of moral consciousness or conscience. These imply the idea of not only knowledge but the ability to discern right from wrong.[7]

Paul used this phrase in his testimony before the Sanhedrin, as is recorded in the book of Acts:

> And looking intently at the Sanhedrin, Paul said, "Men and brothers, I have lived my life in all *good conscience* before God to this day." So the high priest Ananias ordered those standing near him to strike his mouth. (Ac 23:1–2, emphasis added)

Paul is not weighed down by guilt from things he has done in the past, he instead considers his conscience clear. A similar usage is found in *First Clement*:

---

[4] BDAG, p. 489. Occurs 27x in NT, 7x in PE.

[5] BDAG, p. 508. Occurs 156x in NT, 2x in PE: 1Ti 1:5, 2Ti 2:22.

[6] BDAG, p. 3. Occurs 102x in NT, 10x in PE.

[7] BDAG, p. 967. Occurs 30x in NT, 6x in PE: 1Ti 1:5, 19; 3:9; 4:2; 2Ti 1:3; Tt 1:15.

> Each of us, brothers, in his own group, must be pleasing to God, being in *good conscience*, not going beyond the appointed rule of his ministry, with dignity. (*1Cl* 41.1, emphasis added)

In *First Clement*, the "good conscience" helps keep one's mind on the task at hand. It allows one to focus on pursuing what is proper, and to dismiss what is not.

Paul desires for the Ephesian believers to have an innate ability to discern proper teaching from improper. At the time of the writing of this epistle, the Ephesians did not have this ability. They were falling prey to heretical teachers and false prophets. A "good conscience" contributes to the ability to discern proper teaching from improper teaching, hence Paul's desire to instill "a good conscience" in them.

and a faith without hypocrisy

Finally, Paul mentions "a sincere faith." Faith, in this context, carries the sense of trust. The word translated as "sincere" (ἀνυπόκριτος) means 'genuine' or 'sincere' or even 'without play-acting' when taken literally.[8]

The word ἀνυπόκριτος could also be translated as "unfeigned." This implies the idea of genuine, but also conveys the idea in the Greek that rather than simply being genuine, this faith is something more. It is not faked and is not false. The faith unfeigned is real, sincere faith.

Consider also the use of ἀνυπόκριτος in the *Wisdom of Solomon*:

> ... bringing your *sincere* command as sharp sword; and it stood and filled all things with death, and it touched the sky but stood on the earth. (Wis 18:16, emphasis added)[9]

These three components of Paul's goal are connected with conjunctions that indicate these three things—a pure heart, a good conscience, and faith unfeigned—all work together to display the love Paul desires the Ephesians to exhibit.

---

[8] BDAG, p. 91. Occurs 6x in NT, 2x in PE: 1Ti 1:5; 2Ti 1:5.

[9] NRSV translates "authentic."

Some Teach Ignorantly (1Ti 1:6–7)

from which some have deviated, and have turned away into fruitless discussion, wanting to be teachers of the law, although they do not understand either the things which they are saying or the things concerning which they are speaking confidently. (1Ti 1:6–7)

Verse 6

from which some have deviated

In verse 3, Paul implored Timothy to "instruct certain people not to teach other doctrine." In verse 6, Paul uses the same language of "certain people." Verses 3 and 4 make it clear that these "certain people" are teachers, and that they are teaching doctrine different from that of Paul. They want to be teachers but they have no understanding of what they are teaching. This contextual evidence is enough to conclude that the "certain people" in both instances refer to the same group.

These certain people have swerved from Paul's earlier three-fold statement of love; the aim of Paul's teaching.[1] The word translated as "have deviated" (ἀστοχέω) is only found in the Pastoral Epistles.[2] It originally meant to 'miss the mark' and carries this meaning in secular contexts, such as the *Works of Josephus*:

> There also those among them who undertake to foretell things to come, by reading the holy books, and using several sorts of purifications, and being perpetually conversant in the discourses of the prophets; and it is but seldom that *they miss* in their predictions. (Jos., *Wars* 2.159, emphasis added)

When predictions do not come true, they are inaccurate, thus they 'miss the mark.'

In Ephesus, "certain people" had turned or deviated from Paul's teaching. They missed the mark that Paul had established. The word also occurs in *Second Clement*:

> But the righteous who have done what is right and who have endured torments and who have hated the pleasures of the soul, when they observe those who *have deviated* and who have denied Jesus by words or by works, how they are punished with severe torments in unquenchable fire, they shall give glory to their God,

---

[1] See comment on 1Ti 1:5.

[2] BDAG, p. 146. Occurs 3x in NT, all in PE: 1Ti 1:6; 6:21; 2Ti 2:18.

> saying that "There will be hope for the one who serves God with his whole heart." (2*Cl* 17.7, emphasis added)

This usage confirms the sense of deviating from an established standard. Paul has established a clear target: Love from a pure heart, a good conscience and a sincere faith. These "certain people" have missed this target.

and have turned away into fruitless discussion

The phrase "have turned away" is from ἐκτρέπω, which (as with many words) carries both a literal and a figurative sense. It was originally a medical term, having to do with the idea of 'turns itself inside out' and to be 'put out of joint.'[3] It was used to describe dislocations or sprains. Later ἐκτρέπω came to be used figuratively to indicate a turning away, though it still would be used in its technical sense. Only the figurative use is found in the Pastoral Epistles. A similar usage is found in Ignatius' letter to the Magnesians:

> These things were really and truly done by Jesus Christ, our hope, from whom may none of you ever *turn away*. (Ign., *Magn.* 11.1, emphasis added)

Ignatius' interest is in protecting the Magnesian believers; he warns them against turning away from Jesus Christ. The use in 1 Timothy is similar in that it describes a figurative turning away from Paul's teaching.

If these certain people have turned away from Paul's teaching, what teaching have they turned toward? Paul makes this plain to Timothy; they have wandered "into fruitless discussion." The word translated as "fruitless discussion" is ματαιολογία.[4] It is a compound word, consisting of μάταιος and λόγος, both of which are commonly used in the New Testament. The word μάταιος means "of no use" while the word λόγος carries the sense of speaking or discussion. The word ματαιολογία is also used in Polycarp's *Letter to the Philippians*:

> Serve God in reverence and truth, leaving behind empty, *fruitless talk* and the deception of the crowd, believing in the one who raised our Lord Jesus Christ from the dead and gave him glory and a throne at his right hand. (Poly., *Phil.* 2.1, emphasis added)

Here, ματαιολογία is translated "fruitless talk." The context is somewhat different between Polycarp and Paul. Polycarp is exhorting his readers to abandon this futile

---

[3] LSJ, p. 523; cf. BDAG, p. 311. Occurs 5x in NT, 4x in PE: 1Ti 1:6; 5:15; 6:20; 2Ti 4:4. The only other NT usage is in Heb 12:13, where the usage is seemingly metaphorical.

[4] BDAG, p. 621. The word only occurs here in the NT.

reasoning while Paul is noting the state into which the "certain people" have devolved. In both cases, however, the state being described is similar.

VERSE 7

wanting to be teachers of the law

The compound word translated "teachers of the law" (νομοδιδάσκαλος)[5] occurs in both Acts and Luke in the context of Jewish teachers.

> But a certain man stood up in the Sanhedrin, a Pharisee named Gamaliel, *a teacher of the law* respected by all the people, and gave orders to put the men outside for a short time. (Ac 5:34, emphasis added)

The "teacher of the law" here is Gamaliel, a Pharisee, referring to an authoritative teacher of the Jews. [6] The instance of νομοδιδάσκαλος in Luke 5:17 is similar in nature:

> And it happened that on one of the days as he was teaching, Pharisees and *teachers of the law* were sitting there who had come from every village of Galilee and Judea and from Jerusalem, and the power of the Lord was there in order for him to heal. (Lk 5:17, emphasis added)

The phrase "teachers of the law" is the translation of νομοδιδάσκαλος. Again, it refers to a group of authoritative Jewish teachers. These teachers of the law (law = Torah)[7] were respected and their teachings on matters of the law were considered conclusive and authoritative.

But the use of νομοδιδάσκαλος in 1 Timothy is different. Paul does not equate the status of these teachers in Ephesus with teachers such as Gamaliel. Paul instead ridicules them by showing that they cannot be teachers of the law because they have no understanding of the law.

although they do not understand either the things which they are saying

Paul describes why those who want to be teachers of the law fall short. He is very blunt, writing that these teachers do not understand what they are saying. This in

---

[5] BDAG, p. 676. 3x in NT, only here in PE.

[6] *Anchor Bible Dictionary*, 2:904.

[7] The "Torah" is the Jewish name for the law of Moses, also known as the Pentateuch, the first five books of the Hebrew Old Testament. See article "Torah (Pentateuch)" in ABD 6:605.

itself is a damning criticism of the teachers: If they don't understand the law, how can they teach it?[8] This criticism is similar to the reaction of Jesus to Nicodemus:

> Nicodemus answered and said to him, "How can these things be?" Jesus answered and said to him, "Are you the teacher of Israel, and you do not understand these things? (Jn 3:9–10)

Jesus had just finished explaining to Nicodemus what it meant to be born again. He expresses surprise that Nicodemus, a teacher of the Jews, did not quite understand how one could be born again. The situation is similar to those who desire to be teachers of the law in Ephesus, and Paul's reaction is much the same as Jesus.'

The word translated as "understand" (νοέω) has a rather broad meaning. In general it means to 'know, understand, or perceive.'[9] It is used similarly by Paul in his previous letter to the Ephesians:

> so that you may be able when you read to *understand* my insight into the mystery of Christ. (Eph 3:4, emphasis added)[10]

The *Epistle of Barnabas* has a passage similar to 1Ti 1:7, contrasting those who do not know a particular teaching with those who do:

> But how did those people *understand* or comprehend these things? But we, having rightly *understood* the commandments, we speak as the Lord wished. (*Ep. Barn.* 10.12, emphasis added)

The larger context of this quotation from the *Epistle of Barnabas*[11] provides examples of the use of νοέω in contexts similar to 1Ti 1:7. The word is used in conjunction with those who have no understanding of what is considered to be proper teaching and also with those who do have knowledge of the proper teaching. In such contexts, the concept of 'know' or 'understand' is clearly intended.

In short, Paul is rather unambiguously accusing these false teachers of teaching out of ignorance.

---

[8] Cf. comments on 1Ti 6:3–4.

[9] BDAG p. 674; occurs 14x in NT; 2x in PE: 1Ti 1:7; 2Ti 2:7.

[10] See also Ro 1:20.

[11] A strange digression considering split hooves is the larger context of this quotation from the *Epistle of Barnabas*.

or the things concerning which they are speaking confidently

Paul next turns to the method of their teaching, informing Timothy that even though these teachers speak with presumed authority, they are ignorant[12] and should be ignored.

The word translated as "they are speaking confidently" (διαβεβαιόομαι)[13] occurs only twice in the New Testament, both times in the Pastoral Epistles. The word is also used by Josephus, in a context similar to that used by Paul:

> Now, this [man], grammarian as he was, could not *certainly tell* which was the poet Homer's country, no more than he could which was the country of Pythagoras, who lived comparatively but a little while ago; yet does he thus easily determine the age of Moses, who preceded them such a vast number of years, as depending on his ancient men's relation, which shows how notorious a liar he was. (Jos., *Apion* 2.14, emphasis added)

Josephus is making light of Apion's skills as a rhetoretician, asking how Apion can "easily determine" the age of Moses when Apion "could not certainly tell" things more widely known, such as the native countries of Homer and Pythagoras, both of whom lived much more recently than Moses.

The false teachers at Ephesus had apparently done similar things, making confident assertions based on incomplete and erroneous knowledge. Their teaching had no substance; it was empty and false. In swerving from Paul's primary aim—love that issues from a pure heart and a good conscience and a sincere faith—they embraced false teaching. These false teachers had so assimilated the false doctrine they were propagating that they sincerely believed they were being true teachers of the law when, in fact, they were perpetuating a lie. Timothy must counter this false teaching by focusing on the sound doctrine as taught by Paul.

---

[12] Cf. 1Ti 1:13 and Paul's state of ignorance prior to his salvation.

[13] BDAG, p. 226; occurs 2x in NT, both in PE: 1Ti 1:7; Tt 3:8.

The Proper Use of the Law (1Ti 1:8–11)

But we know that the law is good, if anyone makes use of it lawfully, knowing this, that the law is not given for a righteous person but for the lawless and rebellious, for the ungodly and sinners, for the unholy and totally worldly, for the one who kills his father and the one who kills his mother, for murderers, sexually immoral people, homosexuals, kidnappers, liars, perjurers, and whatever else is opposed to sound teaching, according to the glorious gospel of the blessed God that I was entrusted with. (1Ti 1:8–11)

Verse 8

But we know that the law is good, if anyone makes use of it lawfully

The word translated "lawfully" (νομίμως)[1] occurs twice in the New Testament, both times in the Pastoral Epistles. The word means "in accordance with rules or laws" and was also used to describe athletes "competing according to the rules."[2] In Jewish and Christian literature, νομίμως can take on the meaning of acting in accordance with Torah. The word occurs in Fourth Maccabees:

> For it would be especially irrational if, although having lived a life until old age for truth and having guarded *lawfully* a reputation upon them, we should change our ways presently. (4Ma 6:18, emphasis added)

The context in Fourth Maccabees is a story of martyrdom of seven brothers and their mother. They object to personal defilement they consider to be against the law (Torah). The notion is that these martyrs had lived their lives in accordance with the law. There was no inkling in their being that they would not act lawfully. Because they would not transgress the law, they were killed.

Paul was not opposed to the use of the law, but he required that the law be used properly. Only in this way can the law be "good."

---

[1] BDAG, p. 676, occurs 2x in NT, both in PE: 1Ti 1:8; 2Ti 2:5. Note 2Ti 2:5 uses νομίμως in its second sense, that pertaining to athletes.

[2] BDAG, p. 676.

Verse 9

knowing this, that the law is not given for a righteous person

Paul proceeds to explain how the law, the Torah, applies to the people of Ephesus. Paul offers a contrast, describing two groups. The first group is "the righteous," the second group runs afoul of the law. Paul organizes his description of the second group in an arrangement parallel to the Ten Commandments (cf. Ex 20:1–17).[3]

The word translated as "is given" (κεῖμαι)[4] has a few different senses. The word can mean to physically lie down or recline and is actually used of Jesus' body during its short time in the tomb.[5] Euripides uses κεῖμαι to say 'the law is *laid down*.' Aristophanes likewise uses κεῖμαι for 'the *established* laws.' Other classical writers use κεῖμαι in the same sense when discussing law.[6] The word also occurs in the *Shepherd of Hermas*:

> "I commanded you," he said, "in the first commandment that you keep the faith and the fear and the self-control." "Yes sir," I said. "But now I want you," he said, "to also make known their abilities so that you might understand which of them has which ability and function, for their functions are two-fold. Therefore *they relate* to righteousness and unrighteousness. (Hermas, *Mandates*, VI, i, 1, emphasis added)

The word κεῖμαι is used in this same sense of establish. Paul uses κεῖμαι in this same manner, to indicate that the law has been established.

The word translated as "just" (δίκαιος) is a common word in the New Testament.[7] The primary sense is that of being 'in accordance with high standards.'[8] In this context the high standard is the law. It has been "laid down ... for the lawless and disobedient." Those who run afoul of the law are in most need of its corrective nature.

Paul proceeds to list one of several catalogues of vices contained in his epistles, describing those for whom the law has been established. Each component of this catalogue is listed and discussed in turn.

---

[3] This is shown more plainly at the end of the section commenting on v. 10.

[4] BDAG, p. 537. Occurs 24x in NT, only here in PE.

[5] Cf. Mt 28:6; Lk 23:53; Jn 20:12 for mentioned usage.

[6] LSJ, p. 934, sense IV. All classical citations garnered from this article.

[7] 79x in NT, 3x in PE: 1Ti 1:9; 2Ti 4:8; Tt 1:8.

[8] BDAG, p. 246.

but for the lawless and rebellious

The "lawless" are those who are literally 'without law' (ἄνομος,)[9] while the "rebellious" are classed as 'pertaining to being rebelliously disobedient' (ἀνυπότακτος)[10]. The difference between the two is that the lawless do not know or recognize the law, but the rebellious have some knowledge of the law and still are not in conformity with it.

for the ungodly and sinners

The word translated as "ungodly" (ἀσεβής) pertains to 'violating norms for a proper relation to deity;'[11] hence ungodly. This describes those who are irreverent toward God. The word "sinners" (ἁμαρτωλός) refers to those who do not adhere or measure up to community religious or moral standards.[12] In this case, it means those who do not follow the law that was established.

for the unholy and totally worldly

The "unholy" are those who are the opposite of holy, or in opposition to God.[13] The "totally worldly" are those who have made the holy things cheap and common.[14] They have devalued the things of God and are in need of the law.

for the one who kills his father and the one who kills his mother

The ESV translation "strike" is weak as the Greek words (πατρολῴας and μητρολῴας) literally mean "father-killer"[15] and "mother-killer."[16]

---

[9] BDAG, p. 85. This is the only occurrence of ἄνομος in the PE. Note this is simply the word for law (νομος) with an alpha prepended, thus indicating the opposite of the law, or "lawless."

[10] LN 36.26; vol. 1 p. 468; cf. BDAG, p. 91. Used 3x in PE; 1Ti 1:9; Tt 1:6, 10.

[11] BDAG, p. 141. ἀσεβής occurs 9x in the NT, only here in PE.

[12] BDAG, p. 51. ἁμαρτωλός occurs 2x in PE; 1Ti 1:9, 15.

[13] BDAG, p. 86. ἀνόσιος occurs 2x in NT, both are in the PE: 1Ti 1:9; 2Ti 3:2.

[14] BDAG, p. 173. βέβηλος occurs 5x in the NT, four of which are in the PE: 1Ti 1:9; 4:7; 6:20; 2Ti 2:16 as well as Heb 12:16.

[15] BDAG, p. 789. *hapax.*

[16] BDAG, p. 649. *hapax.*

for murderers

The word translated as "murderers" (ἀνδροφόνος) means "man-slayer," however the word was used classically of one who kills women and children as well.[17] "Father-killers" and "mother-killers" are distinguished from other sorts of murderous acts, but those who commit murderous acts of any sort are in need of the law.

Verse 10

sexually immoral people

This word (πόρνος)[18] is rather broad in scope. Some older translations use terms such as "whoremongers" (KJV) or "fornicators" (1901 ASV) to translate πόρνος in this instance. The specificity of the word is dependent on context. As the context here is a catalogue of vices, the word is most likely intended in its general sense. The general sense does not limit itself to adultery but refers broadly to sexual immorality.

homosexuals

Even with the generic nature of the term "the sexually immoral" used immediately previous, Paul includes ἀρσενοκοίτης, drawing attention to a particular vice: that of a male having intercourse with another male.[19] The word ἀρσενοκοίτης is a compound word. Its root components are the word for "male" and the word for "bed." When words denoting people are combined with the word for "bed," the common meaning of the compound has a sexual nature.[20] This word is also used First Corinthians:

> Or do you not know that the unrighteous will not inherit the kingdom of God? Do not be deceived! Neither sexually immoral people, nor idolaters, nor adulterers, nor passive homosexual partners, nor *dominant homosexual partners*, (1Co 6:9, emphasis added)

Similar usage occurs in Polycarp's letter to the Philippians:

> Likewise also, the younger men must be blameless in all things; above all being concerned about purity and holding themselves in check from all evil. For it is

---

[17] BDAG, p. 76. *hapax*.

[18] BDAG, p. 855. 10x in NT, only once in PE.

[19] BDAG, p. 135. 2x in NT. 1Co 6:9; 1Ti 1:10. LSJ glosses ἀρσενοκοίτης as "sodomite" (cf. LSJ p. 247).

[20] BDAG, p. 135.

> good to abstain from sinful passions in the world because all sinful passion wages war against the spirit, and neither the sexually immoral, nor the passive homosexual partner, nor *the dominant homosexual partner* will inherit the kingdom of God; nor those who engage in perversity. Therefore it is necessary to refrain from all these things, being subject to the presbyters and deacons as to God and Christ. (Poly., *Phil.* 5.3, emphasis added)

Polycarp is careful to state his primary motive: a concern for purity and blamelessness will lead one to abstain from things that "war against the spirit." He sees engaging in homosexual activity as one of those things.

kidnappers

This term (ἀνδραποδιστής) was historically used to describe one who sold men as slaves, even those who kidnapped men to sell them as slaves.[21] Whatever the method of acquisition, these men trafficked in men, selling them as cattle to make a profit.

Translating ἀνδραποδιστής as "kidnappers"[22] causes one to think of fanciful images of classic heists, ransom notes, and the Lindbergh baby. In light of later discussion on the role of slaves within the community,[23] Paul's inclusion of ἀνδραποδιστής in a list of vices is significant. The significance is lost when translated with a term like "kidnappers" that, in today's vernacular, will merit little attention. Consider the following excerpt from Philo, *On the Special Laws*:

> A *kidnapper* also is a thief; but he is, moreover, a thief who steals the very most excellent thing that exists upon the earth. … but man, as it seems, has been assigned the most pre-eminent position among the animals, being, as it were, a near relation of God himself, and akin to him in respect of his participation in reason; which makes him immortal, although he is liable to death. On which account every one who feels any admiration of virtue is full of exceeding anger, and is utterly implacable against *kidnappers*, who for the sake of most iniquitous gain dare to inflict slavery on those who are free by birth, and who partake of the same nature as themselves. (Philo, *Spec. Laws* IV 13–14, emphasis added)

The one who steals men to sell them into slavery in this context is the "kidnapper."

---

[21] BDAG p. 76. *hapax*.

[22] NET Bible, NASB95, RSV, NKJV all use "kidnappers." NIV and NRSV have some variant of "slave traders." ESV uses "enslavers."

[23] Cf. comments on 1Ti 6:1–2.

liars, perjurers

The word translated "liars" (ψεύστης) is fairly clear and unambiguous. The word translated as "perjurers" (ἐπίορκος) indicates "falseness in oath-taking."[24] These are men who bear false witness; men who cannot be taken at their word. Philo, in his *Treatise on the Decalogue*, writes concerning perjurers:

> "What sayest thou?" I should say to the perjured man, "will you dare to go to any one of your own acquaintances and say, 'My friend, come and bear witness for me that you have seen and heard, and been present at a whole catalogue of things which you have neither seen, nor heard?' I think not; for that would be an act of incurable insanity; with what face can you while sober, and while appearing to be master of yourself look upon your friend, and say, 'By reason of our acquaintance and companionship, act unjustly, violate the law, commit impiety for my sake;' for it is plain that if he heard such a request, he would quickly renounce that companionship which you now believe to exist, reproaching himself for having ever had any friendship at all with a man of such a character as you, and would flee from you, as from a savage, and maddened, wild beast." (Philo, *Decalogue* 88–89)

In ridiculing the perjurer, Philo accurately describes the damage such men do. These are men in need of the law.

Paul indicates that the law was established for all of these, and that the proper use of the law is to make those who practice these actions aware of the degree to which they fall short of God's perfect law. Many of the vices listed in the above catalog bear direct resemblance to prohibitions in the Ten Commandments (Ex 20:1–17). Paul's list contains references to sexual immorality, liars, bearing false witness and not honoring one's father or mother. Considering Paul's upbringing and education, this allusion is in all likelihood intended.

---

[24] BDAG, p. 376. *hapax*.

Ten Commandments (Ex 20:1–17)	**Paul's List of Vices (1Ti 1:9–10)**
Commandments concerning honoring God.	"for the lawless and rebellious, for the ungodly and sinners, for the unholy and totally worldly" (v. 9)
Honor your father and mother	"for the one who kills his father and the one who kills his mother" (v. 9)
You shall not murder	"for murderers" (v. 9)
You shall not commit adultery	"sexually immoral people, homosexuals" (v. 10)
You shall not steal	"kidnappers" (those who steal freedom, v. 10)
You shall not bear false witness.	"liars, perjurers" (v. 10)

The ungodly and sinners need the law in order to be restored to the proper path. The unholy and profane need the law in order to be brought into right relationship with God, to make holy again what they have profaned. Those who strike their fathers and mothers need the law as they obviously act outside of the law and are in need of correction. Murderers are obviously in need of knowing the law; both to stop their actions and to prosecute their wrongdoings. The sexually immoral and men who practice homosexuality are in need of the law as they need to repent and forsake sinful and immoral sexual relationships. The kidnappers are in need of the law for correction, as they misunderstand the value of people that God loves and has sacrificed so much for. The liars and perjurers are in need of correction, they are in need of a respect of honesty and trust. The law has been laid down to provide this, to establish a standard so that people with no standards have something to base their actions on.

and whatever else is opposed to sound teaching

Paul completes his list with a catch-all: "and whatever else is opposed to sound teaching." This reiterates his primary concern to teach and disseminate proper doctrine. The law has been laid down not only to establish a standard in all of the above-mentioned situations, but in general the law has been laid down for those who find themselves on the wrong side of "sound doctrine."

The phrase "whatever else is opposed to" hinges on the word translated as "opposed to." This word (ἀντίκειμαι) carries the sense of 'be in opposition' or 'be opposed.'[25] Note that ἀντίκειμαι is the opposite of the word translated "laid down" in 1Ti 1:9 (κεῖμαι). The law was laid down (κεῖμαι); actions opposed to the law are contrary (ἀντίκειμαι) to what was laid down.

Paul uses this same word (ἀντίκειμαι) in his epistle to the Galatians when he writes:

> For the flesh desires against the Spirit, and the Spirit against the flesh, for these *are in opposition to* one another, so that whatever you want, you may not do these things. (Ga 5:17, emphasis added)

In the same way, the things contrary to sound teaching are opposed to the sound teaching itself.

The phrase "sound teaching" is unique to the Pastoral Epistles.[26] It is made up of two Greek words. The first word, typically translated 'sound,' 'healthy,' or 'correct;' is ὑγιαίνω.[27] In the Pastoral Epistles, ὑγιαίνω always occurs with the figurative sense of "sound" or "correct" and never with the medical sense of "healthy." The second word, διδασκαλία, carries the meaning of 'teaching' or 'instruction.'[28] The phrase "sound teaching" conveys the idea of 'correct instruction' or 'healthy teaching.'

The sound doctrine appeals to the standard of the law. The items in Paul's catalogue of vices are contrary to the law and thus contrary to sound doctrine.

VERSE 11

according to the glorious gospel of the blessed God

In the New Testament, the "gospel" (εὐαγγέλιον) generally carries the meaning of 'good news' or 'gospel,'[29] typically in the context of God's good news to man regarding redemption. The word translated "glorious" (δόξα) is another noun that simply means splendor or glory or brightness.[30] It is a common word in the New Testament that occurs in many different contexts.

---

[25] BDAG, p. 88. Occurs 8x in NT, 2x in PE.

[26] The phrase "sound doctrine"occurs 5x in the PE: 1Ti 1:10; 6:3; 2Ti 4:3; Tt 1:9; 2:1.

[27] BDAG, p. 1023. Occurs 12x in NT, 8x in PE.

[28] BDAG, p. 240. Occurs 21x in NT, 14x in PE.

[29] BDAG, p. 402. Occurs 79x in NT, 4x in PE: 1Ti 1:11; 2Ti 1:8, 10; 2:8.

[30] BDAG, p. 256. Occurs 166x in NT, 6x in PE: 1Ti 1:11, 17; 3:16; 2Ti 2:10; 4:18; Tt 2:13.

This glorious gospel is the gospel "of the blessed God." The word translated "blessed" (μακάριος)[31] is an adjective that describes God. Paul is in the process of completing his thought concerning the proper use of the law, concluding that the law is used properly when it is used in accordance with the good news of God.

that I was entrusted with

Paul, as an ambassador of God and Christ Jesus, was entrusted with the responsibility of ensuring the proper application of the law. The word translated as "was entrusted" (πιστεύω) occurs frequently, ranging in meaning from 'believe' to 'trust.'[32] Paul has been entrusted with the glorious gospel of the blessed God.

---

[31] BDAG, p. 610. Occurs 50x in NT, 3x in PE: 1Ti 1:11; 6:15; Tt 2:13.

[32] BDAG, p. 816. Occurs 241x in NT. See also comment on 1Ti 1:18.

The Example of Paul (1Ti 1:12–17)

> *I give thanks to the one who strengthens me, Christ Jesus our Lord, because he considered me faithful, placing me into ministry, although I was formerly a blasphemer and a persecutor and a violent man, but I was shown mercy because I acted ignorantly in unbelief, and the grace of our Lord abounded with the faith and love that are in Christ Jesus. The saying is trustworthy and worthy of all acceptance: Christ Jesus came into the world to save sinners, of whom I am the foremost. But because of this I was shown mercy, in order that in me foremost, Christ Jesus might demonstrate his total patience, for an example for those who are going to believe in him for eternal life. Now to the King of the ages, immortal, invisible, to the only God, be honor and glory forever and ever. Amen. (1Ti 1:12–17)*

Verse 12

I give thanks to the one who strengthens me, Christ Jesus our Lord

Prior to being justified, Paul lived under the burden of the law, attempting to meet its standard. Knowing this, Paul offers thanks to Christ Jesus, who is the source of his strength.

"Christ Jesus our Lord" is described by Paul as "the one who strengthens me." The Greek word translated "strengthens" is ἐνδυναμόω.[1] Christ Jesus is the one who strengthens Paul. Paul testifies to this, giving the glory to Christ Jesus for enabling him to meet the tasks set before him.

Paul realizes the power of this external strength. He testifies to the strengthening of Christ Jesus in his letter to the Philippians:

> I am able to do all things by the one who *strengthens* me. (Php 4:13, emphasis added)

Paul knows that he must rely upon Christ Jesus for strength. He does not have the strength to make it on his own. This idea of relying on Christ Jesus for strength also appears in Ignatius' letter to the Smyrnaeans:

---

[1] BDAG, p. 333. Occurs 7x in NT, 3x in PE: 1Ti 1:12; 2Ti 2:1; 4:17.

> For if these things were accomplished by our Lord in appearance only, I also am a prisoner in appearance only, and why also have I allowed myself to be given over to death, to fire, to the sword, to beasts? Instead nearer to the sword is nearer to God; in the midst of beasts is in the midst of God. I endure all things in the name of Jesus Christ alone so that I may suffer with him; the perfect human himself *strengthening* me. (Ign., *Smyrn.* 4.2, emphasis added)

The same word for 'empower,' ἐνδυναμόω, is used here by Ignatius, in much the same way as Paul used it, indicating a strengthening or empowerment from an external source. Ignatius believed that Jesus Christ would strengthen him to enable him to face the horrible physical persecution that he was destined for.[2] For both Paul and Ignatius, the external source of empowerment is Jesus Christ.

because he considered me faithful

Paul now begins explaining why he needs the strength offered to him by Christ Jesus. First, Paul writes, "he considered me faithful." The word translated "considered" (ἡγέομαι) in this context means 'to judge or consider.'[3] As with the previous phrase, Christ Jesus is the one performing the action and Paul is the recipient of the action. Christ Jesus is the one who judges or considers Paul to be faithful.

placing me into ministry

Paul, strengthened by Christ and found faithful, has been called into the service of the one who has done so much for him. The word τίθημιis translated "placing." Various senses include 'lay, put, sense, and place.'[4] Christ Jesus is performing the action, and Paul is the recipient.

Paul is appointed to the ministry of Christ Jesus. The word translated "ministry" is the Greek word διακονία, which is variously translated as 'ministry' or 'service.'[5] Paul had earlier written that he was serving as an apostle at the command of Christ Jesus (v. 1) and later notes that he was appointed (τίθημι) as an apostle to the Gentiles (1Ti 2:7).[6] In these instances, service (διακονία) is a role one is appointed to. This sense of διακονία is also used to describe the ministry of apostles in the book of Acts, notably in the first chapter:

---

[2] Ignatius was a prisoner of Rome, on his way from Smyrna to Rome as he wrote this letter. He knew he would die the death of a martyr, which sheds some light on his comments.

[3] BDAG, p. 434. Occurs 28x in NT, 2x in PE: 1Ti 1:12; 6:1.

[4] BDAG, p. 1003. Occurs 100x in NT, 3x in PE: 1Ti 1:12; 2:7; 2Ti 1:11.

[5] BDAG, p. 230. Occurs 34x in NT, 3x in PE: 1Ti 1:12; 2Ti 4:5, 11.

[6] See comment on 1Ti 2:7.

> And they prayed and said, "You, Lord, who know the hearts of all, show clearly which one of these two you have chosen to take the place in this *ministry* and apostleship from which Judas turned aside to depart to his own place." And they cast lots for them, and the lot fell on Matthias, and he was added to serve with the eleven apostles. (Ac 1:24–26, emphasis added)[7]

Though not referring to Paul, the idea is the same. Matthias is chosen to fulfill the "ministry and apostleship" left open by Judas' betrayal and subsequent death. Ministry, in this instance, is not a vague idea but is a specific task appointed to a specific person, who has a responsibility to carry out the task of service in the name of the one who appointed him, Jesus Christ.

Another example of διακονία occurs in Ignatius' letter to the Philadelphians:

> Since, according to your prayers and according to the compassion which you have in Christ Jesus, it has been reported to me the church which is in Antioch of Syria is at peace, it is fitting for you as a church of God to appoint a deacon to go on a mission there as God's ambassador to rejoice with those gathered together and to glorify the name. Blessed in Jesus Christ is he who will be considered worthy of such *a ministry* and you yourselves will be glorified. And if you have the will it is not impossible for you to do this on behalf of the name of God as also the churches nearby have sent bishops, and others have sent presbyters and deacons. (Ign., *Phld.* 10.1–2, emphasis added)

Ignatius' word "ministry" is the same word used here in v. 12. The context is similar, that of one chosen sent on a mission (errand) in the name of Jesus Christ.

Verse 13

although I was formerly a blasphemer

Before Paul was strengthened by Christ Jesus, before he was judged to be faithful, before he was appointed into the service of Christ Jesus, Paul "was a blasphemer" (βλάσφημος). Paul identifies himself as one who slandered and defamed the name

---

[7] See also Ac 1:15–17.

of God.[8] He uses serious language to describe his life before the strengthening offered by Christ Jesus.

The semantic boundaries of blasphemy are wide, but in Christian literature the basic notion is that of questioning or refuting God's status or action. "In the NT the concept of blasphemy is controlled throughout by the thought of violation of the power and majesty of God."[9] Likewise, blasphemy is found in denying the Messiahship of Jesus Christ, "for Christians it is blasphemy to throw doubt on the lawful Messianic claim of Jesus, to deride Christ in His unity with the Father and as the Bearer of divine majesty."[10] This sense of blasphemy was understood from the earliest times of the Christian era, as evidenced by the *Martyrdom of Polycarp*:

> But when the proconsul persisted and said, "Take the oath and I will release you. Revile Christ." Polycarp responded, "Eighty-six years I have served him and he has done me no wrong. How could *I blaspheme* my king who saved me?" (*Mart. Poly.* 9.3, emphasis added)

Here Polycarp clearly equates denial of Christ with blasphemy. Paul, who persecuted Christians for professing faith in Christ Jesus, sees himself as a blasphemer for similar reasons.

As a former Pharisee (Ac 23:6), Paul no doubt understood exactly what he was saying when he professed to being a blasphemer. Paul also would have understood the degree to which he had been saved by Christ Jesus. This change, ascribed to the strengthening of Christ Jesus, would be a powerful testimony.

and a persecutor

Paul also describes himself as a former "persecutor." This word (διώκτης) only occurs here in the NT, however the meaning[11] is relatively certain. One sense of the

---

[8] There are three words used in the NT that are directly related to blasphemy. The verb βλασφημέω (34x in NT; 4x in PE, see note on 1Ti 1:20) which means to blaspheme, the noun βλασφημία (18x in NT; once in PE) which is the speech or content of the blasphemy or simply blasphemy, and the noun βλάσφημος (4x in NT; 2x in PE) which describes the one doing the blasphemy or the blasphemer though it may simply be an adjective. This instance is this latter word.

[9] Gerhard Kittel and Gerhard Friedrich, eds., *Theological Dictionary of the New Testament*, 10 vols. (Grand Rapids: W. B. Eerdmans, 2006). Vol. 1 p. 622.

[10] TDNT 1:623.

[11] BDAG, p. 253. *hapax*.

verbal form of διώκτης is that of persecution due to one's beliefs.[12] Paul's role as a persecutor is testified to in the book of Acts:[13]

> But Saul, still breathing threats and murder against the disciples of the Lord, went to the high priest and asked for letters from him to the synagogues in Damascus, so that if he found any who were of the Way, both men and women, he could bring them tied up to Jerusalem. Now as he proceeded, it happened that when he approached Damascus, suddenly a light from heaven flashed around him. And falling to the ground, he heard a voice saying to him, "Saul, Saul, why *are you persecuting* me?" So he said, "Who are you, Lord?" And he said, "I am Jesus, whom *you are persecuting*! But get up and enter into the city, and it will be told to you what you must do." (Ac 9:1–6, emphasis added.)

Paul even reminded the Galatian church that he was, in fact, one of the parties responsible for persecution of the church:

> For you have heard about my former way of life in Judaism, that to an extraordinary degree *I was persecuting* the church of God, and trying to destroy it, and was progressing in Judaism beyond many contemporaries in my nation, because I was a far more zealous adherent of the traditions handed down by my forefathers. (Ga 1:13–14, emphasis added.)

Paul was unquestionably a persecutor prior to his salvation. He punished Christians for their beliefs. He attempted to destroy the fledgling church as it was being started.

and a violent man

Paul next describes himself as having formerly been violent. He is not painting a flattering picture of himself. The word translated "a violent man" (ὑβριστής)[14] is not complimentary. One lexicon offers a list of potential glosses: 'violent, wanton, licentious, insolent man.'[15] Another lexicon notes that ὑβριστής 'emphasizes the element of outrageous disregard of other men's rights.'[16] Paul uses this word in Romans, in a catalogue of vices that describes those who do not acknowledge God:

> They are gossipers, slanderers, haters of God, *insolent*, arrogant, boasters, contrivers of evil, disobedient to parents, (Ro 1:29b–30, emphasis added)

[12] διώκω. BDAG, p. 253. Ga 1:13–14 (quoted below) uses this form.

[13] In this excerpt, "Saul" = Paul.

[14] BDAG, p. 1022. Occurs 2x in NT: Ro 1:30; 1Ti 1:13.

[15] LSJ, p. 1841.

[16] M-M, p. 647.

The insolent or violent man does not keep good company. Yet Paul describes his pre-Damascus-road self as a ὑβριστής.

Josephus uses ὑβριστής to describe the nature of the sons of the high priest Eli:

> These sons of Eli were guilty of *injustice towards* men, and of impiety towards God, and abstained from no sort of wickedness. Some of their gifts they carried off, as belonging to the honorable employment they had; others of them they took away by violence. They also were guilty of impurity with the women that came to worship God [at the tabernacle], obliging some to submit to their lust by force, and enticing others by bribes; nay, the whole course of their lives was no better than tyranny. (Jos., *Ant.* 5.339, emphasis added)[17]

Once again, the context is not complimentary. Yet Paul — this blasphemer, this persecutor, this violent man — had somehow been appointed into the service of Christ Jesus.

but I was shown mercy

Paul confirms what he has just said in vv. 8–11, that the law was "not given for the righteous" but for those doing whatever is "contrary to sound teaching." Those who are acting contrary to sound teaching have no understanding; they act ignorantly and in unbelief. Paul classifies himself as one of these.

Yet Paul "was shown mercy." This word (ἐλεέω) simply means to have compassion, mercy, or pity.[18] The mercy has already been bestowed upon Paul, he did not demand mercy or reach out and take it. He is the recipient.

Paul calls this "mercy" as he was on the wrong side of the law. He was aligned with the lawless and disobedient, the ungodly and sinners, the unholy and profane, and those who acted contrary to sound doctrine. Yet Paul, through the mercy granted him, was rescued from this state.

because I acted ignorantly in unbelief

The verb "I acted" is ποιέω, which literally means 'to act or to do.'[19] In this instance it means that while Paul was the recipient of the mercy, he was the doer of actions done in ignorance and unbelief.

This helps in understanding the "because" relationship between these two phrases, "but I received mercy" and "I had acted ignorantly and in unbelief." Paul was in need

---

[17] Cf. 1Sa 2:12–36 regarding Eli's sons and their unrighteousness.

[18] BDAG, p. 315. Occurs 28x in NT, 2x in PE: 1Ti 1:13, 16.

[19] BDAG, p. 839. Occurs 568x in NT.

of mercy because he was in a state of unbelief and ignorance. He was shown mercy not because he demanded it, but because mercy was necessary for his salvation. The gift of mercy rescued Paul from the punishment of ignorance and unbelief.

The Greek word translated "ignorantly" is ἀγνοέω, which means 'without knowledge.'[20] The book of Acts records the same word in one of Peter's sermons:

> And now, brothers, I know that you acted in *ignorance*, just as your rulers did also. (Ac 3:17, emphasis added)

Peter is speaking of the crucifixion of Jesus (Ac 3:14–15). Those who called for the crucifixion of Jesus did so out of ignorance. As they didn't understand that Christ Jesus really was the Son of God, they didn't truly know what they were asking for when they demanded the crucifixion of Jesus. Paul uses this same word, in the same sense, to describe his previous life of persecuting the church.

His previous actions were also grounded "in unbelief" (ἀπιστία).[21] Paul's unbelief was such that he didn't recognize God within Christianity as he persecuted it. Paul was in great need of mercy.

Paul, of course, understands all of this. In his earlier discussion on the proper use of the law[22] he noted two groups: the just and the unjust. He noted that the law was intended for the unjust, for those who lived in either ignorance or disregard of both the law and its giver. Paul has placed his pre-Damascus-road self squarely in the column of the unjust. Trained from youth in matters of the law, Paul knew the law but used it unlawfully. Paul used the law to persecute the just. This shows his earlier ignorance of the proper use of the law.

Paul now testifies to the merciful intervention of Christ Jesus in his life. Paul needed this mercy, he needed the correction, otherwise the law he knew so well would condemn him. Christ Jesus acted mercifully and erased Paul's ignorance. He was an unbeliever, but now by the mercy of Christ Jesus is entrusted with the law.[23] The one who was living in ignorance and unbelief now has now been entrusted with promoting the message of the gospel, addressing the problems of ignorance and unbelief. Such a complete turnaround could only happen with the merciful intervention of Christ Jesus.

---

[20] BDAG, p. 12. Occurs 22x in NT; only here in PE.

[21] BDAG, p. 103. 11x in NT; only here in PE.

[22] In 1Ti 1:8–11; see above.

[23] The word for "unbelief" is ἀπιστία; the word for "entrusted"(v. 11) is πιστεύω "to believe or trust." The one who was an unbeliever now believes.

Verse 14

and the grace of our Lord abounded

The concept of overflowing is the key to understanding the picture. The Greek word is ὑπερπλεονάζω, which means 'to run over or overflow.'[24] The word is used of a vessel or cup that becomes too full and ends up overflowing. It occurs infrequently; only here in the New Testament.

The word appears in the *Psalms of Solomon*:

> Blessed is he whom God remembers in due proportion to sufficiency; if the person *abounds too much*, he sins. (*Ps. Sol.* 5:18–19, emphasis added)

This translation illustrates the sense of redundancy in the word. To "abound too much" seems like an unnecessary expansion of meaning. What does this say that a simple "abound" does not communicate? It is this superfluous aspect that makes the word ὑπερπλεονάζω precisely the right word to explain how generous the grace of God really is. It doesn't simply fill; it inundates.

with the faith and love that are in Christ Jesus

Paul has nothing within himself that merits "the faith and love that are in Christ Jesus." It is through the grace of God that Paul is able to partake in this super-abounding faith and love. It is through such grace that Paul has been saved.

The "faith and love that are in Christ Jesus" are the contents of Paul's vessel; they are what he is overflowing with because they have been presented to him in such abundance. Paul has been saved by grace, through faith that he himself did not muster yet still has in super-abundance. This faith was given to him (cf. Eph 2:8–9). This reception of faith is indicative of the mercy that Paul received; it is what transformed him from a blasphemer, persecutor, and insolent opponent into an apostle of Christ Jesus. Paul didn't transform Paul; Christ Jesus did with a gracious gift: a generous portion of faith and love.

---

[24] BDAG, p. 1034. *hapax*. M-M, p. 654 "abound exceedingly."

Verse 15

The saying is trustworthy and worthy of all acceptance

Paul next moves from the specific example of his own redemption to a general principle. He uses the words "this saying is trustworthy and worthy of all acceptance" to introduce this principle.[25] This serves as a key to emphasize the balance of this section.

Christ Jesus came into the world to save sinners

The general principle stressed by Paul is "Christ Jesus came into the world to save sinners." After offering himself as an example of this principle, Paul elucidates the general truth for the benefit of both Timothy and his readers.

Jesus' purpose in coming into the world was to save sinners. Sinners are those who are unable to live up to the standard of the law.[26] Paul has just shown that even though he had been trained as a Pharisee since his youth, he was unable to keep the law. All are sinners, all are in need of salvation.

Yet Christ Jesus' purpose is to save those who, through the proper use of the law, see that they are unable to keep the law. This is why the proper use of the law is so important to Paul. The law, used properly, erases ignorance and allows people to plainly see that they have no hope of keeping the law.

Christ Jesus is the one who gave Paul strength, he is the one who appointed Paul to his service. But this was only possible after Paul relied on Christ for strength, after Christ had saved Paul on the Damascus road.

The word translated "to save" (σῴζω) has several different senses in the New Testament. In this instance, the meaning is 'salvation from certain death.'[27] For Christians this means salvation from the eternal death of hell and entrance into eternal life. The gospels are quite clear in establishing the purpose of Christ's saving his own:[28]

---

[25] In the PE, the phrase "The saying is trustworthy" (πιστὸς ὁ λόγος) is formulaic. It occurs five times in the NT, and all five of these instances are in the PE.

[26] Cf. comments on 1Ti 1:9.

[27] BDAG, p. 982. Occurs 106x in NT.

[28] The examples are from the gospels; similar examples exist in the PE, but those will be discussed in place, cf. comments on 2Ti 1:9; 4:18; Tt 3:5.

> And she will give birth to a son, and you will call his name 'Jesus,' because *he will save* his people from their sins." (Mt 1:21, emphasis added)

> For the Son of Man came to seek and *to save* those who are lost." (Lk 19:10, emphasis added)

> And if anyone hears my words and does not observe them, I will not judge him. For I have not come to judge the world, but *to save* the world. (Jn 12:47, emphasis added)

Consider also the words attributed to Polycarp. He obviously believed that his king, Christ Jesus, had saved him from eternal death, he was therefore unafraid of being killed by the proconsul:

> But when the proconsul persisted and said, "Take the oath and I will release you. Revile Christ." Polycarp responded, "Eighty-six years I have served him and he has done me no wrong. How could I blaspheme my king who *saved* me?" (*Mart. Poly.* 9.3, emphasis added)

Polycarp was sure in his salvation; he knew that Christ Jesus had saved him.

of whom I am foremost

After establishing the general principle that Christ Jesus had come to save sinners, Paul offers that he is the "foremost" of sinners. While the word translated "foremost" (πρῶτος) literally means 'first,' [29] Paul is not claiming to be the first or primary sinner. The sense is that of 'most prominent' or perhaps 'worst' of the sinners. This is less of a boast and more of an effort to establish a very high bar that all can pass under.

Paul's testimony is exceptional (cf. 1Co 15:9–11). His purpose here is to show that if Christ Jesus can save him, then the salvation offered by Christ Jesus is available to anyone else.

---

[29] πρῶτος, BDAG, p. 893. Occurs 155x in NT; 10x in PE.

Verse 16

But because of this I was shown mercy, in order that in me foremost, Christ Jesus might demonstrate his total patience,

The first part is "that ... Christ Jesus might demonstrate." The word translated "might demonstrate" (ἐνδείκνυμι) means 'to show or demonstrate.'[30] The same word is used in Paul's epistle to the Romans:

> For the scripture says to Pharaoh, "For this very reason I have raised you up, so that *I may demonstrate* my power in you, and so that my name might be proclaimed in all the earth." (Ro 9:17, emphasis added)[31]

In this example, the power of God is being displayed through Pharaoh. The observer of Pharaoh becomes familiar with the power of God as it is shown. Paul makes the case that the same sort of thing happens to him. The perfect patience of Jesus Christ is on display through Paul. As such, those who witness Paul, and who are aware of Paul's background, become much more familiar with the patience of Jesus Christ. They become convinced that Jesus Christ could be patient with them if he was able to patiently work in the life of Paul.

his total patience

The second part is the patience of Christ. The word translated "total" is ἅπας, which has to do with 'the whole of something' or 'all of something.'[32] When used of concepts instead of objects, it takes on the sense of 'ultimate' or 'perfect.' The word translated "patience" is μακροθυμία. It can mean patience, as in 'a calm tranquil state;' or it can mean patience as in 'forbearance toward others.'[33] In this case, it is used of Christ's forbearance to those who will believe in him. Christ is able to deal with those who are his, despite their many shortcomings and frustrations. The same word is used in similar context in Peter's second epistle:

> And regard the *patience* of our Lord as salvation, just as also our dear brother Paul wrote to you, according to the wisdom that was given to him, (2Pe 3:15, emphasis added)

---

[30] BDAG, p. 331. Occurs 11x in NT; 4x in PE.

[31] This is a quotation of Ex 9:16 (LXX).

[32] BDAG, p. 98. Occurs 34x in NT; only here in PE.

[33] BDAG, p. 612. Occurs 14x in NT; 3x in PE: 1Ti 1:16; 2Ti 3:10; 4:2.

Here the patience of Jesus Christ has been equated with salvation. Jesus Christ is patient in dealing with those who will believe. Christ's patience is on display in the way he worked to save Paul. The impatient option would have been to smite Paul. However, showing patience, Jesus Christ saved Paul and transformed him into the apostle to the Gentiles. Paul says that if Jesus Christ has the patience to do this, then this patience is the epitome of patience and can work to transform all of those who will believe.

for an example for those who are going to believe in him for eternal life

The conversion of Paul is an example of how the total patience of Jesus Christ has been demonstrated. The word "example" is ὑποτύπωσις, which may be translated as either prototype, example or standard.[34] Of this particular instance, one lexicon notes, "as prime recipient of extraordinary mercy in view of his infamous past, Paul serves as a model for the certainty of availability of mercy to others."[35] This same word is also used in Second Timothy:

> Hold fast to *the pattern* of sound words which you heard from me, in the faith and love that are in Christ Jesus. (2Ti 1:13, emphasis added)

The word also occurs in the works of Philo:

> In order, therefore, that he may the more firmly establish the sight which has thus been presented to him in his mind, the sacred word says to him, "My good friend, great things are often made known by slight *outlines*, at which he who looks increases his imagination to an unlimited extent (Philo, *Abraham* 71)

The conversion of Paul is more than a simple example. Christ Jesus' display of total patience in saving Paul provides a model or pattern for how Christ Jesus will act in the lives of others.

This example is "for those who are going to believe in him for eternal life." The word μέλλω occurs frequently in the NT and has to do with what is to occur in the future.[36] In this case, "were" points to the future and is not descriptive of something in the past. The verb, "to believe" (πιστεύω), provides the action that will take place.[37]

First Clement uses the same exact words (μελλόντων πιστεύειν) used in First Timothy:

---

[34] BDAG, p. 1042. Occurs 2x in NT, both occurrences are in PE: 1Ti 1:16; 2Ti 1:13.

[35] BDAG, p. 1042.

[36] BDAG, p. 628. Occurs 109x in NT; 4x in PE: 1Ti 1:16; 4:8; 6:19; 2Ti 4:1.

[37] BDAG, p. 816. Occurs 241x in NT.

> Therefore, preaching among regions and cities, they appointed their first fruits, testing them by the Spirit to be bishops and deacons *of the future believers*. (*1Cl* 42.4, emphasis added)

A note is included in the translation indicating that "of the future believers" could be more literally translated, "of those who are going to believe." The context points to the converts that would come about as a result of the nascent ministry in the area. This isn't a particular group, chosen by some divine foresight peeking down through the annals of time. It is rather a way to speak of those who would become Christians as a result of the ministry before the conversions actually take place.

In the same way, Paul's conversion is an example to those who will come along later and believe.

The result of believing in Jesus Christ as Savior is "eternal life." This is, simply put, life into the ages or life without end. It is salvation from eternal death, from receiving the penalty of the law. The proper use of the law makes one aware of sin and also makes one aware of his inability to break free from the sin in his life. Only through the mercy of God, which Paul exemplifies, can one be saved from the penalty of sin.

Paul's example of complete conversion from persecutor and blasphemer into apostle of Jesus Christ puts the total patience of Jesus on display for all to see; prompting those who would believe in Jesus Christ to actually believe and be saved, taking part in eternal life.

Verse 17

Now to the King of the ages, immortal, invisible, to the only God, be honor and glory forever and ever. Amen.

Paul offers a short benediction to end this section. It is simple yet profound, briefly mentioning some obvious and important attributes of God.

Paul offers his benediction to "the King of the ages." God is eternal (αἰών),[38] he has always been and always will be. He is the King of eternity. He is the King of those who have received eternal life through the grace and mercy of Jesus Christ.

As the King of eternity, God is "immortal" (ἄφθαρτος). This word is variously glossed as 'imperishable, incorruptible, and immortal.'[39] Paul uses this same word in First Corinthians:

---

[38] BDAG, p. 32. Occurs 122x in NT; 8x in PE.

[39] BDAG, p. 155. Occurs 11x in NT; only here in PE.

> Do you not know that those who run in the stadium all run, but one receives the prize? Run in such a way that you may win. And everyone who competes exercises self-control in all things. Thus those do so in order that they may receive a perishable crown, but we an *imperishable* one. (1Co 9:24–25, emphasis added)

In this passage, the victor's wreath is described as "perishable" (φθαρτός). The wreath desired by Christians is just the opposite, "imperishable" (ἄφθαρτος).[40] It indicates something that does not perish, wilt, or die. When ἄφθαρτος is used to describe God, it carries the sense of 'immortal,' as God cannot perish. He is not mortal, he is not subject to the bonds of death.

God is also "invisible." That is, the person of God is not physically visible to humans; he cannot be seen, yet he nonetheless exists and is active. Paul mentions this attribute of God in his epistle to the Colossians:

> He [Jesus] is the image of the *invisible* God, the firstborn of all creation. (Col 1:15, emphasis added)

This quality (ἀόρατος)[41] is also mentioned in some benedictions in the Apostolic Fathers. Consider the *Epistle to Diognetus*:

> But he, truly the Almighty and all-creating and *invisible* God himself, he established the truth and the holy and incomprehensible word from heaven among people, and fixed it firmly in their hearts (*Ep. Diog.* 7.2a, emphasis added)

In addition to being immortal and invisible, God is alone. He is the "only God;" there are no others. Consider *Second Clement*, which also combines these words to describe God:

> To the *only invisible* God, Father of truth, who sent to us the Savior and Originator of immortality, through whom also he made known to us the truth and the heavenly life, to him *be* the glory forever, amen. (2*Cl* 20.5, emphasis added)

To this eternal, immortal, invisible God, the only God, Paul ascribes "honor and glory forever and ever." He has been saved from eternal death by Christ Jesus. As such, he offers honor and glory to his God and Savior.

---

[40] That is, the word for "perishable" is the same as the word for "imperishable," only "imperishable" uses an alpha prefix for negation.

[41] Occurs 5x in NT, only here in PE.

Timothy's Charge (1Ti 1:18–20)

I am setting before you this instruction, Timothy my child, in accordance with the prophecies spoken long ago about you, in order that by them you may fight the good fight, having faith and a good conscience, which some, because they have rejected these, have suffered shipwreck concerning their faith, among whom are Hymenaeus and Alexander, whom I have handed over to Satan, in order that they may be taught not to blaspheme. (1Ti 1:18–20)

Verse 18

I am setting before you this instruction

Paul instructs Timothy to weed out those teachers who teach contrary to Paul. The word translated "I am setting before" is παρατίθημι, meaning to 'entrust for safekeeping or transmission.'[1] Paul is transferring responsibility of right teaching from himself to Timothy.

The word translated "instruction" is the same word as used in verse 5, παραγγελία, generally translated as "charge" or "instruction."[2] The verb form of this word is used in verse 3. The use of the same word in vv. 5 and 18 along with the general flow of the chapter make it clear that all three of these instances (vv. 3, 5, 18) refer to the same instruction or charge.

Paul puts his trust in Timothy to properly transmit this charge to the Ephesians. Timothy is to remove false teachers and refute false doctrine with the goal of a solid foundation built on "love that issues from a pure heart and a good conscience and a sincere faith" (v. 5).[3] In acting faithfully to preach and teach this to the Ephesians, Timothy will keep the charge.

---

[1] BDAG p. 722. Occurs 19x in NT; 2x in PE: 1Ti 1:18; 2Ti 2:2. See comment on 1Ti 1:18.

[2] BDAG p. 760. Occurs 5x in NT: Ac 5:28; 16:24; 1Th 4:2; 1Ti 1:5, 18.

[3] See comment on 1Ti 1:5.

Timothy my child

Paul reminds his readers of his relationship with Timothy with the phrase "Timothy my child."[4] Paul is Timothy's mentor and instructor in matters of faith and doctrine. When correcting the Ephesians' unsound doctrine, Timothy will be bringing them into alignment with the doctrine and teaching of his mentor, Paul.

in accordance with the prophecies spoken long ago about you

Paul's trust of Timothy is no accident. Paul reminds Timothy that his trust agrees with "prophecies spoken long ago" concerning him. In First Timothy, the sort of prophecy (προφητεία)[5] is rather clear as it is discussed later in the epistle:

> Do not neglect the gift that is in you, that was granted to you through *prophecy* with the laying on of hands by the council of elders. (1Ti 4:14, emphasis added)

These "prophecies" mentioned by Paul had been "spoken long ago." The Greek word used is προάγω. It generally means 'to go before,' but depending on the context can mean anything from 'lead the way' to 'precede.'[6] The word is usually used to describe movement, but here the word is used in a temporal manner, describing an event that happened to Timothy in the past. A similar usage occurs in the *Martyrdom of Polycarp*:

> For nearly all the things *that happened previously* happened in order that the Lord might demonstrate to us again a martyrdom in accordance with the gospel. (*Mart. Poly.* 1.1b, emphasis added)

The sense is that events happened prior to the current situation. The word προάγω is used to indicate when the events under discussion occurred.

---

[4] See comment on 1Ti 1:2.

[5] BDAG, p. 889. Occurs 19x in NT; 2x in PE: 1Ti 1:18; 4:14. See comment on 1Ti 4:14 for a fuller discussion of this "prophecy."

[6] BDAG, p. 864. Occurs 20x in NT, 2x in PE: 1Ti 1:18; 5:24.

in order that by them you may fight the good fight

Paul uses the metaphor of warfare to describe Timothy's task: "in order that … you may fight the good fight."[7]

The phrase "you may fight" is from the Greek word στρατεύω, which is defined as "serve in the army" or "fight in a conflict."[8] The word is a military word, though it is used figuratively here.

The word στρατεύω is used in the LXX in a similar vein:

> "Imitate me, brothers," he said. "Do not desert my ages nor renounce my high spirited brotherhood with you. *Fight* the holy and noble fight concerning godliness through which the just providence of our fathers in being merciful to our nation might aid us against the accursed tyrant." (4Ma 9:23–24, emphasis added)

The passage from Fourth Maccabees is translated as "*wage* a holy and honourable war on behalf of righteousness" in one lexicon.[9] In the case of Fourth Maccabees, the war was an actual, physical war. Timothy's war is that of a different realm, but the basic idea is the same. Timothy is to work on behalf of the right, to fight the fight against those who teach contrary doctrine.

First Clement also uses the word στρατεύω:

> Therefore *let us wage war*, men and brothers, with all earnestness under his faultless commands. (*1Cl* 37.1, emphasis added)

In *First Clement* the fight is more like the usage in First Timothy. The commands of God (Timothy's charge, supplemented by the prophecies made concerning him) are the impetus to action. They are to guide Timothy while he is waging war, to assure proper action.

Timothy's fight is to be a "good fight." The word for "fight" is the noun form of the word used for "fight" earlier in the phrase, στρατεία. It has to do with a military

---

[7] The ESV, NKJV, and KJV use language similar to "wage the good warfare." "Wage the good warfare" reflects the military language of the metaphor. Note that other occurrences of the English phrase "fight the good fight" in the PE (1Ti 6:12, 2Ti 4:7) do not use the military terminology used here, but rather use words indicative of a struggle. This accounts for ESV's use of "wage the good warfare" here and "fight the good fight" in 1Ti 6:12 and 2Ti 4:7. See comment on 1Ti 6:12 for more discussion of this difference.

[8] BDAG, p. 947. Occurs 7x in NT, 2x in PE: 1Ti 1:18; 2Ti 2:4.

[9] Lust, J., Eynikel, E., & Hauspie, K. (2003). *A Greek-English Lexicon of the Septuagint: Revised Edition*. Deutsche Bibelgesellschaft: Stuttgart. Emphasis added.

engagement or campaign.[10] The fight is "good" in the sense that it is warfare on the side of the right, for the proper purpose, in response to the command of God.

Philo of Alexandria uses similar language in his tractate on *Allegorical Interpretation*:

> And he is thought worthy of grace, for *having fought the good fight* in behalf of virtue he never ceases from warring till he sees the pleasures overthrown and baulked of their object. (Philo, *Alleg. Interp.* III 14, emphasis added)

Evidence of literal and figurative usage of the phrase "fight the good fight" is readily available from literature from the same era. Paul's use of this metaphor was not innovative. It would be familiar to the recipients of this letter in Ephesus. They would understand that Paul was speaking figuratively yet seriously. Paul was not exhorting Timothy to physical warfare. He was instead exhorting Timothy to work seriously and diligently toward the promotion of sound doctrine within the Ephesian fellowship. This is the warfare Timothy is to wage.

Verse 19

having faith with a good conscience

While fighting the battle, Timothy is to act honorably, with faith and a good conscience on his side. The translation "having faith" consists of the word ἔχω, which generally means to 'hold, possess, or have;'[11] and the typical word for faith, πίστις.[12] In this context, having faith means that one fights the battle without compromising one's faith.

The syntax of the phrase "good conscience" indicates that it as well is to be held onto by Timothy as he fights the battle. Not only must Timothy remain uncompromising in his faith while completing his task, he must do this in such a way that his conscience is clear.

Such language is reminiscent of Paul's three-fold charge in v. 5 and serves to remind Timothy of his duty to keep this charge while addressing the problem of false teachers.

---

[10] BDAG, p. 947. Occurs 2x in NT: 2Co 10:4; 1Ti 1:18.

[11] BDAG, p. 420. Occurs 708x in NT, a very common word. Note the NET New Testament's translation of "holding firmly" in this particular instance.

[12] BDAG, p. 818. Occurs 243x in NT.

which some, because they have rejected these

Paul next mentions that some have rejected faith and a good conscience. This is reminiscent of v. 6, where Paul notes that some have swerved from the goal he set. As such, some similarities between vv. 5–6 and vv. 18–19 can be seen.

The Charge	The Rejection
Verse 5: But the goal of our instruction is love from a pure heart and a good conscience and a faith without hypocrisy,	**Verse 6:** from which some have deviated, *and* have turned away into fruitless discussion,
Verse 18–19a: I am setting before you this instruction, Timothy *my* child, in accordance with the prophecies spoken long ago about you, in order that by them you may fight the good fight, having faith and a good conscience,	**Verse 19b:** which some, *because they* have rejected *these,* have suffered shipwreck concerning their faith,

Some sort of consequence is incurred by rejecting Paul's charge. The word translated "rejecting" is ἀπωθέω, which is glossed as 'push aside' or 'reject' or 'repudiate.'[13] Paul uses ἀπωθέω in his epistle to the Romans:

> Therefore I say, God has not *rejected* his people, has he? May it never be! For I also am an Israelite, from the descendants of Abraham, of the tribe of Benjamin. God has not rejected his people, whom he foreknew! Or do you not know, in the passage about Elijah, what the scripture says—how he appeals to God against Israel? (Ro 11:1–2, emphasis added)

In Romans 11, ἀπωθέω is used of God potentially rejecting his people. Paul's point is that God did not reject his people. The context in First Timothy, however, is of people rejecting faith and good conscience.

The word ἀπωθέω is used multiple times in Acts. Acts 7:39[14] is representative of these instances:

> to whom our fathers were not willing to become obedient, but *rejected* him and turned back in their hearts to Egypt, (Ac 7:39, emphasis added).

---

[13] BDAG, p. 126. Occurs 6x in NT, only here in PE.

[14] The word also occurs in Ac 7:27, 13:46.

In the above context, "him" refers to Moses, whose authority "the fathers" were rejecting. Paul is making much the same point here in First Timothy. This rejection of faith and good conscience is akin to apostasy and it has a consequence: the destruction of one's faith.

have suffered shipwreck concerning their faith

Paul uses the word translated "have suffered shipwreck" (ναυαγέω)[15] figuratively, but not lightly. He had been shipwrecked before; he was well acquainted with the situation. He uses the word in a literal sense in 2 Corinthians:

> Three times I was beaten with rods. Once I received a stoning. Three times *I was shipwrecked.* A day and a night I have spent in the deep water. (2Co 11:25, emphasis added)

The phrase "made shipwreck of their faith" may seem like a strange metaphor initially, but it is used elsewhere. Consider Philo:

> … if we have fallen in with ever so slight a breeze which bears us towards the good fortune, immediately set all sail and became greatly elated, and being full of great and high spirits, hurry forward with all our speed to the indulgence of our passions, and never will check our unbridled and immoderately excited desires until *we run ashore and are wrecked as to the whole vessel* of our souls. (Philo, *Names* 215, emphasis added)

In the above instance, the nautical metaphor implies complete destruction of one's soul as a result of indulging one's passion and then not being able to manage the resultant course. The indulgence of passion continues and eventually runs the whole metaphorical ship aground, completely destroying it.

Paul makes much the same case. In rejecting Paul's charge[16] and pursuing false doctrine some have run their faith aground and destroyed it.

VERSE 20

among whom are Hymenaeus and Alexander

Paul next provides examples of those who made shipwreck of their faith, "Hymenaeus and Alexander." These are men with whom Timothy was sure to be acquainted.

---

[15] BDAG, p. 666. Occurs 2x in NT: 2Co 11:25; 1Ti 1:19.

[16] cf. 1Ti 1:5.

The name "Hymenaeus" is mentioned again in 2Ti 2:17. Both instances are assumed by many to be the same person:

> "That the references are to the same Hymenaeus is generally agreed since in each instance he is characterized as having deviated from the faith."[17]

The name "Alexander" is mentioned twice in the Pastoral Epistles.[18] As Alexander was a common name, there is no certainty that both instances refer to the same person.

> There is no firm evidence to identify this Alexander [from 2Ti 4:14] with either of the two men of the same name in Acts 19:33 and 1 Tim 1:20. The name itself was common in the Hellenistic and Roman periods.[19]

Though little is known of the biographies of these two men, they are indisputable examples of men who "made shipwreck of their faith." These are men who rejected the teaching of Paul, pursued false doctrine and styled themselves as teachers of the law when they were wholly ignorant of such things. They have been devastated and are of no further use as teachers or leaders to the Ephesian community. In this way, they are shipwrecked. Their faith has been destroyed. Their teaching is unsound. They are not to be trusted.

whom I have handed over to Satan

The Greek word translated as "handed over" is παραδίδωμι, which means to 'hand over,' 'give over,' 'hand down,' 'pass on,' or 'allow.'[20] It is used elsewhere in the New Testament, notably in the Gospels, when Judas proposes "delivering over" Jesus to the Pharisees:

> and said, "What are you willing to give me if I in turn *deliver* him to you?" So they set out for him thirty silver coins. And from that time on, he began seeking a favorable opportunity in order that he could betray him. (Mt 26:15–16, emphasis added).

In handing over Jesus to the synagogue authorities Judas betrayed Jesus. Though from a different perspective, the action is the same; the "handing over" or "delivering" from one party to another party.

---

[17] ABD 3:348.

[18] Here and 2Ti 4:14.

[19] ABD 1:151. Addition of bracketed text mine.

[20] BDAG p. 762. Occurs 119x in NT, only here in PE.

This usage is not unique to the New Testament; it is an acceptable use of παραδίδωμι in the LXX as well. The term is used three times to describe how the Lord handed Job over to the devil:

> And the Lord said to the devil, "Behold, *I deliver* him to you; only guard carefully his life." (Job 2:6, emphasis added)

> For they have been *handed over* to the hands of the wicked.'
> He covers the faces of judges.
> And if it is not he, who is it? (Job 9:24, emphasis added)

> For the Lord *gave me up* into the hands of the unrighteous and threw me upon the wicked. (Job 16:11 [LXX 16:12], emphasis added)

The meaning is much the same as in the New Testament instances. This sense of παραδίδωμι is also attested in the apocryphal book of Judith:

> Then Holofernes commanded his slaves, who were attending him in his tent, to take hold of Achior and to bring him to Bethulia and *to hand him over* into the hands of the children of Israel. (Jdt 6:10, emphasis added).

Alexander and Hymenaeus have been handed over "to Satan."[21] Paul uses similar language, even including use of the word παραδίδωμι, in First Corinthians:

> I have decided *to hand over* such a person to Satan for the destruction of the flesh, in order that his spirit may be saved in the day of the Lord. (1Co 5:5, emphasis added)

The context in First Corinthians is that of a man engaged in sexual immorality with his father's wife. Paul instructs the Corinthian congregation to hand the offender over to Satan. In both situations, Paul advocates the release of the troublemaker from the church in a last-ditch effort to convince the offender of his wrongdoing and bring him to repentance.

In the case of Hymenaeus and Alexander, Paul exercised discipline on behalf of the church (cf. Mt 18:15–17) and removed the persisting offenders from the body. In the case of the Corinthians, Paul commands the church to remove the offender. The language of delivering the offender "to Satan"[22] is unusual to 21st century eyes, but is not out of place. If one who professed Christ yet remained persisting in sin was removed from the fellowship, then he ended up with, for lack of a better term, sinners—exactly as described in Mt. 18:17. These are people who are *de facto* aligned

---

[21] Both the 1Co 5:5 and 1Ti 1:20 instances, UBS5 upper-cases Σατανᾶς, while NA28 lower cases to σατανᾶς.

[22] NA28 has τῷ σατανᾷ (lower-case) while UBS5 has τῷ Σατανᾷ (upper-case). It is preferable to follow NA28 and translate with "to the adversary" instead of using a named entity, "Satan."

with Satan as they are not aligned with believers in Christ. In removing Hymenaeus and Alexander from the fellowship of believers, they have been "handed over to Satan" for the express purpose of discipline.

in order that they may be taught not to blaspheme

The handing over of Hymenaeus and Alexander to Satan was a result of perpetuating and persisting in false doctrine, even after attempts at correction. Despite the tough language of handing people over to Satan, Paul earnestly desires for these people to repent and to return to right relationship with Christ and his body. Paul desires correction, not excommunication.

The word translated as "they may learn" is παιδεύω. This is a versatile word and can be interpreted a number of ways, meaning anything from educate to discipline; the sense of discipline may also include some sort of punishment.[23] The context here indicates that the idea of discipline is intended. The punishment is that of removal from the fellowship through handing over to Satan.

In this case, the punishment is intended as a corrective action, causing those so punished to learn and apply the truth. A similar instance of παιδεύω is used in *First Clement*:

> Therefore you who laid the foundation of the rebellion, you be subject to the presbyters and *be disciplined* to repentance, bending the knees of your hearts. (*1Cl* 57.1, emphasis added)

This instance in *First Clement* explicitly states that discipline of those who acted contrary to proper teaching is done with the intent of leading to repentance.

The Greek word translated "to blaspheme" is βλασφημέω, which means to slander, revile, or defame.[24] By teaching false doctrine and misrepresenting the gospel, Hymenaeus and Alexander have blasphemed God.

Hymenaeus and Alexander must learn not to blaspheme. If they are unable to learn this lesson, they will be unable to return to the fellowship.

---

[23] BDAG, p. 749. Occurs 13x in NT, 3x in PE: 1Ti 1:20; 2Ti 2:25; Tt 2:12.

[24] BDAG, p. 178. Occurs 34x in NT, 4x in PE: 1Ti 1:20; 6:1; Tt 2:5; 3:2. See comment on 1Ti 1:13.

Paul Urges Prayer (1Ti 2:1–2)

Therefore, I urge first of all that petitions, prayers, requests, and thanksgiving be made on behalf of all people, on behalf of kings and all those who are in authority, in order that we may live a tranquil and quiet life in all godliness and dignity. (1Ti 2: 1–2)

Verse 1

Therefore I urge first of all

Paul focuses on practical things that believers in Ephesus can do to exhibit their faith. He writes "first of all," which serves as a transition.[1] This statement sets this section in distinction to the previous section and signals that Paul will be discussing new things.

The phrase "I urge" is from the Greek word παρακαλέω. This word was used in this same sense earlier, in 1Ti 1:3. On his way to Macedonia, Paul had "urged" Timothy to deal with the problem of false doctrine. Paul now implores the readers of his letter to proper practice in prayer.

that petitions, prayers

The Greek word translated "petitions" is δέησις. The word may mean simply prayer when it occurs by itself, but when it occurs with προσευχή (as it does here) then δέησις usually takes the more specific meaning of petition or supplication.[2] A petition is a request. When the request is made of God, it is made through prayer. It occurs frequently in the Old Testament,[3] always in the sense of an entreaty or cry for help.[4]

If "petitions" refers to a specific type of prayer, the word προσευχή refers very generally to prayer made to any deity, though in this instance the prayer is offered

---

[1] πρῶτος ("first") occurs 155x in NT; πᾶς ("of all") occurs 1243x in NT.

[2] BDAG, p. 213. Occurs 18x in NT, 3x in PE: 1Ti 2:1; 5:5; 2Ti 1:3.

[3] Occurs 58x in LXX.

[4] BDAG, p. 213.

specifically to God.[5] Some semantic overlap exists between the words δέησις and προσευχή as they both indicate a very general form of prayer. These words occur together four times in the Pauline epistles,[6] usually translated as "prayer and supplication." Paul uses this language in his epistle to the Philippians:

> Let your gentleness be made known to all people. The Lord is near. Be anxious for nothing, but in everything by *prayer and supplication* with thanksgiving let your requests be made known to God. (Php 4:5–6, emphasis added)[7]

The words δέησις and προσευχή occur together with some frequency in the Old Testament too.[8] Consider Solomon, as recorded in First Kings:

> And it came to pass when Solomon completed praying to the Lord all this *prayer and entreaty*, he rose from before the altar of the Lord, having knelt on his knees and having spread out his hands to heaven. (1Ki 8:54 [LXX 3 Kgdms 8:54], emphasis added)

These words are also found in close proximity in Ignatius' *Letter to the Magnesians*:

> Do not even attempt anything that appears reasonable to yourselves, but, for the common purpose, one *prayer*, one *petition*, one mind, one hope in love in the blameless joy, which is Jesus Christ, nothing is better than him. (Ign., *Magn.* 7.1b)

Prayers and supplications are complimentary ideas. When these words occur together, they should be seen as a group, with "prayers" typically representing the general idea of prayer to God, and "supplications" representing specific entreaties made to God through prayer.

requests

The word "requests" is a translation of the Greek word ἔντευξις. In the New Testament, this word typically connotes intercessory prayer.[9] Of this word, Deissmann writes:

> In the New Testament writings ἔντευξις is used only in 1 Tim 2:1 and 4:5, having in both passages the sense of *petitionary prayer*. This usage is commonly explained

---

[5] BDAG, p. 878. Occurs 36x in NT; 2x in PE: 1Ti 2:1; 5:5.

[6] Eph 6:18; Php 4:6; 1Ti 2:1; 5:5.

[7] Note that Php 4:5–6 also mentions thanksgiving, which is discussed in more detail below.

[8] The two words occur in the same verse 22x in the LXX.

[9] BDAG, p. 339. Occurs 2x in NT, both times in PE: 1Ti 2:1; 4:5. It occurs in the LXX once (2Ma 4:8) but the context there is not of prayer, it aligns with BDAG's first sense.

> by the employment of the word in the sense of *petition* which is found in extra-biblical literature from the time of Diodorus and Josephus.[10]

Milligan provides a quotation using ἔντευξις in this sense from a petition dating back to 163 B.C.

> On a former occasion when you were in residence at Memphis and had gone up to the temple to sacrifice, we petitioned you, and gave in a *petition*, bringing before you our plea that we are not receiving the contribution of necessaries which it is fitting should be given to us both … [11]

In the above quote, "we petitioned you" is the verb form of ἔντευξις, while "petition" is the noun form that is also used here in the Pastoral Epistles. Milligan defines it as " … properly the act of approaching the king, and thence the petition addressed to him."[12] Here the petition (ἔντευξις) is made to the king with the anticipation that, if the petition is granted, the king himself will intervene to make the situation right.

In the context of prayer to God ἔντευξις carries the same connotation. The intercession is a prayer of request to God that he intercede in some situation to help the requesting believer and to bring glory upon himself.

and thanksgiving

The word εὐχαριστία is translated as "thanksgiving." The word is versatile, it need not mean a type of prayer. It typically refers to the attitude of thankfulness, or the act of giving thanks.[13] Paul uses this same word in his second epistle to the Corinthians:

> being made rich in every way for all generosity, which is producing through us *thanksgiving* to God, because the service of this ministry is not only supplying the needs of the saints, but also is overflowing through many *expressions of thanksgiving* to God. (2Co 9:11–12, emphasis added)

Thanksgivings are a response to God, giving glory to God for the blessings one receives. As mentioned above, Paul has used this term in similar contexts, most notably in Php 4:5–6.

Paul is not providing a catalogue of different types of prayer; he is instead using different words with overlapping meanings to express a comprehensive view of

---

[10] Gustav Adolf Deissmann, *Bible Studies: Contributions, Chiefly from Papyri and Inscriptions, to the History of the Language, the Literature, and the Religion of Hellenistic Judaism and Primitive Christianity* (T. & T. Clark, 1923), 121.

[11] Milligan, *Selections from the Greek Papyri*, 13. Emphasis added.

[12] Ibid. note 5.

[13] BDAG, p. 416. Occurs 15x in NT, 3x in PE: 1Ti 2:1; 4:3, 4.

prayer. This view also happens to be rhetorically satisfying, leaving little if any possibility for readers of the letter to find an excuse to abstain from praying as directed.

be made on behalf of all people

The word translated "be made" is ποιέω, a common word with many senses that carries a general meaning of make or do.[14] The phrase "on behalf of all people" is translated from a prepositional phrase that simply means 'on behalf of all people.'[15] This group is not limited. Paul intends it to be inclusive, instructing the Ephesians to pray for all people, considering both spiritual and physical needs of their fellow citizens, employers, rulers and others.

VERSE 2

on behalf of kings and all those who are in authority

The word translated "kings" is βασιλεύς. This word is generically used of the highest-level ruler of a realm, which is typically an emperor or king.[16] Paul just used this term (1Ti 1:17) to describe God as "the King of the ages." God is certainly King of all. Here in 1Ti 2:2 Paul uses the term to describe rulers in their earthly realms; those in positions of civil and political authority as a result of their position.

The phrase "high positions" is translated from ὑπεροχή, which in this context means authority or official in high rank.[17] The word may also convey superiority, but as the immediate context contains βασιλεύς ("kings") the sense of authority or official is preferred. The word also occurs in Second Maccabees:

> The high priest indicated that there were deposits both from widows and orphans, and also that a certain Hyrcanus the son of Tobias, a man exceeding in *dignity*, was storing some money there. It was not as the impious Simon misinformed, and the total amount was four hundred talents of silver and two hundred of gold. And that wrongs should happen to those who trusted in the sanctity of the place and in

---

[14] BDAG, p. 839. See comment on 1Ti 1:13.

[15] The word translated "people" is ἄνθρωπος. As a plural in this context, it is obviously referring not only to males but to humans in general (i.e. mankind), thus the translation "people" instead of "men" in a generic sense. See comment on 1Ti 2:4 for more discussion on this phrase.

[16] BDAG, p. 169. Occurs 115x in NT, 3x in PE: 1Ti 1:17; 2:2; 6:15.

[17] BDAG, p. 1034. Occurs 2x in NT: 1Co 2:1; 1Ti 2:2. The verb form, ὑπερέχω, occurs 5x in the NT (e.g. Php 4:7), none of which are in the PE.

> the dignity and inviolability of the temple, which is honored throughout the whole world, was completely impossible. (2Ma 3:10–12, emphasis added)

In this instance, ὑπεροχή denotes the high rank[18] of Hyrcanus. The word also occurs in Josephus' *Antiquities*:

> He also constituted judges in every one of the cities of his kingdom; and charged them to have regard to nothing so much in judging the multitude as to do justice, and not to be moved by bribes, nor by the dignity *of men eminent for either their riches or their high birth*, but to distribute justice equally to all, as knowing that God is conscious of every secret action of theirs. (Jos., *Ant.* 9.3, emphasis added)

In evaluating the above, the picture of the ὑπεροχή becomes evident. These are men who are in some position of prominence within their communities. Their prominence is due to nobility, office, or wealth. Paul desires the Ephesians to pray specifically for such people, in addition to generally praying "on behalf of all people."

in order that we may live a tranquil and quiet life

The phrase "we may lead … life" is from the Greek word διάγω, which has the sense of 'to spend one's life,' or 'live one's life,' or simply 'to live.'[19] Paul is speaking of the life lived as a Christian. Consider Ignatius, writing in his *Letter to the Trallians*:

> Therefore it is necessary (just as you already do) for you to do nothing without the bishop, but be subject also to the council of elders as to the apostles of Jesus Christ our hope. If *we live* in him, we will be found in him. (Ign., *Trall.* 2.2, emphasis added)

Ignatius is not simply speaking of living in a biological sense, but is rather speaking of the fullness of life lived in Christ.

The word translated "tranquil" is ἤρεμος, an NT *hapax* which means tranquil or quiet.[20] The word translated "quiet" is ἡσύχιος, an adjective. In this instance, it carries the sense of 'without turmoil'[21] instead of the more common sense of 'to be silent.' Peter uses ἡσύχιος in his first epistle to describe what Christian women are "adorned" with:

> Let your adornment not be the external kind, braiding hair and putting on gold jewelry or putting on fine clothing, but the hidden person of the heart, with the

---

[18] The NRSV translates ὑπεροχή as "prominent position."

[19] BDAG, p. 227. Occurs 2x in NT, both in PE: 1Ti 2:2; Tt 3:3.

[20] BDAG, p. 439. *hapax*.

[21] BDAG, p. 440. Occurs 2x in NT: 1Ti 2:2; 1Pe 3:4. The related noun ἡσυχία appears in 1Ti 2:11 and 12.

> imperishable quality of a gentle and *quiet* spirit, which is highly valuable in the sight of God. (1Pe 3:3–4, emphasis added)

Consider also the following from the *Psalms of Solomon*, where ἡσύχιος describes one's soul:

> May the Lord guard the *quiet* soul that hates the unrighteous, and may the Lord guide the man who makes peace in the house. (*Ps. Sol.* 12:6, emphasis added)

The life recommended by Paul is a tranquil life that is properly grounded. It is a life that does not seek attention, but does not compromise itself under the burden of attention.

in all godliness and dignity

The word translated as "godly" is εὐσέβεια, which has to do with godliness or piety.[22] This is a life of unadvertised worship, devotion and piety that manifests itself externally in a subtle yet powerful way. The word occurs in the LXX, in Fourth Maccabees:

> You mock our philosophy as if living by it was not with prudence. But it thoroughly teaches us good judgment so as to rule over all the pleasures and desires and courage; to train so as to endure willingly all pain. And it educates us in justice so as to act fairly through all activity and to teach *piety*, so as to worship the only God who exists reverently. (4Ma 5:22–24 NRSV, emphasis added)

The citation from Fourth Maccabees is interesting in that not only does it mention εὐσέβεια but it plainly shows the effect of εὐσέβεια: " ... so as to worship the only God who exists reverently." The word εὐσέβεια is also used by Josephus:

> Pythagoras, therefore, of Samos, lived in very ancient times, and was esteemed a person superior to all philosophers in wisdom and *piety* towards God. Now it is plain that he did not only know our doctrines, but was in very great measure a follower and admirer of them. (Jos., *Apion* 1.162, emphasis added)

As Josephus makes plain, the effect of εὐσέβεια (piety) is seen by others. The word occurs in *First Clement* as well:

> And we, therefore, having been called through his will in Christ Jesus, we are not justified through ourselves, or through our wisdom or understanding or *piety* or deeds which we accomplished in holiness of heart, but through the faith by which

---

[22] BDAG, p. 412. Occurs 15x in NT, 10x in PE: 1Ti 2:2; 3:16; 4:7, 8; 6:3, 5, 6, 11; 2Ti 3:5; Tt 1:1. The other NT occurrences are, apart from an instance in Ac 3:12, all in Second Peter: 2Pe 1:3, 6, 7; 3:11.

> all those since the beginning the Almighty God has justified to him be the glory forever, amen. (*1Cl* 32.4, emphasis added)

The examples from Josephus and *First Clement* make clear that one's godliness is evidenced in the way one leads his life. Piety or godliness that one purposefully draws attention to with hopes of praise from others is neither piety nor godliness; it is hypocrisy. Philo writes concerning this:

> … and these are the doctrines, not of men who are halting between two opinions, but of those who are occupied in a firm and sure faith; since, even now, there are some persons among those who make a show and pretence of *piety*, who calumniate the literal meaning of this saying, saying that it is neither pious nor safe to speak of God as the inheritance of a man. (Philo, *Planting* 70)

This quality of godliness, εὐσέβεια, comes about as a result of a life of worship and devotion.

The life Paul desires the Ephesians to lead is not only godly, but is also to be "dignified." The word "dignified" is a translation of the Greek word σεμνότης. The definition offered for this word is "a manner or mode of behavior that indicates one is above what is ordinary and therefore worthy of special respect."[23] Paul desires that Christians live their lives not simply in accordance with the standards of their community, but above those standards. He desires the Ephesians to be visibly different in the way they live their lives.

One of the primary methods to achieve this difference is for the Ephesian Christians to be in prayer constantly for those around them and specifically for their leaders. In reconciling with neighbors and respecting leaders, the Ephesian Christians will display evidence of godly and dignified lives.

---

[23] BDAG, p. 919. When used of a deity, σεμνότης has the sense of "holiness," when used of people the sense of "dignity." Occurs 3x in NT, all three are in PE: 1Ti 2:2; 3:4; Tt 2:7.

The Rationale for Requiring Prayer (1Ti 2:3–7)

> *This is good and acceptable before God our Savior, who wants all people to be saved and to come to a knowledge of the truth. For there is one God and one mediator between God and human beings, the man Christ Jesus, who gave himself a ransom for all, the testimony at the proper time, for which I was appointed a herald and an apostle—I am speaking the truth, I am not lying—a teacher of the Gentiles in faith and truth. (1Ti 2:3–7)*

Verse 3

This is good

Paul exhorts his readers to offer prayer on the behalf of all men and to specifically pray for those in positions of authority. This effort in prayer reaps benefits for the Ephesian believers, making a quiet and peaceful life more likely. So when Paul opens up verse 3 with "This is good," he is referring to the content of verses 1 and 2. It is good that the Ephesian Christians pray for all people and also for those in authority.

and acceptable before God our Savior

The word translated "acceptable" is ἀπόδεκτος,[1] but might be better translated as "pleasing" (ESV). The word is also used in 1Ti 5:4, where LEB does translate "pleasing":

> But if any widow has children or grandchildren, they must learn to show profound respect for their own household first, and to pay back recompense to their parents, for this is *pleasing* in the sight of God. (1Ti 5:4, emphasis added)

The word translated as "before" is the preposition ἐνώπιον, which typically carries the meaning of before or in front of.[2] It also refers to the sense of being under the evaluation of someone. Paul uses this word in Second Corinthians:

---

[1] BDAG, p 109. Occurs 2x in NT, both in PE: 1Ti 2:3; 5:4.

[2] BDAG, p. 342. Occurs 94x in NT, 9x in PE.

> We are trying to avoid this, lest anyone should find fault with us in this abundant gift that is being administered by us. For we are taking into consideration what is honorable not only *before* the Lord, but also *before* people. (2Co 8:20–21, emphasis added).

In the above example, the word ἐνώπιον occurs twice. The deeds of Christians are on display before both God and man. The word is also used in *First Clement*:

> Beloved, take care that his many kindnesses may not come to judgment on us if, leading a life not worthy of him we should do good and pleasing things *before* him in harmony. (*1Cl* 21.1, emphasis added)

Though not the primary sense of ἐνώπιον, this sense is well attested. The prayer of the Ephesian Christians for their neighbors and also for those in authority over them is pleasing in the sight of God.

Paul next uses the phrase "God our Savior"[3] to remind both Timothy and the readers of the epistle of the one offering approval for the action of prayer; the same God who commissioned Paul to the office of apostle. The God who saves is the one these prayer are offered to, and they are not offered in vain.

VERSE 4

who wants all people to be saved

The word translated "desires" is θέλω, which occurs frequently in the New Testament.[4] In this instance, as in 1Ti 1:7, the general meaning of want, wish, or desire is intended. As Paul testified earlier in 1Ti 1:15,[5] "Christ Jesus came into the world to save sinners." Paul declared that this saying is "trustworthy and worthy of all acceptance."

The inclusion of the phrase "all people" (πάντας ἀνθρώπους) is important because it points back to the same phrase that occurs in verse 1. Paul implores the Ephesians to make petitions, prayers, requests, and thanksgivings for all people because God desires for all people to be saved. In praying for those around them, the Ephesians will build a desire for those around them to be saved.

---

[3] cf. notes on 1Ti 1:1.

[4] cf. 1Ti 1:7, " … desiring to be teachers of the law … "

[5] See comment on 1Ti 1:15, specifically on the word "saved."

and to come to a knowledge of the truth.

The second part of Paul's description has to do with coming to a "knowledge of the truth."[6] Salvation and knowledge of the truth are tied together. If one does not come into knowledge of the truth (as described in vv. 5–6a) then one is not saved.[7] Paul was fairly explicit about this in chapter one, focusing on the need to correct false teachers. Paul also focused on the proper use of the law, establishing that the law is to be used correctively to enlighten men of their inadequacy to meet God's standard.

Prior to his encounter with Jesus, Paul was a blasphemer, persecutor, and insolent opponent of Christ. Paul describes how in spite of his sin he was shown mercy and how his salvation serves as an example for the salvation of others. When one begins to understand the depth of his own depravity, as Paul testifies he did, one is left at the mercy of God. Salvation only occurs through Jesus Christ. Outside of Christ there is no forgiveness of sin and therefore no manner of escaping death and hell. Those who disregard the law and remain ignorant of sin cannot be saved because they do not rely on Jesus Christ for salvation. They are doomed. They have no knowledge of the truth.

Yet Paul desires for the Ephesian Christians to be aligned with the desires of God—that all people are saved and come to knowledge of the truth. Therefore Paul urges them to focus on praying for the people around them and their leaders. In offering petitions, prayers, requests, and thanksgivings, the Ephesian Christians will mature and develop a sincere desire for the salvation of those for whom they are praying.

---

[6] The phrase "knowledge of the truth" occurs 4x in the PE. 4x, 1Ti 2:4; 2Ti 2:25; 3:7; Tt 1:1. cf. also Heb 10:26. It is explained by Paul in vv. 5–6.

[7] Note that John 14:21 implies that the one who loves Jesus and keeps his commandments will be loved by the Father and by Jesus, and that Jesus will "disclose" (NASB) or "manifest" (ESV) himself to the one who loves him. This seems to allow for a non-consecutive nature of salvation (loving Jesus) and coming into knowledge of the truth (instruction from Jesus). The point of 1Ti 2:4, however, is that the one who is saved will—eventually—come into knowledge of the truth described in 1Ti 2:5–6a. Those teaching contrary to that knowledge of the truth are to be removed from the fellowship as false teachers.

VERSE 5

Verses 5 and 6 are in all likelihood part of an early hymn or creed.[8] Paul was appealing to a source known in common to establish the content of the "knowledge of the truth."

For there is one God

The first line of the creed evokes memories of Deut. 6:4, "Hear O Israel: The LORD our God, the LORD is one" (ESV)[9]. There is only one God, and salvation, as Paul has so ably shown, depends on living to the standard expected by God.

However, as Paul has also rather ably shown, people are unable to meet that standard. People are unable to live up to the law of God. Even Paul was unable to do this; he required the intervention of Jesus Christ in order to be saved. Paul holds the intervention of Christ in his life as an example for others. "Christ Jesus came into the world to save sinners" is a trustworthy saying, according to Paul—and he ought to know.

and one mediator between God and human beings

The second line is a realization of the inadequacy of people to present themselves before God. People need an intermediary. Just as there is one God, there is one mediator—not two or three mediators, only one mediator. Salvation is available through one path. The word translated as one is εἷς, the standard numerical term for one.[10]

The word translated "mediator" comes from the Greek word μεσίτης, which traditionally means 'intermediary,' 'mediator,' or 'arbitrator.'[11] Paul uses this word in his letter to the Galatians:

> Why then the law? It was added on account of transgressions, until the descendant should come to whom it had been promised, having been ordered

---

[8] Scholars differ on division and extent of the source; it will be presented here as two stanzas, with each stanza comprised of two lines. For simplicity's sake, it will be referred to as a creed for the balance of this work.

[9] ESV quoted because LEB is less familiar: "Hear, Israel, Yahweh our God, Yahweh is unique." Deut 6:4, LEB

[10] BDAG, p. 291. Occurs 345x in NT.

[11] BDAG, p. 634. Occurs 6x in NT, once in PE (here). Other NT occurrences are Ga 3:19–20; Heb 8:6; 9:15; 12:24.

> through angels by the hand *of a mediator*. Now *the mediator* is not for one, but God is one. (Ga 3:19–20, emphasis added)

The μεσίτης is the one acting on behalf of God to put the law into place, so that people may benefit by it. The intermediary, in the above context, is the one working between the parties.

the man, Christ Jesus

As the third line of the creed states, this mediator, the one who stands between God and people, is "the man, Christ Jesus." The epistle to the Hebrews discusses Christ's mediation of the new covenant:

> And because of this, he [Jesus Christ] is *the mediator* of a new covenant, in order that, because a death has taken place for the redemption of transgressions committed during the first covenant, those who are the called may receive the promise of the eternal inheritance. (Heb 9:15, emphasis added)

The previous verses in Hebrews (Heb 9:13–14) are essential to understanding the role of the mediator of the new covenant:

> For if the blood of goats and bulls and the ashes of a young cow sprinkled on those who are defiled sanctify them for the ritual purity of the flesh, how much more will the blood of Christ, who through the eternal Spirit offered himself without blemish to God, cleanse our consciences from dead works to serve the living God? (Heb 9:13–14)

This passage from Hebrews states that Christ offered himself to God in order to purify people. Christ acted on behalf of people to satisfy the requirements of God. In this way Christ is the one mediator[12] between God and people.

---

[12] The translation of "mediator" is not without its problems. In modern usage, a mediator is one who meets with parties that have some dispute and arranges a settlement. The settlement typically involves both sides making compromises to arrive at a solution. This is most emphatically not the case with a person's relationship with God. God makes no compromise, his standard is not breeched in order to allow people to partake of salvation. Instead, Christ Jesus fully satisfies the requirements of God, without exception or compromise. Christ Jesus propitiates (1Jn 2:1–2)[12] the wrath of God on our behalf. This satisfaction allows men to approach God through the one who stands before God on our account, Jesus Christ. This is the mediation of the new covenant spoken of in Hebrews 9.

Verse 6

who gave himself a ransom for all

The word translated as "ransom" is ἀντίλυτρον.[13] This word only occurs here in the New Testament. However, the concept of "ransom" is used elsewhere in the New Testament to much the same effect. The TDNT article for ἀντίλυτρον states, "Materially ἀντίλυτρον is the same as λύτρον."[14] The word λύτρον occurs in the Gospels, in Mk 10:45:[15]

> For even the Son of Man did not come to be served, but to serve, and to give his life as *a ransom* for many. (Mk 10:45, emphasis added.)

The verse in Mark may very well serve as the basis for this line of the creed. The death of Christ was a ransom that freed many men for salvation. Christ effectively bought their way with his sacrifice. This concept is outstanding in light of Psalm 49 [48 LXX]:

> A brother is not *redeemed*. Will a person *redeem*? He will not give to God his ransom, and the price of the ransoming of his life, even though he labor forever. But he will live in the end because he will not see destruction (Ps 49:7–9 [LXX 48:8–10])[16]

No man has sufficient means to ransom another man from eternal suffering, according to the Psalmist. Yet Christ has come to offer his life as a ransom for many. Paul is familiar with these words of Christ in the gospel of Mark. In his epistolary greeting to the Galatians, Paul bestows grace from the Lord Jesus Christ:

> who gave himself for our sins in order to rescue us from the present evil age, according to the will of our God and Father, (Ga 1:4).

Ga 2:20 similarly notes that Christ "gave himself for me." Ro 4:25 notes that Christ "... was handed over on account of our trespasses and was raised up in the interest of our justification." Paul wrote similarly to the Ephesians:

---

[13] BDAG, p. 89. *hapax*.

[14] TDNT, 4:349.

[15] See the parallel passage, Mt 20:28, for the other instance of λύτρον in the NT. Other references: Isa. 53:10; Dan. 9:26; John 10:15; 11:51, 52; Rom. 4:25; Gal. 1:4; 2:20; 1 Pet. 1:18, 19 (ESV marginal x-refs)

[16] The word translated "redeem" by the *Lexham English Septuagint* is the verb λυτρόω, related to the noun under discussion. The word translated "ransom" is ἐξίλασμα, which refers more specifically to the payment as ransom or bribe.

> and live in love, just as also Christ loved us, and gave himself for us an offering and sacrifice to God for a fragrant smell. (Eph 5:2)

Paul continually describes himself as a "slave of Christ,"[17] and also notes that he has been bought at a price and set free.[18] Paul himself has been ransomed by Christ. Deissmann ties it all together nicely when he writes,

> ... when anybody heard the Greek word λύτρον, "ransom," in the first century, it was natural for him to think of the purchase-money for manumitting slaves.[19]

Prior to this statement, Deissmann examined in some detail the practice of manumission: slaves purchasing their own freedom through the pagan temples.

> What was this custom? Among the various ways in which the manumission of a slave could take place by ancient law we find the solemn rite of fictitious purchase of the slave by some divinity. The owner comes with the slave to the temple, sells him there to the god, and receives the purchase money from the temple treasury, the slave having previously paid it in there out of his savings. The slave is now the property of the god; not, however, a slave of the temple, but a protégé of the god. Against all the world, especially his former master, he is a completely free man; at the utmost a few pious obligations to his old master are imposed upon him.[20]

When Paul mentions "ransom," he is referring at least obliquely to the practice of manumission. And he is doing it in language that the commonest of people in Ephesus would have understood. Again, an extended passage from Deissmann:

> I would rather point out that St. Paul, in expanding and adapting to the Greek world the Master's old saying about ransom, was admirably meeting the requirements and the intellectual capacity of the lower classes. For the poor saints of Corinth, among whom there were certainly some slaves, he could not have found a more popular illustration of the past and present work of the Lord. A Christian slave of Corinth going up the path to the Acrocorinthus about Eastertide, when St. Paul's letter arrived, would see towards the north-west the snowy peak of Parnassus rising clearer and clearer before him, and everyone knew that within the circuit of that commanding summit lay the shrines at which Apollo or Serapis or Asclepius the Healer *bought slaves with a price, for freedom.* Then in the evening assembly was read the letter lately received from Ephesus, and straightway the new Healer was present in spirit with His worshippers, giving them freedom from another slavery, *redeeming with a price* the bondmen of sin

---

[17] cf Ro 1:1. Deissmann writes "The expression δοῦλος Χριστοῦ (slave of Christ) is so common in St. Paul that there is no need to give its instances." LAE, 325..

[18] cf. 1Co 6:20; 7:23.

[19] LAE, 327.

[20] Ibid., 322.

> and the law – and that price no pious fiction, first received by Him out of the hard-earned denarii of the slave, but paid by Himself with the redemption-money of His daily new self-sacrifice, rousing up *for freedom* those who languished in slavery.[21]

Jesus Christ has paid the price of the ransom, buying freedom for his own. Paul argues using similar cultural knowledge in First Corinthians:

Were you called while a slave? Do not let it be a concern to you. But if indeed you are able to become free, rather make use of it. For the one who is called in the Lord while a slave is the Lord's freedperson. Likewise the one who is called while free is a slave of Christ. You were bought at a price; do not become slaves of people.

> Were you called while a slave? Do not let it be a concern to you. But if indeed you are able to become free, rather make use of it. For the one who is called in the Lord while a slave is the Lord's freedperson. Likewise the one who is called while free is a slave of Christ. *You were bought at a price; do not become slaves of men.* (1Co 7:21–23, emphasis added)

Here Paul speaks of the redemption performed by Christ in terms of manumission, noting that the believers in Corinth were "bought with a price," and that they must remember this and not fall back, to "become slaves of men."

the testimony at the proper time,

Paul is referring to the death of Christ, the ransom, as "the testimony." The word translated as "testimony" is the Greek word μαρτύριον.[22] It is used in the LXX in Ge 31:44, to describe the covenant made between Jacob and Laban.[23]

> Now then come, let us establish a covenant, I and you, and it will be for a *testimony* between me and you." He said to him, "Look, Jacob, no one is with us; see, God is witness between me and you." (Ge 31:44 [LXX])

This took place after Jacob and his family (Rachel, Leah, and children) left Laban to return to the promised land. In this verse, the covenant itself is a testimony to the agreement made, with God as a witness, between Jacob and Laban.

The death and resurrection of Christ serves as testimony to the fact that Christ now stands in the role of mediator between God and man. Man is in need of salvation. Paul established this earlier by saying that Christ came to save sinners. Paul held up

---

[21] Ibid., 328–329.

[22] BDAG, p. 619, μαρτύριον. Occurs 19x in NT, 2x in PE: 1Ti 2:6; 2Ti 1:8.

[23] The LXX version of this verse is longer than the Hebrew equivalent that is used as the basis of most English versions.

his own life as prototypical, showing how the only way to be saved was for Christ to do it, for Christ to intercede on behalf of men to present them before God. And Christ did exactly that. He interceded by paying the ransom demanded, freeing men from sin. He "...who gave himself for us, in order that he might redeem us from all lawlessness and purify for himself a people for his own possession, zealous for good deeds." (Tt 2:14).

VERSE 7

or which I was appointed a herald and an apostle

Paul once again notes that he was appointed to his current role.[24] His appointed role involves being "a herald and an apostle."[25] Paul is an apostle[26] though his role as apostle requires him to preach and to teach effectively.

The word translated "herald" is κῆρυξ, which is typically translated as 'herald,' 'proclaimer,' or 'preacher.'[27] The author of *First Clement* uses κῆρυξ to describe Paul's work:

> Because of jealousy and strife, Paul pointed the way to the prize of endurance. Having borne chains seven times, having been exiled, having been stoned, having been *a preacher* in both the east and in the west, he received the noble fame of his faith. (*1Cl* 5.5–6, emphasis added)

The word κῆρυξ is also used in the *Corpus Hermeticum*[28] where it is helpfully defined in context:

> HERMES: He filled a mighty Cup with it, and sent it down, joining a *Herald* [to it], to whom He gave command to make this proclamation to the hearts of men (*Corpus Hermeticum* 4.4, emphasis added)[29]

This citation is helpful as it shows the herald to be one who is given a proclamation. Upon receipt of the proclamation, the herald's role is to make the proclamation

---

[24] See comment on 1Ti 1:12.

[25] See comment on 2Ti 1:11, which uses the same phrase.

[26] See comment on 1Ti 1:1 for more information on Paul's apostleship.

[27] BDAG p. 543. Occurs 3x in NT: 1Ti 2:7; 2Ti 1:11; 2Pe 2:5.

[28] The *Corpus Hermeticum* is a gnostic document and should not be misconstrued as a document to be read for Christian edification. But it was most likely composed sometime in the 2nd or 3rd century A.D., which makes it helpful to examine for insight on words used infrequently in the NT.

[29] Online: http://www.gnosis.org/library/hermet.htm.

known—in the case of the *Corpus Hermeticum*, "to the hearts of men." Paul had been tasked by Jesus in much the same way. Paul was to proclaim (preach) the word to the Gentiles.

I am speaking the truth, I am not lying

This is a parenthetical note from Paul, confirming his status as apostle and preacher. The phrase is interesting for its redundancy. Both "I am telling the truth" and "I am not lying" use different language to say the same thing; one using positive language and the other using negation.

There is no reason to doubt Paul's call as apostle or as preacher. As he has clearly stated in his salutation to Timothy and in other epistolary salutations, his apostleship is a result of the command of God.[30]

a teacher of the Gentiles in faith and truth

As an apostle and preacher, Paul is responsible to accurately teach this testimony. This explains his insistence earlier in the epistle regarding sound doctrine.[31] His appointment as preacher and apostle is not a general appointment, he is specifically responsible to teach "the Gentiles in faith and truth."

The word translated "Gentiles" is the Greek word ἔθνος. This is a common word and its meaning is different depending on context. In the context of Paul's apostleship, the meaning of non-Jews is typically intended.[32] Paul is to carry out his appointed tasks to the Gentiles "in faith and truth." Earlier, Paul exhorted Timothy to carry out the task of teaching sound doctrine in faith and good conscience.[33] Paul is to have a similar outlook. He is to properly represent the testimony (v. 6b) to the Gentiles.

---

[30] See comment on 1Ti 1:1.

[31] cf. 1Ti 1:3.

[32] BDAG p. 276. Occurs 162x in NT, 3x in PE: 1Ti 2:7; 3:16; 2Ti 4:17.

[33] cf. 1Ti 1:19, "faith with a good conscience."

Women in the Fellowship (1Ti 2:8–15)

> *Therefore I want the men in every place to pray, lifting up holy hands without anger and dispute. Likewise also the women should adorn themselves in appropriate clothing, with modesty and self-control, not with braided hair and gold jewelry or pearls or expensive clothing, but with good deeds which are fitting for women who profess godliness. A woman must learn in quietness with all submission. But I do not permit a woman to teach or to exercise authority over a man, but to remain quiet. For Adam was formed first, then Eve, and Adam was not deceived, but the woman, because she was deceived, came into transgression. But she will be saved through the bearing of children, if she continues in faith and love and holiness with self-control. (1Ti 2:8–15)*

After focusing on God's desire for the Ephesians (and all Christians) to pray, Paul transitions into the subject of women in the fellowship.

Verse 8

Therefore I want the men in every place to pray

Paul offers a short application of the previous emphasis on prayer. The word "want" was used earlier, in verse 4, to communicate God's desire for "all people to be saved and to come to knowledge of the truth."[1] In that situation, the Greek word θέλω was translated as "[God] wants."

In verse 8, however, a different Greek word is translated "I want." Here, the Greek word is βούλομαι.[2] The word, in this sort of context, covers much of the same semantic range as θέλω, though there are some differences. LN differentiate the nuance between the two by noting that βούλομαι speaks of planned intentions; 'to purpose, to plan, to intend'[3] while θέλω is 'to purpose, generally based upon a preference and desire.'[4]

The word βούλομαι is also used in 1Ti 5:14:

---

[1] See comment on 1Ti 2:4.

[2] BDAG, p. 182. Occurs 37x in NT, 4x in PE: 1Ti 2:8; 5:14; 6:9; Tt 3:8.

[3] LN 30.56; vol. 1 p. 356.

[4] LN 30.58; vol. 1 p. 356.

> Therefore *I want* younger widows to marry, to bear children, to manage a household, to give the adversary no opportunity for reproach. (1Ti 5:14, emphasis added)

In the above verse, βούλομαι is used to express Paul's desire for younger widows to marry and establish a family. This is Paul's intention, though through distance he can do very little to enact his intentions. Paul uses this same sort of structure[5] in his letter to the Philippians:

> Now *I want* you to know, brothers, that my circumstances have happened instead for the progress of the gospel, (Php 1:12, emphasis added)

In these sorts of situations, Paul is expressing his own desire and goal. He wants to communicate a particular desire to a particular group.

Josephus, in his *Antiquities of the Jews*, uses βούλομαι in similar fashion with θέλω in close succession. The first italic instance represents βούλομαι; the second θέλω:

> Caius Phanius, the son of Caius, imperator and consul, to the magistrates of Cos, sendeth greeting. *I would have* you know that the ambassadors of the Jews have been with me, and desired they might have those decrees which the senate had made about them: which decrees are here subjoined. *My will is*, that you have a regard to and take care of these men, according to the senate's decree, that they may be safely conveyed home through your country. (Jos., *Ant.* 14.233, emphasis added)

In this short example, βούλομαι is used to express a want or desire—that the reader of the letter know about the Jewish ambassadors and their interaction with the senate—while θέλω is used to express the strong hopes of Caius Phanius that the senate decree be adhered to, and that the safety of the Jewish ambassadors be thus guaranteed.

Paul's desire, his wish, is that in "every place the men should pray." Based on the emphasis on prayer in verses 1–4,[6] this makes sense. The word for "every" (πᾶς) is the same word used for "all" in verses 1 and 4[7]. The word "place" is translated from the Greek word τόπος. This word means, most generically, 'place, position or region.'[8] It forms the root from which English words such as "topography" are derived. Paul is expressing his desire that men pray in all places. The word "pray" in

---

[5] Βούλομαι, followed by an accusative and infinitive. This happens with βούλομαι in 1Ti 2:8; 5:14; Tt 3:8 and Php 1:12.

[6] See comments on 1Ti 2:1–4.

[7] "all people," in both instances.

[8] BDAG p. 1011. Occurs 94x in NT, only here in PE.

this phrase is the Greek word προσεύχομαι. The meaning of the word is simply 'pray' or 'to petition deity.'[9]

lifting up holy hands

Paul describes this prayer as taking place by "lifting up holy hands without anger or dispute." The Greek word for "lifting" is ἐπαίρω, typically meaning 'lift up' or 'hold up.'[10] In this instance "holy hands" are lifted. The Greek word for "holy" is ὅσιος, typically meaning 'holy' or 'pleasing to God'[11] and the word translated "hands" is the standard word for 'hand,' χείρ,[12] in the plural.

The picture of "lifting hands" occurs elsewhere in the New Testament. Luke records an instance at the end of his Gospel, immediately previous to the ascension:

> And he led them out as far as Bethany, and *lifting up his hands*, he blessed them. And it happened that while he was blessing them, he parted from them and was taken up into heaven. And they worshiped him and returned to Jerusalem with great joy. And they were continually in the temple courts praising God. (Lk 24:50–53, emphasis added)

In this instance, the lifting up of hands was part of the act of blessing; a sort of body language that indicates the blessing.

This sort of image also occurs in the LXX, typically implying worship, praise or blessing. Below is an example from Psalms:

> Behold, surely bless the Lord, all servants of the Lord, who stand in the courts of the house of our God. In the nights *lift up your hands* to the holy place and bless the Lord. (Ps 134:1–2 [133:1–2 LXX])

Similar images appear in Sirach:

> Then, going down, *he lifted up his hands* over all the assembly of the children of Israel to give a blessing to the Lord from his lips and to boast in his name. (Sir 50:20 [LXX])

---

[9] BDAG p. 879. Occurs 85x in NT, only here in PE. Note, however, the noun form of this word occurs in 1Ti 2:1.

[10] BDAG, p. 357. Occurs 19x in NT, only here in PE.

[11] BDAG, p. 728. Occurs 8x in NT, 2x in PE: 1Ti 2:8; Tt 1:8.

[12] BDAG, p. 1082. Occurs 177x in NT.

without anger or dispute

The statement's corollary is that hands are to be lifted "without anger or dispute." That is, the hands are to be lifted up in the sense of blessing, not in the sense of violence or quarrelling. Consider Second Samuel:

> "This is not the reason! For there is a man from the hill country of Ephraim; Sheba son of Bichri is his name. And *he has raised his hand against* King David. Give him to me alone and I will depart from the city." And the woman said to Joab, "Look, his head will be thrown to you through the wall." (2Sa 20:21 [LXX 2Kgdms 20:21])

Sheba had "raised his hand" against King David, which implies that Sheba was acting against King David. This is why Joab wanted to destroy him. In this case, the lifting up of Sheba's hand carries a negative connotation.[13]

Paul was only interested in the lifting up of holy hands in blessing and encouragement, not in anger or quarreling. The word translated "anger" is the Greek word ὀργή, which typically means 'anger' or 'wrath.' [14] The word translated "quarreling" is διαλογισμός, meaning 'dispute' or 'argument' in contexts like this,[15] merits further discussion. Paul's letter to the Philippians contains a similar phrase using διαλογισμός:

> Do all things without grumbling or *disputing*, (Php 2:14, emphasis added)

Moulton and Milligan have entries for both διαλογισμός and the related verb διαλογίζομαι, relating the judicial nature of the term:

> The verb and its derivative noun are conspicuous in Egyptian documents to describe the *conventus*, the judicial "circuit" of the Praefect.[16]

In such instances, the word διαλογισμός describes the disputing or arguing that occurs within in a judicial court. Moulton and Milligan go on to note that Php 2:14 and 1Ti 2:8 are passages "where the thought of outward disputing and discussion is uppermost."[17] It is possible that the disputing, quarreling and questioning indicated in these two NT passages is indicative of disputing in a judicial context. This sort of

---

[13] There appears to be a trend for the "lifting of hands" (plural) to be something positive, with the "lifting of a hand" (singular) to be negative.

[14] BDAG p. 720. Occurs 36x in NT, only here in PE.

[15] BDAG p. 232. Occurs 14x in NT, only here in PE.

[16] M-M, p. 151. Note, however, that this "judicial" sense of the verb διαλογίζομαι is not found in the NT.

[17] Ibid.

bickering is not to be accepted, and is certainly not to have any part in the offering of prayers to God.

Verse 9

Paul next addresses the women of the community of believers. His hope is that women will express themselves in a modest and godly manner. He begins explaining this by addressing the appearance of women in the fellowship.

Likewise also the women should adorn themselves

The key to understanding verses 9–10 is the concept of "adorning." The Greek word is κοσμέω, and in this passage the word functions both literally and figuratively.[18] It describes both a literal adorning (the negative items) and a figurative adorning (the positive non-physical items).

The word κοσμέω occurs in its literal sense at the end of Revelation:

> And I saw the holy city, new Jerusalem, coming down out of heaven from God, prepared like a bride *adorned* for her husband. (Re 21:2, emphasis added)

Here, the adornment is a reference to the desire of a bride to look her best for her husband. Consider also the *Testament of Judah*:

> After this, while Tamar was a widow she heard two years later that I was going up to shear sheep. *Decking herself* in bridal array she sat at the entrance of the inn in the city of Enan, for there was a law among the Amorites that a woman who was widowed should sit in public like a whore. (*T. Judah* 12.1–2, emphasis added)

Here as well the adornment is in reference to matrimonial practice, though in this case it is in the pseudepigraphal re-telling and expansion of the episode between Judah and Tamar.[19]

The apocryphal *Apocalypse of Peter* uses κοσμέω in a context specifically dealing with women who have committed adultery:

> And there were also others, women, hanged by their hair above that mire which boiled up; and these were *they that adorned themselves* for adultery. And the men that were joined with them in the defilement of adultery were hanging by their feet, and had their heads hidden in the mire, and said: We believed not that we should come unto this place. (*Apocalypse of Peter* 24, emphasis added)

---

[18] BDAG, p. 560. Occurs 11x in NT, only here in PE.

[19] cf. Gen. 38.

Adornment outside of matrimonial practice is also referred to in the *Works of Josephus*:

> for he went up thither to worship in a pompous manner, and *adorned* with royal garments, and had his followers with him in their armor. (Jos., *Wars* 2.444, emphasis added)

When one physically adorns oneself, the adornment is with attire intended to create a positive impression. The impression may be intended to beautify; as in stimulating the desire of a newly-married husband. One may also adorn oneself with a regal air in an attempt to show strength or worthiness. In short, one "adorns" oneself with external accoutrements in an attempt to portray oneself in the best possible light for the situation at hand; perhaps sometimes even manipulatively to attain a particular goal or desire or elicit a particular response.

Based on the above citations, it appears that the literal, physical "adornment" of women was primarily that of women presenting themselves to their husbands attempting to present themselves in the best light possible for the situation.

The figurative "adornment" is similar, only instead of being adorned with material, the adornment is that of character or idea. This sort of adorning is discussed in First Peter:

> For in the same way formerly the holy women also, who hoped in God, *used to adorn* themselves by being subject to their own husbands, like Sarah obeyed Abraham, calling him lord, whose children you have become when you do good and are not frightened with respect to any terror. (1Pe 3:5–6, emphasis added)

In this instance, women adorn themselves through their own actions. The word κοσμέω occurs in similar fashion in the *Martyrdom of Polycarp*:

> And when the funeral pyre was prepared, he took off all his own clothes, and having loosed his belt, he tried also to take off shoes by himself, not having done this before, because each of the faithful always were zealous, which might touch his skin more quickly. For *he had been adorned* with every good thing because of his way of life, even before his martyrdom. (*Mart. Poly.* 13.2, emphasis added)

This instance speaks of the blessings received by Polycarp due to his faith and example in life. Such things, though they were not all physical or tangible, adorned Polycarp. Another example occurs in *First Clement*:

> Let us consider that all the righteous *have been adorned* with good works; and even the Lord himself, *having adorned* himself with good works, rejoiced. (*1Cl* 33.7, emphasis added)

In *First Clement* the adornment is with "good works;" exactly what Paul will recommend godly women adorn themselves with.[20] The figurative sense of κοσμέω is that of taking on these good qualities and ways of living and thus becoming inwardly and morally attractive.

in appropriate clothing

The word translated "appropriate" (κόσμιος) implies 'appropriate' or 'modest' in this context.[21] It is coupled with "apparel" (καταστολή), which typically means 'attire' or 'clothing,'[22] however, BDAG notes:

> Like the verb καταστέλλω, the basic idea is keeping something in check, hence the use of this term in the sense of 'reserve, restraint' … The verb στέλλω means to 'furnish, equip,' a sense that extends itself to the putting on of garments. Hence καταστολή readily serves to express outward attire, either the character one exhibits in personal deportment or something to cover the body.[23]

These words (κόσμιος and καταστολή) are taken as a unit. This unit can be understood either literally or figuratively. It is best to see the "appropriate clothing" as both literal and figurative to make the most sense of this passage. Paul isn't simply making a comment about the manner in which women dress, but he also isn't only referring to a figurative adornment of women. He means both.

with modesty and self control

Paul desires women to clothe themselves "with modesty with self-control." The word translated 'modesty' is αἰδώς,[24] which only occurs here in the NT and is absent from the Apostolic Fathers. TDNT discusses αἰδώς in Christian usage, mentioning it:

> … denotes the "modest demeanour" of the wife, as in Greek, and the linking with σωφροσύνη and κοσμεῖν is wholly in line with Greek usage.[25]

---

[20] See comment on 1Ti 2:10.

[21] BDAG, p. 561; TDNT 3.895 is especially helpful. Occurs 2x in NT, both in PE: 1Ti 2:8; 3:2. See note on 1Ti 3:2, where the word has a slightly different sense. Also interesting is the close proximity of κόσμιος with the related verb κοσμέω, leading to something that could read like "adorn themselves with respectable adornment." Lastly, note also the variant κοσμίως (an adverb) in place of κοσμίῳ (a feminine dative adjective) in several important MSS.

[22] BDAG p. 527; TDNT 7.595. NT *hapax*.

[23] BDAG p. 527.

[24] BDAG p. 24. TDNT 1.170–171. NT *hapax*.

[25] TDNT 1:171.

The word occurs outside of the New Testament. Consider Third Maccabees:

> And even those who had been recently arrayed for all those now appointed, and neglecting the *modesty* befitting them, they gathered together, running in a disorderly fashion. (3Ma 1:19, emphasis added)

The sense of the occurrence in Third Maccabees is more in line with the classical sense of the word. In earlier times, αἰδώς carried a sense of shame. A lexicon of the Septuagint provides glosses of 'shame,' 'modesty,' and 'reserve.'[26] The idea of "modesty" is still present in the word, yet the modesty is based on concealing shame or inappropriateness. Modesty (αἰδώς) prevented one from acting in shame.

Some development had taken place by NT times, however. Instead of primarily indicating shame,[27] the word takes on the positive aspect of modesty. Consider BDAG:

> This term expresses the opposite of considering or treating something in a common or ordinary manner; a respect for convention.[28]

This word is combined with "self-control" (σωφροσύνη) to provide a picture of how women should adorn themselves. The word, in this context, means something like 'good judgment' or 'moderation.'[29] This implies that one is acting with consideration to circumstance, acting appropriately given the expectations and constraints of the situation.

As women adorn themselves both literally and figuratively, they are to exercise both modesty and self-control. Paul addresses this next.

not with braided hair and gold jewelry or pearls or expensive clothing

Literally, women are to exercise modesty and self-control in their adornment by avoiding overly glamorous or risqué clothing and accessories.

The word translated "braided hair" is πλέγμα, which has to do with something woven or braided; typically hair when used of a person.[30] Of this practice, *A Handbook on Paul's Letters to Timothy and to Titus* notes:

---

[26] LEH αἰδώς.

[27] e.g. 3Ma 4:5.

[28] BDAG p. 24.

[29] BDAG p. 987. Occurs 3x in NT: Ac 26:25; 1Ti 2:9, 15.

[30] BDAG p. 824. NT *hapax*.

> *Braided hair* was considered a work of art and was very popular among Greek and Roman ladies, with the braided hair rising some inches above the head, and often intertwined with chains of gold or strings of pearls.[31]

Such ostentatiously coiffed hair is not indicative of the modesty and self-control that Paul describes. Humility, not superiority, is the proper attitude.

Paul further lists gold, pearls, and costly attire as items for Christian women to avoid in their dress and presentation. The word translated "gold" is χρυσίον, and it has a range of meaning from simple, raw gold to gold ornamentation to coinage made of gold.[32] In this context, as applied to the apparel of women, the idea of gold ornamentation or jewelry is in mind. The word translated "pearls" is μαργαρίτης.[33] While the word is used figuratively in the New Testament (cf. Mt 7:6) here the context is clear and the literal sense is intended.

The phrase translated "costly attire" consists of two Greek words. First is ἱματισμός, meaning simply 'clothing' or 'apparel.'[34] Second is πολυτελής, which is glossed as '(very) expensive, costly.'[35] Paul's concept of respectable apparel does not include expensive clothing that has the primary function of showing off the wealth of the wearer. A sense of the degree of costliness provided by πολυτελής is provided in Mark's gospel:

> And while he was at Bethany in the house of Simon the leper, as he was reclining for a meal, a woman came holding an alabaster flask of *very costly* perfumed oil of genuine nard. After breaking the alabaster flask, she poured it out on his head. (Mk 14:3, emphasis added)

Paul does not endorse an absolute prohibition on things like jewelry or nice clothes. He is instead reminding women to present themselves with modesty and self-control in all things. Women who profess Christianity should constantly be aware of the difference between respectable apparel and ostentatious or immodest dress.

---

[31] Daniel C.; Hatton Arichea, *A Handbook on Paul's Letters to Timothy and to Titus* (New York: United Bible Societies, 1995), 57.

[32] BDAG p. 1092. Occurs 12x in NT, only here in PE.

[33] BDAG p. 616. Occurs 9x in NT, only here in PE.

[34] BDAG p. 475. Occurs 5x in NT: Lk 7:25; 9:29; Jn 19:24; Ac 20:33; 1Ti 2:9.

[35] BDAG p. 850. Occurs 3x in NT: Mk 14:3; 1Ti 2:9; 1Pe 3:4.

Verse 10

but with good deeds which are fitting for women who profess godliness

Paul next focuses on how women are to adorn themselves in a figurative sense. The word translated "proper" is πρέπω, glossed as 'be fitting, be seemly/suitable.'[36] The author of Hebrews uses the word twice:

> For *it was fitting* for him for whom are all things and through whom are all things in bringing many sons to glory to perfect the originator of their salvation through sufferings. (Heb 2:10, emphasis added)

> For a high priest such as this indeed *is fitting* for us, holy, innocent, undefiled, separated from sinners, and having become exalted above the heavens, (Heb 7:26, emphasis added)

In these settings the actions of Jesus are seen as "fitting" or "proper" for his person to accomplish. The word πρέπω is used similarly in the Third Maccabees:

> Therefore, being persuaded rightly even by proofs that these people are ill-disposed to us in every way, and taking thought, lest a sudden disorder arise against us afterward, and we have these wicked traitors and barbarous enemies behind our back, we have given an order that as soon as this letter arrives, immediately you are to send to us those living amongst you with their wives and children with hardship and cruel treatment, being locked up with chains made of iron on every side, for a cruel and infamous slaughter *befitting* enemies. (3Ma 3:24–25, emphasis added)

Here, the "proper" or "fitting" action is applied to the "traitors."[37] Those viewed as traitors are to be dealt with accordingly.

The word is used in a different sort of way in *Ignatius to the Ephesians*:

> Apart from this one, let nothing *be pleasing* to you, in whom I carry about these chains, my spiritual pearls, in which may it be granted to me to rise up in your prayer, of which may it be granted to me always to be a sharer, that I may be

---

[36] BDAG p. 861. Occurs 7x in NT, 2x in PE: 1Ti 1:10; Tt 2:1.

[37] The context: This is a letter from King Ptolmey Philopator to his army requiring them to persecute those who harbor Jews as traitors.

> found in the lot of the Christians of the Ephesians, who also have always agreed with the apostles in the power of Jesus Christ. (Ign., *Eph.* 11.2, emphasis added)[38]

Here, πρέπω is used as a sort of weighted judgment. Apart from Jesus Christ, writes Ignatius, nothing should seem "proper" or "fitting." A similar meaning is intended by Paul. Understanding that they are to adorn themselves appropriately, both literally and figuratively, women are to seek fitting attire.

Paul next qualifies exactly whom he intends to receive these instructions: "women who profess godliness." The word translated "profess" is the Greek word ἐπαγγέλλομαι, which here implies 'profess' or 'lay claim to.'[39] The word is used in a similar sense in the Wisdom of Solomon:

> *He claims* to have knowledge of God, and he calls himself a child of the Lord. (Wis 2:13, emphasis added)

The idea of ἐπαγγέλλομαι in such contexts involves the claiming of something, be it tangible or ethereal. Consider also *Ignatius to the Ephesians*:

> No one *professing* faith sins, nor possessing love hates. "The tree is known by its fruit," so those who profess to be Christ's will be seen through what they do. For the deed is not a matter of what one now professes but if one be found in the power of faith to the end. (Ign., *Eph.* 14.2, emphasis added)

In verse 10, the women are claiming or professing "godliness." The Greek word is θεοσέβεια, a 'reverence for God or set of beliefs and practices relating to interest in God.'[40] Moulton and Milligan note " … it is practically equivalent to εὐσέβεια (ver. 2)."[41]

Though θεοσέβεια occurs only here in the New Testament, it does occur in the Septuagint. An example is in Genesis:

> Abraham said, "For I said, 'As it seems, there is no *fear of God* in this place; and they will kill me on account of my wife.' " (Ge 20:11 [LXX])

Abraham clearly understood that one who fears God will act accordingly. Another example of this word occurs in *Second Clement*:

---

[38] The bit about the Ephesian Christians "who have always agreed with the apostles" seems strange in light of 1 Timothy's emphasis on correction of misapplied apostolic doctrine, though at the same time seems to confirm that Timothy completed the task set before him and got the Ephesian Christians back on the track of sound doctrine.

[39] BDAG p. 356. Occurs 15x in NT, 3x in PE: 1Ti 2:10; 6:21; Tt 1:2.

[40] BDAG p. 452. NT *hapax*.

[41] M-M p. 288. See comment on 1Ti 2:2 regarding εὐσέβεια.

> None of the righteous received a reward quickly, but waits for it. For if God promptly paid the wages of the righteous, we would immediately engage in commerce and not *godliness*, for we would seem to be righteous, pursuing not piety but profit. And because of this, divine judgment injures a spirit that is not righteous and weighs it down with chains. (*2Cl* 20.3–4, emphasis added)

The author of *Second Clement* realizes that true godliness is devotion that affects action despite the immediate response. It is following God, wherever he leads, despite the repercussions.

Women who claim to be godly are to figuratively adorn themselves with "good works." This agrees with what is written in First Peter:

> Let your adornment not be the external kind, braiding hair and putting on gold jewelry or putting on fine clothing, but the hidden person of the heart, with the imperishable quality of a gentle and quiet spirit, which is highly valuable in the sight of God. For in the same way formerly the holy women also, who hoped in God, used to adorn themselves by being subject to their own husbands, like Sarah obeyed Abraham, calling him lord, whose children you have become when you do good and are not frightened with respect to any terror. (1Pe 3:3–6)

Rather than dress in an extravagant manner with jewels on display, Christian women are to dress appropriately and respectably. Their physical presentation is to match and properly reflect their spiritual attitude of devotion to God.

Verse 11

Paul next discusses the role of women in the fellowship. The context has not changed; Paul previously discussed how women should present themselves, both literally and figuratively. Paul now discusses how these women are to interact within the fellowship.

A woman must learn in quietness with all submission

The phrase "must learn" is translated from the Greek word μανθάνω, a multipurpose word having to do with gaining or acquiring information, be it from deduction or from a teacher or from some other source.[42] There is no reason to prevent a woman from learning the things of sound doctrine. If women desire to learn then they must be taught. This may have been at issue, based on earlier writings of Paul to the Corinthians:

---

[42] BDAG p. 615. Occurs 25x in NT, 6x in PE.

> As in all the churches of the saints, the women must be silent in the churches, for it is not permitted for them to speak, but they must be in submission, just as the law also says. But if they want *to learn* something, let them ask their own husbands at home, for it is shameful for a woman to speak in church. (1Co 14:33b-35, emphasis added)

According to Paul, women are to learn but they are to do it quietly. The word translated "quietness" is the Greek word ἡσυχία, which can indicate a 'state of undisturbed quietness or rest' or a 'state of silence.'[43] The meaning in this instance (and the following instance in verse 12) is the latter, that of silence. The word occurs in this sense in Proverbs:

> The one who lacks understanding mocks neighbors, but a wise man remains *quiet*. (Pr 11:12 [LXX], emphasis added)

Based on the contextual and topical similarity of this passage with 1Co 14:33b–35, this instance of ἡσυχία most likely means "silence" during times of instruction.

Paul also recommends the women learn "with all submission." The word translated "all" is the same word used for "all" in vv. 2 and 4.[44] The word translated "submission" is ὑποταγή and has to do with 'subjection' or 'subordination.'[45] This word occurs three other times in the New Testament:

> Through the proven character of this service they will glorify God because of the *submission* of your confession to the gospel of Christ and the generosity of your participation toward them and toward everyone, (2Co 9:13, emphasis added)

> ... to whom not even for an hour did we yield in *subjection*, in order that the truth of the gospel might remain continually with you. (Ga 2:5, emphasis added)

> ... managing his own household well, having children in *submission* with all dignity (1Ti 3:4, emphasis added)

In all of these instances, ὑποταγή is used to describe yielding of some sort. In 2Co 9:13 the yielding is seen positively, submitting to God's will in giving toward the contribution. In Ga 2:5 there is no yielding as submission would be improper in this context. In the last example, 1Ti 3:4, the submission of children to their father is seen as positive for both the father and the children. Consider also *First Clement*:

> Let us take our body, the head is nothing without the feet, likewise the feet are nothing without the head. Even the smallest parts of our body are necessary and

---

[43] BDAG p. 440. Occurs in 4x in NT, 2x in PE: 1Ti 2:11, 12. Note also the adjective ἡσύχιος in 1Ti 2:2.

[44] See comment on 1Ti 2:2.

[45] BDAG p. 1041. Occurs 4x in NT: 2Co 9:13; Ga 2:5; 1Ti 2:11; 3:4.

> useful to the whole body, but all work together and experience a mutual *subjection*, to save the whole body. (*1Cl* 37.5, emphasis added)

This sort of submission or "renunciation of initiative"[46] is the same sort of idea as that presented in 1Co 14:33b–35. Paul's goal is not to quell a woman's initiative to learn. He hopes that women will learn in the proper setting. The setting in which one learns is important. The Ephesian fellowship was having problems with false teachers and propagation of unsound doctrine.[47] Paul desires a structure that will ensure the teaching of sound doctrine by the leaders of the church.[48]

VERSE 12

But I do not permit a woman to teach

The phrase "I do not permit" is a translation of the Greek verb ἐπιτρέπω with a negative particle preceding the verb. The general sense of the word is 'allow' or 'permit.'[49] The word also occurs in Luke:

> Now there was a large herd of pigs feeding there on the hill, and they implored him that *he would permit* them to enter into those pigs. And *he permitted* them. (Lk 8:32, emphasis added)

In this verse from Luke, the word ἐπιτρέπω occurs twice, first with the demons asking permission of Jesus to enter the pigs on the hillside, next with Jesus giving his permission allowing the demons to enter the pigs. The demons cannot do this unless the one in authority, Jesus, allows them.

The word also occurs in Josephus:

> When Hadad heard in Egypt that both David and Joab were dead, he came to Pharaoh, and desired that *he would permit him* to go to his own country; upon which the king asked what it was that he wanted, and what hardship he had met with, that he was so desirous to leave him; and when he was often troublesome to him, and entreated him to dismiss him, he did not then do it. (Jos., *Ant.* 8.202, emphasis added)

---

[46] TDNT 8.46.

[47] cf. 1Ti 1:3–7. Also note younger widows' particular susceptibility to false teachers, cf. 1Ti 5:11–15.

[48] This may be one reason why the next major section (1Ti 3:1–13) has to do with church leadership.

[49] BDAG, p.384. Occurs 18x in NT, only here in PE.

Here, Pharaoh, who is in a position of authority, is asked by Hadad for permission to return to his own country. Hadad is bound by the will of Pharaoh and cannot do this thing[50] without Pharaoh's permission.

The phrase "to teach" is a translation of the Greek word διδάσκω. The word means 'teach' or 'provide instruction.'[51] The word is common and its meaning is relatively unambiguous. The word διδάσκω occurs five times in the Pastoral Epistles, and each of these occurrences is in the context of teaching things of doctrine.[52] In the present context, Paul rather clearly states that he does not permit women to teach men (ἀνήρ).[53]

The question, of course, concerns the nature of the teaching. What is it that women are not to teach? Douglas J. Moo addresses this:

> In sum, "teaching" according to Paul involves the careful transmission of the tradition concerning Jesus Christ and His significance and the authoritative proclamation of God's will to believers in light of that tradition.[54]

In these areas, Paul's practice is that women are free to learn[55] but they are not free to instruct the men of the fellowship.

or to exercise authority over a man

In addition to Paul's prohibition of women from teaching, in his practice women are also not "to exercise authority" over men. The Greek word is αὐθεντέω, which implies 'having authority or power over.'[56] One of the latest comprehensive surveys

---

[50] Without penalty, that is.

[51] BDAG, p. 241. Occurs 97x in NT, 5x in PE: 1Ti 2:12; 4:11; 6:2; 2Ti 2:2; Tt 1:11

[52] Tt 1:11 speaks of "teaching … for the sake of dishonest gain," though the larger context is that of false teachers teaching improper doctrine. Tt 1:11 is still about teaching doctrine, albeit false doctrine.

[53] BDAG, p. 79. Occurs 216x in NT. This is not a prohibition against all women teaching anything to anyone. It is instead a prohibition of Paul against women teaching men the things of doctrine.

[54] Douglas J. Moo, "1 Timothy 2:11–15: Meaning and Significance," Trinity J. 1 (1980): 66.

[55] Apparently from either women or men. 1Co 14:33b–35 indicates women are, in Paul's view, to learn from their husbands at home; though Tt 2:3–4 indicates that (again, in Paul's view) older women are to teach younger women.

[56] LSJ, p. 275; BDAG p. 150. NT *hapax*. This word is exceedingly rare in literature contemporaneous with or before the first century AD, but it occurs in patristic literature after this date with some frequency.

of αὐθεντέω is that of H. Scott Baldwin.[57] He narrows the intended sense in this passage down to the following senses with the caveat that further syntactic studies are necessary to make any further determination on the issue:[58]

- To control, to dominate
- To compel, to influence something
- To assume authority over
- To flout the authority of

According to Baldwin, in 1Ti 2:12, the "root meaning [of αὐθεντέω] involves the concept of authority."[59]

In a separate survey,[60] Al Wolters examines the translations of αὐθεντέω in the early versions[61] of 1Ti 2:12, reporting:

> The Old Latin of this verse has a variety of renderings (dated to the third century and later), all of which are related to a Latin word designating someone in authority. … The Sahidic Coptic version uses a verb meaning 'to be lord,' and the Bohairic another Coptic verb meaning 'to be head.' The Gothic version of Ulfilas has a verb derived from the regular Gothic word for 'lord.' Only the Peshitta seems to break this pattern, since the printed editions of 1Ti 2:12 all have the Aphel verb *mrah*, meaning 'to venture' or 'be rash,' which does not seem to fit the Greek very well. … Consequently, a good case can be made for the thesis that all these ancient versions (with the possible exception of the Peshitta) reflect an accurate understanding of αὐθεντέω in 1Ti 2:12 as a denominative verb based on αὐθέντης 'master.' Furthermore, it is to be noted that all these versions (with the same possible exception) understand the verb in a non-pejorative sense.[62]

In looking at how early versions handle this difficult word some insight can be gained as to how it was understood.

---

[57] H. Scott Baldwin, "A Difficult Word: αὐθεντέω in 1 Timothy 2:12," in *Women in the Church: An Analysis and Application of 1 Timothy 2:9–15*, ed. Andreas J. Köstenberger and Thomas R. Schreiner, Second Edition. (Grand Rapids: Baker Academic, 2005), 288. Baldwin surveys known lexicons from the classical period onward and examines every known, available usage of αὐθεντέω from before the 10th century.

[58] Ibid., 73, 79–80. I've surmised/paraphrased this.

[59] Ibid., 79.

[60] Al Wolters, "A Semantic Study of αὐθέντης and Its Derivatives," JGRChJ 1 (2000): 145–75.

[61] The "early versions" are ancient translations from the Greek. They provide a witness to how the text was understood by translators of these editions.

[62] Wolters, "Semantic Study," 164–165.

but to remain quiet

The alternative to exercising authority, for women, is "to remain quiet." The phrase "to remain" comes from the present active infinitive form of εἰμί, the verb for 'to be.' The word "quiet" is translated from ἡσυχίᾳ.[63] This is not referring to a state of inner peace or solitude; the quality of silence is intended. This is clear from context; in situations where women could exercise authority over men, which would be vocal, women are to instead remain quiet.

VERSE 13

Paul next offers a justification for his dictum concerning women, teaching, and authority. Paul appeals to the creation order.

For Adam was formed first, then Eve,

The primary word in this phrase to consider is the verb, "was formed." The Greek verb is πλάσσω, which has to do with 'forming' or 'molding.'[64] Paul uses the word in Romans:

> On the contrary, O man, who are you who answers back to God? Will what is *molded* say to the one who molded it, "Why did you make me like this?" (Ro 9:20, emphasis added)

In this case[65] there is no specific reference to Adam or Eve, yet the idea that God has formed or molded man is communicated. The same word, πλάσσω, is used in the Septuagint version of the creation narrative:

> And God *formed* the human with earth from the land and blew into his face the breath of life, and the human came into being as a living soul. (Ge 2:7 [LXX], emphasis added)

> The Lord God took the human that he *formed*, and he placed him in the paradise to work and to keep it. (Ge 2: 15 [LXX], emphasis added)

Paul uses πλάσσω, just as the Septuagint account of creation does, to indicate the process by which humans were created. This word seems to be the standard method one uses to refer to human creation. Consider Second Maccabees:

---

[63] See comment on 1Ti 2:11 for fuller discussion on ἡσυχίᾳ.

[64] BDAG, p. 823. Occurs 2x in NT: Ro 9:20; 1Ti 2:13.

[65] This is a quotation of Is 29:16, which, in the LXX, also uses the word πλάσσω.

> Now then, the creator of the world, the one who *formed* the family of humanity and who devised the generation of all things, will with mercy restore to you again both your spirit and your life because now you are disregarding yourselves on account of his laws. (2Ma 7:23, emphasis added)

The word is used in similar context by Josephus, in his *Antiquities*:

> And on the fifth day he produced the living creatures, both those that swim and those that fly; the former in the sea, the latter in the air: he also sorted them as to society and mixture, for procreation, and that their kinds might increase and multiply. On the sixth day he created the four-footed beasts, and made them male and female: on the same day *he* also *formed* man. (Jos., *Ant.* 1.32, emphasis added)

Josephus speaks of creative action many times in this verse: "he produced," "he created," "made them." Yet only when speaking of the creation of man does Josephus use the word πλάσσω.

In discussing the creation account from Genesis, Paul likely had this word (and thus the account from Genesis 2 and 3)[66] in mind. He recalls the creation account in a sort of shorthand to establish his rationale for not permitting women to teach or be in positions of authority over men.

Verse 14

and Adam was not decieved

The word translated "deceived" is the Greek word ἀπατάω, which typically means 'deceive' or 'mislead.'[67] This word is also used in Ephesians:

> Let no one *deceive* you with empty words, for because of these things the wrath of God is coming on the sons of disobedience. (Eph 5:6, emphasis added)

Here it is clear that a deception predicated on a lie is in mind. Someone (or some party) is using a lie to elicit a response. Paul urges the Ephesians to be on their guard and not let such lies lead them into improper or unfortunate actions.

The word also occurs in the pseudepigraphical *Testament of Judah*, describing Tamar as she approached Judah in his drunken state:

---

[66] See comment on 1Ti 2:14 for application of Genesis 3.

[67] BDAG, p. 98. Occurs 3x in NT: Eph 5:6; 1Ti 2:14; Jam 1:26.

> Since I was drunk with wine, I did not recognize her and her beauty *enticed* me because of her manner of tricking herself out. (*T. Judah* 12.3, emphasis added)[68]

A deception was perpetrated upon Judah. In this instance, the deception was achieved by Tamar, whose appearance was enhanced both by her adornment and by Judah's drunken state.

Regarding Adam, Paul states that the deception of the serpent was not perpetrated against Adam,[69] thus "Adam was not deceived." This accords with the account in Genesis that Paul would have been familiar with:

> And Lord God summoned Adam and said to him, "Adam, where are you?" He said to him, "I heard the sound of you walking about in the paradise, and I was afraid because I am naked, and I hid." He said to him, "Who announced to you that you are naked? Unless you have eaten from the tree of which I commanded you 'From this one alone, do not eat.' " Adam said, "The woman whom you gave with me, she gave to me from the tree, and I ate." (Ge 3:10–13 [LXX 3:9–12])

but the woman, because she was deceived,

A slightly different word (ἐξαπατάω) is used for "was deceived" in this phrase. TDNT has no differentiation; it treats them both under the same head.[70] This second form of the word occurs in a similar statement from Paul in 2 Corinthians:

> But I am afraid lest somehow, as the serpent *deceived* Eve by his craftiness, your minds may be led astray from the sincerity and the purity of devotion to Christ. (2Co 11:3, emphasis added)

Paul uses the same word of himself in Romans:

> For sin, seizing the opportunity through the commandment, *deceived* me and through it killed me. (Ro 7:11, emphasis added)

As Paul uses ἐξαπατάω to describe how he had been deceived by sin, one can be relatively sure that ἐξαπατάω does not imply more culpability in a deception on the part of the one being deceived. That is, one cannot conclude that Paul considers Eve to have greater responsibility in the fall based on the use of ἐξαπατάω as Paul uses the same word of his own succumbing to the deception of sin.

This as well reflects the creation account from Genesis 3:

---

[68] Cf. Ge 38 for Biblical account.

[69] Not that Adam wasn't responsible for his action in taking of the forbidding fruit, only that Adam's action was not a result of the deception of the serpent.

[70] TDNT 1:384. Occurs 6x in NT, only here in PE. A variant noted in the NA28 apparatus indicates some MSS (notably the Byzantine tradition) have ἀπατάω here instead of ἐξαπατάω.

> The Lord God said to the woman, "What is this you have done?" The woman said, "The serpent *deceived* me, and I ate." (Ge 3:13 [3:14 LXX])

The word "deceived" in Ge 3:13 is translated from the word ἀπατάω. Given these parallels between the two accounts, it seems likely that Paul had the creation and fall account in mind when composing this letter.

came into transgression

Paul not only mentions that the woman had been deceived, he goes on to say that she "came into transgression." The word "transgression" is from the Greek word παράβασις, which is typically defined as 'overstepping' or 'transgression.'[71] The woman, Eve, has transgressed (sinned) based on her response to the serpent's deception.

Paul uses this same word, παράβασις, to describe Adam's action in the fall:

> Because of this, just as sin entered into the world through one man, and death through sin, so also death spread to all people because all sinned. For until the law, sin was in the world, but sin is not charged to one's account when there is no law. But death reigned from Adam until Moses even over those who did not sin in the likeness of the *transgression* of Adam, who is a type of the one who is to come. (Ro 5:12–14, emphasis added)

Indeed, far from considering the woman solely at fault for the fall, in Romans Paul indicates that sin and death—the result of the fall—came in the world "through one man."

The current passage (1Ti 2:12–15) is not about establishing blame for the fall. Instead, Paul is providing his rationale for prohibiting women from taking positions of leadership or teaching in the community.

VERSE 15

But she will be saved through the bearing of children

Paul follows up his quick overview of the result of the fall with a comment that is somewhat cryptic.

---

[71] BDAG, p. 758. Occurs 7x in NT, only here in PE.

One factor that complicates the examination of this verse lies in the usage of the word σῴζω.[72] In the Pastoral Epistles, σῴζω occurs seven times. All of these occurrences, including this one, have to do with salvation in a religious sense.[73] The eternal state of the soul is at stake when σῴζω is used in the Pastoral Epistles. And in this phrase, Paul appears to be stating that the salvation of women is dependent upon childbearing (τεκνογονία),[74] and even then is further dependent upon living in the manner stipulated in verses 9–10.

However, this is not the case. As with the previous verses, this verse relies upon reading it in the light of Genesis 3.

> I will place enmity between you and between the woman, and between your seed and between her seed; he will watch carefully your head, and you will watch carefully his heel." He said to the woman, "Multiplying, I will multiply your pain and your moaning. In pain you will bring forth children, and your recourse will be to your husband, and he will be master over you." And to Adam he said, "Because you obeyed the voice of your wife and ate from the tree of which I commanded you, 'From this one alone, do not eat,' from that you ate, the land is accursed in your work. In pain you will eat it all the days of your life. (Ge 3:14–16 [3:15–17 LXX])

There are two items to note that bear importance for the exposition of 1Ti 2:15. First, painful childbirth is part of the curse of the fall for women. Secondly, the prophecy concerning the seed of woman, a child that will be born in the future, will avenge the serpent for his deception of the woman.

Paul hints at this interpretation in his epistle to the Galatians:

> But when the fullness of time came, God sent out his Son, *born of a woman*, born under the law, in order that he might redeem those under the law, in order that we might receive the adoption. (Ga 4:4–5, emphasis added)

---

[72] See comment on 1Ti 1:15 for statistics on NT occurrences of σῴζω. See also comments on 1Ti 2:4.

[73] The seven instances are: 1Ti 1:15; 2:4, 15; 4:16; 2Ti 1:9; 4:18; Tt 3:5. These are all categorized in LN 21.27.

[74] BDAG, p. 994. NT *hapax.*

It is by the seed of woman, through the birth of Jesus, that the serpent who deceived the woman will receive justice.[75]

if she continues in faith and love and holiness with self-control

This promise of salvation, however, is not reason to dismiss responsibility. Until that final day, men and women both must be diligent. This is why Paul reminds his readers that women, even though salvation is assured through the birth, death and resurrection of Christ, are still subject to the curse and thus are to remain constant in their efforts to live responsibly and properly as Christians, emulating what Paul has instructed in verses 9–12.

The word translated "she continues" is μένω, typically glossed as 'remain,' 'continue,' or 'abide.'[76] Here it involves remaining in a particular realm or sphere; not a physical location or state. It is used similarly in Second Timothy:

> But you *continue* in the things which you have learned and are convinced of, because you know from whom you learned them, (2Ti 3:14, emphasis added)

Similar usage occurs in Ignatius' letter to Polycarp:

> If anyone is able *to remain* in purity to honor the flesh of the Lord, let him do so without boasting. If he boasts, he has been lost; and if it becomes known to any beyond the bishop, he is ruined. But it is fitting for men and women who marry with the consent of the bishop to make their union, that the marriage may be in accordance with the Lord and not in accordance with lust. Let all things be done for the honor of God. (Ign., *Poly.* 5.2, emphasis added)

Use of the word μένω to indicate continuance in a non-physical state or sphere is a common use of the word.

The section ends with a reminder to women, imploring them to continue in the sorts of things that Paul has been discussing in verses 9–12 (self-control, proper attire and attitudes, etc.). Paul also asks women to continue in the same sorts of things he has been discussing through the whole letter; particularly 1Ti 1:12–14, which professes:

> I give thanks to the one who strengthens me, Christ Jesus our Lord, because he considered me faithful, placing me into ministry, although I was formerly a

---

[75] This verse (1Ti 2:15) is a difficult verse. Several complicating grammatical and syntactical features of the text must be dealt with in the interpretation. For a survey of these issues, see Porter, Stanley E., "What Does it Mean To Be 'Saved By Childbirth' (1 Timothy 2:15)" in *Studies in the Greek New Testament: Theory and Practice*. Peter Lang: New York, 1996. The essay isolates and provides insight on the grammatical and syntactical problems in this verse.

[76] BDAG, p. 630. Occurs 118x in NT; 4x in PE: 1Ti 2:15; 2Ti 2:13; 3:14; 4:20.

> blasphemer and a persecutor and a violent man, but I was shown mercy because I acted ignorantly in unbelief, and the grace of our Lord abounded with the faith and love that are in Christ Jesus. (1Ti 1:12–14)

Paul exhorts women to continue in the same faith and love that he received by the grace of God.

Qualifications of Overseers (1Ti 3:1–7)

The saying is trustworthy: if anyone aspires to supervision, he desires a good work. Therefore the overseer must be irreproachable, the husband of one wife, temperate, self-controlled, respectable, hospitable, skillful in teaching, not addicted to wine, not a violent person, but gentle, peaceable, not loving money, managing his own household well, having children in submission with all dignity (but if someone does not know how to manage his own household, how will he take care of the church of God?), not newly converted, lest he become conceited and fall into the condemnation of the devil. But he must also have a good testimony from those outside, in order that he may not fall into disgrace and the trap of the devil. (1Ti 3:1–7)

Verse 1

The saying is trustworthy

This phrase is formulaic, declaring a surrounding "saying" to be worthy of the reader's attention.[1] Exactly which saying is trustworthy is at issue in this instance. It could be either the previous saying at the end of chapter 2 regarding women and childbirth; it could be this next saying regarding the desire of one who wishes to be an overseer. The statement following the formula (the balance of verse 1) is usually understood as the trustworthy saying.[2]

If anyone aspires to supervision

Paul proceeds to the topic of leadership; specifically the leadership office of overseer. The words "aspires to" come from the Greek ὀρέγω, generally meaning 'aspire to,' 'strive to,' or 'desire.'[3] The word is also used in the Epistle to the Hebrews:

---

[1] See comment on 1Ti 1:15

[2] Note NA28 and UBS5 both attach the chapter break and πιστὸς ὁ λόγος at the end of chapter 2 and insert the paragraph break after λόγος. From this one can only assume these editions consider the faithful saying to be 1Ti 2:15.

[3] BDAG p. 721. Occurs 3x in NT, 2x in PE: 1Ti 3:1; 6:10; He 11:16.

> But now *they aspire* to a better land, that is, a heavenly one. Therefore God is not ashamed of them, to be called their God, for he has prepared for them a city. (Heb 11:16, emphasis added)

In Hebrews, the word ὀρέγω indicates the desire that Christians have for the heavenly city. It is also semantically similar to a word that occurs in the next clause of 1Tim. 3:1, "desires" (ἐπιθυμέω).[4] Both words are used in the *Letter of Aristeas*, with a king is answering a question about the "essence of kingship." The first italicized word represents ἐπιθυμέω, the second ὀρέγω:

> The king agreed with him and said to the next guest, "What is the definition of kingship?" The reply was, "Real self-mastery, not being carried away by wealth and glamour, nor having, as a result, overweening or unworthy *ambitions*—that would be kingship if you reasoned well. You have everything you need at hand. God likewise does not want anything and yet is merciful. You too must think in human terms, do not *desire* overmuch, but only what is sufficient for reigning." (*Let. Arist.* 211, emphasis added)

In the *Letter of Aristeas* the advice of the king is to guard against strong ambitions (ἐπιθυμέω), and to "become a man" and "desire" (ὀρέγω) what is necessary to rule effectively.

Both of these instances (Hebrews and *Letter of Aristeas*) indicate that the act of "aspiring" (ὀρέγω) is not a wish or want but instead a serious desire focused on the state in question. The same is true of the desire or aspirations of the office of overseer, when seriously held. The word ὀρέγω does not indicate some wistful thought of serving in such a role one day in the future. Accomplishing the desired goal is in mind. Indeed, the use of ὀρέγω by Theocritus in the third century BC seems to be of the same nature when he uses it to describe "fish, *who rise* at the bait."[5] In this instance, the fish desire the bait and pursue it in order to achieve it.

The object of this focused desire is "the supervision." The Greek word is ἐπισκοπή, which has the sense of of 'position of responsibility' or 'supervision.'[6] The position is a leadership role in the community of believers. Consider *First Clement*:

> And our apostles knew through our Lord Jesus Christ that there would be strife concerning *the title of bishop*. (*1Cl* 44.1, emphasis added)

The usage in *First Clement* simply refers to the office, not the holder of the office. And this is the sense of the word as used in v. 1.

---

[4] See comment on ἐπιθυμέω below.

[5] LSJ, p. 1247, citing Theoc.21.44.

[6] BDAG, p. 379. Occurs 4x in NT; only here in PE: Lk 19:44; Ac 1:20; 1Ti 3:1; 1Pe 2:12.

he desires a good work

The one who desires to hold the office of overseer, Paul writes, "desires a good work." The word translated "he desires" is the Greek word ἐπιθυμέω.[7] The word means 'desire' or 'long for.'[8] It may also mean 'lust after' in certain contexts.[9] While it is important to note the sense of 'strong desire' evident in the word, the sense of 'lust after' is not used here. This word also occurs in Acts:

> "And now I entrust you to God and to the message of his grace, which is able to build you up and to give you the inheritance among all those who are sanctified. *I have desired* no one's silver or gold or clothing! You yourselves know that these hands served to meet my needs and the needs of those who were with me. (Ac 20:32–34, emphasis added)

The context of the desire in Ac 20:33 is negative; this is why ἐπιθυμέω some translations such as ESV translate as "I coveted." But the sense of desiring something (either accepted, forbidden, or morally questionable) is the primary sense of the word. The word occurs a few times in *Second Clement*:

> And you know, brothers, that the sojourn, the one in this world, of this flesh is small and of short duration, but the promise of Christ is great and wonderful: the rest of the coming kingdom and life eternal. Therefore, what are we to do to obtain them, except to conduct ourselves reverently and rightly, and to consider these worldly things as foreign and not *to desire* them? For when *we desire* to acquire these things, we fall away from the way of the righteous. (*2Cl* 5.5–7, emphasis added)

The author of *Second Clement* exhorts his readers to not yearn or long after the things of the world, and to instead focus on Christ. The word occurs with much the same meaning in the *Shepherd of Hermas*:

> But accomplish your own extravagance in which you are able to rejoice and not counterfeit or touch what belongs to another, or *lust after* it, for it is evil *to lust after* what belongs to another, but do your own work and you will be saved." (Hermas, *Similitudes* I, 11, emphasis added)

This same word, ἐπιθυμέω, is used to show the positive desire or longing one may have for a position of leadership in the church. This desire is "a good work," writes Paul. The phrase involves the word for 'good' (καλός)[10] and the word for 'work' or

---

[7] See discussion above on ὀρέγω.

[8] BDAG, p. 371. Occurs 16x in NT, only here in PE.

[9] e.g., Mt 5:28.

[10] BDAG, p. 504. Occurs 101x in NT.

'deed' (ἔργον).[11] Other English versions translate this phrase as "a noble task" (ESV) or "a fine work" (NASB95).

VERSE 2

Therefore the overseer

Paul next provides a list of qualifications for those who desire to be overseers. This list is long, running from here through the end of verse 7. It has much in common with the parallel list in Tt 1:6–9.[12]

must be irreproachable

One who serves as a leader of the fellowship must not be subject to accusations of impropriety. The phrase translated "must be" is a combination of two Greek words, δεῖ and εἰμί. These words are not contiguous in the Greek text, they stand at the start and end of the phrase. Yet they combine together and convey the meaning of "he must be." Paul uses similar phraseology in other verses:

> For *it is necessary* for the overseer *to be* blameless as God's steward, not self-willed, not quick-tempered, not addicted to wine, not violent, not greedy for dishonest gain, (Tt 1:7, emphasis added)

> And the slave of the Lord *must* not quarrel, but be kind toward everyone, skillful in teaching, tolerant, (2Ti 2:24, emphasis added)

> For in the first place, when you come together as a church, I hear there are divisions among you, and in part I believe it. For indeed *it is necessary* that *there be* factions among you, in order that those who are approved may become evident among you. (1Co 11:18–19, emphasis added)

The requirement is for the overseer to be "irreproachable." The Greek word is ἀνεπίλημπτος, which typically means 'irreproachable.'[13] Paul uses this word in 1Ti 5:7:

> And command these things, in order that they may be *irreproachable*. (1Ti 5:7, emphasis added)

In the context of 1Ti 5:7, "these things" are detailed in 1Ti 5:4–6; they have to do with guidelines for widows in the church. If these guidelines are followed, says Paul,

---

[11] BDAG, p. 390. Occurs 169x in NT.

[12] Similar lists of attributes occur in *Did.* 15.1–2 and Poly., *Phil.* 4–5.

[13] BDAG, p. 77. Occurs 3x in NT, all of these are in the PE: 1Ti 3:2; 5:7; 6:14.

then the widow will be "irreproachable." In the present context, Paul's desire is for those who will become overseers to already be without reproach. The later work *Life of Polycarp*[14] provides another witness to ἀνεπίλημπτος, recalling this passage from First Timothy. The setting is that of Polycarp's ordination to the office of bishop over Smyrna. The text purports to be from Polycarp's ordination address, which is a homily on the Pastoral Epistles.[15]

> ... for I well know that no man could fulfil it well, except he hath first received it from the Lord in heaven, as the blessed Apostle Paul hath shown in his epistles, showing in a single word the whole life of one who is appointed to office, when he speaks of it as *blameless*. This I think cannot have escaped the ears of anyone, but must have been impressed upon his inmost soul wholly and completely. (*Life of Polycarp* 23, emphasis added)

Paul requires those who would lead the fellowship to be above reproach and free of lingering accusations.

the husband of one wife

Many debates on the role of women in the fellowship have turned on this one phrase. The phrase in the Greek is simple; it is the words for "one," "woman," and "man" (in that order). The words for "one" (εἷς) and "woman" (γυνή) agree in case, number, and gender.[16] The word translated "man" is ἀνήρ, which most generically represents an adult male. This has led many to translate this phrase in a substitutionary manner as "a one-woman man."

As is the case with many simple and seemingly literal interpretations, there is more to this situation than meets the eye. The word γυνή, in some contexts, also indicates 'wife.'[17] The same is true for ἀνήρ, which may indicate 'husband.'[18]

---

[14] The *Life of Polycarp* is estimated to have been written circa 250, reputed to be authored by Pionus. The content of this document is not reliable, but the interpretation of the use of ἀνεπίλημπτος in this instance does provide some witness as to how this passage was understood at this relatively early point in the history of the Christian church.

[15] cf. *Life of Polycarp* 22, "Now the lesson was on the Epistles of Paul to Timothy and to Titus, in which he says what manner of man a bishop ought to be."

[16] The case is genitive, the number is singular and the gender is feminine.

[17] BDAG, p. 208. Occurs 215x in NT.

[18] BDAG, p. 79. Occurs 216x in NT.

The words ἀνήρ and γυνή occur frequently in the New Testament and are translated various ways, according to context. When both of these words occur together, and when both are singular nouns[19] the context is usually that of marriage.

Given that these words have some sort of grammatical relationship, and realizing that when they occur in close proximity elsewhere in the NT with similar form the context of marriage is usually assumed, it is appropriate to apply similar understanding here. The text does not speak of man and woman in some sort of generic relation, the relationship is that of marriage, between a husband (the overseer) and his wife. Therefore the phrase should be rendered "husband of one wife."

This may also be seen as a prohibition against polygamy. Reading any more (or less) into the phrase is not wise. The plain meaning is that of a monogamous marriage between a man (the overseer) and a woman. Using this phrase as justification that an overseer need only be married (thus can be either male or female) or simply monogamous inside or outside of marriage is a stretch, particularly in light of the opposite of this phrase used in 1Tim. 5:9:

> Let a widow be put on the list if she is not less than sixty years old, *the wife of one husband,* (1Ti 5:9, emphasis added)

Here the opposite relationship, "the wife of one husband," is stated as the discussion is concerning widows. The phrase, both in 1Ti 3:2 and 5:9, is not formulaic or aphoristic, but changes form to emphasize the primary member in the relationship under discussion. In 1Ti 5:9, the primary subject is the widow, who is also the wife. In 1Ti 3:2, the primary subject is the overseer, who is also the husband.

Temperate, self-controlled

The Greek word is νηφάλιος, which has both literal and figurative senses. Literally, it means 'temperate' or 'sober,' having to do with moderation of the consumption of alcoholic beverages. The figurative sense is to be 'self-controlled' or 'level-headed.'[20] In this case, the sense is most likely figurative as the phrase "not addicted to wine" occurs in v. 3 as part of the same list.

---

[19] 27 verses: Mk 10:2; Lk 16:18; Jn 4:17; Ac 5:1; Ro 7:2; 1Co 7:2, 3, 4, 10, 11, 13, 14, 16, 34, 39; 11:3, 7, 8, 9, 11, 12; Eph 5:23, 33; 1Ti 2:12; 3:2; 5:9; Tt 1:6. It is questionable whether 1Ti 2:12 is in the context of marriage, though it is quite possible.

[20] BDAG, p. 672. Occurs 3x in NT, all are in PE: 1Ti 3:2, 11; Tt 2:2.

"Self-controlled" comes from the Greek word σώφρων, which is translated variously as 'prudent,' 'thoughtful,' 'self-controlled.'[21] This word may also be translated "wisely," as in the Wisdom of Solomon:

> For she knows and understands all things,
> and she will lead me in my actions *wisely*,
> and she will watch me in her glory. (Wis 9:11, emphasis added)

A similar passage occurs in Fourth Maccabees:

> For at the time God made humans, he implanted their emotions and habits. And at that time, he enthroned the mind as the sacred guide among the sensory organs over all the rest. And he gave to this the law, according to which the one who lives will be king over both a *sensible* kingdom and a just, good, and courageous one. (4Ma 2:21–23, NRSV, emphasis added)

These Greek words found adjacently in 1Ti 3:2 (νηφάλιος and σώφρων) convey similar meaning and overlap somewhat in their semantic range. The overall sense of their juxtaposition is that of being thoughtful and wise in a situation.

respectable

The Greek word is κόσμιος, which here has the sense of 'respectable' or 'honorable.'[22] BDAG cites an inscription that uses κόσμιος, dated around 40 A.D.,[23] showing that the term was used in a public fashion to honor someone. Moulton & Milligan gloss the word as 'orderly' or 'virtuous' and further note κόσμιος " … is common as an epithet of honour in the inscriptions."[24] As this instance occurs in a list of virtues, the sense of virtue or respect is appropriate.

hospitable

"Hospitable" is translated from the Greek word φιλόξενος,[25] a compound word consisting of the word for 'love' or 'friendship' and the word for 'stranger/foreigner' respectively. The word occurs in First Peter:

> Be *hospitable* to one another without complaining. (1Pe 4:9, emphasis added)

---

[21] BDAG, p. 987. Occurs 4x in NT, all are in PE: 1Ti 3:2, Tt 1:8; 2:2, 5.

[22] BDAG, p. 561. Occurs 2x in NT, both times in PE: 1Ti 2:9, 3:2. See note on 1Ti 2:9, where the word has a slightly different sense.

[23] BDAG, p. 561, citing *Inscriptiones Graecae* IV2/1, 82, 27

[24] M-M, p. 356.

[25] BDAG, p. 1058. Occurs 3x in NT: 1Ti 3:2; Tt 1:8; 1Pe 4:9. The Tt 1:8 occurrence is in a parallel list of qualities of an overseer.

The word φιλόξενος also occurs in the *Works of Josephus*:

> When, therefore, silence was made by the whole multitude, I spake thus to them:—"O my countrymen! I refuse not to die, if justice so require. However, I am desirous to tell you the truth of this matter before I die; for as I know that this city of yours [Taricheae] was a city of *great hospitality*, and filled with abundance of such men as have left their own countries, and are come hither to be partakers of your fortune, whatever it be, I had a mind to build walls about it, out of this money, for which you are so angry with me, while yet it was to be expended in building your own walls." (Jos., *Life* 1.141–142, emphasis added)

This excerpt[26] provides some context that assists in evaluating the semantic range of φιλόξενος. From Josephus' perspective, the city in question (Taricheae) has some sort of population of foreigners[27] who are not rejected by the city. Josephus' statement contains a bit of irony in that he is praising the citizens of the city while also pleading for hospitality to be extended to him. He is hoping for the citizens of Taricheae to show him mercy.[28] By referencing that Taricheae "... was a city of great hospitality," Josephus intends to kindle their renowned hospitality that he may benefit from it.[29]

Thus φιλόξενος, in at least one sense, has to do with showing kindness of some degree to foreigners sojourning among the native population. A similar sense is found in *First Clement*:

> Because of faith and hospitality Rahab the prostitute was rescued. For the spies were sent out by Joshua the son of Nun to Jericho, the king of the land knew that they had come to spy out their land, and he sent out men who were to seize them, so that having seized them, they might put them to death. Therefore the *hospitable* Rahab, having welcomed them, hid them in the upper level, under the stalks of flax. (*1Cl* 12.1–3, emphasis added)

Rahab was "hospitable" in her actions toward the spies from Joshua. She, a citizen of Jericho, showed kindness to the Israelite spies. Another instance that sheds light on the meaning of φιλόξενος is found in the *Shepherd of Hermas*:

> Bishops and *hospitable ones* who always gladly welcome the servants of God into their own houses without hypocrisy. And the bishops always unceasingly protected the needy ones and the widows by their own ministry and always

[26] In which φιλόξενος is the superlative φιλοξενωτάτην, thus "great hospitality" or "greatly hospitable" or even "greatest hospitality."

[27] "... such men as have left their own countries, and are come hither to be partakers of your fortune."

[28] "I refuse not to die, if justice so require."

[29] The reader of Josephus' *Life* needs to remember that Josephus tends to recall events in the light most beneficial to himself. This particular anecdote likely reflects this tendency.

> conducted themselves in purity. (Hermas, *Similitudes* IX, xxvii, 2, emphasis added)

In this instance, φιλόξενος is clarified as applying to those who allowed fellow Christians to stay in their homes as need be.

skillful in teaching

The Greek word is διδακτικός, 'skillful in teaching' or 'able to teach.'[30] This word also occurs in Second Timothy:

> And the slave of the Lord must not quarrel, but be kind toward everyone, *skillful in teaching*, tolerant, (2Ti 2:24, emphasis added)

In light of Paul's comments regarding false teachers who infiltrated the church and misled Christians with heresy,[31] the ability to teach is an important skill for leaders of the church to have. If the leaders are not able to properly instruct the church in the ways of Christ, then the church will be lost.

VERSE 3

not addicted to wine

"Not addicted to wine" is a translation of the Greek word πάροινος. Standard glosses include 'addicted to wine' and 'drunkard.'[32] M-M translate instances in the Pastoral Epistles as meaning "one given to too much wine."[33] This quality in overseers is not equivalent with teetotalism; it instead draws attention to the ability of the overseer to act responsibly in all aspects, including his use or abstention from alcohol.

not a violent person, but gentle

The Greek word translated "a violent person" is πλήκτης, typically indicating 'bully' or 'pugnacious person.'[34] The word has to do with one who easily comes to blows, or

---

[30] BDAG, p. 240. Occurs 2x in NT, both in PE: 1Ti 3:2; 2Ti 2:24.

[31] e.g. 1Ti 1:3–7.

[32] BDAG, p. 780. Occurs 2x in NT, both in PE: 1Ti 3:3; Tt 1:7; both of these are in lists of virtues describing overseers.

[33] M-M, p. 496.

[34] BDAG, p. 826. Occurs 2x in NT, both in PE: 1Ti 3:3; Tt 1:7; both of these are in lists of virtues describing overseers.

one who tends to desire to solve problems by resorting to aggressive means earlier rather than later in a negotiation.

The Greek word translated "gentle" is ἐπιεικής, glossed as 'kind,' 'courteous,' 'tolerant,' or 'yielding.'[35] This offers a contrast to "not violent." A similar contrast occurs in First Peter:

> Domestic slaves, be subject to your masters with all respect, not only to those who are good and *gentle*, but also to those who are unjust. (1Pe 2:18, emphasis added)

Here slaves are told to obey their masters whether their masters are "good and gentle" or whether they are "unjust." Josephus also uses this word in his treatise *Against Apion*:

> However, there are other things which our legislator ordained for us beforehand, which of necessity we ought to do in common to all men; as to afford fire, and water, and food to such as want it; to show them the roads; and not to let anyone lie unburied. He also would have us treat those that are esteemed our enemies *with moderation*: for he doth not allow us to set their country on fire, nor permit us to cut down those trees that bear fruit: nay, farther, he forbids us to spoil those that have been slain in war. He hath also provided for such as are taken captive, that they may not be injured, and especially that the women may not be abused. (Jos., *Apion* 2.211–212) [36]

Here Josephus uses the word ἐπιεικής and then provides several examples of the "moderation" that was exercised: not setting the country on fire, not cutting down fruit-bearing trees, not plundering the dead, and so on. From the perspective of a triumphal conqueror, these are not small concessions, thus it is "moderation" or some form of gentleness or yielding to do such things.

Paul requires overseers that do not exhibit violence when challenged. He instead wants them to treat situations with a serious gentleness, addressing issues properly while considering those who happen to be involved in them.

peaceable

The Greek word translated "peaceable" is ἄμαχος; it could also be translated as "not a fighter." The word is glossed as 'disinclined to fight' and 'not contentious.'[37] This is most likely reiterating the previous entry in the list, "not violent, but gentle."

---

[35] BDAG, p. 371. Occurs 5x in NT: Php 4:5; 1Ti 3:3; Tt 3:2; Jas 3:17; 1Pe 2:18.

[36] The entire section (through Jos., *Apion* 2.214) is worth examining.

[37] LSJ, p. 78.

not loving money

This phrase is translated from one compound Greek word,[38] ἀφιλάργυρος. The meaning of 'not loving money' or 'not greedy' is appropriate.[39] This word is the opposite of φιλάργυρος, which occurs in 1Ti 6:10. The word ἀφιλάργυρος also occurs in Hebrews:

> Your lifestyle must be *free from the love of money*, being content with what you have. For he himself has said, "I will never desert you, and I will never abandon you." (Heb 13:5, emphasis added)

Instead of seeking for more money or things that money provides, the author of Hebrews urges his readers to be content. In this letter to Timothy, Paul is requiring a similar perspective for those who would be overseers. This qualification persisted through the early church, as is evident in the *Didache*:

> Therefore, appoint for yourselves overseers and deacons worthy of the Lord, men who are gentle and *not lovers of money* and truthful and well-proven, for to you they themselves also minister the ministry of the prophets and teachers. (*Did.* 15.1, emphasis added)[40]

VERSE 4

Paul has ended his list of virtues, but continues with qualifications for overseer. Some explanation is provided for each requirement; before he was simply listing criteria as they came to mind.[41] Paul recommends that the potential overseer's household management be evaluated for insight as to how he might function in the role of overseer.

managing his own household well

The Greek word translated "He must manage" is προΐστημι, which in this instance has the sense of 'rule' or 'direct'[42] and occurs both here and in v. 5. The word literally means to 'come forward' or 'stand before.' Thus it has to do with having a position of

---

[38] Combining the alpha prefix for negation and adding φιλέω (love) and ἄργυρος (money).

[39] BDAG, p. 157. Occurs 2x in NT: 1Ti 3:3; Heb 13:5. Cf. also φιλάργυρος in 1Ti 6:10.

[40] Also see Poly., *Phil.* 4 and 5, which have parallels with 1Ti 3:8–13 and 1Ti 6:7–10.

[41] Hence the reason for the apparent duplication. In 1Ti 3:2, 'temperate,' 'self-controlled' and 'respectable' have some degree of semantic overlap.

[42] BDAG, p. 870. Occurs 8x in NT, 6x in PE: 1Ti 3:4, 5, 12; 5:17; Tt 3:8, 14.

leadership (standing before something in the sense of leading or directing). Paul uses προΐστημι in Romans:

> if it is one who exhorts, by exhortation; one who gives, with sincerity; *one who leads*, with diligence; one who shows mercy, with cheerfulness. (Ro 12:8, emphasis added)

Here προΐστημι is a participle used substantively. The word also occurs in First Maccabees:

> And he ordered them, saying, "*Take charge* of these people, and you should not join in battle against the nations until our return." (1Ma 5:19, emphasis added)

The word is used by Josephus as well:

> However, I assured them that I would entirely forgive them for the time to come, if they would send ten of the *ringleaders* of the multitude to me; and when they complied readily with this proposal, and sent me the men forementioned, I put them on board a ship, and sent them away to Taricheae, and ordered them to be kept in prison. (Jos., *Life* 168, emphasis added)

This verb is also used in the context of church leadership in the *Shepherd of Hermas*:

> Therefore you are to write two little books and you will send one to Clement and one to Grapte. Then Clement will send his to the outer cities, for that is his duty. And Grapte will instruct the widows and the orphans. But you, Hermas, you will read *yours* in this city with the elders who *lead* the church." (Hermas, *Visions* II, iv, 3, emphasis added)

The sort of leadership represented by προΐστημι may be military (1Ma 5:19), nefarious (Jos., *Life* 168) or well-intentioned (Hermas, *Visions* II, iv, 3). Here Paul applies προΐστημι to a household, noting that the state of the household must reflect proper management. One measure of how well a potential overseer runs his household is to examine how his children behave.

having children in submission with all dignity

The word translated "dignity" is σεμνότης,[43] which Paul used earlier in 1Ti 2:2, "...that we may live a tranquil and quiet life in all godliness and *dignity*." The meaning of the word is much the same in this verse; that the man's dignity is evident through the manner in which his children are submissive to him.

---

[43] BDAG, p. 919. Occurs 3x in NT: 1Ti 2:2; 3:4; Tt 2:7. See discussion on 1Ti 2:2.

The word translated "submissive" is ὑποταγή[44] which in 1Ti 2:11 describes the manner in which women are to learn. The same sort of relationship between father and child is being described here. The rearing of a child is a process. For the process to be effective, the parents must be in control. If a man is being evaluated as a potential overseer, yet his children are not under control, this reflects poorly on his ability to function as an effective overseer.

The potential overseer must keep his children submissive while retaining his "dignity." That is, one's children must not be submissive or respectful due solely to fear of punishment. Those who would condition their children in such a way would not be able to retain dignity. Instead, the one qualified to be an overseer manages his household and his children in such a way as to retain dignity.

Verse 5

but if someone does not know how to manage his own household

Paul next adds a parenthetical remark to reinforce his point, explicitly linking a well-managed household with the likelihood that one will be able to serve well as an overseer. The phrase "manage his own household" in verse 5 is a mirror of the same phrase in verse 4, using a different form of the verb προΐστημι.[45] The word conveys the same meaning in both verses, that of managing or supervising, with the different inflections of the verb providing the different senses ("he must manage" vs. "how to manage") in each verse.

The thrust of verses 4–5a is an emphasis on the ability of the overseer to manage his own household, which serves as an indicator of how he will serve in the management of the church. One's household management skill can be evaluated by examining both how his children behave ("keeping his children submissive") and how his treatment of his children reflects on him ("with all dignity").

Examining the potential overseer in these areas is important because it reflects directly upon his potential ability in leadership of the church. There is not an exact correspondence; one who manages his household well will not always be a good candidate for overseer. However, one who manages his household poorly will always be a bad candidate for overseer.

---

[44] BDAG, p. 1041. Occurs 4x in NT: 2Co 9:13; Ga 2:5; 1Ti 2:11; 3:4. See comment on 1Ti 2:11.

[45] The instance in v. 4 is a present middle participle masculine accusative singular; the instance in v. 5 is an aorist active infinitive.

how will he take care of the church of God

The phrase "how will he take care of" is a combination of the adverb πῶς, which typically is translated 'how,' and the word ἐπιμελέομαι, which has the sense of 'care for' or 'take care of.'[46] The word ἐπιμελέομαι also occurs in the gospel of Luke, in the parable of the good Samaritan:

> But a certain Samaritan who was traveling came up to him and, when he saw him, had compassion. And he came up and bandaged his wounds, pouring on olive oil and wine, and he put him on his own animal and brought him to an inn and *took care of him.* And on the next day, he took out two denarii and gave them to the innkeeper, and said, "*Take care of him*, and whatever you spend in addition, I will repay to you when I return." (Lk 10:33–35, emphasis added)

In this passage, ἐπιμελέομαι occurs twice, both times having to do with the Samaritan's attending to the needs of the wounded traveler. The same word is used in Genesis, in Judah's account to Joseph (now a ruler in Egypt) of their earlier trip to Joseph:

> Lord, you asked your servants, saying, 'Tell me if you have a father or brother?' And we said to our lord, 'We have an elderly father, and there is a younger child from his old age, and his brother died. He alone is left to his father. Indeed, his father loved him.' You said to your servants, 'Bring him down to me, and *I will take care of him.*' (Ge 44:19–21 [LXX])

The "servants" in this passage are Joseph's brothers; they are petitioning Joseph for help during the famine. Joseph's response, as recounted by Judah, was to ask his brothers (who were, of course, unaware of Joseph's true identity) to bring this younger brother to him so that he could take care of the younger brother. Here again, the word has to do with the physical care of a person.

But Paul uses ἐπιμελέομαι to describe the care and oversight that one has for "God's church." Rather than physical care of a person or care for a person's economic welfare, Paul uses the term to indicate the type of oversight the overseer must administer in order to be a faithful steward of God's church.

The word translated "church" is ἐκκλησία, a much-studied word.[47] The broadest sense of ἐκκλησία is that of an assembly gathered together for some common reason;

---

[46] BDAG, p. 375. Occurs 3x in NT: Lk 10:34, 35; 1Ti 3:5.

[47] For an excellent study on ἐκκλησία, see Fenton John Anthony Hort, *The Christian Ecclesia: A Course of Lectures on the Early History and Early Conceptions of the Ecclesia* (London: Macmillan & Co, 1897). See particularly the introductory chapter and pp. 171–217 which discuss the idea of the ἐκκλησία in the Pastoral Epistles.

an 'assembly duly summoned.'[48] In New Testament usage, ἐκκλησία has three primary senses: a summoned 'assembly,' a casually gathered 'assemblage,' and a 'congregation' of people with shared beliefs.[49] The vast majority of New Testament usage involves this third sense.

The word ἐκκλησία occurs two other times in the Pastoral Epistles, both in First Timothy:

> I am writing these things to you, hoping to come to you in a short time. But if I am delayed, I am writing in order that you may know how one must conduct oneself in the household of God, which is the *church* of the living God, the pillar and mainstay of the truth. (1Ti 3:14–15, emphasis added)

> If any believing woman has widows, she must help them, and the *church* must not be burdened, in order that it may help those who are truly widows. (1Ti 5:16, emphasis added)

Both of these instances use the word ἐκκλησία in the sense of a congregation or body of people gathered together with shared beliefs. One passage (1Ti 3:14) defines the ἐκκλησία as the "household of God" and further describes it as "a pillar and mainstay of the truth."[50] In the context of First Timothy, the ἐκκλησία is generally representative of a gathering of like-minded people who share belief that Jesus Christ is Savior. In 1Ti 5:16, the idea of "church" may be localized to a specific group: the one needing to care for the widow. In the current verse, however, the "church" is the church in general or the "universal" church.

The word ἐκκλησία is used to describe large groups such as this. In the LXX, the word ἐκκλησία is used of the assembly of Israelites:

> And Moses spoke into the ears of all *the assembly* the words of this song until the end: (De 31:30 [LXX])

The phrase "church of God" is found in the epistles of Ignatius as well:

> And it is also necessary that those who are deacons of the mysteries of Jesus Christ please everyone in every way. For they are not deacons of food and drink but servants of the church of God. Therefore they must guard against accusation as against fire. (Ign., *Trall.* 2.3, emphasis added)

> Since, according to your prayers and according to the compassion which you have in Christ Jesus, it has been reported to me the church which is in Antioch of Syria is at peace, it is fitting for you as a *church of God* to appoint a deacon to go on a

---

[48] LSJ, p. 509. Occurs 114x in NT; 3x in PE: 1Ti 3:5, 15; 5:16.

[49] BDAG, p. 303.

[50] See comment on 1Ti 3:14.

> mission there as God's ambassador to rejoice with those gathered together and to glorify the name. (Ign., *Phld.* 10.1, emphasis added)
>
> Ignatius, who is also called "God-bearer," to the *church of God* the Father and of the beloved Jesus Christ, which has obtained mercy in every gift, which has been filled with faith and love, which is not lacking in any gift, most worthy of God and bearing holy things, which is in Smyrna of Asia, abundant greetings in a blameless spirit and the word of God. (Ign., *Smyrn. inscriptio*)

Ignatius typically uses the phrase in a local context, either speaking in the context of the actions of a particular assembly or the "church of God" in a specific locale.

The context here is similar. Paul's comments apply to each local ἐκκλησία as it evaluates the worthiness of potential overseers. But Paul's words do not only apply to the local ἐκκλησία, they apply to each ἐκκλησία that together makes up the universal church.

Some have attempted to generally render ἐκκλησία as 'called-out ones,' [51] yet this is a most unlikely translation. F.J.A. Hort discusses this (in the context of usage of ἐκκλησία in the LXX) in his book *The Christian Ecclesia*:

> There is no foundation for the widely spread notion that ἐκκλησία means a people or a number of individual men *called out* of the world or mankind. In itself the idea is of course entirely Scriptural, and moreover it is associated with the word and idea 'called,' 'calling,' 'call.' But the compound verb ἐκκαλέω is never so used, and ἐκκλησία never occurs in a context which suggests this supposed sense to have been present in the writer's mind.[52]

Paul's parenthetical comment "if someone does not know how to manage his own household, how will he care for God's church?" provides one test that must be applied to prospective overseers. If one desires to be an overseer, his track record of managing his own household must be evaluated and used to help determine if he is qualified for the office of overseer.

---

[51] e.g. E. W. Bullinger, *The Companion Bible*, Enlarged Type edition. (Grand Rapids, Mich.: Kregel Publications, 1999). Appendix 186.

[52] Hort, *Christian Ecclesia*, 5.

Verse 6

not newly converted

The word translated as "newly converted" is νεόφυτος. Its usage here is figurative as its literal meaning is 'newly planted.'[53] The word occurs four times in the LXX,[54] one of them in Job:

> For there is hope for a tree, for if it is cut down yet it shall bloom, and its shoot shall not die. For if its root should grow old in the earth, and its stump should die in rock, from the smell of water it shall bloom and shall create a crop as though *newly planted*. (Job 14:7–9 [LXX]).

Outside of and previous to the use of νεόφυτος in 1 Timothy, evidence of usage is strictly literal. Moulton and Milligan note:

> This word, which in its metaphorical sense of "newly-converted" is confined to Christian literature (cf. 1Ti 3:6), is of frequent occurrence in the papyri in the original meaning of "newly-planted."[55]

Despite the lack of previous evidence of figurative usage, the meaning of "newly planted" is well enough established that the intended figurative meaning of "newly converted" is clear. Paul desires overseers who have had experience in their faith.

lest he become conceited

The Greek word translated "he become conceited" is τυφόω, which typically carries the sense of 'be puffed up, conceited' in the NT.[56] Paul uses the word in a similar list in 2Ti 3:4, describing some of the poor qualities of people in the last days, noting that some will be "conceited." Paul also uses the word to describe false teachers:

> If anyone teaches other doctrine and does not devote himself to the sound words of our Lord Jesus Christ and the teaching that is in accordance with godliness, *he is conceited*, understanding nothing, but having a morbid interest concerning controversies and disputes about words, from which come envy, strife, slanders, evil suspicions, constant wrangling by people of depraved mind and deprived of the truth, who consider godliness to be a means of gain. But godliness with contentment is a great means of gain. (1Ti 6:3–6, emphasis added)

---

[53] BDAG, p. 669. Only occurs here in NT.

[54] Ps 128:3 [127:3 LXX]; 144:12 [143:12 LXX]; Is 5:7; Job 14:9.

[55] M-M, p. 425.

[56] BDAG, p. 1021. Occurs 3x in NT, all three in PE: 1Ti 3:6; 6:4; 2Ti 3:4.

This word is used similarly in the *Life of Flavius Josephus*:

> Varus accused this messenger also, when he came, of telling a falsehood, and slew him; for he was puffed up by the Syrians that were at Caesarea, and had great expectations; for they said that Agrippa would be slain by the Romans for the crimes which the Jews had committed, and that he should himself take the government, as derived from their kings; for Varus was, by the confession of all, of the royal family, as being a descendant of Sohemus, who had enjoyed a tetrarchy about Libanus; for which reason it was that *he was puffed up*, and kept the letters to himself. He contrived also that the king should not meet with those writings, by guarding all the passes, lest anyone should escape, and inform the king what had been done. He moreover slew many of the Jews, in order to gratify the Syrians of Caesarea. (Jos., *Life* 52–53, emphasis added) [57]

Here, Josephus' point is that Varus, due to being a part of the royal family, was "puffed up" or conceited. Varus thought more of himself than he should have.

A particularly enlightening use of τυφόω is found in Philo's tractate *On Mating with the Preliminary Studies*:

> And it often happens that he who professes some one of the indifferent branches of knowledge, when he meets with a pupil of good natural qualifications, boasts of his success in teaching, thinking that he, by himself and alone, is the cause of his pupil's facility in learning. And then, becoming elated and puffing himself up, he holds his head high, and draws his eyebrows and becomes full of pride, and asks very high terms from those who desire to become his pupils; but those whom he perceives to be poor but still to be eager for instruction, he rejects and repels, as if he were the only person who had found a treasure of wisdom. This is the meaning of the expression, "to conceive," namely, to be full of pride, and *to be puffed up with arrogance beyond all moderation*, on which account some persons have appeared to dishonour the queen of all the intermediate and indifferent branches of knowledge, virtue, who deserves to be honoured, even for her own sake. (Philo, *Prelim. Studies* 127–128, emphasis added)

In this example, τυφόω is defined in context. The instructor is chastised for considering the innate skill of the student to be a result of his effort. This instructor has been "puffed up with arrogance beyond all moderation" in that he has taken credit for a result which he did not cause. He subsequently held students with no similar innate ability to the standard of the innately-skilled student, considering them (instead of himself) at fault when their skills did not develop in the same manner.

---

[57] Note the phrase "he was puffed up" occurs in 1.52, but the underlying Greek is not the word τυφόω. Instead, it is the phrase ἐπῆρτο μέγα φρονεῖν.

Paul's fear of the overseer becoming "puffed up with conceit" is similar. If a recent convert becomes an overseer, he may consider his own skill in doctrine or practice to be superior. His lack of a solid and tested foundation in the things of doctrine may cause him to be swayed by false teaching much more easily than that of an overseer who has experience in the faith and has been tested in these things.

and fall into the condemnation of the devil

The recent convert may "fall into the condemnation of the devil" as a result of being conceited. The phrase "fall into" is a translation of the Greek word ἐμπίπτω, which means to fall either literally or figuratively.[58] The word occurs again in verse 7, "fall into disgrace and the trap of the devil."

This figurative use of the word ἐμπίπτω occurs in the book of Hebrews:

> For we know the one who said, "Vengeance is mine, I will repay," and again, "The Lord will judge his people." It is a terrifying thing *to fall into* the hands of the living God. (Heb 10:30–31, emphasis added)

Here the act of judgment is described as falling into "the hands of the living God." The word also occurs in the LXX, this instance in Proverbs:

> By the sin of his lips the sinful *falls into* traps, but the righteous escapes from them. (Pr 12:13 [LXX]).

Josephus also uses the word in his *Antiquities of the Jews*:

> But as he was fallen to a fatal choice of great miseries, he was in trouble, and sorely confounded; and when the prophet had said that he must of necessity make his choice, and had ordered him to answer quickly, that he might declare what he had chosen to God, the king reasoned with himself, that in case he should ask for famine, he would appear to do it for others, and without danger to himself, since he had a great deal of corn hoarded up, but to the harm of others; that in case he should choose to be overcome [by his enemies] for three months, he would appear to have chosen war, because he had valiant men about him, and strongholds, and that therefore he feared nothing therefrom: so he chose that affliction which is common to kings and to their subjects, and in which the fear was equal on all sides; and said this beforehand, that it was much better *to fall into* the hands of God, than into those of his enemies. (Jos., *Ant.* 7.322–323, emphasis added)

[58] BDAG, p. 324. Occurs 7x in NT, 3x in PE: 1Ti 3:6, 7; 6:9.

In this example, the king calculates that it is better for him to "fall into" the hands of God instead of the hands of his enemies. This occurrence is almost in the sense of 'being delivered into.'

Ignatius uses ἐμπίπτω figuratively in his *Letter to the Magnesians*:

> And I say these things, my beloved, not because I have learned that any from you are acting in this way, but as less than you, I desire to protect you, that you not *be snagged* by the fishhooks of worthless delusion, but to be fully convinced of the birth and the suffering and the resurrection, which took place in the time of the rule of Pontius Pilate. These things were really and truly done by Jesus Christ, our hope, from which may none of you ever turn away. (Ign., *Magn.* 11, emphasis added)

The picture of "being snagged by the fish hooks of worthless delusion" is particularly vivid. Ignatius urges the Magnesians to remain convinced of the essential points of faith so that worthless ideas will not entice them. If they are properly grounded, then the worthless ideas will have no ability to snag them.

Ignatius' logic here is similar to that of Paul in 1Ti 3:6. Those without experience or grounding, no matter how impressive their other qualifications, are more susceptible to being enticed by false doctrine presented in an appealing and seemingly innocuous manner.

The danger is that the ungrounded will fall into "the condemnation of the devil." The word translated "condemnation" is the Greek word κρίμα and has to do with judgment, usually in a legal context.[59] In the NT, God is the legal authority who renders this judgment. The word is used frequently in this sort of context:

> But refuse younger widows, for whenever their physical desires lead them away from Christ, they want to marry, thus incurring *condemnation* because they have broken their former pledge. (1Ti 5:11–12, emphasis added)

> Let every person be subject to the governing authorities, for there is no authority except by God, and those that exist are put in place by God. So then, the one who resists authority resists the ordinance which is from God, and those who resist will receive *condemnation* on themselves. (Ro 13:1–2, emphasis added)

This word also occurs in *First Clement*:

> For having gone away with him, [Lot's] wife changed her mind and was not in harmony; a sign was made to this end so that she became a pillar of salt even to this day to make known to all that the double-minded and those who doubt

---

[59] BDAG, p. 567. Occurs 27x in NT, 2x in PE: 1Ti 3:6; 5:12.

> concerning the power of God will be for *judgment* and for a warning to all generations. (*1Cl* 11.2, emphasis added)

The condemnation/judgment entered into is that "of the devil." The word translated devil is διάβολος. When διάβολος occurs with an article, as it does here, it is typically translated as 'the slanderer' or 'the devil.'[60]

The trap the recent convert may fall into isn't simply "condemnation," it is the "condemnation of the devil." The phrase "of the devil" is added to qualify the sort of condemnation that could easily befall the recent convert. Until the faith of the recent convert is tested and proven true, says Paul, he should not be put into a leadership position.

Verse 7

But he must also have a good testimony from those outside

In addition to being experienced, the overseer "have a good testimony from those outside." The phrase "he must have a good testimony" is an accurate translation, but the English words do not have equally corresponding Greek words. "He must" is reflective of the Greek word δεῖ which, while having a multitude of uses, typically implies the idea of necessity. It is combined with ἔχω, a frequently-used verb which typically means 'have.'[61] The English word "good" comes from the Greek adjective καλός, which typically means 'well,' 'good,' 'beautiful,' or 'useful.'[62] The words "testimony" come from the Greek word μαρτυρία. This word has to do with 'testimony' or statements of approval.[63] This usage occurs elsewhere in the NT:

> Demetrius has been testified to by all, even by the truth itself. And we also testify to him, and you know that our *testimony* is true. (3Jn 12, emphasis added)

The first two instances of the English word "testimony" are translated from verbs ("has been testified to" and "we also testify to him"). The third instance of "testimony" comes from the noun under discussion. While "by all" may be hyperbolic it does imply that there were few who would disapprove of Demetrius' way of life. Paul uses μαρτυρία in his epistle to Titus as well:

---

[60] BDAG, p. 226. Occurs 37x in NT, 6x in PE. Three of these are in chapter 3: 1Ti 3:6, 7, 11.

[61] Regarding the combination of δεῖ and ἔχω, see comments on 1Ti 3:2 where this same sort of usage is discussed (only with δεῖ and εἰμί).

[62] BDAG, p. 504. Occurs 101x in NT.

[63] BDAG, p. 618. Occurs 37x in NT, 2x in PE: 1Ti 3:7; Tt 1:13. The word μαρτυρία occurs in a judicial or legal context in some instances, but that is not the case in the Pastoral Epistles.

> A certain one of them, one of their own prophets, has said, "Cretans are always liars, evil beasts, lazy gluttons." This *testimony* is true, for which reason reprove them severely, in order that they may be sound in the faith, (Tt 1:12–13, emphasis added)

In this instance, Paul provides confirmation of the testimony of Epimenides concerning Cretans. The testimony is not in a legal context, it is a statement of disapproval regarding Cretans.[64]

The overseer must be held in esteem "from those outside." The word "outside" is a translation of the Greek word ἔξωθεν, an adverb, here used substantively, that functions in a number of ways but typically implies something outside of or external to something else.[65] A similar usage is found in Josephus' *Wars of the Jews*:

> Although I must say that submission to *foreigners* may be borne because fortune hath already doomed us to it, while submission to wicked people of our own nation is too unmanly, and brought upon us by our own consent. (Jos., *Wars* 4.179, emphasis added)[66]

Josephus uses ἔξωθεν to mean "foreigners," showing that submission to those outside of the nationality of the speaker is meant. The same sort of relationship is intended by Paul here; those who are outside of the fellowship must think highly of the overseer, just as those who are in the fellowship do.

in order that he may not fall into disgrace

Paul's reason for requiring that the overseer be well thought of by those outside the fellowship is "in order that he may not fall into disgrace." The phrase "fall into" is from the Greek word ἐμπίπτω, which was used in similar fashion in v. 6.[67]

The word "disgrace" is a translation of the Greek word ὀνειδισμός, which typically carries the sense of 'reproach' or 'revile.'[68] All of the NT instances of ὀνειδισμός, apart from this instance, have to do with reproach or disgrace heaped upon Christians as a result of their identification with Christ or the reproach Christ received.

---

[64] While Cretans may have been known for deceit and laziness, Epimenides was most likely posing a paradox, and Paul was most likely playing along with it.

[65] BDAG, p. 354. Occurs 13x in NT, only here in PE. The sense used here is not the primary sense of the word. However, ἔξωθεν occurs in a sense similar to that used here in a variant reading of Mark 4:11 (found in codex Vaticanus, a highly regarded Greek uncial MS of the fourth century), in place of ἔξω.

[66] The word is used similarly in Jos., *Ant.* 15.316.

[67] See comment on 1Ti 3:6.

[68] BDAG, p. 710. Occurs 5x in NT: Ro 15:3; 1Ti 3:7; Heb 10:33; 11:26; 13:13.

> By faith Moses, when he was grown up, refused to be called the son of Pharaoh's daughter, choosing instead to be mistreated with the people of God rather than to experience the transitory enjoyment of sin, considering *reproach* endured for the sake of Christ greater wealth than the treasures of Egypt, for he was looking to the reward. (Heb 11:24–26, emphasis added)

The other two instances in Hebrews (10:33 and 13:13) are similar in that the reproach they describe is received on a basis of identification with Christ. Paul has similar usage in his epistle to the Romans:

> Let each one of us please his neighbor for his good, for the purpose of edification. For even Christ did not please himself, but just as it is written, "The *insults* of those who insult you have fallen on me." For whatever was written beforehand was written for our instruction, in order that through patient endurance and through the encouragement of the scriptures we may have hope. (Ro 15:2–4, emphasis added)

Yet in First Timothy, Paul does not use this word in this manner; he uses it to indicate disgrace that the overseer may be susceptible to if he doesn't have a proper foundation. If the overseer acts rashly or imprudently he may bring disgrace upon himself in the eyes of the community. The *Testament of Reuben* offers a similar example:

> For until my father's death I never had the courage to look him in the face or speak to any of my brothers because of *my disgraceful act*. Even until now my conscience harasses me because of my impious act. (*T. Reub.* 4.2–3, emphasis added)

In this excerpt from the *Testament of Reuben*, ὀνειδισμός seems to be a sense of shame or guilt in this case due to one's own previous actions.[69] Paul's concern is that the neophyte overseer may similarly compromise himself. While still a danger with those who have a firm foundation in the faith, in Paul's mind the problem is much less likely.

and the trap of the devil

There are dangers in addition to disgrace, namely, falling into "the trap of the devil." The word translated "trap" is the Greek word παγίς, meaning 'trap' either literally or

---

[69] Ge 35:22: "While Israel lived in that land, Reuben went and lay with Bilhah his father's concubine. And Israel heard of it." The *Testament of Reuben* expands on this story in 3:9–4:4.

figuratively.[70] Here the meaning is figurative, speaking of a "trap of the devil." The same phrase occurs in Second Timothy:

> And the slave of the Lord must not quarrel, but be kind toward everyone, skillful in teaching, tolerant, correcting those who are opposed with gentleness, seeing whether perhaps God may grant them repentance to a knowledge of the truth, and they will come to their senses again and escape from the *trap of the devil*, being held captive by him to do his will. (2Ti 2:24–26, emphasis added)

However, this phrase "the trap of the devil" is problematic. Is it a separate thing from the disgrace, or is it epexegetical, explaining the disgrace? Knight addresses this issue:

> The first aspect of this concern is that he will fall into "reproach" (ὀνειδισμός). From whom will the reproach come? That is to say, is ὀνειδισμός qualified by the genitive τοῦ διαβόλου or is it used absolutely? For the former, it is argued that the preposition εἰς is not repeated before παγίδα. For the latter, it is argued that the reproach follows from the potential bishop not having a good testimony from those outside and so is not restricted exclusively to the διάβολος. That consideration is more in line with the context.[71]

According to Knight, then, the trap of the devil is something separate from the disgrace; one who has been disgraced may then fall into the snare of the devil. Charles Ellicott, writing in the mid-1800's, arrived at the same basic conclusion:

> ... the absence of the article before παγίδα being perhaps due to the preposition; comp. Winer, *Gr.* 19.2, p. 114. The exact connexion is somewhat doubtful, as the genitive may depend (*a*) on both, or (*b*) only on the last of the two substantives. The omission of the prep. before παγίδα (De W.) is an argument in favour of (*a*); the isolated position however of ὀνειδισμός and the connexion of thought in ch. 5:14, 15, seem to preponderate in favour of (*b*), ὀνειδισμός being thus absolute, and referring to 'the reproachful comments and judgment,' whether of those without (Chrys.) or within the Church. ... The expression παγίδα τοῦ διαβόλου ('snare laid by the devil;' apparently *gen. originis*, contrast ver. 6), occurs again in 2Ti 2:26; so similarly in 1Ti 6:9. It is here added to ὀνειδισμός, not epexegetically

---

[70] BDAG, p. 747. Occurs 5x in NT: Lk 21:35; Ro 11:9; 1Ti 3:7; 6:9; 2Ti 2:26. On "of the devil" see comment on 1Ti 3:6 above which treats the same phrase.

[71] George W Knight, *The Pastoral Epistles: A Commentary on the Greek Text*, New International Greek Testament Commentary (Grand Rapids, Mich.; Carlisle, England: W.B. Eerdmans; Paternoster Press, 1992), 165.

> … but rather as marking the temptations that will be sure to follow the loss of character.[72]

One danger or "trap" is that church leaders may become targets of persecution and the objects of baseless allegation from those outside of the fellowship. Such accusations are less likely to stick if the overseer has built rapport among non-Christians in the larger community. Ignatius, in his *Letter to the Trallians*, offers a similar warning:

> And it is also necessary that those who are deacons of the mysteries of Jesus Christ please everyone in every way. For they are not deacons of food and drink but servants of the church of God. *Therefore they must guard against accusation as against fire.* (Ign., *Trall.* 2.3, emphasis added)

Paul desires overseers firmly grounded and tested in the faith and thought well of by those outside of the church, that the leadership of the fellowship may be certain.

---

[72] Charles J Ellicott, *The Pastoral Epistles of St. Paul: With a Critical and Grammatical Commentary, and a Revised Translation.* (Bellingham, WA: Logos Research Systems, Inc., 2008), 45.

DEACONS IN THE FELLOWSHIP (1Ti 3:8–13)

Deacons likewise must be dignified, not insincere, not devoted to much wine, not fond of dishonest gain, holding the mystery of the faith with a clear conscience, and these also must be tested first; then let them serve if they are above reproach. The wives likewise must be dignified, not slanderous, temperate, faithful in all things. Deacons must be husbands of one wife, managing their children and their own households well. For those who have served well acquire a good standing for themselves, and great boldness in the faith that is in Christ Jesus. (1Ti 3:8–13)

VERSE 8

Deacons likewise must be dignified

The Greek word translated "deacons" is διάκονος, which here has the sense of 'assistant.'[1] In other contexts, διάκονος may be translated as "servant" or perhaps "minister,"[2] but here, in the context of discussing roles of responsibility in the fellowship, the sense of "deacon" is most likely.

However, the translation of "deacon," taken directly into English from the Greek word, is problematic because of the lexical freight it carries. Different denominations and traditions have roles or offices that are labeled "deacon," yet the scope of responsibility of a "deacon" varies from tradition to tradition. Thus one cannot start with a modern-day conception of "deacon" and then consider this list of qualifications as proper for the sort of deacon that his tradition utilizes. [3]

While the present-day role of those known as deacons is varied, this section uses the term in the consistent sense of an office or established role of some sort in the

---

[1] BDAG, p. 230. Occurs 29x in NT, 3x in PE: 1Ti 3:8, 12; 4:6.

[2] See comment on 1Ti 4:6.

[3] The term "deacon" will be used for the balance of this work, despite its inadequacies. Note also that Poly., *Phil.* 5.2 also lists qualifications for deacons.

community. Ignatius, in his *Letter to the Magnesians*, provides some insight to the role of διάκονος as practiced in the late first century/early second century:[4]

> Therefore, since I have been considered worthy to see you through Damas, your godly bishop, and through your worthy presbyters Bassus and Apollonius and my fellow slave, the *deacon* Zotion, who I would enjoy because he is subject to the bishop as to the grace of God, and to the council of elders as to the law of Jesus Christ. (Ign., *Magn.* 2, emphasis added)

The role of deacon is one that serves the bishop/overseer and (at least in Ignatius' time) the presbytery. Deacons serve in the role of assistant to those in leadership positions. Ignatius also writes in his *Letter to the Magnesians*:

> Therefore, since I have by faith seen and loved, in the people mentioned above, the whole congregation. I urge you: be eager to do everything in the harmony of God, the bishop presiding in the place of God, and the presbyters in the place of the council of the apostles, and the *deacons*, who to me are especially dear, entrusted with the ministry of Jesus Christ, who before the ages was with the Father and has been revealed at the end. (Ign., *Magn.* 6.1, emphasis added)

Here Ignatius notes that the deacons have been "entrusted with the ministry of Jesus Christ." While the responsibility of serving Christ falls on all those who profess his name, the deacon has some sort of additional responsibility to ensure that the "ministry of Jesus Christ" is pursued through assistance given to the overseer.

The transitioning word "likewise" (ὡσαύτως) is used to relate the qualifications of deacons with the earlier provided qualifications for the overseer. Because deacons are involved to some degree in the leadership of the fellowship, it is important to be equally stringent in their selection. Therefore Paul provides criteria to guide the selection of deacons.[5] He begins by noting that deacons "must be dignified." The word translated "dignified" is the Greek word σεμνός, which may be glossed 'worthy of respect' or 'dignified' or perhaps even 'noble.'[6] Paul uses this term to describe older men in the fellowship in his epistle to Titus:

---

[4] Ignatius' views on the role of deacon progress from the role of deacon in the New Testament. The Ignatian conception of deacon is the result of development and practice of the proto-apostolic church. As such, it is valuable to examine the state of Ignatian deacons as this may provide insight to the Pauline conception of deacons in the apostolic church.

[5] Many of the qualifications are similar. Note also *Did.* 15, which provides an abbreviated list for "bishops and deacons."

[6] BDAG, p. 919. Occurs 4x in NT: Php 4:8; 1Ti 3:8, 11; Tt 2:2. Only the PE occurrences apply σεμνός to humans.

> Older men are to be temperate, *worthy of respect*, self-controlled, sound in faith, in love, and in endurance. (Tt 2:2, emphasis added)

Josephus uses this term to describe a man called Ananus.

> I should not mistake if I said that the death of Ananus was the beginning of the destruction of the city, and that from this very day may be dated the overthrow of her wall, and the ruin of her affairs, whereon they saw their high priest, and the procurer of their preservation, slain in the midst of their city. He was on other accounts also a *venerable*, and a very just man; and besides the grandeur of that nobility, and dignity, and honor, of which he was possessed, he had been a lover of a kind of parity, even with regard to the meanest of the people; he was a prodigious lover of liberty, and an admirer of a democracy in government; and did ever prefer the public welfare before his own advantage, and preferred peace above all things; for he was thoroughly sensible that the Romans were not to be conquered. (Jos., *Wars* 4.317–320a, emphasis added)

The extent and kindness of Josephus' description of Ananus reinforces what sort of person can be called σεμνός, or "dignified." Deacons in the service of the church are to have a similar quality.

not insincere

The word translated "insincere" is the Greek word δίλογος. The word literally means 'double-speaking.'[7] Polycarp uses the word in his discussion on qualifications of deacons:

> Likewise, deacons must be blameless in the presence of his righteousness, as servants of God and Christ and not of people, not slanderers, not *insincere*, not lovers of money, but self-controlled in all things, compassionate, careful, walking according to the truth of the Lord, who became the servant of all. (Poly., *Phil.* 5.2a, emphasis added)

Deacons are to be sincere in their interactions with those whom they serve.

not devoted to much wine

As in the English, this is a phrase in the Greek, not a single word. The significant word is προσέχω, which is translated "devoted." This word has multiple senses,

---

[7] BDAG, p. 250. *hapax.*

ranging in meaning from 'take care' to 'pay attention to' to 'occupy oneself with' or even 'apply oneself to.'[8]

The sort of personal devotion or occupation implied by this sense of προσέχω is strong. Paul uses the word in this same sense later in First Timothy:

> Until I come, *pay attention* to the public reading, to exhortation, to teaching. (1Ti 4:13, emphasis added)

In this case the devotion is positive, to the public reading of Scripture. In the current context, however, the devotion is negative, leading to the sense of addiction. This passage, as with 1Ti 3:3, does not command complete abstention from alcohol. It does, however, mandate responsibility on the part of those who partake of alcohol.

not fond of dishonest gain

The Greek word αἰσχροκερδής is translated "fond for dishonest gain." The sense is that of 'avaricious.'[9] Paul uses the same word in the same sense (though in reference to the overseer) in the epistle to Titus:

> For it is necessary for the overseer to be blameless as God's steward, not self-willed, not quick-tempered, not addicted to wine, not violent, not *greedy for dishonest gain*, (Tt 1:7, emphasis added)

The plain meaning of both passages is that greed or desire of material goods must not motivate the one who is in a leadership position. The word also occurs in the pseudepigraphal *Testament of Judah*:

> Take care to be temperate with wine, my children; for there are in it four evil spirits: desire, heated passion, debauchery, and *sordid greed*. (*T. Judah* 16.1, emphasis added)

In the *Testament of Judah*, avarice or "sordid greed" is an effect of too much wine. Each of the "four evil spirits" are undesirable and obviously are to be avoided. In First Timothy, however, the desire for dishonest gain is not necessarily tied to the consumption of alcohol, it is a quality to generally be avoided, particularly in the lives of leaders of the fellowship.

---

[8] BDAG, p. 880. Occurs 24x in NT; 5x in PE: 1Ti 1:4; 3:8; 4:1, 13; Tt 1:14. See comments on 1Ti 1:4 and 4:1 for discussion on alternate senses of the word.

[9] BDAG, p. 29. Occurs 2x in NT, both in PE: 1Ti 3:8; Tt 1:7, though the adverbial form of this word is used in 1Pe 5:2.

VERSE 9

holding the mystery of the faith

The word "holding" is from the Greek word ἔχω, which has been discussed previously.[10] In this situation, ἔχω carries the sense of "holding fast to matters of transcendent importance."[11] The word is also used in Second Timothy:

> *Hold fast to* the pattern of sound words which you heard from me, in the faith and love that are in Christ Jesus. (2Ti 1:13, emphasis added)

The sense of ἔχω in these two verses is similar. In Second Timothy, Paul urges Timothy to "hold fast" or adhere to the teaching he knows from Paul. In First Timothy, Paul urges Timothy to select deacons who are "holding the mystery of the faith."

The Greek word μυστήριον is translated as "mystery," in the sense of a 'secret' or 'something transcending normal understanding.'[12] The same sort of phrase occurs just a few verses later, in verse 16:

> And most certainly, great is the *mystery* of godliness: Who was revealed in the flesh, was vindicated by the Spirit, was seen by angels, was proclaimed among the Gentiles, was believed on in the world, was taken up in glory. (1Ti 3:16, emphasis added)

In such contexts, the "mystery" is something that moves beyond the common view of reality. Consider the *Epistle to Diognetus*:

> For as I have said this is no earthly discovery handed over to them, nor do they desire to guard a mortal thought so carefully, nor have they been entrusted with the management of human *mysteries*. But he, truly the Almighty and all-creating and invisible God himself, he established the truth and the holy and incomprehensible word from heaven among people, (*Ep. Diog.* 7.1–2a, emphasis added)

The action of God as described by the author of the *Epistle to Diognetus* is mysterious, unable to be "comprehended by humans."

---

[10] See comment on 1Ti 1:12.

[11] BDAG, p. 420.

[12] BDAG, p. 662. Occurs 28x in NT, 2x in PE: 1Ti 3:8, 16.

The mystery described by Paul in 1Ti 3:9 is that of "the faith." The Greek word is πίστις, which has been discussed previously.[13] Here, "the faith" refers to the Christian faith.

with a clear conscience

The word "clear" is translated from the Greek word καθαρός, here occurring in the sense of 'clean' or 'pure.'[14] The word translated "conscience" is from συνείδησις.[15] The phrase "clear conscience" also occurs in Second Timothy:

> I am thankful to God, whom I have served *with a clear conscience* as my ancestors did, when I remember you constantly in my prayers night and day. (2Ti 1:3, emphasis added)

Paul indicates he serves "with a clear conscience." He has no reason to second-guess his service, no reason for it to be called into question. His conscience is clear. Paul desires the same clarity of conscience for deacons. In order to properly serve the community, deacons must believe the essentials of faith (the sound doctrine) with no regrets and no second-guessing. Their consciences must be clear.

The author of *First Clement* uses this phrase as well:

> Ananias and Azariah and Mishael were shut up inside the furnace of fire by those who ministered to the magnificent and glorious worship of the Most High? By no means may this be granted! Who, therefore, were those who accomplish these things? The despicable ones, and full of all evil were roused to such anger that those who served God with holy and unblemished purpose they tortured cruelly not knowing that the Most High is defender and protector of those who serve his most excellent name *with a pure conscience*, to whom be the glory forever, amen. (*1Cl* 45.7, emphasis added)

The general thought in *First Clement* is much the same as that of the Pastoral Epistles, with the "pure conscience" indicating a conscience sure of the verity of Most High God.

It is possible, through use of the words "clear," "conscience" and "faith" that Paul is recalling (from 1Ti 1:5) his three-fold charge of love issued "from a pure heart and a good conscience and a sincere faith."

---

[13] See comment on 1Ti 1:2.

[14] See comment on 1Ti 1:5.

[15] See comment on 1Ti 1:5.

VERSE 10

and these also must be tested first

The Greek word for "must be tested" is δοκιμάζω, which in this context has to do with 'put to the test' or 'examine.'[16] As with the overseers who must not be new converts but must have some experience and testing in their life and doctrine, Paul indicates that deacons are also to "be tested first," prior to their service. Paul uses this same word twice in his first epistle to the Thessalonians:

> For our exhortation is not from error or from impurity or with deceit, but just as we have been *approved* by God to be entrusted with the gospel, thus we speak, not as pleasing people but God, who *examines* our hearts. (1Th 2:3–4, emphasis added)

In the above citation, the second instance is more in line with the sense under discussion. A similar sense occurs in the *Didache*, in an exhortation to examine traveling prophets for genuineness of spirit.

> But everyone who comes in the name of the Lord, let him be welcomed. And then, *having tested* him you will know him. Then you will be able to distinguish whether he is true or false. (*Did.* 12.1, emphasis added)

The word also occurs in *First Clement*:

> Therefore, preaching among regions and cities, they appointed their first fruits, *testing them* by the Spirit to *be* bishops and deacons of the future believers. (*1Cl.* 42.4, emphasis added)

The sense of δοκιμάζω is not one of a formal, objective test of skill or knowledge. Instead, potential deacons are to be examined to see if they live in a manner worthy of the office.

then let them serve

The phrase "let them serve" comes from the Greek word διακονέω.[17] This word typically has to do with the general concept of service. Here, in the context of

---

[16] BDAG, p. 255. Occurs 22x in NT, only here in PE. LSJ (p. 442) cites secular usage of the word in the context of political offices; that of 'approve after scrutiny as fit for an office,' from authors as early as 4 BC.

[17] The noun διάκονος (translated "deacon" in this section) and this verb, διακονέω, are similar in sound and meaning.

appointing deacons to general service, the sense is that of minister or servant carrying out the service of deacon.[18] The same word occurs later, in v. 13:

> For those *who have served well* acquire a good standing for themselves, and great boldness in the faith that is in Christ Jesus. (1Ti 3:13, emphasis added)

This word is used in a similar yet negative context in the *Shepherd of Hermas*:

> Those having spots are deacons *who ministered* poorly and thoroughly plundered the livelihood of widows and orphans, and made profit for themselves from the ministry which they received to administer. If, then, they continue in the same desires, they are dead and have no hope of life in them. But if they turn and fulfill their ministry purely, they will be able to live. (Hermas, *Similitudes* IX, xxvi, 2, emphasis added)

The word διακονέω, then, refers to the act of service or ministry that the prospective deacon will be appointed to.

if they are above reproach

The word translated "above reproach" is the Greek word ἀνέγκλητος, which has the sense of 'irreproachable.'[19] Also interesting is a Platonic usage of the word to indicate 'giving no ground in a dispute,'[20] that the one who is ἀνέγκλητος cannot have blame ascribed to him in an argument as the blame has no merit. This word is used twice in short succession in the epistle to Titus:

> If anyone is *blameless*, the husband of one wife, having faithful children, not accused of dissipation or rebellious. For it is necessary for the overseer *to be blameless* as God's steward, not self-willed, not quick-tempered, not addicted to wine, not violent, not greedy for dishonest gain. (Tt 1:6–7, emphasis added)

Deacons are to be appointed to service if they are above reproach. This echoes the same call for overseers to "be above reproach" in 1Ti 3:1.[21] If these potential deacons are found blameless as a result of their testing, then they are to be appointed to service as deacons.

---

[18] BDAG, p. 229. Occurs 37x in NT; 3x in PE: 1Ti 3:10, 13; 2Ti 1:18.

[19] BDAG, p. 76. Occurs 5x in NT: 1Co 1:8; Col 1:22; 1Ti 3:10; Tt 1:6, 7.

[20] LSJ, p. 129.

[21] See comment on 1Ti 3:1. This is a parallel in thought; both passages use different words to state essentially the same concept.

Verse 11

The wives likewise

The Greek word translated "wives" is γυνή, which may mean either 'woman' or 'wife.'[22] The translation is wholly dependent on context. Of the usage of γυνή in the Pastoral Epistles, Knight writes:

> Both usages occur in the PE and especially in 1 Timothy ("woman" in 2:9, 10, 11, 12, 14; "wife" in 3:2, 12; 5:9; cf. Tt 1:6).[23]

There are two primary interpretations for this passage. One interpretation prefers to read the word as "wives" and sees this verse as establishing a strong role of the wife in the support of her husband in the role of deacon. A variation of this interpretation translates the word as "women" yet sees these women as diaconal assistants, not (necessarily) as wives of deacons. Given Paul's focus on marital fidelity (1Ti 3:2, 12; 5:9), his earlier position on issues of teaching and authority between men and women (1Ti 2:11–12) and on preventing false teachers from preying on younger widowed women (1Ti 5:9–16), it seems unlikely that Paul would recommend such a close and involved working relationship between unmarried deacons and female assistants.

The other interpretation prefers to read the word as "women" or perhaps even "deaconesses" and sees the establishment of a separate office for women similar to that of deacon. The following discussion assumes the translation of "wives" is correct in this instance.

A short list of virtues that are to be exemplified by the deacon's wife is provided next.

must be dignified

The word translated as "dignified" is σεμνός, which was used in 1Ti 3:8 with similar meaning.[24]

not slanderous

The Greek word διάβολος is translated as "slanderous."[25] This word also occurs in verses. 6 and 7, where it is translated "devil." In that context, however, the word is in

---

[22] BDAG, p. 208.

[23] Knight, *The Pastoral Epistles : A Commentary on the Greek Text*, 171.

[24] See comment on 1Ti 3:8.

[25] BDAG, p. 226. Occurs 37x in NT; 6x in PE. See below note for occurrences.

the singular. When διάβολος occurs in the singular in the New Testament, it refers to a particular "slanderer," usually associated with Satan.[26] The noun, in the singular, has effectively become a title or name. When in the plural, however, the general meaning of "slanderers" is appropriate.

In this verse διάβολος occurs in the plural, allowing the association of the wives of deacons as those who are not slanderous. This word is used by Polycarp in his *Epistle to the Philippians* in a section dealing with deacons:

> Likewise, deacons *must be* blameless in the presence of his righteousness, as servants of God and Christ and not of people, not *slanderers*, not insincere, not lovers of money, *but* self-controlled in all things, compassionate, careful, walking according to the truth of the Lord, who became the servant of all. If we please him in this present age, we will receive also that which is to come, just as he promised us, to raise us from the dead, and that if we conduct our lives in a manner worthy of him, we will also reign with him, if indeed we have faith. (Poly., *Phil.* 5.2, emphasis added)

temperate, faithful in all things

The term "temperate" is a translation of the Greek word νηφάλιος. This word is used in the same sense in 1Ti 3:2.[27]

The wives of deacons are also to be "faithful in all things." The word translated "faithful" is πιστός, and has been previously discussed.[28] The idea of "all things" is a catch-all,[29] filling out the list.

VERSE 12

Deacons must be husbands of one wife

Paul has transitioned back to providing qualifications for deacons. The phrasing of this statement is similar to the requirement for overseers given in v. 2 above.[30] Paul requires overseers to be "the husband of one wife" and he has the same requirement

---

[26] διάβολος has 34 occurrences in the singular: Mt 4:1, 5, 8, 11; 13:39; 25:41; Lk 4:2, 3, 6, 13; 8:12; Jn 6:70; 8:44; 13:2; Ac 10:38; 13:10; Eph 4:27; 6:11; 1Ti 3:6, 7; 2Ti 2:26; Heb 2:14; Jam 4:7; 1Pe 5:8; 1Jn 3:8, 10; Jd 9; Re 2:10; 12:9, 12; 20:2, 10. There are three occurrences of διάβολος in the plural. All three of these are in the PE: 1Ti 3:11; 2Ti 3:3; Tt 2:3.

[27] See comment on 1Ti 3:2.

[28] See comment on 1Ti 1:12.

[29] See comment on 1Ti 1:10.

[30] See comment on 1Ti 3:2.

for deacons. In addition to this requirement, Paul has described the responsibilities of the deacon's wife in the previous verse. Not only are the deacons to be married, but the deacons are to be married to women who fit the requirements given in v. 11.

managing their children and their own households well

This phrase echoes verses 4–5, using the same words for "managing" and "their own households."[31] As with the overseer, a deacon's worthiness for the office can be discovered by examining how he manages his household and how he interacts with his family. If he is trustworthy and proven reliable in these things, he may be fit for office as a deacon.

VERSE 13

For those who have served well

The word translated "served well" is the Greek word διακονέω. This word is used similarly in v. 10 above.[32]

acquire a good standing for themselves

The word translated "acquire" is the Greek word περιποιέω. Here it has the meaning of 'gain for oneself.'[33] The word is used in Acts:

> Be on guard for yourselves and for all the flock among which the Holy Spirit has appointed you as overseers, to shepherd the church of God which *he obtained* through the blood of his own Son. (Ac 20:28, emphasis added)

In Acts, περιποιέω is used to refer to God's obtaining of the church through his own blood. This is something that God has taken possession of. The same word is used by Josephus:

> But now Cassius, after Crassus, put a stop to the Parthians, who were marching, in order to enter Syria. Cassius had fled into that province, and when *he had taken possession* of the same, he made a hasty march into Judea; and, upon his taking Taricheae, he carried thirty thousand Jews into slavery. He also slew Pitholaus,

---

[31] Though v. 4 has "his own household" (singular) and v. 12 has "their own households" (plural). See comments on 1Ti 3:4–5.

[32] See comment on 1Ti 3:10.

[33] BDAG, p. 804. Occurs 3x in NT: Lk 17:33; Ac 20:28; 1Ti 3:13.

> who had supported the seditious followers of Aristobulus; and it was Antipater who advised him so to do. (Jos., *Wars* 1.180, emphasis added)

Josephus uses περιποιέω to indicate taking possession of another land. Paul uses the same word to speak of gaining or acquiring a "good standing."

The phrase "good standing" is translated from the Greek word βαθμός. The literal sense of βαθμός is that of a 'step' or 'stage.'[34] This is not the sort of step one takes when walking, but more along the lines of a step in a staircase. LSJ offers some interesting glosses:

- *rung* of a ladder (Lucian)
- *degree* on a dial (2Ki 20:9 [LXX])
- *interval* on a musical scale (Iamblichus)[35]

In this instance, βαθμός has to do with 'a stage in intellectual or spiritual progress.'[36] The word is used in this sense in Philo's tractate *On the Eternity of the World*:

> For the very moment that the first man was born there was a necessity for his receiving growth in accordance with the previously defined measures and numbers of time, for nature has arranged the different ages as certain *steps* along which man in a manner ascends and descends; he ascends while he is growing, and he descends at the period when he is lessening; and the boundary of the uppermost steps is the prime of life at which when a man has arrived he no longer makes any further advance; but as runners who run the *diaulos* turn back again upon the same path which they have already travelled, so too does man retrace his steps, giving back in the weakness of old age what he has received from vigorous youth; but to fancy that any one has ever been born absolutely perfect is the part of those who are ignorant of the laws of nature, which are unchangeable ordinances. (Philo, *Eternity* 58, emphasis added)

In this excerpt from Philo, the "steps" are seen as stages which man progresses through during the process of his life. This word is also used in the *Corpus Hermeticum*:

> Now fourth, on Continence I call, the Power against Desire. ... This *step*, my son, is Righteousness' firm seat. For without judgement see how she hath chased Unrighteousness away. We are made righteous, son, by the departure of Unrighteousness. (*Corpus Hermeticum* 8.9, emphasis added)

---

[34] BDAG, p. 162. *hapax*.

[35] LSJ, p. 300.

[36] BDAG, p. 162.

In this instance in the *Corpus Hermeticum*, βαθμός is used similarly to its Philonic usage. The "step" is action by the initiate in an effort to progress further along in the Hermetic practice.

In First Timothy, the sense is similar. Those who "serve well" gain a better standing (or "step") for themselves. They have progressed both in their practice of leadership and also in their application and understanding of the sound doctrine that is so important to Paul. Hort sums this up well:

> The last verse, 3:13, has been often understood to say that excellent discharge of the duties of a διάκονος would rightly entitle him to promotion to a higher kind of work, doubtless that of an Elder. Βαθμός undeniably means a step, and so might easily be used for a grade of dignity and function. But the rest of the verse renders this interpretation unnatural; and the true sense doubtless is that διάκονοι by excellent discharge of their duties may win for themselves an excellent vantage ground, a "standing" (R.V.) a little, as it were, above the common level, enabling them to exercise an influence and moral authority to which their work *as such* could not entitle them.[37]

This is not a step up along a chain of leadership, it is an enhanced perspective based on having served well (as opposed to simply having served) in the capacity as deacon.

and great boldness in the faith that is in Christ Jesus

The word "great" (πολύς) was used earlier in v. 8, "not addicted to *much* wine." The meaning here is similar, that of 'much' or 'great.'[38] This describes "boldness," translated from the Greek word παρρησία. The word has to do with boldness in social situations, hence 'courage,' 'confidence,' and 'fearlessness.'[39] The same word is used in Hebrews:

> Therefore let us approach with *confidence* to the throne of grace, in order that we may receive mercy and find grace to help in time of need. (Heb 4:16, emphasis added)

> Therefore do not throw away your *confidence*, which has great reward. (Heb 10:35, emphasis added)

This word is also used in *First Clement*:

---

[37] Hort, *Christian Ecclesia*, 202.

[38] BDAG, p. 847.

[39] BDAG, p. 781. Occurs 31x in NT, only here in PE.

> Let our boast and *confidence* be in him. Let us be subject to his will. Let us consider the whole multitude of his angels, how standing by they serve his will. (*1Cl* 34.5, emphasis added)

In all of these instances, παρρησία is not confidence that exists due to one's own merit or virtue, instead it exists as a result of something external. Paul uses the word in the same sense here. Confidence or boldness is bolstered as a result of serving well as a deacon.

The Fellowship and God (1Ti 3:14–16)

I am writing these things to you, hoping to come to you in a short time. But if I am delayed, I am writing in order that you may know how one must conduct oneself in the household of God, which is the church of the living God, the pillar and mainstay of the truth. And most certainly, great is the mystery of godliness: Who was revealed in the flesh, was vindicated by the Spirit, was seen by angels, was proclaimed among the Gentiles, was believed on in the world, was taken up in glory. (1Ti 3:14–16)

Verse 14

I am writing these things to you

The word translated "I am writing" is the Greek word γράφω which typically means 'write,' 'record,' or 'write down.'[1] Paul uses similar language in his first epistle to the Corinthians:

> *I am* not *writing* these things to shame you, but admonishing you as my dear children. (1Co 4:14, emphasis added)

The word γράφω is used frequently in John's first epistle:

> Dear friends, *I am* not *writing* a new commandment to you, but an old commandment which you have had from the beginning. The old commandment is the message which you have heard. Again, *I am writing* a new commandment to you, which is true in him and in you, because the darkness is passing away and the true light already is shining. (1Jn 2:7–8, emphasis added)

Paul writes Timothy to ensure that they are of one mind concerning the progress of the ministry in Ephesus. The substance of Paul's writing, "these things," is the letter, particularly the preceding text (ch. 1–3).

---

[1] BDAG, p. 206. Occurs 191x in NT.

hoping to come to you in a short time

Paul desires to visit Timothy soon.[2] The word translated "hoping" is ἐλπίζω, which here has the sense of 'expect' or 'look forward to.'[3] He uses this sort of language elsewhere in his epistles:

> For I do not want to see you now in passing, for *I hope* to remain some time with you, if the Lord allows it. (1Co 16:7, emphasis added)

> But *I hope* in the Lord Jesus to send Timothy to you soon, so that I also may be encouraged when I know your circumstances. (Php 2:19, emphasis added)

Ignatius uses the word in similar fashion in his *Letter to the Romans*:

> Since by praying to God I have managed to see your godly faces, as even more than I asked to receive, for being imprisoned in Christ Jesus *I hope* to greet you, if indeed it be his will to consider me to be worthy to the end. (Ign., *Rom.* 1.1, emphasis added)

Paul's hope is "to come" to visit Timothy. This is a translation of the Greek word ἔρχομαι. It is a fairly common word and need not be discussed in detail[4] apart from noting that the combination of the infinitive ἔρχομαι with ἐλπίζω gives the sense of "hope/hoping to [*infinitive verb*]" that is found with some frequency in the Pauline epistles.[5]

Paul's hope is to come "soon." This is a translation of the Greek word τάχος, which usually has to do with 'speed,' 'quickness,' or 'haste;' but here has the sense of 'soon' or 'in a short time.'[6] This word is used similarly in Acts:

> Then Festus replied that Paul was being kept at Caesarea, and he himself was about to go there *in a short time*. (Ac 25:4, emphasis added)

It is also used in *First Clement*:

> Now those who were sent from us, Claudius Ephebus and Valerius Bito also along with Fortunatus, send them back to us *very soon* in peace with joy, so that they

---

[2] The pronoun translated "you" is in the singular.

[3] BDAG, p. 319. Occurs 31x in NT, 4x in PE: 1Ti 3:14; 4:10; 5:5; 6:17. This is the verb form of the noun ἐλπίς, which is used in 1Ti 1:1 and elsewhere throughout the PE.

[4] BDAG, p. 393. Occurs 632x in NT.

[5] In addition to 1Co 16:7 and Php 2:19 (cited above), other Pauline instances of ἐλπίζω + infinitive (not necessarily ἔρχομαι) are found in Ro 15:24; 1Co 5:11 and Php 2:23. The combination is also found in Lk 6:34; Lk 23:8; Ac 26:7; 2Jn 12 and 3Jn 14.

[6] BDAG, p. 992. Occurs 8x in NT, only here in PE.

> may report quickly the peace and harmony prayed for and greatly desired by us, so that we also may soon rejoice about your stability. (*1Cl* 65.1, emphasis added)

The language here indicates that Paul hopes to come and see Timothy sooner rather than later.

Verse 15

But if I am delayed

The word translated "I am delayed" is the Greek word βραδύνω. The word has the sense of 'hesitate' or 'delay.'[7] This word also occurs in Peter's second epistle:

> The Lord is not *delaying* the promise, as some consider slowness, but is being patient toward you, because he does not want any to perish, but all to come to repentance. (2Pe 3:9, emphasis added)

In Second Peter, the idea is that the Lord will not delay or hesitate to fulfill his promise. The word occurs in the *Martyrdom of Polycarp* as well:

> And again he said to him, "I will cause you to be consumed by fire, since you despise the beasts, unless you repent." But Polycarp replied, you threaten with fire that burns for a while, and after a little time is extinguished. For you are ignorant of the fire of the coming judgment and eternal punishment, reserved for the ungodly. But why *do you wait*? Bring about what you wish." (*Mart. Poly.* 11.2, emphasis added)

Polycarp is urging the proconsul not to delay the implementation of his threat. He knows he will not be convinced to "repent," thus he urges the proconsul to hurry up (that is, to not delay) and make good on his threat.

Paul's idea of delay is similar, though the context is different. That is, Paul indicates that his travel may be delayed or postponed.

in order that you may know how one must conduct oneself

The phrase "you may know" is a translation of the Greek word οἶδα, which was used similarly in verse 5.[8]

---

[7] BDAG, p. 183. Occurs 2x in NT: 1Ti 3:15; 2Pe 3:9.

[8] See note on 1Ti 3:5.

Timothy is to know "how one must conduct oneself." The Greek translated "conduct oneself" is ἀναστρέφω, which has several senses. The sense in use here is that of 'act,' 'behave' or 'conduct oneself.'[9] The word occurs in First Peter:

> And if you call on him as Father who judges impartially according to each one's work, *conduct yourselves* with fear during the time of your temporary residence, (1Pe 1:17, emphasis added)

In First Peter, the word is used to indicate how those who claim God as Father are to then act; what their behavior is to be like. Deissmann provides an inscription found in Pergamum:

> The people honoured Apollodorus, the son of Pyrrhus, with a golden crown and a brazen image by reason of his virtue and goodwill towards them, and because of his good and glorious *behaviour* when he was Gymnasiarch.[10]

In this context, ἀναστρέφω indicates the manner in which Apollodorus conducted himself during his tenure as Gymnasiarch.

Paul's use of ἀναστρέφω in 1Ti 3:15 is similar to the above instances. The Ephesians are in need of instruction regarding their behavior "in the household of God." Paul provides Timothy with the apostolic endorsement needed to address this problem.

in the household of God, which is the church of the living God

Paul desires that the Ephesians know how to conduct themselves "in the household of God." The word translated "household" is οἶκος, which is used in this same way earlier, in verses 4–5.[11] Here, however, the household is that of God instead of that of the prospective overseer.

The "household of God" is further qualified as "the church of the living God." The word translated church is ἐκκλησία, the same word used earlier in verse 5.[12] Here, however, the participle form of ζάω modifies the noun supplying the idea of a "living" God. Hort comments on this concept:

> Often the (a) living God is spoken of in contrast to dead idols: but sometimes (e.g. Heb 3:12; 9:14; 12:22) it implies a contrast with the true God made practically a dead deity by a lifeless and rigid form of religion; with the God in short in whom

---

[9] BDAG, p. 72. Occurs 9x in NT, only here in PE.

[10] Deissmann, LAE, 312. Inscription described as "Marble Pedestal from Pergamum with an Inscription in honour of the Gymnasiarch Apollodorus of Pergamum. Roman Period. Original still at Pergamum." Deissmann dates the inscription "after 133 B.C."

[11] See comments on 1Ti 3:4–5.

[12] On the phrase "church of God," see comments on 1Ti 3:5.

> too many of the Jews virtually believed. Such is probably the force here as it evidently is in 4:10.[13]

the pillar and mainstay of the truth

The household of God, which is the church of the living God, is further described as "the pillar and mainstay of truth." The word "pillar" is a translation of the Greek word στῦλος. In this instance, the meaning is 'pillar' or 'support' in a representative sense.[14] The word is used in Paul's epistle to the Galatians:

> But these, when they saw that I had been entrusted with the gospel to the uncircumcision, just as Peter to the circumcision (for the one who was at work through Peter for his apostleship to the circumcision was at work also through me for the Gentiles), and when James and Cephas and John—those thought to be *pillars*—acknowledged the grace given to me, they gave to me and Barnabas the right hand of fellowship, in order that we should go to the Gentiles and they to the circumcision. (Ga 2:7–9, emphasis added)

The word is used in a similar manner in *First Clement*:

> Because of jealousy and envy, the greatest and most righteous *pillars* of the church were persecuted and they competed until death. (*1Cl.* 5.2, emphasis added)

In Galatians and *First Clement* στῦλος is applied to people whose service is foundational to the church. In First Timothy, however, στῦλος is applied to "the church of the living God." Instead of describing how people are "pillars" in relation to the church, Paul now describes how the church serves as a "pillar" to the truth—which fits with his overarching theme of sound doctrine and proper teaching.

Paul also uses the term "mainstay" to describe the church's relationship with the truth.[15] This is a translation of the Greek word ἑδραίωμα, defined as 'that which provides a firm base for something.'[16] Of this word, Hort writes:

> There are few passages of the New Testament in which the reckless disregard of the presence or absence of the article has made wilder havoc of the sense than this. To speak of either *an* Ecclesia or *the* Ecclesia, as being *the* pillar of the truth, is to represent the truth as a building, standing in the air supported on a single column. Again there is no clear evidence that the rare word ἑδραίωμα ever means 'ground'

---

[13] Hort, *Christian Ecclesia*, 173–174.

[14] BDAG, p. 949. Occurs 4x in NT: Ga 2:9; 1Ti 3:15; Re 3:12; 10:1. The word frequently occurs in the LXX with its literal meaning.

[15] Some translations, e.g. ESV, translate as "bulwark."

[16] BDAG, p. 276. *hapax*. The word does not occur in the LXX.

> = "foundation." It is rather, in accordance with the almost universal Latin rendering *firmamentum*, a "stay" or "bulwark."[17]

Thus ἑδραίωμα ("mainstay") is akin to a physical structure that protects from external forces or pressure; much like a sea wall protects from battering waves. In this context, the church is the structure that protects the truth; the church proclaims and teaches the truth. The article in TDNT for ἑδραίωμα continues along this line of thought:

> In 1 Tm. 3:15 the ἐκκλησία is called στῦλος καὶ ἑδραίωμα τῆς ἀληθείας. A Church is established which protects and defends the truth against the confusion of myths. It gives the faith and thinking of individuals a sure ground in confession (cf. 3:16 etc.). No longer God alone, but also the Church of God, now guarantees the permanence of the ἀλήθεια. The steadfastness of faith has now become loyalty to the Church and the confession.[18]

For the church to remain pure, it must protect the truth it proclaims from falsehood; it must proclaim the truth accurately and forthrightly.

VERSE 16

And most certainly, great is the mystery of godliness

The word translated "great" is the adjective μέγας. This accounts for the degree or extent of the "mystery of godliness." The extent is confirmed with the Greek word ὁμολογουμένως, which the LEB translates "most certainly." The word is defined as 'pertaining to being a matter on which there is general agreement.'[19] It is an adverb related to the verb ὁμολογέω, which has the basic sense of 'confess.'[20] TDNT provides a note on this instance:

> The common Hellenistic term ὁμολογουμένως occurs only once in the Pastorals, where it serves to introduce the hymn to Christ in 1 Tm. 3:16: ὁμολογουμένως μέγα, "confessedly great" (Vg *manifeste magnum*) is the mystery of the Christian

---

[17] Hort, *Christian Ecclesia*, 174.

[18] TDNT 2.364.

[19] BDAG, p. 709.

[20] BDAG, p. 708. A sixth-century uncial (D [06], housed in Paris) and a tenth-century minuscule (1175) have ὁμολογοῦμεν ὡς (plural verb + conjunction) instead of ὁμολογουμένως (adverb) in this instance. If the ESV translation committee prefers this reading, it may also account for the addition of "we confess." A translation more respecting of word order may be "Confessedly great is the mystery of godliness."

> faith. The mystery of Jesus Christ is declared in the worship of heaven and earth, angels and men.[21]

This word also occurs in Josephus' *Antiquities of the Jews*:

> Hereupon it was that Thermuthis imposed this name Moses upon him from what had happened when he was put into the river; for the Egyptians call water by the name of Mo, and such as are saved out of it, by the name of Uses; so by putting these two words together, they imposed this name upon him; and he was, *by the confession of all*, according to God's prediction, as well for his greatness of mind, as for his contempt of difficulties, the best of all the Hebrews; for Abraham was his ancestor of the seventh generation. For Moses was the son of Amram, who was the son of Caath, whose father, Levi, was the son of Jacob, who was the son of Isaac, who was the son of Abraham. (Jos., *Ant.* 2.228–229, emphasis added)

Josephus uses ὁμολογουμένως to confirm the views or testimony of witnesses concerning Moses. Paul uses the word in a similar sense, to confirm the greatness of the mystery of godliness. The word translated "mystery" is μυστήριον, which is discussed above.[22] The word translated "godliness" is εὐσέβεια, which occurs with some frequency in the Pastoral Epistles.[23] This "mystery of godliness" may have some relation to the "mystery of the faith" Paul discussed earlier in regard to deacons:

> holding *the mystery of the faith* with a clear conscience, (1Ti 3:9, emphasis added)

In both of these instances, the appending of "mystery" to the term ("faith" or "godliness") is a device that draws out the importance of the term under discussion. That is, there is no actual "mystery" of faith, the concept of faith itself is under discussion in 1Ti 3:9. The same holds for 1Ti 3:16. There is no "mystery" of godliness as the supposed mystery is spelled out in the balance of verse 16. That is, the mystery of why Christians are godly and pious is explained. TDNT notes the following:

> The transition from the hidden event to its proclamation in the term μυστήριον explains the formal use in 1 Tm. 3:9: τὸ μυστήριον τῆς πίστεως, and 3:16: τὸ τῆς εὐσεβείας μυστήριον. In the first case it simply means πίστις and in the second εὐσέβεια, but the phrase derives its point from the reference to the eschatological manifestation of Christ, as may be seen from the quasi-confessional hymn in 3:16.[24]

---

[21] TDNT 5:213.

[22] See comment on 1Ti 3:9.

[23] See comment on 1Ti 2:2. Note that in this instance εὐσέβεια may also be translated as "the key to our piety" or perhaps "the secret of our devotion to God" (BDAG, p. 412).

[24] TDNT 4:822.

Who was manifested in the flesh[25]

The reference to "Who" is textually uncertain. The reading for "Who" (the relative pronoun ὅς) is, according to Metzger, "The reading which, on the basis of external evidence and transcriptional probability, best explains the rise of the others."[26] Other possibilities are θεός[27] and the definite article ὅ.

Whatever the original reading, the subject is clear. This hymn is Christological in nature; it describes Jesus. It is offered as explanation of "the mystery of godliness," a further description of the "truth" which the church of God supports.

The word translated "was manifested" is the Greek word φανερόω; meaning 'show' or 'reveal oneself' or 'be revealed.'[28] Paul uses the word similarly in Second Timothy:

> but *has* now *been disclosed* by the appearing of our Savior Jesus Christ, who has abolished death and brought to light life and immortality through the gospel, (2Ti 1:10, emphasis added)

In Second Timothy, a "holy calling" is what has been manifested (2Ti 1:8). The word is also used in the salutation of the epistle to Titus:

> but at the proper time *has disclosed* his message in the proclamation with which I was entrusted according to the command of God our Savior, (Tt 1:3, emphasis added)

In the example from Titus, "eternal life" is being manifested (Tt 1:2). In both of these instances, a concept or idea is somehow "manifested" or revealed. In 1Ti 3:16, however, Christ is manifested "in the flesh." This is far more than a concept or idea, it is a testimony to the reality of the incarnation of Christ.

The Greek word σάρξ is translated as "the flesh." The phrase "manifested in the flesh"[29] occurs several times in the *Epistle of Barnabas*.

> Learn! The Prophets, having grace from him, prophesied of him, and he, that he might abolish death and demonstrate the resurrection from the dead, because it

---

[25] The hymn is six lines. Different translations portray the structure in different ways. NA28 has three doublets, UBS5 has two triplets; other commentators see different structures. Note also that each line of the hymn contains an aorist passive verb and a dative noun.

[26] Bruce M. Metzger, ed., *A Textual Commentary on the Greek New Testament*, Second Revised ed. (London; New York: United Bible Societies, 1994), 573.

[27] The Byzantine text (thus KJV, NKJV) prefer this reading.

[28] BDAG, p. 1048. Occurs 49x in NT; 3x in PE: 1Ti 3:16; 2Ti 1:10; Tt 1:3.

[29] That is, the verb φανερόω with a prepositional phrase consisting of at least the words ἐν and σάρξ.

> was necessary for him *to be manifested in the flesh.* (*Ep. Barn.* 5.6, emphasis added)[30]

The testimony that the Christ had been manifested in the flesh was foundational to the early church. Similar language occurs in Ignatius' *Letter to the Ephesians*:

> By this all magic was destroyed, and every bond of wickedness disappeared. Ignorance was torn down. The old kingdom was annihilated. God, *being made known in human form* to the newness of eternal life, and that which had been prepared by God received its beginning. From then on, all things were stirred up because the abolition of death was taking place. (Ign., *Eph.* 19.3, emphasis added)

Indeed, the New Testament explicitly testifies to the coming of the Messiah in the flesh, and the identification of Jesus with the Messiah:

> What was from the beginning, what we have heard, what we have seen with our eyes, what we have looked at and our hands have touched, concerning the word of life—*and the life was revealed, and we have seen and testify* and announce to you the eternal life which was with the Father and was revealed to us—what we have seen and heard, we announce to you also, in order that you also may have fellowship with us, and indeed our fellowship is with the Father and with his Son Jesus Christ. And these things we write, in order that our joy may be complete. (1Jn 1:1–4, emphasis added)[31]

Here the testimony confirms that Jesus was seen, was touched; that the life was "revealed." Similar language regarding manifestation in the flesh occurs in Second Corinthians, though in this context the idea is that the life of Jesus is manifested in the flesh of believers:

> But we have this treasure in earthenware jars, in order that the extraordinary degree of the power may be from God and not from us. We are afflicted in every way, but not crushed; perplexed, but not despairing; persecuted, but not abandoned; struck down, but not destroyed; always carrying around the death of Jesus in our body, *in order that the life of Jesus may also be revealed in our body.* For we who are alive are continually being handed over to death because of Jesus, *in order that the life of Jesus may also be revealed in our mortal flesh.* (2Co 4:7–11, emphasis added)

---

[30] This phrase also occurs in *Ep. Barn.* 6.7, 9, 14; 12.10.

[31] Similar testimony occurs in the prologue to John's gospel, particularly Jn 1:14.

was vindicated by the Spirit

The word translated "vindicated" is the Greek word δικαιόω, which here carries the sense of 'prove to be right.'[32] The word is used similarly in Romans:

> May it never be! But let God be true but every human being a liar, just as it is written, "In order that you *may be justified* in your words, and may prevail when you are judged." (Ro 3:4, emphasis added)

In Romans (quoting Ps. 51:4 [LXX 50:6]) God has spoken and his words will prove him true. They will "vindicate" him. A similar instance occurs in Matthew:

> For John came neither eating nor drinking, and they say, 'He has a demon!' The Son of Man came eating and drinking, and they say, 'Behold, a man who is a glutton and a drunkard, a friend of tax collectors and sinners!' But wisdom *is vindicated* by her deeds." (Mt 11:18–19, emphasis added)

Thus, in First Timothy, Jesus is proven true or vindicated "by the Spirit." The phrase translated "by the Spirit" could be woodenly translated as "in spirit," but this approach is misleading. Knight discusses this issue:

> The next use of πνεῦμα in the PE (4:1, without qualification, as here) refers to the Holy Spirit (see also Tt 3:5; 2Ti 1:14; probably 1:7) and not the human spirit (as indicated by ὑμῶν in 2Ti 4:22), and there is no indication of shift in meaning, which favors that same identification here. If this understanding is correct, then ἐν is used with the meaning "by," indicating means, in contrast to the preceding line where it is used with the meaning "in," indicating place. The nearly identical format of each line should not be construed as requiring the same meaning for each instance of ἐν and each dative.[33]

According to Knight, the Spirit is the means of "vindicating" the one manifested in the flesh. This is in agreement with part of Paul's prologue in his letter to the Romans:

> who was declared Son of God in power according to the Holy Spirit by the resurrection from the dead of Jesus Christ our Lord, (Ro 1:4)

While the exact words of "vindicated by the Spirit" are not reproduced in Romans, the idea is similar. The Spirit has some role in the "vindication" of Christ. This is seen in John 16:

> But I tell you the truth, it is better for you that I go away. For if I do not go away, the Advocate will not come to you; but if I go, I will send him to you. And when he comes, he will convict the world concerning sin and concerning righteousness

---

[32] BDAG, p. 249.

[33] Knight, *The Pastoral Epistles : A Commentary on the Greek Text*, 185.

> and concerning judgment: concerning sin, because they do not believe in me, and concerning righteousness, because I am going away to the Father and you will see me no more, and concerning judgment, because the ruler of this world has been condemned. (Jn 16:7–11)

In John 16, Jesus prophesies that the "Advocate" (the Holy Spirit) will come after he has ascended to the right hand of the Father. That is, the presence of the Spirit on earth is testimony to the fact that Jesus is with the Father.[34] This is how the Spirit "vindicates" the divinity of Jesus.

was seen by angels

The Greek word translated "was seen" is the verb ὁράω, which here has the sense of 'become visible' or 'appear.'[35] BDAG notes that this sense of the word is used "Mostly of beings that make their appearance in a transcendent manner, almost always with dative of the person to whom they appear."[36] A similar usage occurs in Luke's gospel:

> And they got up that same hour and returned to Jerusalem and found the eleven and those with them assembled, saying, "The Lord has really been raised, and *has appeared* to Simon!" (Lk 24:33–34, emphasis added)

This instance of ὁράω in Luke is the same inflected form as the instance in the current context.[37] The adjoining nouns, in both instances, are in the dative case. Christ had appeared to angels, thus he had been seen by angels.

The word translated "angels" is the word ἄγγελος, which may mean 'messenger,' 'envoy,' or 'angel.'[38] The angels are the ones who have "seen" the Christ. Paul uses this word later in First Timothy:

> I testify solemnly before God and Christ Jesus and the elect *angels* that you observe these things without prejudice, doing nothing according to partiality. (1Ti 5:21, emphasis added)

Paul exhorts Timothy to adhere to his guidelines, reminding him that God, Christ Jesus and the "elect angels" are witnesses to his actions. This concept of angels as witnesses is also found in the *Testament of Levi*:

---

[34] Whether this vindication took place at resurrection (Paul?), or at ascension (John?), is questionable. The basic idea is that as a result of Christ's action, the Spirit is present on earth, and this vindicates Christ.

[35] BDAG, p. 719.

[36] BDAG, p. 719. Note that ἄγγελος here is in the dative.

[37] An aorist passive indicative, third person singular.

[38] BDAG, p. 8.

> "And now, my children, you have heard everything. Choose for yourselves light or darkness, the Law of the Lord or the works of Beliar." And his sons replied, "Before the Lord we will live according to his Law." And their father said to them, "The Lord is my witness and *his angels are witnesses*, and you are witnesses, and I am witness concerning the word from your mouth." (*T. Levi* 19.1–3, emphasis added)

Josephus also invokes angels as witnesses in his *Jewish Wars*:

> I call to witness your sanctuary, and the holy *angels* of God, and this country common to us all, that I have not kept back anything that is for your preservation; and if you will follow that advice which you ought to do, you will have that peace which will be common to you and to me; but if you indulge your passions, you will run those hazards which I shall be free from." (Jos., *Wars* 2.401, emphasis added)

Calling to mind the presence of angels as witnesses in an effort to keep one vigilant in actions or response does not appear to be unusual. The instance of "seen by angels" could be a variation of this, using the testimony of angels as additional confirmation of the incarnation of God as Christ.

was proclaimed among the Gentiles

The Greek word κηρύσσω is translated as "proclaimed." The word has to do with 'making an announcement.' It can be used for official announcements or for other sorts of announcements.[39] This same word is used by Paul in a command to Timothy to preach or proclaim the word of God:

> I solemnly charge you before God and Christ Jesus, who is going to judge the living and the dead, and by his appearing and his kingdom, *preach* the word, be ready in season and out of season, reprove, rebuke, exhort, with all patience and instruction. (2Ti 4:1–2, emphasis added)

The above is an instance of a non-official (non-governmental) proclamation. However, the proclamation still calls to mind the idea of a transcendent being as a witness.

The *Martyrdom of Polycarp* contains an example of an official pronouncement:

> But saying these and many other words, [Polycarp] was filled with courage and joy, and his face was full of grace, so that not only did he not collapse, having been

---

[39] BDAG, p. 543. The word κῆρυξ, discussed earlier in 1Ti 2:7, is a noun form of this word meaning 'proclaimer' or 'preacher' or 'herald.' See comment on 1Ti 2:7 (particularly the citation from the *Corpus Hermeticum*) for more background.

> disturbed by what was said to him, but instead the proconsul was dumbfounded and sent his own herald into the middle of the stadium to *proclaim* three times: "Polycarp has confessed himself to be a Christian." (*Mart. Poly.* 12.1, emphasis added)[40]

In this hymn in First Timothy, the proclamation of the message is "among the Gentiles." This sort of proclamation is also found in other literature. Consider the *Shepherd of Hermas*:

> "Listen," he said, "this great tree which covers fields and mountains and all the earth is the law of God which was given to the whole world. And this law is the Son of God *being preached* to the ends of the earth. And the people under the shade are those who have heard the preaching and believed in him. (Hermas, *Similitudes* VIII, iii, 2, emphasis added)

Similar language is found in the *Epistle to Diognetus*:

> For this reason he sent the Word, so that he might be made manifest to the world, who was dishonored by the chosen people, *preached* by apostles, he was believed in by Gentiles. (*Ep. Diog.* 11.3, emphasis added)

The word translated "Gentiles" in the hymn is ἔθνος. This is the same word that is translated "Gentiles" in the above excerpt from *Diognetus*. It is used frequently and its meaning is dependent on context, meaning anything from 'nations' or 'peoples' to 'Gentiles.'[41] As the context here is general as well (and most likely a citation of a hymn of some sort) the sense is general as well, thus "nations" or "peoples." This brings to mind the Great Commission, recorded at the end of Matthew's gospel:

> And Jesus approached and spoke to them, saying, "All authority in heaven and on earth has been given to me. Therefore, go and make disciples of all the *nations*, baptizing them in the name of the Father and of the Son and of the Holy Spirit, teaching them to observe everything I have commanded you, and behold, I am with you all the days until the end of the age." (Mt 28:18–20, emphasis added)[42]

was believed on in the world

The word translated "was believed" is the Greek word πιστεύω, which usually means 'believe.'[43] The usage here is similar to usage in Second Thessalonians:

---

[40] Note that "herald" is a translation of the word κῆρυξ here as well.

[41] BDAG, p. 276. Occurs 162x in NT.

[42] Note also Ac 1:8, which also contains the idea proclamation the nations.

[43] BDAG, p. 816. Occurs 241x in NT.

> who will pay the penalty of eternal destruction, away from the presence of the Lord and from the glory of his strength, whenever he should come to be glorified on that day by his saints and to be marveled at by all who *believe*, because our testimony *was believed* among you, (2Th 1:9–10, emphasis added)

The word πιστεύω occurs twice in the above excerpt from Second Thessalonians. The sense is the same here as in 1Ti 3:16, that of believing testimony or proclamation.

This proclamation is believed "in the world." The word "world" is a translation of the Greek word κόσμος. It has several different context-dependent meanings.[44] The sense found here is similar to that used in 1Ti 1:15:

> The saying is trustworthy and worthy of all acceptance: Christ Jesus came into *the world* to save sinners, of whom I am the foremost. (1Ti 1:15, emphasis added)

The word is used similarly in 1Ti 6:7:

> But godliness with contentment is a great means of gain. For we have brought nothing into *the world*, so that neither can we bring anything out. (1Ti 6:6–7, emphasis added)

In these verses, κόσμος has to do generally with "the world," the sphere in which humans interact in time with other humans. In the world, humans are sinners and Christ has come to save them. The world is the sphere in which humans may believe on or have faith in Christ and be saved from the penalty of sin.

was taken up in glory

The word translated "was taken up" is the Greek word ἀναλαμβάνω, a verb that typically means 'lift up.'[45] When used in the aorist tense and passive voice (as it is here), speaking of Christ,[46] the language points toward the transfiguration:

> Then the Lord Jesus, after he had spoken to them, *was taken up* into heaven and sat down at the right hand of God. (Mk 16:19, emphasis added)

> until the day *he was taken up*, after he had given orders through the Holy Spirit to the apostles whom he had chosen, (Ac 1:2, emphasis added)

> who also said, "Men of Galilee, why do you stand there looking into the sky? This Jesus who *was taken up* from you into heaven like this will come back in the same way you saw him departing into heaven!" (Ac 1:11, emphasis added)

---

[44] See BDAG, p. 561. Occurs 186x in NT, 3x in PE: 1Ti 1:15; 3:16; 6:7.

[45] BDAG, p. 66. Occurs 13x in NT, 2x in PE: 1Ti 3:16, 2Ti 4:11.

[46] One other example is Ac 10:6, though this does not speak of Christ it does speak of something being "taken up" to heaven.

> beginning from the baptism of John until the day on which *he was taken up* from us—one of these men must become a witness of his resurrection together with us." (Ac 1:22, emphasis added)

In First Clement, ἀναλαμβάνω is used similarly, though speaking of the apostle Paul:

> Having taught righteousness to the whole world and having come to the limits of the west and having given his testimony before the rulers, thus he was set free from the world and *was taken up* to the holy place, having become the greatest example of endurance. (*1Cl* 5.7, emphasis added)

In such constructions and context the word is clearly used to refer to the "taking up" of a being to heaven. The Christological context of 1Ti 3:16 indicates similar meaning is intended here. He was taken up "in glory," noting the nature of the event of the transfiguration. An account is recorded in the book of Acts:

> And after he had said these things, while they were watching, he was taken up, and a cloud received him from their sight. And as they were staring into the sky while he was departing, behold, two men in white clothing stood by them who also said, "Men of Galilee, why do you stand there looking into the sky? This Jesus who was taken up from you into heaven like this will come back in the same way you saw him departing into heaven!" (Ac 1:9–11)

False Requirements (1Ti 4:1–3)

> *Now the Spirit explicitly says that in the last times some will depart from the faith, paying attention to deceitful spirits and teachings of demons, by the hypocrisy of liars, who are seared in their own conscience, who forbid marrying and insist on abstaining from foods that God created for sharing in with thankfulness by those who believe and who know the truth, (1Ti 4:1–3)*

Verse 1

Now the Spirit explicitly says

The Greek word translated "Spirit" is πνεῦμα, which generally means 'spirit' or 'breath' or 'blowing.'[1] Here the word occurs with an article, allowing specific identification with "Spirit" or the Holy Spirit (unlike in 1Ti 3:16). A similar instance occurs in Romans:

> And likewise also, the Spirit helps us in our weakness, for we do not know how to pray as one ought, but *the Spirit* himself intercedes for us with unexpressed groanings. And the one who searches our hearts knows what the mindset of the Spirit is, because he intercedes on behalf of the saints according to the will of God. (Ro 8:26–27, emphasis added)

In the above example from Romans, the Spirit is actively involved in the lives of believers. Similar language occurs in the letters to the churches in Revelation:

> The one who has an ear, let him hear what *the Spirit* says to the churches. To the one who conquers, I will grant to him to eat from the tree of life which is in the paradise of God.' (Re 2:7, emphasis added)[2]

The same concept of the Spirit acting in the lives of believers is also seen in the *Didache*:

> Do not command your male slave or female slave who are hoping in the same God in your bitterness, lest they cease to fear the God over you both, for he does

---

[1] BDAG, p. 832. Occurs 379x in NT. Cf. comments on 1Ti 3:16.

[2] The same sentence occurs in Re 2:7, 11, 17, 29; 3:6, 13, 22; at the end of each of the letters to the churches, confirming the status of the message given through the agency of the Spirit.

> not come to call with partiality but to whom *the Spirit* prepares. (*Did.* 4.10, emphasis added)

In this epistle to Timothy, the language is similar to that of the letters to the churches of Revelation, with one small difference: the Spirit "explicitly says" something. The word "explicitly" is a translation of the Greek word ῥητῶς. Only occurring here in the New Testament, ῥητῶς typically means 'distinctly' or 'expressly.'[3] Josephus uses it in the sense of "distinctly" or "specifically" in *Against Apion*:

> Now, in another copy it is said that this word does not denote Kings but, on the contrary, denotes Captive Shepherds, and this on account of the particle Hyc; for that Hyc, with the aspiration, in the Egyptian tongue again denotes Shepherds, and that *expressly* also: and this to me seems the more probable opinion, and more agreeable to ancient history. (Jos., *Apion* 1.83, emphasis added)

Philo uses ῥητῶς to describe speech in much the same way that it is used in First Timothy:

> And of this tree Moses *expressly* says, that it is placed in the middle of the paradise; but as to the other tree, that namely of the knowledge of good and evil, he has not specified whether it is within or outside of the Paradise; but after he has used the following expression, "and the tree of the knowledge of good and evil," he says no more, not mentioning where it is placed, in order that any one who is uninitiated in the principles of natural philosophy, may not be made to marvel at his knowledge. (Philo, *Alleg. Interp.* I 60, emphasis added)

The word ῥητῶς is an adverb, describing the manner of speaking or speech under examination. In First Timothy, the speaking attributed to the Spirit is specific and distinct, not to be misunderstood.

This short preface to verses 2–3 serves as an attention-getter and a warning to those reading, that they had better take note of the following words as they contain special importance.

that in the last times

The Greek word translated "last" is the adjective ὕστερος.[4] This is its only adjectival use in the NT, though the use of ὕστερος as an adjective in temporal relation is sufficiently testified to in classical literature.[5] Plato has a similar prepositional phrase

---

[3] LSJ, p. 1569. *hapax*. ῥητῶς is the adverbial form of the noun ῥητός, under which LSJ lists the gloss.

[4] BDAG, p. 1044. Occurs 12x in NT, only here in PE.

[5] LSJ, p. 1096.

in *Leges*, 9.865a to say "in future periods/times;" but Plato uses χρόνος instead of Paul's καιρός.[6]

The word also occurs in the *Psalms of Solomon*:

> because he rejected him in dishonor.
> He did not consider that he was a human,
> and he did not consider what comes after. (*Ps. Sol.* 2:32, emphasis added)[7]

In this LXX instance, the word ὕστερος is a temporal reference, pointing to "the end." The word modified by ὕστερος is the noun καιρός, which also occurs in 1Ti 2:6, "a witness at the proper *time*." In the current context, καιρός agrees in case, number and gender with ὕστερος, thus the translation "in the last times."

However, this translation does not mean that the practices mentioned in following verses are destined to take place in the future relative to the time of the writing. Paul is instead reminding the recipients (Timothy and the Ephesian church) of an earlier prophecy with the implication that the earlier-prophesied time has now come to pass. The "last times" of the prophecy are, therefore, contemporary with the writing of the letter.

some will depart from the faith

The word translated "some" is the indefinite pronoun τὶς. It has no antecedent so those who will "depart from the faith" cannot be specifically identified.

The Greek word ἀφίστημι is translated as "will depart." The word is glossed as 'go away, withdraw.'[8] This word also occurs in Second Timothy:

> However, the solid foundation of God stands firm, having this seal: "The Lord knows those who are his," and "Everyone who names the name of the Lord *must abstain* from unrighteousness." (2Ti 2:19, emphasis added)

The word ἀφίστημι occurs in the *Shepherd of Hermas*:

> But those who are falling into the fire and being burned, these are those who *completely revolted against* the living God and it has entered no longer into their heart to repent because of the lust of their licentiousness and the wicked deeds which they have done. (Hermas, *Visions* III, vii, 2, emphasis added)

---

[6] This reference to Plato is cited in both LSJ and BDAG articles. The above translation is the author's, and it is made without any knowledge of the surrounding context of the phrase.

[7] BDAG specifically translates this instance as "the end" in its definition for ὕστερος (BDAG, p. 1044). Some editions of *Ps. Sol.* have this content as *Ps. Sol.* 2:28.

[8] BDAG, p. 157. Occurs 14x in NT, 2x in PE: 1Ti 4:1; 2Ti 2:19.

The act of departing involves leaving one thing and progressing toward another. In the current context of First Timothy, "the faith" is being left, and something outside of the faith (outside of the sound teaching) will be pursued.

paying attention to deceitful spirits and teachings of demons

The phrase "paying attention to" is a translation from the Greek word προσέχω. This word occurs in 1Ti 1:4 where it is translated similarly, "to pay attention to." In the current instance, προσέχω is followed by "deceitful spirits and teachings of demons." These "deceitful spirits" stand in contrast to the Holy Spirit from whom the prophecy comes.

The word translated "deceitful" is πλάνος, an adjective describing "spirits." As an adjective, the word carries the meaning of 'leading astray' or 'deceitful.'[9] Josephus uses the same word in his *Wars of the Jews*:

> These were such men as *deceived* and deluded the people under pretense of divine inspiration, but were for procuring innovations and changes of the government, and these prevailed with the multitude to act like madmen, and went before them into the wilderness, as pretending that God would there show them the signals of liberty; (Jos., *Wars* 2.259, emphasis added)

The context is helpful in providing the sense of the word. The men who were "deceived" in the above citation are those who were snookered into believing one thing (the men in question acted under "divine insipiration") when another thing was true (the men in question were concerned with changing the government).

The word πλάνος also occurs in the *Testament to Benjamin*:

> The deliberations of the good man are not in the control of the *deceitful* spirit, Beliar, for the angel of peace guides his life. (*T. Benj.* 6.1, emphasis added)

Here πλάνος is used to qualify the Beliar as a deceitful spirit. According to the *Testament of Benjamin*, the "good man" is not under the power of the deceitful spirit.

The word is also used in the LXX, in Jeremiah:

> Because of this, Look! I am against the prophets who prophesy false dreams and have not recited them in detail, and led my people astray by their lies. And with respect to their *leading* my people *astray*, it was not I who sent them, and I did not command them, and they will not help this people with help. (Jer 23:32 [LXX])

---

[9] BDAG, p. 822. Occurs 5x in NT: Mt 27:63; 2Co 6:8; 1Ti 4:1; 2Jn 7 (twice).

Here again, πλάνος is used to describe false and erroneous action. In this instance, it is action on the part of false prophets who deceive people, claiming genuine prophecy when they are not sent by God.

In First Timothy, πλάνος is used to modify the word "spirits," indicating the nature of these "spirits" is deceitful and erroneous.[10] The word translated "spirits" is πνεῦμα. As one primary underlying theme of First Timothy is that of sound doctrine, this phrase "deceitful spirits and teachings of demons" could be seen as the opposite of sound doctrine. As obedience to the Holy Spirit (mentioned earlier in the verse) leads to sound doctrine; obedience to the deceitful spirits leads to disobedience. Instead of devotion to sound doctrine the Ephesians are in danger of devoting themselves to the opposite. The effect will be ruinous.

The "teachings of demons" is in apposition to the "deceitful spirits." These teachings are negative and serve to work against Paul's teaching of sound doctrine.

VERSE 2

by the hypocrisy of liars

The word translated "hypocrisy" is the Greek word ὑπόκρισις, typically meaning 'play-acting,' 'pretense,' or 'outward show.'[11] This word is also used in the epistle to the Galatians:

> But when Cephas came to Antioch, I opposed him to his face, because he was condemned. For before certain people came from James, he used to eat with the Gentiles, but when they came, he withdrew and separated himself, because he was afraid of those who were of the circumcision, and the rest of the Jews also joined in this hypocrisy with him, so that even Barnabas was carried away with them in their *hypocrisy*. But when I saw that they were not being straightforward with the truth of the gospel, I said to Cephas in the presence of them all, "If you, although you are a Jew, live like a Gentile and not like a Jew, how can you try to compel the Gentiles to live like Jews?" (Ga 2:11–14, emphasis added)[12]

In this instance, the surrounding context helps define the word. Cephas (Peter) and "the rest of the Jews" are taken to task by Paul because of their actions toward the

---

[10] Much as πλάνος is used in *T. Benj.* 6.1.

[11] BDAG, p. 1038. Occur 6x in NT, only here in PE.

[12] Note that earlier in the verse, the phrase "acted hypocritically along with him" is the Greek *hapax* συνυποκρίνομαι, which is the verb form of ὑπόκρισις (ὑποκρίνομαι) with the preposition συν attached.

Gentiles. Paul points out the inconsistencies in the actions of this party toward the Gentiles in current company. Paul names this action ὑπόκρισις.

The word is also used in the *Testament of Benjamin*, as part of a series of contrasts where opposites are paired together:

> The good set of mind does not talk from both sides of its mouth: praises and curses, abuse and honor, calm and strife, *hypocrisy and truth*, poverty and wealth, but it has one disposition, uncontaminated and pure, toward all men. There is no duplicity in its perception or its hearing. Whatever it does, or speaks, or perceives, it knows that the Lord is watching over its life, (*T. Benj.* 6.5–6, emphasis added)

Here "hypocrisy" is paired with "truth," showing that these are in a contrastive relation, along with the other elements in the list.[13] Further expansion of ὑπόκρισις is seen in *First Clement*:

> Therefore we should join with those who practice peace with piety and not with those who desire peace with *hypocrisy*. For it says somewhere, "This people honor me with their lips but their heart is far from me." And again, "They blessed with their mouth, but they cursed in their heart." And again it says, "They loved him with their mouth and with their tongue they lied to him; and their heart was not upright with him and they did not show themselves faithful in his covenant." (*1Cl* 15.1–4, emphasis added)

The contrast between proper action and action based in hypocrisy is evident; hypocritical action speaks from one perspective yet thinks or believes another.

In Polycarp's *Letter to the Philippians*, ὑπόκρισις is used similarly to show that there are some who represent the name of the Lord falsely:

> So, then, let us serve him with fear and all reverence, just as he himself has commanded, as did the apostles who proclaimed the gospel to us and the prophets who publicly proclaimed the coming of our Lord. Let us be enthusiasts concerning the good, refraining from those who cause others to stumble and the false brothers and those bearing the name of the Lord in *hypocrisy*, who mislead foolish people. (Poly., *Phil.* 6.3, emphasis added)

Those who claim to preach in the name of the Lord yet proclaim a message against him are in hypocrisy.

In First Timothy, the context is similar. Here, "liars" (ψευδολόγος)[14] are those who, through hypocrisy, are the agents by which some "depart from the faith." These agents advocate, teach and propagate the deceitful teaching mentioned in v. 1. Paul

---

[13] e.g. "sorrow" and "joy" or "quietness" and "confusion."

[14] BDAG, p. 1096. NT *hapax*.

earlier implored the Ephesians to have "faith without hypocrisy,"[15] he now warns the Ephesians to be on watch for those who are insincere or hypocritical liars.

who are seared in their own conscience

Paul discussed "conscience" when he established the goal of his teaching:

> But the goal of our instruction is love from a pure heart and a good *conscience* and a faith without hypocrisy, (1Ti 1:5, emphasis added)

The insincere liars (in contrast with the "faith without hypocrisy" of 1Ti 1:5) are not in possession of good consciences. Rather, their consciences are "seared."

The word translated "seared" is the Greek word καυστηριάζω.[16] In classical literature, καυστηριάζω has a literal meaning of 'to burn with a glowing iron.'[17] Paul here means that these insincere liars, who are agents of the false teaching, have consciences that are seared (or perhaps 'branded') thus marking them as undesirables. TDNT offers one perspective:

> At 1 Tm. 4:2 the false teachers are described as men who have been branded in their consciences, i.e., who bear the mark of slaves.[18]

Paul distinguishes the conscience and sincerity of these agents of false teaching as being out of line with Pauline standards (as described in 1Ti 1:5 and 3:16).

VERSE 3

Paul now moves from a general description of the undesirable qualities of the insincere liars to provide a few specific examples of the improper teaching they advocate.

---

[15] See comment on 1Ti 1:5 where the word translated "insincere" is the word ὑπόκρισις with an alpha prefix.

[16] BDAG, p. 536. NT *hapax*.

[17] TDNT 3:644: "to burn with a glowing iron" or "to supply with a branding mark" in the active voice.

[18] TDNT 3:644.

Who forbid marrying

The word translated "forbid" is the Greek verb κωλύω, glossed as 'hinder, prevent, forbid;'[19] it occurs here in relation to a thing. The word is used similarly in First Corinthians in respect to tongues:

> So then, my brothers, desire to prophesy, and do not *prevent* speaking with tongues. (1Co 14:39, emphasis added)

Luke also uses κωλύω:

> And they began to accuse him, saying, "We have found this man misleading our nation and *forbidding* us to pay taxes to Caesar, and saying he himself is Christ, a king!" (Lk 23:2, emphasis added)

The word is also used in the *Epistle to Diognetus*:

> And to falsely accuse God, as *forbidding* to do something good on the Sabbath day, how is this not impious? (*Ep. Diog.* 4.3, emphasis added)

Forbidding or frustrating a particular action is typically in mind when κωλύω is used in relation to a thing or practice. As the context of this section in First Timothy is about the erroneous teaching of liars whose consciences are branded, indicating they are filled with falsehood, it makes sense to understand κωλύω in this context as forbidding a particular practice, such as marriage.[20] The practice is not simply being frustrated, or allowed but hindered; these teachers forbid it.

and insist on abstaining from foods

The words "insist on abstaining" are translated from the Greek word ἀπέχω. This word has a number of senses, but the sense intended here is that of 'keep away, abstain, refrain from.'[21] The word is used twice in Acts 15:

> Therefore I conclude we should not cause difficulty for those from among the Gentiles who turn to God, but we should write a letter to them *to abstain* from the pollution of idols and from sexual immorality and from what has been strangled and from blood. (Ac 15:19–20, emphasis added)

> For it seemed best to the Holy Spirit and to us to place on you no greater burden except these necessary things: that *you abstain* from food sacrificed to idols, and from blood, and from what has been strangled, and from sexual immorality. If

---

[19] BDAG, p. 580. Occurs 23x in NT, only here in PE.

[20] The word translated "marriage" is the Greek word γαμέω. The meaning is straightforward and need not be discussed further here.

[21] BDAG, p. 103. Occurs 19x in NT, only here in PE.

> you keep yourselves from these things you will do well. Farewell. (Ac 15:28–29, emphasis added)

In Acts, abstention from certain foods is required. Earlier in Acts, however, Peter is led to consider all foods clean.[22] The cleanness or uncleanness of certain foods was eventually left as a matter of conscience, with one's practice dictated to be in conformance with what would not cause a fellow believer to stumble.[23]

Yet here in First Timothy, Paul specifies that the teaching of later times (which are actually contemporaneous with First Timothy) will wrongly require abstention from foods.

that God created for sharing in with thankfulness

According to Paul, there is no reason in accordance with sound teaching that would cause one to consider any food unclean. God "created" these things for those "who believe and who know the truth."

The word "created" is a translation of the Greek word κτίζω, which means 'create.'[24] In the NT, κτίζω is used to describe God's creative work,[25] and this instance is no different. Typically it speaks of bringing something into being that had not existed previously. Consider these excerpts from various NT books:

> To me, the least of all the saints, was given this grace: to proclaim the good news of the fathomless riches of Christ to the Gentiles, and to enlighten everyone as to what is the administration of the mystery hidden from the ages by God, who *created* all things, in order that the many-sided wisdom of God might be made known now to the rulers and the authorities in the heavenly places through the church, (Eph 3:8–10, emphasis added)

> because all things in the heavens and on the earth *were created* by him, things visible and things invisible, whether thrones or dominions or rulers or powers, all things were created through him and for him, (Col 1:16, emphasis added)

> For in those days there will be tribulation of such a kind as has not happened from the beginning of the creation that God *created* until now, and never will happen. (Mk 13:19, emphasis added)

---

22 cf. Acts 10:9–16.

23 The specifics of food ethics in the NT are outside of the scope of this work. Cf. 1Co 7:1–13.

24 BDAG, p. 572. Occurs 15x in NT, only here in PE. Note that 1Ti 2:13 uses the word πλάσσω ('formed') to convey much the same meaning as κτίζω. The word πλάσσω may imply existence of previous material; κτίζω seems to represent the generic act of creation, be it ex nihilo or otherwise.

25 Though some instances (e.g. Col 3:10) use it substantively as "our creator."

Paul notes that these items were created "to be received with thanksgiving." The phrase "to be received" is a translation of the Greek word μετάλημψις which here has the sense of 'sharing.'[26] This word is not found elsewhere in the NT or in the LXX, but it is found in at least one of the papyri from Oxyrhynchus, as cited in Moulton and Milligan:

> ... is found in the sense of "concurrence" in the marriage-contract P Oxy X. 1273[39] (A.D. 260) οὐ προσδεόμενος τῆς τοῦ ἑτέρου μεταλήμψεως οὐδὲ ἑτέρας εὐδοκήσεως, "without requiring the concurrence of the other side or any further consent"[27]

In the citation from Oxyrhynchus, the sense of "sharing" is seen in the consent not being shared or agreed to ('concurrent') between the two parties. In First Timothy the sharing takes place in that God has given the food to his people, and his people have "received" it.

The Greek word εὐχαριστία is translated "thanksgiving." This word was used previously,[28] describing "thanksgivings" as a type or aspect of prayer that all in Ephesus are to practice. Those who receive provision from God are to offer thanksgiving to God who provides for all needs.

by those who believe and who know the truth

The recipients of God's provision are "those who believe and who know the truth." The phrase "those who believe" is translated from the word πιστός and its article.

The compound phrase "those who believe and who know the truth" is significant because it echoes 1Ti 2:3–4:

> This is good and acceptable before God our Savior, who wants all people *to be saved and to come to a knowledge of the truth.* (1Ti 2:3–4, emphasis added)

Paul earlier described the desire of God to not only save all men, but to bring them into "knowledge of the truth." Now Paul describes how God provides food to be received by the ones "who believe and know the truth." The same group is being described in the same way from a different perspective:

---

[26] BDAG, p. 639. NT *hapax*.

[27] M-M, p. 403.

[28] See comment on 1Ti 2:1.

1Ti 2:4	1Ti 4:3
to be saved	those who believe
and	and
to come to knowledge of the truth	Who know the truth

Those whom God has saved are those who now believe; those whom he has brought into knowledge of the truth now know the truth.

FREEDOM FROM FALSE REQUIREMENTS (1TI 4:4–5)

because everything created by God is good and nothing is to be rejected if it is received with thankfulness, for it is made holy by the word of God and prayer. (1Ti 4:4–5)

VERSE 4

because everything created by God is good

The word "everything" is a translation of the Greek word πᾶς, a frequently-occurring word that means 'all, each or every.'[1] It modifies "created," which is a translation of the Greek word κτίσμα. The word κτίσμα is not a verb with the meaning of "to create;" it is a noun indicating 'something that has been created' or 'creature.'[2] This combination of words also occurs in Re 5:13:

> And I heard *every creature* that is in heaven and on the earth and under the earth and in the sea and everything in them saying, "To the one who is seated on the throne and to the Lamb be praise and honor and glory and power forever and ever." (Re 5:13, emphasis added)

The word κτίσμα is used similarly in the *Epistle to Diognetus*:

> Although if any of these reasons are acceptable it would also be possible for each one of the remaining *creatures* to likewise be declared God. (*Ep. Diog.* 8.3, emphasis added)

In *Diognetus*, the word is used in much the same way that it is used here in First Timothy, to attribute the creation to God, the creator.

The previous context of First Timothy had to do with practices or items that false teachers forbid. Paul's response is a realization that all things created by God are "good" and therefore are acceptable to be used by those for whom these things have been created. Paul may be reminding the reader of the creation account in Genesis:

---

[1] BDAG p. 782. Occurs 1243x in NT, 55x in PE. The word is briefly discussed in notes on 1Ti 2:1 and 2:4.

[2] BDAG, p. 573. Occurs 4x in NT: 1Ti 4:4; Jam 1:18; Re 5:13; 8:9.

> And God saw everything that he had made and, behold, it was very good. And there was evening, and there was morning, a sixth day. (Ge 1:31)

and nothing is to be rejected

After noting that "everything" created by God is good and therefore acceptable, Paul states that "nothing" is to be rejected. The word "nothing" is a translation of the Greek word οὐδείς, which means 'no one' or 'nothing.'[3] The contrast between "everything" and "nothing" is notable. This contrast occurs in the epistle to the Hebrews as well:

> Pursue peace with *everyone*, and holiness, without which *no one* will see the Lord. (Heb 12:14, emphasis added)

The LXX has more examples of this type of contrast; one of which occurs in Judith:

> And *everyone* departed from view, and *no one* was left in the bedchamber from small to great; and Judith, standing beside his bed, said in her heart, "Lord God of all power, look in this hour upon the works of my hands for the exaltation of Jerusalem. Because now is the time to lay hold of your inheritance and to complete my mission for the destruction of the enemies who rose up against us." (Jdt 13:4–5, emphasis added)

Similar contrast occurs in the *Shepherd of Hermas*:

> And from the fifth mountain, the one having green plants and being rough, the ones who believe such as these are faithful but also slow to learn, arrogant and are pleasers of self, wanting to know *all things* yet they know *nothing at all*. (Hermas, *Similitudes* IX, xxii, 1, emphasis added)

In First Timothy, πᾶς and οὐδείς provide the same sort of contrast, emphasizing the wrongness of the false teachers in their approach restricting certain items from those who are believers.

According to Paul, everything was created by God so nothing need be rejected out-of-hand. The word translated "rejected" in this verse is the Greek word ἀπόβλητος.[4] The word is seldom used in Christian literature. LSJ cites the *Iliad*, noting that ἀπόβλητος there means 'to be thrown away or aside, as worthless.'[5] Those things previously mentioned by Paul—marriage and certain foods—have been created by

---

[3] BDAG, p. 735. Occurs 227x in NT.

[4] BDAG, p. 107. NT *hapax*. According to BDAG, this is a verbal adjective from the verb ἀποβάλλω.

[5] LSJ, p. 193, citing *Iliad* 3.65, "οὔ τοι ἀπόβλητ᾽ ἐστὶ θεῶν ἐρικυδέα δῶρα"

God a gnd are good, and therefore should not be dismissed, or put aside as lacking worth or as evil.

if it is received with thankfulness

There is one qualification, however, to the reception of the provision of God in the area of food. In verse 3, Paul describes these rejected foods as items "... that God created for sharing in with thankfulness by those who believe and know the truth." Here, in verse 4, Paul reiterates this qualification to the Ephesians, noting that food should not be rejected "... if it is received with thankfulness."[6]

VERSE 5

for it is made holy by the word of God and prayer

If the status of the food is questionable,[7] receiving the food with thanksgiving through prayer to God to purify it is all that is required. The food need not be avoided or disposed of, it is the provision of God and through God's blessing it can be restored and eaten.

The phrase "made holy" is a translation of the Greek word ἁγιάζω. In contexts where ἁγιάζω is used in reference to a thing, the sense is usually that of 'consecrate, dedicate.'[8] The word is used in Matthew:

> "Woe to you, blind guides, who say, 'Whoever swears by the temple, it is nothing! But whoever swears by the gold of the temple is bound by his oath.' Fools and blind people! For which is greater, the gold or the temple that *makes* the gold *holy*? And, 'Whoever swears by the altar, it is nothing! But whoever swears by the gift that is on it is bound by his oath.' Blind people! For which is greater, the gift or the altar that *makes* the gift *holy*? (Mt 23:16–19, emphasis added)

In the above context, as well as in First Timothy, the thing[9] is being made holy or sacred. The verb ἁγιάζω is in the passive voice implying that its object is being acted upon; it is not making itself holy or sacred. In First Timothy, this action is prompted "by the word of God and prayer."

---

[6] On the phrase "received with thanksgiving" see comment on 1Ti 4:3.

[7] e.g., perhaps it had been sacrificed or slain in honor of false gods, then sold in the marketplace.

[8] BDAG, p. 9. Occurs 28x in NT, 2x in PE: 1Ti 4:5; 2Ti 2:21.

[9] In these instances: gold, gifts, or food.

The Greek word ἔντευξις is translated "prayer." The word may mean prayer in a general sense, or it could imply some sort of intercession.[10] Here the word likely carries the more general sense and could even have to do with thanksgiving. Verses 3 and 4 clearly use the term "thanksgiving" (εὐχαριστία) as describing the attitude with which the provision is received, so the prayer mentioned in verse 5 may therefore be prayer of thanksgiving for the food with the request (intercession) to make it holy and proper for consumption by a believer.[11]

---

[10] BDAG, p. 339. See comment on 1Ti 2:1.

[11] BDAG, p. 340.

Training for Godliness (1Ti 4:6–10)

By teaching these things to the brothers, you will be a good servant of Christ Jesus, trained in the words of the faith and of the good teaching that you have followed faithfully. But reject those worthless myths told by elderly women, and train yourself for godliness. For the training of the body is somewhat profitable, but godliness is profitable for everything, because it holds promise for the present life and for the life to come. The statement is trustworthy and deserving of complete acceptance. For to this end we labor and suffer reproach, because we have put our hope in the living God, who is the Savior of all people, especially of believers. (1Ti 4:6–10)

Verse 6

By teaching these things

The phrase "By teaching" is a translation of the Greek word ὑποτίθημι. It conveys the sense of to 'make known' or to 'teach.'[1] The sense is not simply that of teaching, but more that of informing. In this situation, Timothy is to take the things noted by Paul in the previous section and put them before the brothers, ensuring that the members of the fellowship know them and are therefore responsible to implement them.

Consider the use of the same word in Josephus' *Wars of the Jews*:

> But now, if any one hath a mind to come over to their sect, he is not immediately admitted, but he *is prescribed* the same method of living which they use, for a year, while he continues excluded; and they give him a small hatchet, and the fore-mentioned girdle, and the white garment. (Jos., *Wars* 2.137, emphasis added)

Here, Josephus uses ὑποτίθημι to describe how a particular sect communicates the basic rules of the community to the proselyte. These instructions or rules are prescribed for the applicant and he is to understand them and integrate them into his new life within the sect. Similarly, Timothy is to make the believers in Ephesus aware of "these things." The phrase "these things" is the demonstrative pronoun οὗτος. It refers to the content of the previous discussion (1Ti 4:1–5).

---

[1] BDAG p. 1042. Occurs 2x in NT: Ro 16:4; 1Ti 4:6.

to the brothers

This phrase comes from the Greek word ἀδελφός. It may specify the relationship between a person and a male sibling, or it may specify a more generic relation. In the plural it can refer to a group of males and females. Thus glosses of 'brother,' 'fellow member' or even 'associate' could be proper in a given context.[2] The LEB uses "brothers" as a generic term, intending to include both males and females in the group. In general contexts such as this, the plural instance of ἀδελφός may likely be best translated as "brother and sisters" or perhaps "fellow believers."

you will be a good servant of Christ Jesus

The phrase "you will be" is a translation of the Greek verb εἰμί. This verb is common as its basic meaning is 'to be.'[3] Here εἰμί is a future middle indicative in the second person, leading to the translation "you will be." As the verb is also in the singular, Timothy is the addressee. He is the one whom Paul indicates will "be a good servant" if he makes the teaching known.

The phrase "good servant" is a combination of the word for good (καλός)[4] and the word for servant (διάκονος).[5] The word καλός occurs 22 times in the Pastoral Epistles. Of those instances, 20 directly modify a noun declaring something as being "good":

- the law is good: 1Ti 1:8
- good fight: 1Ti 1:18; 6:12; 2Ti 4:7
- good work (or works): 1Ti 3:1; 5:10, 25; 6:18; Tt 2:7, 14; 3:8, 14
- good testimony: 1Ti 3:7
- good standing: 1Ti 3:13
- created (by God) is good: 1Ti 4:4
- good servant: 1Ti 4:6
- good teaching: 1Ti 4:6
- good confession: 1Ti 6:13
- good deposit: 2Ti 1:14
- good soldier: 2Ti 2:3

---

[2] BDAG p. 18. Occurs 343x in NT.

[3] BDAG, p. 282. Occurs 2462x in NT.

[4] For more on καλός , see comment on 1Ti 3:7.

[5] This is the same noun translated as "deacon" earlier. As this context is not explicitly about serving in an official capacity, the translation of "servant" seems more appropriate than "deacon," though perhaps "minister" would be appropriate as well.

The word καλός functions here as it usually does throughout the Pastoral Epistles, as an adjective modifying a noun. As Timothy passes along what Paul has taught him, he will become a "good servant" of Christ Jesus. Paul next describes what is involved in being a "good servant."

trained

The good servant evidences his previous instruction and training. The word "trained" is a translation of the Greek word ἐντρέφω. The word typically means 'train in.'[6] This word also occurs in Philo's tractate *Legatio ad Gaium*:

> If, therefore, both the objects on account of which we were sent are overthrown, perhaps some one will say, What then, did they not know that they had to negotiate for a safe return? But I would reply to such a man, You either have not the genuine feelings of a nobly born man, or else you were not educated like one, and have never *been trained in* the knowledge of the sacred scriptures; for men who are truly noble are full of hope, and the laws too implant good hopes in all those who do not study them superficially but with all their hearts. (Philo, *Embassy* 195–196, emphasis added)

Philo uses the word ἐντρέφω to specifically refer to the training one receives "in the knowledge of the sacred scriptures." He discusses how true study of the law has a visible effect on the student. Paul uses the word similarly, noting that a good servant is one whose training is reflected in his action. Timothy's training will be made evident in how he carries out Paul's instruction.

the words of the faith and of the good teaching

Timothy's instruction has been (and continues to be) two areas: faith and doctrine. The phrase "words of the faith" consists of the word λόγος (typically meaning 'word,' 'statement,' or 'saying')[7] and the word πίστις (typically meaning 'faith' or 'firm commitment');[8] the group thus meaning "in the words of the faith." It is followed by the phrase translated "of the good teaching." The training is not in the words of the faith and also in good doctrine, but in the words of the faith and in the words of the good doctrine.

Paul uses a construction similar to this one later in this epistle:

---

[6] BDAG, p. 341. NT *hapax*. See comment on 1Ti 4:7 having to do with "train yourself for godliness," where "train" is a translation of γυμνάζω.

[7] BDAG, p. 598.

[8] BDAG, p. 819.

> If anyone teaches other doctrine and does not devote himself to *the sound words of our Lord Jesus Christ and the teaching that is in accordance with godliness*, he is conceited, understanding nothing, but having a morbid interest concerning controversies and disputes about words, from which come envy, strife, slanders, evil suspicions, constant wrangling by people of depraved mind and deprived of the truth, who consider godliness to be a means of gain. But godliness with contentment is a great means of gain. (1Ti 6:3–6, emphasis added)

In this later instance,[9] Paul uses the standard of "the sound words of our Lord Jesus Christ and the teaching that accords with godliness" as the basis to compare the doctrine offered by other teachers. Unlike the one who has been properly trained (1Ti 4:6), the one teaching doctrine contrary to the sound doctrine is "puffed up and understands nothing." Paul desires the Ephesians to be properly anchored, to be evidence of correct training in faith and doctrine.[10] Paul wants them to be like Timothy.

that you have followed faithfully

Paul has observed Timothy through the years and knows that he has adhered to Paul's teaching of faith and doctrine. The phrase "you have followed faithfully" is a translation of the Greek word παρακολουθέω. In the current context, glosses of 'follow faithfully' or 'follow as a rule' are appropriate.[11] LSJ provide general glosses of 'follow closely,' 'attend closely,' and 'dog one's steps.'[12] This word is used in the second epistle to Timothy in a similar context:

> But you *have faithfully followed* my teaching, way of life, purpose, faith, patience, love, endurance, persecutions, and sufferings that happened to me in Antioch, in Iconium, and in Lystra, what sort of persecutions I endured, and the Lord delivered me from all of them. (2Ti 3:10–11, emphasis added)

The sense of Timothy adhering to and thus following the teaching and example of Paul in faith and doctrine is reiterated.

---

[9] See comments on 1Ti 6:3–6.

[10] Regarding proper doctrine, see comment on 1Ti 1:10.

[11] BDAG, p. 767. Occurs 4x in NT: Mk 16:17; Lk 1:3; 1Ti 4:6; 2Ti 3:10.

[12] LSJ, p. 1313.

Verse 7

But reject those worthless myths told by elderly women

The phrase "reject" is translated from the Greek word παραιτέομαι. When used with accusative objects (as it is here) the typical meaning is that of 'refuse' or 'reject.'[13] Similar instances occur elsewhere in the Pastorals:

> But *avoid* foolish and uninformed controversies, because you know that they produce quarrels. (2Ti 2:23, emphasis added)

> *Reject* a divisive person after a first and second admonition, (Tt 3:10, emphasis added)

In these examples, the accusative objects (controversies, divisive people) are the things to be avoided or rejected. Josephus' *Antiquities* contains similar instances:

> But Moses *refused* all that honor which he saw the multitude ready to bestow upon him, and attended to nothing else but the service of God. He went no more up to Mount Sinai; but he went into the tabernacle, and brought back answers from God for what he prayed for. His habit was also that of a private man; and in all other circumstances he behaved himself like one of the common people, and was desirous to appear without distinguishing himself from the multitude, but would have it known that he did nothing else but take care of them. (Jos., *Ant.* 3.212, emphasis added)[14]

In the example from Josephus, Moses has been offered something which he actively refused; he requested that the honor not be given him. The examples from the Pastorals have a similar dynamic; Paul instructs his readers to refuse practices or things which are apparently readily available for them to accept.

Timothy is to avoid "worthless myths told by elderly women." The word "worthless" is a translation of the Greek word βέβηλος. In context such as this, it typically means 'pointless' or 'worthless.'[15] Similar usage occurs later in the epistle:

> O Timothy, guard what has been entrusted to you. Turn away from *pointless* empty talk and contradictions of what is falsely called knowledge, (1Ti 6:20, emphasis added)

---

[13] BDAG, p. 764. 12x in NT, 4x in PE: 1Ti 4:7, 5:11; 2Ti 2:23; Tt 3:10. Note that all instances in the PE are in the same morphological form, παραιτοῦ, which is a present middle imperative second person singular verb.

[14] Also see Jos., *Ant.* 5.237.

[15] BDAG, p. 173. Occurs 5x in the NT: 1Ti 1:9, 4:7, 6:20; 2Ti 2:16; He 12:16.

The word occurs in similar context in Second Timothy:

> But avoid *pointless* chatter, for it will progress to greater ungodliness, (2Ti 2:16, emphasis added)

The "worthless" communication is pointless and lacks edification. It is also framed as "told by elderly women." The Greek word is γραώδης, meaning 'characteristic of an elderly woman.'[16] Both βέβηλος and γραώδης modify the word μῦθος.[17] These words all combine to be used idiomatically, meaning something like "pointless tales told by old women." In contrasting these worthless myths with the good teaching,[18] Paul finds the myths worthy of ridicule. This communication is not worthy of one's attention, it is instead to be treated as one treats folk wisdom based in superstition and ignorance: it is to be ignored.

and train yourself for godliness

Instead of concerning oneself with "worthless myths told by elderly women" one should pursue other things. And Paul does not note a simple preference for other things, he specifies for Timothy and the community at Ephesus a specific object of pursuit: godliness.

Godliness is to become part of the regular routine of the Ephesian community. One is to "train" oneself in it. The Greek word translated "train" is γυμνάζω, generally meaning 'to train' or 'undergo discipline.'[19] This word is different from the word translated 'being trained' in verse 6, ἐντρέφω.[20]

Originally γυμνάζω had to do with physical training, "gymnastic exercise in the nude"[21] But in the New Testament, γυμνάζω is primarily used in a figurative sense, that of training or disciplining oneself in thought or morality. This is similar to the sense used in Hebrews:

> But solid food is for the mature, who because of practice *have trained* their faculties for the distinguishing of both good and evil. (Heb 5:14, emphasis added)

The author of Hebrews refers to the training of "faculties." The method of training is "practice … for the distinguishing of both good from evil." In evaluating situations

---

[16] BDAG, p. 207. *hapax*.

[17] See comment on 1Ti 1:4.

[18] That is, the "words of the faith and the good teaching you have followed faithfully" in 1Ti 4:6.

[19] BDAG, p. 208. Occurs 4x in NT: 1Ti 4:7; Heb 5:14, 12:11; 2Pe 2:14.

[20] See comment on 1Ti 4:6.

[21] BDAG, p. 208.

and distinguishing between things that are good and things that are evil, "faculties" are developed, or trained. Exercising one's critical faculty will result in a better ability to discern.

Philo uses similar language regarding "training":

> But while he was preparing to display the decision which he was about to pronounce, Moses was devoting himself to all the labours of virtue, having a teacher within himself, virtuous reason, by whom *he had been trained* to the most virtuous pursuits of life, and had learnt to apply himself to the contemplation and practice of virtue and to the continual study of the doctrines of philosophy, which he easily and thoroughly comprehended in his soul, and committed to memory in such a manner as never to forget them; and, moreover, he made all his own actions, which were intrinsically praiseworthy, to harmonise with them, desiring not to seem wise and good, but in truth and reality to be so, because he made the right reason of nature his only aim; which is, in fact, the only first principle and fountain of all the virtues. (Philo, *Moses* I 48, emphasis added)

This training, however, need not only be in pursuit of the good. The word γυμνάζω is also used in Second Peter:

> But these persons, like irrational animals born only with natural instincts for capture and killing, blaspheming about things they do not understand, in their destruction will also be destroyed, being harmed as the wages of unrighteousness. Considering reveling in the daytime a pleasure, they are stains and blemishes, carousing in their deceitful pleasures when they feast together with you, having eyes full of desire for an adulteress and unceasing from sin, enticing unstable persons, and having hearts *trained* for greediness. Accursed children! By leaving the straight path, they have gone astray, because they followed the way of Balaam the son of Bosor, who loved the wages of unrighteousness, but received a rebuke for his own lawlessness: a speechless donkey, speaking with a human voice, restrained the prophet's madness. (2Pe 2:12–16, emphasis added)

In this chapter of Second Peter, no scorn is spared from those who teach falsely. Particularly, in regard to the use of γυμνάζω in First Timothy, the false teachers have "hearts trained in greed." As they have been seeking after greed, they have conditioned their hearts to be greedy and have therefore become even greedier.

In First Timothy, Paul intends for Timothy to model godliness[22] to the Ephesians. In consciously and purposefully pursuing godliness, Timothy will not only develop his own personal habits of godliness, but he will provide an example for the Ephesians

---

[22] For εὐσέβεια ("godliness") see 1Ti 2:2. "Godliness" is the primary subject of 1Ti 2:1–7.

to follow. In this way, Timothy will begin to train the Ephesians in godliness, they will begin to exercise the ways of godliness and further develop their abilities.

Verse 8

For training of the body is somewhat profitable

After introducing the concept of training in godliness, Paul contrasts this concept with that of "training of the body." The same cognate word used for "training" (γυμνασία)[23] was used earlier; the difference being the realm of training. Josephus uses the word in this sense:

> He was also such a warrior as could not be withstood; many men therefore there are who have stood amazed at his readiness in his *exercises*, when they saw him throw the javelin directly forward, and shoot the arrow upon the mark; and then, besides these performances of his depending on his own strength of mind and *body*, fortune was also very favorable to him, for he seldom failed of success in his wars; and when he failed, he was not himself the occasion of such failings, but he either was betrayed by some, or the rashness of his own soldiers procured his defeat. (Jos., *Wars* 1.430, emphasis added)

In the excerpt from Josephus, the exercises described are those having to do with the body. Both the body and the mind have been properly trained, and this training is reflected in the skill shown during the exercises.

Profitable though it may be, according to Paul bodily training is only "somewhat profitable." The word translated "somewhat" is the Greek word ὀλίγος, here meaning 'little' or 'slight.'[24] The Greek word ὠφέλιμος is translated "profitable." In this context it carries the meaning of 'useful,' 'beneficial,' or 'advantageous.'[25] Josephus uses this word in the superlative to distinguish something as most beneficial or great:

> And for any great or royal work that he ever did, which might be for the present or future ages, nobody can name any such, but only the haven that he made about Rhegium and Sicily, for the reception of the ships that brought corn from Egypt; which was indeed a work without dispute very great in itself, and of *very great advantage* to the navigation. (Jos., *Ant.* 19.205–206a, emphasis added)

---

[23] Here "training" is the noun γυμνασία (which only occurs here in the NT) instead of the verb γυμνάζω used in the above verse.

[24] BDAG, p. 703. Occurs 40x in NT, 2x in PE: 1Ti 4:8; 5:23.

[25] BDAG, p. 1108. Occurs 4x in NT: 1Ti 4:8 (twice); 2Ti 3:16; Tt 3:8.

Paul does not dispute the worthiness of bodily training, he simply sees training in godliness as having more value.

but godliness is profitable for everything, because it holds promise for the present life and for the life to come.

Training in godliness provides benefits in every way while bodily training has partial benefit. Paul now explains the difference between partial benefit and full benefit. Bodily exercise reaps benefits only for the "present life," while the pursuit of godliness reaps benefit not only for the present life but also for "the life to come." Godliness has physical and eschatological benefits. The list of contrasts can now be expanded:

Statement #1	Statement #2
bodily training	godliness
of some value	of value in every way
(value in) the present life	(value in) the present life and the life to come

The *Epistle of Barnabas* offers a similar contrast between the present and the time to come:

> Therefore, it is necessary for us, doing careful investigation concerning the present, to seek out the things which are able to save us. Therefore, let us flee completely from all the works of lawlessness, so that the works of lawlessness do not overcome us, *and let us hate the deception of the present time, so that we may be loved in what is to come.* Let us give no freedom to our own soul, so that it has the ability to join with sinners and evildoers, lest we become like them. (*Ep. Barn.* 4.1–2, emphasis added)

VERSE 9

The statement is trustworthy and deserving of complete acceptance

Paul confirms that the distinction between bodily training and training in godliness is one that should be embraced.[26] This is identical to the text of 1Ti 1:15.

[26] This text is formulaic and has been discussed elsewhere (cf. notes on 1Ti 1:15).

Verse 10

For to this end we labor and suffer reproach

The "end"[27] Paul mentions is the result of being trained in godliness as described in the second part of 1Ti 4:6. This result is what is being worked toward; it is what is toiled and suffered on behalf of.

The Greek word translated "we toil" is κοπιάω, typically meaning 'work hard,' 'toil,' 'strive,' or 'struggle.'[28] Paul uses κοπιάω in his epistle to the Colossians:

> for which purpose also *I labor*, striving according to his working which is at work powerfully in me. (Col 1:29, emphasis added)

In First Timothy, κοπιάω occurs along with the Greek word ὀνειδίζω, indicating 'reproach,' 'revile,' or 'mock.'[29] This word is often used in the context of Jesus' suffering; as Paul uses it in Romans, which quotes from Ps 69:9:

> For even Christ did not please himself, but just as it is written, "The insults of those who *insult* you have fallen on me." (Ro 15:3, emphasis added)[30]

The same word occurs in the *Gospel of Peter*:

> But one of the criminals *reprimanded* them, saying, "We have suffered in this way for the evil that we did, but this man, being the Savior of men, how has he wronged you?" (*Gospel of Peter* 4.13, emphasis added)

The notion of suffering reproach, then, is one of perspective. The one receiving the reproach perceives it as an insult or as scorn; the one giving the reproach can see it as a reprimand. In First Timothy, the invective received by those doing the work of the gospel is scorn or reproach.

---

[27] Implied in the Greek text, "end" is not explicitly stated. "For this we labor and suffer reproach …" may be a more literal rendition.

[28] BDAG, p. 558. Occurs 23x in NT, 3x in PE: 1Ti 4:10; 5:17; 2Ti 2:6.

[29] BDAG, p. 710. Occurs 10x in NT, only here in PE. Note that SBLGNT follows MSS of the Byzantine tradition (and thus KJV and NKJV) with ονειδιζομεθα ("suffer reproach") instead of the NA28/UBS5 ἀγωνιζόμεθα. The variant is discussed in some detail by Metzger (TCGNT 574). The Byzantine tradition along with most early versions (Latin, Coptic, Syriac, Armenian and Ethiopic) support ονειδιζομεθα while most prominent uncials (including Sinaiticus' original reading and Alexandrinus) and minuscules support ἀγωνιζόμεθα.

[30] Note that "The insults" translates ὀνειδισμός, which the nominal form of ὀνειδίζω.

because we have put our hope in the living God

The phrase translated "we have put our hope" is from the Greek word ἐλπίζω. This word also occurs in 1Ti 3:14,[31] however the usage here is somewhat different. In 1Ti 3:14, Paul expressed his own desire to visit the Ephesians soon. Something different is intended here. Consider similar instances that occur later in First Timothy:

> But the widow who is one truly, and is left alone, *has put her hope in God* and continues in her petitions and prayers night and day. (1Ti 5:5, emphasis added)

> Command those who are rich in this present age not to be proud and not *to put their hope in* the uncertainty of riches, but in God, who provides us all things richly for enjoyment, (1Ti 6:17, emphasis added)

In these instances, Paul expresses that God is the object of hope. God is the only one worthy of being relied upon to fulfill the eschatological hope of those who follow him. The *Epistle of Barnabas* uses hope in this sense both negatively and positively:

> And he says again to Moses, when Israel was warred upon by foreigners, and in order that he might remind them, being warred upon, that because of their sins they were delivered to death; the spirit says to the heart of Moses, that he should make a type of the cross and the one about to suffer, because he says *unless they place their hope upon him*, they will be warred upon forever. Therefore Moses put one shield upon another in the midst of the fight and being stood up higher than them all, he stretched out his hands and thus again Israel was victorious. Then whenever he lowered them, they began to perish. (*Ep. Barn.* 12.2, emphasis added)

> "But it will be built upon the name of the Lord." And pay attention, in order that the temple of the Lord might be built in splendor. Learn how. Having received the forgiveness of sins, and *having hoped upon the name*, we have become new again, being created from the beginning. Therefore in our dwelling place God truly dwells in us. (*Ep. Barn.* 16.8, emphasis added)

Paul encourages the readers of the letter to set their hopes on "the living God." Paul used similar language earlier in 1Ti 3:15, reminding the Ephesians how Christians are to behave in "the church of the living God."[32] Similar phrases[33] are found elsewhere in the New Testament:

---

[31] See comment on 1Ti 3:14. Here ἐλπίζω is a perfect active indicative verb; in 1Ti 3:14 it is a participle.

[32] See comment on 1Ti 3:15.

[33] These are phrases where the noun θεός and the verb (participle) ζάω agree in case and number, and the case is dative. Several more examples (14, including 1Ti 3:15) occur in the genitive case.

> For they themselves report about us, what sort of welcome we had with you, and how you turned to God from idols to serve *the living* and true *God*, (1Th 1:9, emphasis added)

> For if the blood of goats and bulls and the ashes of a young cow sprinkled on those who are defiled sanctify them for the ritual purity of the flesh, how much more will the blood of Christ, who through the eternal Spirit offered himself without blemish to God, cleanse our consciences from dead works to serve *the living God*? (Heb 9:13–14, emphasis added)

who is the Savior of all people

The titles "God" and "Savior" were used equivalently earlier in the epistle.[34] Here, the living God who is the object of hope is also seen as Savior. This is similar to 1Ti 2:1 and 2:3–4:

> Therefore, I urge first of all that petitions, prayers, requests, and thanksgiving be made on behalf of *all people*, (1Ti 2:1, emphasis added)

> This is good and acceptable before *God our Savior*, who wants *all people to be saved* and to come to a knowledge of the truth. (1Ti 2:3–4, emphasis added)

As in 1Ti 2:3–4, "all people" are saved by the one who saves. In 2:1, "all people" are the object of the prayers of the Ephesian believers. In 2:3, the goal is to build the desire to evangelize to all people, to spread the gospel message to all whom they encounter. As God desires all to be saved, the Ephesians must build this desire within themselves and reach out to those around them. Similarly here, part of the training for godliness involves desiring the salvation of all people, with one's actions and efforts testifying to this end.

especially of believers

This phrase is a translation of two Greek words. The first word is μάλιστα, a superlative adverb meaning 'most of all,' 'above all,' or 'especially.'[35] The second word is πιστός, 'believer' or 'one who believes.'[36]

While the Ephesians are to consider God able to save all people and therefore they are to pray and desire the salvation of all people, Paul notes particularly that the living God saves those who believe. Two further instances of πιστός as a substantive adjective occur in First Timothy:

---

[34] In the epistolary salutation, cf. 1Ti 1:1 and 1Ti 2:3.

[35] BDAG, p. 613. Occurs 12x in NT, 5x in PE: 1Ti 4:10; 5:8, 17; 2Ti 4:13; Tt 1:10.

[36] BDAG, p. 821.

> If any *believing woman* has relatives who are widows, let her care for them. Let the church not be burdened, so that it may care for those who are really widows. (1Ti 5:16, emphasis added)

> Those who have believing masters must not be disrespectful on the ground that they are brothers; rather they must serve all the better since those who benefit by their good service are *believers* and beloved. (1Ti 6:2, emphasis added)

The "ones who believe" mentioned in 1Ti 4:10 are distinguished from the others who are "saved." The saving action of God is more specifically focused on those who are believers. In life and ministry believers are not to presuppose or pre-judge the salvific status of those to whom they minister, they are to equally and passionately proclaim the good news of Christ to all.

LEAD WITH AUTHORITY AND EXAMPLE (1TI 4:11–13)

Command these things and teach them. Let no one look down on your youth, but be an example for the believers in word, in conduct, in love, in faith, in purity. Until I come, pay attention to the public reading, to exhortation, to teaching. (1Ti 4:11–13)

VERSE 11

Command these things and teach them

The word translated "command" is the Greek word παραγγέλλω.[1] The word is generally glossed as 'command' or 'instruct.'[2] Timothy is to assume a position of authority. The word occurs five times in First Timothy; three of those instances (including this occurrence) are imperatives. The other two instances of the imperative are in 1Ti 5:7 and 6:17:

> And *command* these things, in order that they may be irreproachable. (1Ti 5:7, emphasis added)
>
> *Command* those who are rich in this present age not to be proud and not to put their hope in the uncertainty of riches, but in God, who provides us all things richly for enjoyment, (1Ti 6:17, emphasis added)

In both of these instances, Paul provides Timothy with specific exhortation to pass along to the Ephesians.

Timothy is not only to command; he also must "teach." This is the Greek word διδάσκω. A similar occurrence is found in 1Ti 6:2b. In both instances, διδάσκω is in the form of a second person imperative, and in both instances the conjunction καὶ connects διδάσκω with a verb that shares the same form:

---

[1] See comment on 1Ti 1:3.

[2] BDAG, p. 760. Occurs 32x in NT, 5x in PE: 1Ti 1:3; 4:11; 5:7; 6:13, 17.

> Command these things and *teach* them. (1Ti 4:11, emphasis added)
> *Teach* and encourage these things. (1Ti 6:2b, emphasis added)[3]

As mentioned earlier,[4] the Pastoral Epistles use διδάσκω in the context of teaching doctrine. Here as well, Timothy is urged to teach the Ephesian community in what is proper: the pursuit of godliness.

Timothy is to command and teach "these things." The reference is cataphoric; the substance of the teaching is defined in the previous section. Timothy is to be an advocate and model of godliness to the Ephesians.

Verse 12

Let no one look down on your youth

The phrase "Let no one look down on" is a translation of the Greek word καταφρονέω along with μηδείς ('no one' or 'nobody').[5] The word καταφρονέω carries the sense of 'look down on,' 'despise' or 'treat with contempt.'[6] It occurs in the imperative in this instance. Paul uses καταφρονέω similarly in First Corinthians:

> For do you not have houses for eating and drinking? Or *do you despise* the church of God and humiliate those who do not have anything? What shall I say to you? Shall I praise you? In this I will not praise you! (1Co 11:22, emphasis added)

In First Corinthians, the use of καταφρονέω is derogatory, used in conjunction with "humiliate." The same word is also used in the *Epistle to Diognetus*:

> For you, thinking and supposing to praise, do you not *despise* them even more? Do you not instead mock and insult them more, worshiping the unguarded made of stone and clay but locking up those made of silver and gold by night and posting guards by day, so that they might not be stolen? (*Ep. Diog.* 2.7, emphasis added)

In the *Epistle to Diognetus*, the sense of not properly respecting something is at the forefront. The author of *Diognetus* is making a rhetorical point concerning the practice of Greek pagans, showing that while the pagans contend they honor their various gods of metal, wood and clay; in reality they treat them with contempt by

---

[3] The Greek word order for both sentences is different. Translations respecting word order would be "Command these things and teach" (1Ti 4:11) and "These things teach and urge" (1Ti 6:2b).

[4] See note on 1Ti 2:12.

[5] BDAG, p. 642.

[6] BDAG, p. 529. Occurs 9x in NT, 2x in PE: 1Ti 4:12; 6:2.

only guarding the idols made of precious metals. Idols formed from material of lesser innate value are despised; looked down upon because they are not afforded the same protection as the idols made from precious metals even though the pagans would claim them of equal cultic value.

Josephus uses καταφρονέω as well:

> O miserable man! that thou shouldst undergo this bitter absence, and thereby afford a great opportunity for envy to arise against thee, and a long space for such as were laying designs against thee! Yet was I absent, father, on thy affairs, that Sylleus might not *treat thee with contempt* in thine old age. Rome is a witness to my filial affection, and so is Caesar, the ruler of the habitable earth, who oftentimes called me Philopater. Take here the letters he hath sent thee, they are more to be believed than the calumnies raised here; these letters are my only apology; these I use as the demonstration of that natural affection I have to thee. (Jos., *Wars* 1.633, emphasis added)

Josephus' usage is similar to the usage in First Timothy. Josephus uses καταφρονέω to describe contemptable action taken against a man in his old age. In First Timothy, καταφρονέω is used as a reminder for Timothy to not allow rabblerousers to disregard his authority on grounds of his youthfulness.

The reason for potential contempt against Timothy has to do with his age. The word translated "youth" is νεότης, typically meaning 'state of youthfulness' or simply 'youth.'[7] The synoptic gospels use νεότης in the account of the rich young man who asked Jesus how to inherit eternal life:

> And as he was setting out on his way, one individual ran up and knelt down before him and asked him, "Good Teacher, what must I do so that I will inherit eternal life?" So Jesus said to him, "Why do you call me good? No one is good except God alone. You know the commandments: 'Do not murder, do not commit adultery, do not steal, do not give false testimony, do not defraud, honor your father and mother.' " And he said to him, "Teacher, all these I have observed *from my youth*." (Mk 10:17–20, emphasis added)

In Mark, νεότης is used to recall an earlier time in the man's life, the years of his youth. In Acts, νεότης is used in a speech of Paul, defending himself before Agrippa:

> Now all the Jews know my manner of life *from my youth*, that had taken place from the beginning among my own people and in Jerusalem, having known me for a long time, if they are willing to testify, that in accordance with the strictest party of our religion I lived as a Pharisee. (Ac 26:4–5, emphasis added)

---

[7] BDAG p. 669. Occurs 4x in NT: Mk 10:20; Lk 18:21; Ac 26:4; 1Ti 4:12. All four of these instances are genitive singular feminine nouns.

Philo also uses νεότης, helpfully in a list with other terms used to describe children and men at various stages of development:

> For where was my body before my birth? and where will it go when I am departed? And what becomes of the differences of age of that being which at present appears to exist? Where is now the infant?—where the child?—where the boy?—where the youth just arriving at the age of puberty?— where *the young man*?—where is he now whose beard is just budding, the vigorous and perfect man? Whence came the soul, and whither will it go? and how long will it remain with us? and what is its essence, or what may we speak of as such? Moreover, when did we acquire it? Was it before our birth?—But then we ourselves did not exist. Shall we have it after our death?—But then we shall not exist, we who are now a combination of distinctive qualities in combination with our bodies; but rather we shall then be hastening to a regeneration, becoming in combination with incorporeal beings: (Philo, *Cherubim* 114, emphasis added)

In Acts, νεότης is used to describe Paul's earlier years.[8] He testifies that the manner of life he pursued (beginning in the years of his youth) is well known, for he has testified to it previously.[9] He was raised as a Pharisee, and even when he was young his practice among the Pharisees was known. In First Timothy, Paul is recommending that Timothy pursue godliness with similar zeal. Timothy may be younger than the established leaders in the community at Ephesus, but his experience and tutelage under Paul provide an adequate basis for his leadership.[10]

but be an example for the believers in word, in conduct, in love, in faith, in purity

The phrase "be an example" is a translation of γίνομαι[11] and τύπος. Here the usage is similar to that in First Thessalonians:

> You are witnesses, and so is God, how devoutly and righteously and blamelessly *we became to* you who believe, (1Th 2:10, emphasis added)

In First Thessalonians, past conduct is cited. In First Timothy, however, Paul exhorts Timothy to become the example that the Ephesians need. The word "example" is a

---

[8] Paul is described as a "young man" (νεανίας) in Ac 7:58, at the stoning of Stephen. BDAG (p. 667) notes that νεανίας describes a man "fr. about the 24th to the 40th year."

[9] Acts 13:16–41; 14:15–17; 17:22–31; 20:18–35; 22:1–21; 24:10–21; 26:2–23, 25–27; 27:21–26; 28:17–20

[10] See comment on 1Ti 1:1–2 establishing Timothy's authority as Paul's representative.

[11] BDAG, p. 196. Occurs 669x in NT. The word has "numerous nuances relating to being and manner of being" (ibid).

translation of τύπος, which here has the sense of 'type,' 'pattern' or 'model.'[12] This word also occurs in the epistle to Titus:

> concerning everything showing yourself to be *an example* of good deeds, in your teaching demonstrating soundness, dignity, a sound message beyond reproach, in order that an opponent may be put to shame, because he has nothing bad to say concerning us. (Tt 2:7–8, emphasis added)

Indeed, Paul holds up those around him as examples more than once:

> Become fellow imitators of me, brothers, and observe those who walk in this way, just as you have us as *an example*. (Php 3:17, emphasis added)

> And you became imitators of us and of the Lord, receiving the word in much affliction, with the joy of the Holy Spirit, so that you became *an example* to all those who believe in Macedonia and in Achaia, (1Th 1:6–7, emphasis added)

> not that we do not have the right, but so that we may give ourselves as *an example* to you, so that you may imitate us. (2Th 3:9, emphasis added)

Earlier in First Timothy, Paul held himself up as the primary example or prototype (ὑποτύπωσις),[13] Paul now desires Timothy to similarly model behavior to the community in Ephesus, that they may exemplify proper life and doctrine. The ones to whom Timothy is an example are described as "the believers." The word used is πιστός,[14] here referring to the 'faithful ones,' thus 'believers.'[15]

Paul provides five areas[16] for Timothy to model to the believers in Ephesus: speech, conduct, faith, love and purity. This is a series of five prepositional phrases using the preposition ἐν with each noun in the dative case. The sense of "in [*area*]" is direct and unambiguous. These are each in reference to the primary verb γίνομαι (and thus τύπος); so these five areas are all areas in which Timothy is to take the lead and set the example.

in word: The Greek word is λόγος and here refers to the content of one's speech or sayings. This phrase (ἐν λόγῳ) occurs 10 times in the New Testament,[17] notably just a few paragraphs later in First Timothy:

---

[12] BDAG, p. 1020. Occurs 15x in NT, 2x in PE: 1Ti 4:12; Tt 2:7.

[13] See note on 1Ti 1:16.

[14] BDAG, p. 820. Occurs 67x in NT.

[15] Recall the earlier emphasis on believers; see comments on 1Ti 4:10.

[16] Note that texts in the Byzantine tradition add a sixth area, "in spirit" (ἐν πνεύματι). The vast majority of early witnesses (both Alexandrian and Western) do not have this addition. Cf. Metzger, TCGNT p. 574.

[17] Mt 22:15; 1Co 4:20; 2Co 6:7; Co 3:17; 1Th 1:5; 2:5; 4:15; 1Ti 4:12; 5:17; Jam 3:2.

> The elders who lead well must be considered worthy of double honor, especially those who labor *by speaking* and teaching. (1Ti 5:17, emphasis added)

Timothy is not only to provide a model in preaching or speaking, but also in his speech in other contexts as well. This same prepositional phrase is used much more generically in Colossians:

> and everything whatever you do *in word* or in deed, giving thanks for all things in the name of the Lord Jesus to God the Father through him. (Col 3:17, emphasis added)

in conduct: The word translated "conduct" is ἀναστροφή, having the general meaning of 'way of life,' 'conduct,' or 'behavior.'[18] This word is used in the epistle to the Galatians to describe Paul's way of life prior to his encounter with Christ:

> For you have heard about my former *way of life* in Judaism, that to an extraordinary degree I was persecuting the church of God, and trying to destroy it, (Ga 1:13, emphasis added)

Further, ἀναστροφή is used in a comparison between the "old self" and "new self" in Ephesians:

> But you did not learn Christ in this way, if indeed you have heard about him, and you were taught by him (just as truth is in Jesus), that you take off, according to your former *way of life*, the old man, who is being destroyed according to deceitful desires, be renewed in the spirit of your mind, and put on the new man (in accordance with God), who is created in righteousness and holiness from the truth. (Eph 4:20–24, emphasis added)

The "old self," reflective of the life of the Ephesian Christians before they were saved, is provided its anchor point with the term "your former manner of life." This is used to set the comparison of the pre-salvation and post-salvation Ephesians. The way of life pursued by the Ephesians before and after salvation is different. Before, the manner of life (ἀναστροφή) was the environment in which the corrupt and sinful "old self" developed. That is gone; the new manner of life is enveloped in holiness.

Similar usage is found in the *Letter of Aristeas*:

> "You observe," he said, "the important matter raised by *modes of life* and relationships, inasmuch as through bad relationships men become perverted, and are miserable their whole life long; if, however, they mix with wise and prudent

---

[18] BDAG, p. 73. Occurs 13x in NT, only here in PE. Notably, six of the other occurrences of ἀναστροφή are in First Peter, two more of them in Second Peter.

> companions, they rise above ignorance and achieve progress in life. (*Let. Arist.* 130, emphasis added)

In First Timothy, ἀναστροφή has to do with the general manner in which one lives. The immediate context is that of a list. Paul notes areas in which Timothy is to be a positive example to the believers in Ephesus knowing that the example will provide a pattern for others to follow. This is reminiscent of a verse in the epistle to the Hebrews:

> Remember your leaders, who spoke the word of God to you; considering the outcome of their *way of life*, imitate their faith. (Heb 13:7, emphasis added)

Timothy must be aware that he is to provide an example in the way he lives and physically interacts with the Ephesian community.

in love: Timothy is also to model Christian love, which is unsurprising given Paul's frequent association of the faith and love.[19] In 1Ti 1:5, love is exemplified through practice of a "sincere faith" in addition to a "pure heart" and "good conscience."[20]

in faith: The faith Paul mentions is a sincere faith. It is one of his goals for the Ephesian community, and Timothy is to provide an example of it.[21]

in purity: The word translated "purity" is ἁγνεία, which has to do with 'the quality of moral purity.'[22] This word is used just a few verses later in First Timothy:

> Do not rebuke an older man, but appeal to him as a father, younger men as brothers, older women as mothers, younger women as sisters, with all *purity*. (1Ti 5:1–2, emphasis added)

The motives for Timothy's actions toward younger women must be pure and blameless, unable to be construed in an untoward manner.[23] Though the NT witnesses of ἁγνεία are limited, it does occur with some frequency outside of the NT. *First Clement* is one example:

> Let them demonstrate the habit of *purity* worthy of love. Let them display the innocent will of their gentleness. Let them make evident the gentleness of their speech by their silence. Let them give their love devoutly, not according to partiality but equally to all who fear God. (*1Cl* 21.7, emphasis added)

---

[19] Also associated with hope, cf. 1Co 13:13.

[20] See comment on 1Ti 1:5.

[21] See comment on 1Ti 1:5.

[22] BDAG, p. 12. Occurs 2x in NT: 1Ti 4:12; 5:2.

[23] See comment on 1Ti 5:2 for more detail.

In *First Clement*, ἁγνεία is used to describe a characteristic that is proper for wives of believing men to display. The word occurs in Polycarp's *Epistle to the Philippians*, directed toward young men:

> Likewise also, the younger men must be blameless in all things; above all being concerned about *purity* and holding themselves in check from all evil. For it is good to abstain from sinful passions in the world because all sinful passion wages war against the spirit, and neither the sexually immoral, nor the passive homosexual partner, nor the dominant homosexual partner will inherit the kingdom of God; nor those who engage in perversity. Therefore it is necessary to refrain from all these things, being subject to the presbyters and deacons as to God and Christ. The virgins must conduct themselves with a blameless and *pure* conscience. (Poly., *Phil.* 5.3, emphasis added)

In the above three cited references, chastity somehow plays a role in the development or confirmation of purity. Polycarp in particular defines blamelessness and purity through abstention from "the passions of the world." These passions are then listed, and all of them have a sexual connotation. Earlier in his epistle, Polycarp echoes *First Clement*, using ἁγνεία along with the words for "love" and "faith":

> Then also teach your wives to walk in the faith given to them, and in love and *in purity*, feeling affection for their own husbands in all fidelity and loving all others equally in all chastity, and to instruct their children with the instruction of the fear of God. (Poly., *Phil.* 4.2, emphasis added)

Polycarp advocates that men teach their wives to walk "in love and purity." To do this, women must have the proper levels of love and affection to both husbands and also to others they interact with. Again, purity involves a chasteness and propriety in the physical aspects of all relationships. Ignatius underscores this in his own letter to Polycarp:

> If anyone is able to remain *in purity* to honor the flesh of the Lord, let him do so without boasting. If he boasts, he has been lost; and if it becomes known to any beyond the bishop, he is ruined. But it is fitting for men and women who marry with the consent of the bishop to make their union, that the marriage may be in accordance with the Lord and not in accordance with lust. Let all things be done for the honor of God. (Ign., *Poly.* 5.2, emphasis added)

Once again, the context involves chastity. If men or women are unable to maintain a "state of purity," marriage is the proper path. This is reminiscent of Paul's words advocating marriage to those unable to control fleshly lusts.[24] Timothy is to model purity; one primary component of that purity is propriety as he interacts with others.

---

[24] cf. 1Co 7:8–9.

VERSE 13

Until I come, pay attention to the public reading, to exhortation, to teaching

The phrase "until I come" is a combination of the conjunction ἕως (meaning 'till' or 'until'[25]) and the word ἔρχομαι, which is a fairly common word with numerous senses and nuances.[26]

"Pay attention to" is a translation of the word προσέχω.[27] Here it is an imperative verb in the second person singular..

Paul has a three item list of practices that Timothy is to pay attention to (or "devote himself" to) as he ministers to the Ephesians: the public reading of Scripture, exhortation, and teaching. Each item in the list is a noun in the dative case.

public reading: This is a translation of the Greek word ἀνάγνωσις, typically meaning 'reading,'[28] though it often has to do with reading aloud. Consider its use in Acts:

> So after *the reading* from the law and the prophets, the rulers of the synagogue sent word to them, saying, "Men and brothers, if there is any message of exhortation by you for the people, say it." (Ac 13:15, emphasis added)

The use in Second Corinthians is similar:

> But their minds were hardened. For until this very day, the same veil remains upon *the reading* of the old covenant, not being uncovered, because it is done away with in Christ. (2Co 3:14, emphasis added)

Similar usage occurs in 1 Esdras:

> when he unbound the law, they all stood straight and Azariah blessed the Most High, Almighty God. And all the multitude shouted, "Amen, amen!" And lifting up their hands and falling upon the ground they worshiped God. The Levites Joshua and Anniuth and Sherebiah, Jadinus, Iarsouboos, Abtaios, Hodiah, Maiannas and Kalitas, Azariah, Katethzabdos, Hanan, and Pelaiah were teaching the law of the Lord and reading the law of the Lord to the multitude, putting meaning into *the reading* at the same time. (1Esd 9:46–48, emphasis added)

---

[25] BDAG, p. 422.

[26] BDAG, p. 393.

[27] See comment on 1Ti 4:1. Note also that the object of this verb is a dative noun, much like the instance in 1Ti 4:1.

[28] BDAG, p. 61. Occurs 3x in NT: Ac 13:15; 2Co 3:14; 1Ti 4:13.

Here the picture is of Ezra reading the law aloud to the multitude, with assistants translating what Ezra has read (which was in Hebrew) to Aramaic, which the people would understand. The reading of the law was aloud, to the gathered multitude.[29]

exhortation: This is a translation of the Greek word παράκλησις, which means 'encouragement' or 'exhortation.'[30] Consider the use of the same word in First Thessalonians:

> For our *exhortation* is not from error or from impurity or with deceit, but just as we have been approved by God to be entrusted with the gospel, thus we speak, not as pleasing people but God, who examines our hearts. (1Th 2:3–4, emphasis added)

Here παράκλησις refers to the content of the plea Paul makes to the Thessalonians. He prods the Thessalonians to recall the gospel, and to recall his presentation and manner of living among them. He desires the Thessalonians to recall the substance of his preaching, and then to react. Similar use is found in Hebrews:

> And have you completely forgotten *the exhortation* which instructs you as sons? "My son, do not make light of the Lord's discipline, or give up when you are corrected by him. For the Lord disciplines the one whom he loves, and punishes every son whom he accepts." (Heb 12:5–6, emphasis added)

In Hebrews, the substance of the exhortation is included. The exhortation consists of a reminder of the discipline of the Lord, and the motives for such discipline. Exhortation also seems to have a sense of urgency; encouraging the recipient to a recommended course of action. An example from Josephus shows this:

> But then Salome and Alexas, before the king's death was made known, dismissed those that were shut up in the hippodrome, and told them that the king ordered them to go away to their own lands, and take care of their own affairs, which was esteemed by the nation a great benefit; and now the king's death was made public, when Salome and Alexas gathered the soldiery together in the amphitheatre at Jericho; and the first thing they did was, they read Herod's letter, written to the soldiery, thanking them for their fidelity and good will to him, and *exhorting them* to afford his son Archelaus, whom he had appointed for their king, like fidelity and good will (Jos., *Ant.* 17.193–194, emphasis added).

---

[29] Based on NT (all instances cited above) and LXX usage (see also Sirach prologue and Ne 8:8), ἀνάγνωσις appears to refer to public reading of the Law and Prophets as delineated in the Hebrew Bible; though usage in the Apostolic Fathers and OT Pseudepigrapha are not as restricted.

[30] BDAG, p. 766. Occurs 29x in NT; only here in PE.

The letter from Herod exhorts soldiers to transfer the "fidelity and good will" enjoyed by Herod to Herod's son, Archelaus. The exhortation is a request for action on the part of those hearing.

In this instance in First Timothy, exhortation has to do with encouraging or prodding someone or some group along toward an end or goal. Paul wants Timothy to exhort the Ephesians to proper doctrine.

teaching: Paul also desires Timothy to be devoted to teaching. The Greek word is διδασκαλία, which occurs frequently in the Pastoral Epistles as sound teaching is a primary theme.[31]

---

[31] See comment on 1Ti 1:10 regarding "sound doctrine."

Exercise Your Gifts Publicly and with Purpose (1Ti 4:14–16)

> *Do not neglect the gift that is in you, that was granted to you through prophecy with the laying on of hands by the council of elders. Practice these things. Be diligent in these things, in order that your progress may be evident to everyone. Fix your attention on yourself and on your teaching. Continue in them, for by doing this you will save both yourself and those who hear you. (1Ti 4:14–16)*

Verse 14

Do not neglect

The word translated "do … neglect" is the Greek word ἀμελέω, glossed as 'to neglect' or 'be unconcerned.'[1] This instance is in the imperative. Matthew's gospel uses this word:

> Again he sent other slaves, saying, 'Tell those who have been invited, "Behold, I have prepared my dinner; my oxen and fattened cattle have been slaughtered, and everything is ready. Come to the wedding celebration!" ' But *they paid* no *attention* and went away—this one to his own field, that one to his business. And the others, seizing his slaves, mistreated them and killed them. (Mt 22:4–6, emphasis added)

The invitation is disregarded. Though a viable opportunity, it is deemed unworthy of attention and ignored. Similar usage occurs in the epistle to the Hebrews, this time in regard to salvation:

> For if the word spoken through angels was binding and every transgression and act of disobedience received a just penalty, how will we escape if we *neglect* so great a salvation which had its beginning when it was spoken through the Lord and was confirmed to us by those who heard, while God was testifying at the same time by signs and wonders and various miracles and distributions of the Holy Spirit according to his will. (Heb 2:2–4, emphasis added)

Polycarp uses ἀμελέω in a discussion of the role of presybters (overseers):

---

[1] BDAG, p. 52. Occurs 4x in NT: Mt 22:5; 1Ti 4:11; Heb 2:3; 8:9.

> And the presbyters also must be compassionate, merciful to all, turning back those who have gone astray, caring for all sick, *neglecting* neither widow or orphan or the poor, but always taking thought for the good before God and people, refraining from all anger, partiality, unjust judgment, being far removed from all love of money, not quickly believing against anyone, not relentless in judgment, understanding that we are all debtors in the matter of sin. (Poly., *Phil.* 6.1, emphasis added)[2]

Polycarp's usage is helpful because he provides contrast to neglect of "the widow, the orphan, or the poor" with the positive view "always taking thought for what is good before both God and others." Instead of neglecting, the presbyter is to care for those who need the attention.

Likewise, Paul exhorts Timothy not to ignore or disregard the gift he has been given. Instead, Timothy is to develop his gift through use.

the gift that is in you

The word translated "gift" is χάρισμα, glossed as 'favor bestowed' or 'gift.'[3] Paul also uses χάρισμα in Second Timothy:

> for which reason I remind you to rekindle the *gift* of God that is in you through the laying on of my hands. For God has not given us a spirit of cowardice, but of power and love and self-discipline. (2Ti 1:6–7, emphasis added)

In both instances of χάρισμα in the Pastoral Epistles, the gift is provided from God through the laying on of hands (discussed below). The gift itself is something that comes from God and is useful to Timothy in ministry. These sorts of gifts are detailed by Paul in Romans 12 and 1 Corinthians 12. These passages use the body as a metaphor, with different gifts in the church analogous to different parts of the body. *First Clement* uses a similar metaphor in chapters 37 and 38. In the midst of the development of that metaphor, Clement writes:

> Therefore let our whole body be saved in Christ Jesus, and let each of us be subject to his neighbor, according to the *gift* given to him. (*1Cl* 38.1, emphasis added)

These gifts from God, recognized by the leaders of the fellowship, are intended to be used for the edification and health of the fellowship.

---

[2] Note also Ign., *Poly.* 4.1, which also uses ἀμελέω to urge non-neglect of widows.

[3] BDAG, p. 1081. Occurs 17x in NT, 2x in PE: 1Ti 4:14; 2Ti 1:6. See also TDNT (9:402) and EDNT (3:460) for further discussion of χάρισμα.

that was granted to you through prophecy

The Greek word translated "prophecy" is προφητεία, which here has to do with 'inspired statements by Christian prophets' or, more generally, 'prophecy.'[4] The term "prophecy" is somewhat confusing to modern minds; typically read as meaning some sort of future-telling. This, to be sure, is a component of prophecy in general. But it need not always be part of specific prophecy. In a Christian context, prophecy is, very simply, speaking the word of God. God spoke to his prophet (e.g. Isaiah); the prophet then relayed the message of God to the people. One example of the word used in this sense is found in First Thessalonians:

> Do not despise *prophecies*, but examine all things; hold fast to what is good. (1Th 5:20–21, emphasis added)

In First Thessalonians, Paul urges the Thessalonians to test "prophecies" they have received. If someone claims to be a prophet and then claims to speak prophecy (a word from God) then that word should be tested. The result of the test will either confirm that it is to be acted upon or confirm that it is to be ignored.

Timothy's gift, most likely that of teaching and perhaps leadership, are not to be forgotten but used. These gifts, says Paul, were given to Timothy "by prophecy." Timothy's possession of these skills was announced by prophecy and confirmed by witness of Paul.

with the laying on of hands

This text speaks of a gift conferred upon Timothy by a council of elders (see below) at an earlier point in time[5] by the laying on of hands. The phrase "laying on" comes from the Greek word ἐπίθεσις.[6] Paul uses it in his second epistle to Timothy as well, in similar context:

> for which reason I remind you to rekindle the gift of God that is in you through the *laying on of my hands*. For God has not given us a spirit of cowardice, but of power and love and self-discipline. (2Ti 1:6–7, emphasis added)

In both cases (1Ti 4:14 and 2Ti 1:6) the gift to Timothy is a result of the laying on of hands. The same word (along with "hands") occurs in Acts, as part of the commissioning of the original seven deacons:

---

[4] BDAG, p. 889.

[5] Referred to by Paul in 1Ti 1:18, see comment there.

[6] BDAG, p. 371. Occurs 4x in NT: Ac 8:18; 1Ti 4:14; 2Ti 1:6; Heb 6:2.

> So, brothers, select from among you seven men of good reputation, full of the Spirit and wisdom, whom we will put in charge of this need. But we will devote ourselves to prayer and to the ministry of the word." And the statement pleased the whole group, and they chose Stephen (a man full of faith and of the Holy Spirit), and Philip, and Prochorus, and Nicanor, and Timon, and Parmenas, and Nicolaus (a convert from Antioch), whom they stood before the apostles. And they prayed and *placed their hands on* them. (Ac 6:3–6, emphasis added)[7]

The phrase "laying on of hands" was used in similar ceremonial contexts outside of the NT. Philo uses these same Greek words when describing Jacob's blessing of Joseph's sons, Ephraim and Manasses:

> Again, why did the same Jacob when Joseph brought him his two sons, the elder being Manasses and the younger Ephraim, change his hands, and put his right hand upon the younger brother Ephraim, and his left hand upon the elder brother Manasses? And when Joseph thought this a grievous thing, and thought that his father had unintentionally made a mistake in the matter of *the imposition of hands*, Jacob said, "I did not make a mistake, but I knew, my son, I knew that this one should be a father of a nation, and should be exalted; but, nevertheless, his younger brother shall be greater than he." (Philo, *Alleg. Interp.* III 90, emphasis added)[8]

Usage here in First Timothy is similar. The laying on of hands signals an official or ceremonial act. In this case, the act is that of commissioning Timothy for ministry.

by the council of elders

The prophecy (see above) took place, according to Paul, "the council of elders" laid their hands on Timothy. "Council of elders" is a translation of the Greek word πρεσβυτέριον. It has to do with an assembly of leaders or older men. In the NT, the only other usage is in Lukan material:

> And when day came, the *council of elders* of the people gathered, both chief priests and scribes, and they led him away to their Sanhedrin, saying, "If you are the Christ, tell us!" But he said to them, "If I tell you, you will never believe, and if I ask you, you will never answer! (Lk 22:66–68, emphasis added)

> I persecuted this Way to the death, tying up and delivering to prison both men and women, as indeed the high priest and the whole *council of elders* can testify about me, from whom also I received letters to the brothers in Damascus, and was

---

[7] Also cf Ac 8:14–19 and Heb 6:2.

[8] See Ge 48 for Biblical account.

> traveling there to lead away those who were there also tied up to Jerusalem so that they could be punished. (Ac 22:4–5, emphasis added)

In both of these instances, the word πρεσβυτέριον is used in reference to the body known as the Sanhedrin.[9] Therefore πρεσβυτέριον has to do with an overseeing body of some sort, authoritative in judgment. In addition to NT instances, πρεσβυτέριον occurs frequently in the letters of Ignatius,[10] which is not surprising given his emphasis on church order.

VERSE 15

Practice these things

The word translated "practice" is the Greek word μελετάω. Here it means 'practice,' 'cultivate,' or 'take pains with.'[11] Paul desires Timothy and those reading the letter to not skip over the things mentioned in verses 12–14, but to do them. The sense is not that of "practicing" these things until they become perfected, but of doing them. This same word is used in the similar context of the closing lines of the *Epistle of Barnabas*:

> But if there is any remembrance of good, remember me when *thinking about these things*, that even my desire and watchfulness might come to some good. I implore you, asking your kindness. (*Ep. Barn.* 21.7, emphasis added)

The author of the letter provided instruction; at the close of the letter he is desirous that those reading it will heed his call. Paul urges the same heeding from those reading this letter to Timothy.

be diligent in these things

The word translated "be diligent in" is the multifaceted verb εἰμί. In general, the verb means "to be." It is an imperative here; the sense is that of an instruction to Timothy to "be" in these things. This phrase reiterates Paul's desire that his words and instructions are practiced. The word εἰμί is used similarly of hymns by Josephus:

> But the Hebrews were not able to contain themselves for joy at their wonderful deliverance, and destruction of their enemies. Now indeed, supposing themselves firmly delivered, when those that would have forced them into slavery were destroyed, and when they found they had God so evidently for their protector;

---

[9] BDAG, p. 861.

[10] Ign., *Eph.* 2.2; 4.1; 20.2; *Magn.* 2.1; 13.1; *Trall.* 2.2; 7.2; 13.2; *Phld.* 4.1; 5.1; 7.1; *Smyrn.* 8.1; 12.2

[11] BDAG, p. 627. Occurs 2x in NT: Ac 4:25; 1Ti 4:15.

> and now these Hebrews having escaped the danger they were in, after this manner, and besides that, seeing their enemies punished in such a way as is never recorded of any other men whomsoever, were all the night *employed* in singing of hymns, and in mirth. Moses also composed a song unto God, containing his praises, and a thanksgiving for his kindness, in hexameter verse.(Jos., *Ant.* 2.344, emphasis added)

In the excerpt from Josephus, the idea is that the Hebrews were occupied all the night through in singing hymns and mirth. The Greek text just uses the word εἰμί to indicate this. Paul's use is similar; he requires Timothy and those who read the letter to themselves "be" in what he has commanded; hence "devote yourself."

in order that your progress may be evident to everyone

The word translated "evident" is the Greek word φανερός, an adjective meaning 'visible,' 'clear' or 'evident.'[12] Paul uses the word in his epistle to the Galatians:

> Now the deeds of the flesh are *evident*, which are sexual immorality, impurity, licentiousness, idolatry, sorcery, enmity, strife, jealousy, outbursts of anger, selfish ambition, dissension, factions, envy, drunkenness, carousing, and things like these, things which I am telling you in advance, just as I said before, that the ones who practice such things will not inherit the kingdom of God. (Ga 5:19–21, emphasis added)

These things do not simply happen to be seen, they are obvious for all to see; they are "evident." This word also occurs in the *Epistle of Barnabas*:

> And for this reason, things happening thus are *evident* to us but are obscure to them because they do not listen to the voice of the Lord. (*Ep. Barn.* 8.7, emphasis added)

Once again, φανερός is not reflective of the act of witnessing or seeing something; it communicates that the object or trait is immediately evident.

In this example from First Timothy, Paul desires that the "progress" be evident to all. The Greek word is προκοπή, indicating 'progress,' 'advancement,' or 'furtherance.'[13] This word also occurs in Paul's letter to the Philippians:

> And because I am convinced of this, I know that I will remain and continue with all of you for your *progress* and joy in the faith, so that what you can be proud of may increase in Christ Jesus because of me through my return again to you. (Php 1:25–26, emphasis added)

---

[12] BDAG, p. 1047. Occurs 18x in NT; only here in PE.

[13] BDAG, p. 871. Occurs 3x in NT: Php 1:12; 25; 1Ti 4:15.

This instance from Philippians comments on progress in the faith. The idea is that of advancement in some sort of intangible area. An example from a papyrus housed in the Rylands library may provide further light regarding the meaning of προκοπή in this instance:

> I pray, my lord, that I may see your further *advancement* and ripe prosperity.[14]

Paul contends that if Timothy seriously applies himself and does the things recommended in verses 12–14, that he will progress such that there will be noticeable fruit.

Verse 16

Fix your attention on yourself and your teaching

The phrase "fix your attention" is a translation of the Greek word ἐπέχω, here used with the sense of 'hold toward' or 'aim at.'[15] Similar usage occurs in Acts:

> And a certain man was being carried who was lame from birth. He was placed every day at the gate of the temple called "Beautiful," so that he could ask for charitable gifts from those who were going into the temple courts. When he saw Peter and John about to go into the temple courts, he began asking to receive alms. And Peter looked intently at him, together with John, and said, "Look at us!" So *he fixed his attention* on them, expecting to receive something from them. (Ac 3:2–5, emphasis added)

In this instance in Acts, the lame man, after being instructed by Peter, focuses upon Peter and John. This was not a casual glance, but involved intentional action on the part of the lame man to keep his attention upon Peter and John. He did this in expectation of a gift.

The usage in First Timothy is another instance of an imperative verb. Paul exhorts Timothy to be mindful of his own actions and also of what he is teaching. The translation BDAG provides for this phrase, "take pains with yourself,"[16] is helpful. Paul wants Timothy to intently focus on his own actions and the substance of his teaching so that others may benefit.

---

[14] P.Ryl. II.233.16, cited in M-M p. 542. Greek text is: εὔχομαί σε τὸν κύριον ἰδεῖν ἐν μείζοσι προκοπαῖς, ἐν ἁδραῖς εὐημερίαις.

[15] BDAG, p. 362. Occurs 5x in NT: Lk 14:7; Ac 3:5; 19:22; Php 2:16; 1Ti 4:16.

[16] BDAG, p. 362.

The word translated "teaching," is the same word used three times previously in this chapter (cf. vv. 1, 6, and 13), διδασκαλία.[17]

Continue in them

The Greek word ἐπιμένω is translated "continue in." The sense here is to 'continue' or 'persevere,'[18] doing the same thing over a period of time. A similarly structured passage using ἐπιμένω is found in Josephus' *Antiquities*:

> But although Solomon was become the most glorious of kings, and the best beloved by God, and had exceeded in wisdom and riches those that had been rulers of the Hebrews before him, yet *did not he persevere in this* happy state till he died. Nay, he forsook the observation of the laws of his father, and came to an end no way suitable to our foregoing history of him. (Jos., *Ant.* 8.190, emphasis added)

The pronoun is different (τούτοις in Josephus, αὐτοῖς in First Timothy), but they are both dative plurals. They both refer to items stated previously. In Josephus, the antecedent is Solomon's state of exceeding wisdom, riches and belovedness. In First Timothy, the antecedent involves the "these things" of verse 15.

for by doing this

This simple phrase reiterates the action Paul has focused on in the preceding verses; providing rationale for being so diligent and intentional in life and doctrine. The phrase transitions from instruction to the result of the instruction.

you will save both yourself and those who hear you

The phrase "you will save" is a translation of the Greek word σῴζω[19] Here, as in every other instance in the Pastoral Epistles, σῴζω refers to salvation in a Christian sense; the saving of one's soul from eternal damnation.

The entire phrase "you will save both yourself and those who hear you" is curious. Timothy is not in control of the eternal destiny of those who may happen to hear him in any context at any time. This instead applies to the sound teaching that Paul has been exhorting Timothy to both preach and adhere to. Timothy is the conduit through which the message that saves will be proclaimed. The message (the sound teaching) is the message that will save those who truly hear it.

---

[17] See note on 1Ti 1:10.

[18] BDAG, p. 375. Occurs 16x in NT, only here in PE.

[19] See comment on 1Ti 1:15 for further discussion on the word σῴζω.

Similar phrases occur in other writings of this era, particularly in the writings of Ignatius:

> Do not be deceived, my brothers; destroyers of families will not inherit the kingdom of God. Therefore if those who do this according to the flesh die, how much more if someone corrupt the faith of God with evil teaching, for which Jesus Christ was crucified! Such a person, having made himself foul, will go to the unquenchable fire; *so too the one who listens to him.* (Ign., *Eph.* 16.1–2, emphasis added)

Here, Ignatius notes that the one who teaches heresy will negatively influence the listener, condemning the listener in the process. This idiom occurs with some frequency in the document known as *Second Clement*:

> And if they alone were doing these things, it would be bearable, but now they persist teaching evil to innocent souls, not knowing that they will receive a double punishment, *both themselves and those who listen to them.* (*2Cl* 10.5, emphasis added)

> And I do not think that I have given unimportant advice about self control. Whoever does it will not regret it, *but also will save himself and I who advise him.* For it is no small reward to return a wandering and perishing soul to salvation. (*2Cl* 15.1, emphasis added)

> So then, brothers and sisters, with the God of truth, I am reading to you a request to pay attention to what is written, *that you may save both yourselves and your reader.* For the reward I ask you to repent with *your* whole heart, giving yourselves salvation and life. For having done this, we will set a goal for all the younger ones who desire to devote themselves to the piety and the goodness of God. (*2Cl* 19.1, emphasis added)

The same idiom occurs later, in the document known as the *Life of Polycarp*, punctuating the effect of the ministry of Polycarp as bishop of Smyrna:

> Thus speaking in this way from time to time, and being persistent in his teaching, he edified and *saved both himself and his hearers.* (*Life of Polycarp* 25)

The meaning of this idiom is plain: The teacher has responsibility to properly and accurately teach the gospel of Jesus Christ. Those who hear the teacher will, if sincere, apply what they have been taught. Therefore the teacher has special responsibility to ensure proper doctrine, as his understanding affects not only himself but also those who hear him and adhere to his teaching.

RELATIONS WITHIN THE FELLOWSHIP (1TI 5:1–2)

> *Do not rebuke an older man, but appeal to him as a father, younger men as brothers, older women as mothers, younger women as sisters, with all purity. (1Ti 5:1–2)*

VERSE 1

Do not rebuke an older man

The word translated "rebuke" is the Greek word ἐπιπλήσσω. This is the only occurrence of ἐπιπλήσσω in the New Testament. The word is typically translated 'rebuke' or 'reprove.'[1] Philo uses the word in a discussion concerning Genesis 30:

> And he is but a foolish person who thinks that any thing is in true reality made out of the mind, or out of itself. Do you not see that even in the case of Rachel (that is to say of outward sensation) sitting upon the images, while she thought that her motions came from the mind, he who saw her *reproved* her. For she says, "Give me my children, and if you give them not to me I shall die." And he replied: "Because, O mistaken woman, the mind is not the cause of any thing, but he which existed before the mind; namely God." On which account he adds: "Am I equal to God who has deprived you of the fruit of your womb?" (Philo, *Alleg. Interp. II* 46, emphasis added)

The word ἐπιπλήσσω is used to convey the idea that God reproved or rebuked Rachel through withholding children from her womb. It was some sort of punishment or judgment. Josephus uses the word as well:

> With this intention [Jacob] went to the well, and desired the maidens to give him some water to drink; but while the others refused, on pretense that they wanted it all at home, and could spare none for him, one only of the company *rebuked* them for their peevish behavior towards the stranger; and said, What is there that you will ever communicate to anybody, who have not so much as given the man some water. (Jos., *Ant.* 1.246, emphasis added)

---

[1] BDAG, p. 377. This is an NT *hapax.*

Josephus uses ἐπιπλήσσω in his account of this story[2] to describe how Rebekah chided the other women drawing water at the well for refusing to draw water for Jacob and his animals.

In First Timothy, ἐπιπλήσσω has much the same sense of rebuke; though the context is negative. Instead of directly rebuking, Timothy is to gently correct.

The Greek word translated "an older man" is πρεσβύτερος. This word can mean that one is aged, or it may indicate an elder or presbyter.[3] In this case, as the context includes references to different age groups (younger men, older women, and younger women), the sense of "older man" is appropriate. This sort of contrast between older and younger men occurs in Acts:

> 'And it will be in the last days,' God says, 'I will pour out my Spirit on all flesh, and your sons and your daughters will prophesy, *and your young men will see visions, and your old men will dream dreams.* And even on my male slaves and on my female slaves I will pour out my Spirit in those days, and they will prophesy. (Ac 2:17–18, emphasis added)

This contrast between younger and older also occurs in *First Clement*:

> For you did all things impartially, and you walked in the lawful ways of God, being obedient to your rulers and rendering appropriate honor to the *older ones* among you. You instructed the *younger ones* to think both moderate and honorable thoughts. You commanded the women to accomplish all things with a blameless, honorable and pure conscience, feeling appropriate affection for their own husbands and you taught them being in the rule of obedience to manage the things of the household honorably, with all sensibility. (*1Cl* 1.3, emphasis added)

In *First Clement*, the words translated "older" and "young people" are both in the plural, which leads to some potential ambiguity in determining if the groups referred to consist only of males or are mixed. In First Timothy, however, the word is singular and in the dative case. The πρεσβύτερος is an older man; one who is not to be harshly rebuked.

but appeal to him

Instead of rebuking the older man, Timothy is to appeal to him. The word "appeal" is translated from the Greek word παρακαλέω. This word occurs earlier in First Timothy (1:3; 2:1) with the sense of 'exhort' or 'urge.' Here, however, the sense appears to be a bit gentler. The older man is worthy of respect, therefore should be

---

[2] cf. Ge 24:10–28 for the Biblical account of the same episode.

[3] BDAG, p. 862. Occurs 66x in NT, 5x in PE: 1Ti 5:1, 2, 17, 19; Tt 1:5.

respected even when deserving of stiff rebuke. This sense of παρακαλέω is used elsewhere in the New Testament. Paul uses it in First Thessalonians:

> just as you know how we treated each one of you, like a father his own children, exhorting and *consoling* you and insisting that you live in a manner worthy of God, who calls you to his own kingdom and glory. (1Th 2:11–12, emphasis added)

Paul's usage in First Thessalonians is tempered. The appeal is likened to the same way in which a father consoles his children. The same word is also used by Luke:

> But he became angry and did not want to go in. So his father came out and *began to implore* him. But he answered and said to his father, 'Behold, so many years I have served you, and have never disobeyed your command! And you never gave me a young goat so that I could celebrate with my friends! But when this son of yours returned—who has consumed your assets with prostitutes—you killed the fattened calf for him!' (Lk 15:28–30, emphasis added)

In Luke the picture is of the father pleading with his son, not ordering him to do something. The father clearly wants his son to join the feast and urges him to do so, but the father is not pulling rank and ordering the son to join the feast.

Similarly, Timothy is not to "pull rank" and harshly exhort the older men; he is instead to encourage them toward the proper teaching.

as a father

This encouragement is to take place "as [you would appeal to] a father." The word translated "father" is the Greek word πατήρ, typically translated 'father,' referring to one's male parent or to older persons who have provided moral, intellectual or spiritual guidance.[4] In the same way that one would approach a father in need of correction, Timothy is to approach older men of the fellowship.

younger men as brothers

The verb "appeal to" describing how Timothy is to relate to older men, also governs Timothy's action in his relationships with younger men. The relationships described in verses 1–2 comprise a list. The relationship is described in the first element of the list (encourage/correct older men with respect) and then assumed for the balance of the list.

---

[4] BDAG, p. 786. Occurs 413x in NT.

The phrase "younger men" is a translation of the Greek word νέος. Here it is used substantively, not as a simple adjective.[5] The word is used similarly in the epistle to Titus:

> Likewise, exhort the *young men* to be self-controlled, (Tt 2:6, emphasis added)

Similar usage occurs in Polycarp's *Epistle to the Philippians*:

> Likewise also, the *younger men* must be blameless in all things; above all being concerned about purity and holding themselves in check from all evil. (Poly., *Phil.* 5.3a, emphasis added)

The younger men are to be encouraged "like brothers." The word translated "like" is the particle ὡς, with the sense of 'as' or 'like' or 'likewise.' The Greek word ἀδελφός is translated "brothers." Here the meaning is that of a male sibling. The text uses familial relations to direct the type of interaction Timothy is to have with these different groups. Timothy's relationship with older men is to be like that one would have with a father; therefore Timothy's relationship with younger men is to be like the relationship one would have with a brother.

Verse 2

older women as mothers

Paul's list specifying relationships with groups in the fellowship continues, here indicating that Timothy is to be in relationships with older women as if they were mothers to him.

The word translated "older women" is the feminine form of πρεσβύτερος, discussed above. The word translated "mothers" is μήτηρ. The primary meaning of μήτηρ describes the maternal relationship of 'mother' but it can also indicate a relationship like that of a mother.[6] The gospel of John uses μήτηρ in this manner:

> So Jesus, seeing his mother and the disciple whom he loved standing there, said to his mother, "Woman, behold your son!" Then he said to the disciple, "Behold your *mother*!" And from that hour the disciple took her into his own home. (Jn 19:26–27, emphasis added)

Paul uses μήτηρ similarly in Romans, equating Rufus' mother as his own:

---

[5] BDAG, p. 669.Occurs 24x in NT, 6x in PE (4x in this chapter: 1Ti 5:1, 2, 11, 14).

[6] BDAG, p. 649. Occurs 83x in NT, 2x in PE: 1Ti 5:2; 2Ti 1:5.

> Greet Rufus, the chosen one in the Lord, and his *mother* and mine. (Ro 16:13, emphasis added)

Timothy is to interact with older women under the assumption that they are in a motherly relationship with him.

younger women as sisters

The word translated "younger women" is the feminine form of νέος. Here, as above, νέος is used substantively. The word "sisters" is a translation of ἀδελφή. Timothy is to be in relationship with the younger women of the fellowship as if they were sisters of his.

with all purity

This is a prepositional phrase that further qualifies the relationship Timothy is to have with the younger women.[7] Timothy is to guard against false accusations[8] and therefore must be careful in his dealings with younger women of the fellowship.

The word translated "purity" is the Greek word ἁγνεία, meaning 'purity' or even 'chastity.'[9] Earlier in First Timothy (4:12), ἁγνεία was used to specify that Timothy act "in purity" as an example to the Ephesian believers. There, the sense of "purity" is best even though use of ἁγνεία does seem to involve "chastity" to some degree. Here, however, as the relationship is between Timothy and younger women, the sense of chastity plays a larger role. Timothy is to revere and honor these younger women, instructing them and reproving them when necessary. But his involvement with the younger women as a teacher is never to be questioned. He must be diligent and not allow such involvement to spiral into something beyond that of church leader to suppliant.

---

[7] It is possible that the prepositional phrase refers to all four groups, but more likely that it further qualifies the relationship with younger women. Cf. Knight, *The Pastoral Epistles: A Commentary on the Greek Text*, 214.

[8] Which is one of the qualifications of an overseer, cf. notes on 1Ti 3:7 above.

[9] BDAG, p. 12. Occurs 2x in NT, both in PE: 1Ti 4:12; 5:2. See comment on 1Ti 5:2 for further discussion of the word.

Honor True Widows (1Ti 5:3)

Honor widows who are truly widows. (1Ti 5:3)

Verse 3

Honor widows

The Greek word τιμάω, typically meaning 'honor' or 'revere,'[1] occurs here in the second person imperative. The previous instructions to Timothy in the imperative mood, concentrated in 1Ti 4:11–16 and 1Ti 5:1–2, are continued. He is to honor widows. Paul uses τιμάω in Ephesians:

> "*Honor* your father and mother" (which is the first commandment with a promise), "in order that it may be well with you, and you may live a long time on the earth." (Eph 6:2–3, emphasis added)[2]

The word τιμάω is used similarly in Sirach:

> *Honor* a physician for his services with honors,
> for the Lord created him also.
> For healing is from the Most High,
> and he will receive a gift from the king. (Sir 38:1–2, emphasis added)

The same concept appears in Isaiah, only the honor is false:

> And the Lord said, "This people approaches me with their mouth, and with their lips they *honor* me, but their heart remains far from me. And they are pious to me to no avail, teaching human rules and instructions. Because of this, Look! I will continue to change this people, and I will change them, and I will destroy the wisdom of the wise, and I will hide the intelligence of the intelligent." (Is 29:13–14, emphasis added)

The Isaiah passage is quoted in *Second Clement*, after a short discussion on the extent to which the Lord is to be honored:

> And he himself also says, "The one who confesses me before people, I will confess him before my Father." Therefore this is our reward, if only we confess him

---

[1] BDAG p. 1004. Occurs 21x in NT; only here in PE.

[2] This is a quotation of Ex 20:12, which (in the LXX) also uses τιμάω for "honor."

> through whom we are saved. But how do we confess him? By doing what he says and not disobeying his commandments, and by not only *honoring* him with our lips but with our whole heart and with our whole mind. And he also says in Isaiah, "This people *honors* me with their lips, but their heart is far away from me." (*2Cl* 3.2–5, emphasis added)

In the excerpt from *Second Clement*, the extent of true honor is described. Some honor does exist in obedience because obedience clearly shows one's master. But to truly honor involves much more: "by not only honoring him with our lips but with our whole heart and with our whole mind."

Thus, the honor of widows described in First Timothy consists of more than kind words and attitudes; the extent of honor is seen in action.

The word translated "widows" is the Greek word χήρα. The word is generally used to describe a woman whose husband has died, though metaphorical usage (e.g. La 1:1 [LXX]; Re 18:7) is also possible.[3] In the current verse, χήρα is used twice. The first instance uses the general sense, widow.[4] This general sense is well attested throughout the New Testament. A good example is found in Luke:[5]

> And there was a prophetess, Anna the daughter of Phanuel of the tribe of Asher (she was advanced in years, having lived with her husband seven years after her marriage, and herself as a *widow* up to eighty-four years) who did not depart from the temple with fastings and prayers, serving night and day. And at that same hour she approached and began to give thanks to God, and to speak about him to all those who were waiting for the redemption of Jerusalem. (Lk 2:36–38, emphasis added)

Anna lived with her husband for seven years, when he apparently died. She was left as a widow from that point onward; until her death at age 84.[6]

who are truly widows

The concept of "true" widows appears in verses 3, 5 and 16. Only those widows who meet the ecclesial criteria of widowhood qualify for this honor. The word translated

---

[3] BDAG p. 1084. Occurs 26x in NT; 8x in PE, all eight in 1Ti 5: verses 3 (twice), 4, 5, 9, 11, 16 (twice)

[4] The second instance is discussed in the subsequent section, "who are truly widows."

[5] Luke uses the term χήρα several times: Lk 2:37; 4:25, 26; 7:12; 18:3, 5; 20:47; 21:2, 3; Ac 6:1; 9:39; 9:41.

[6] A valid alternate reading would be to read the text as if Anna lived for 84 years as a widow. If that reading is proper, Anna would be well advanced in years with her actual age unknown, having lived 91 years (84 + 7) after being married to her husband.

"truly" is the adverb ὄντως, which typically is translated as 'really,' 'certainly,' or 'in truth.'[7] The word is used similarly in 1Ti 6:19:

> Command those who are rich in this present age not to be proud and not to put their hope in the uncertainty of riches, but in God, who provides us all things richly for enjoyment, to do good, to be rich in good works, to be generous, sharing freely, storing up for themselves a good foundation for the future, in order that they may take hold of what is *truly* life. (1Ti 6:17–19, emphasis added)

In 1Ti 6:17–19, a distinction is made for the rich. They should not focus on physical, material reality (riches) as life, but should focus elsewhere in order to grasp that which is "truly life." Both reflect "life" in some way, but the latter description better reflects "true" life.

A similar distinction is made in the *Epistle to Diognetus*:

> Then you will see, while being upon the earth, that God lives in heaven; then you will begin to speak of the mysteries of God; then you will both love and admire those being punished because they will not deny God; then you will condemn the deceit and the deception of the world, when you know what is the true[8] life in heaven, when you despise the apparent death in this place, when you fear the *true* death, which is kept for those who will be condemned to the eternal fire, which will punish those handed over to it until the end. (*Ep. Diog.* 10.7, emphasis added)

Again, the contrast is made between something that appears to be (physical death) and something that is (eternal death).

Paul uses ὄντως to make a similar distinction on the topic of widows. There are women who have been widowed. There is among them a subset of "true" widows; widows deserving of special attention by the larger community of believers.

Regarding true widows, distinction is made in later verses, particularly verses 4–5:

> But if any widow has children or grandchildren, they must learn to show profound respect for their own household first, and to pay back recompense to their parents, for this is pleasing in the sight of God. But the widow who is one *truly*, and is left alone, has put her hope in God and continues in her petitions and prayers night and day. (1Ti 5:4–5, emphasis added)

The true widow is one without immediate family who has "set her hope on God" and who has committed to and actively partakes in prayer and supplication. Of these true widows, Ignatius writes in his letter to Polycarp:

---

[7] BDAG p. 715. Occurs 10x in NT, 4x in PE: 1Ti 5:3, 5, 16; 6:19

[8] This instance is ἀληθῶς, not ὄντως.

> Do not let the widows be neglected. After the Lord, you yourself be their protector. Let nothing happen without your consent, nor do anything yourself without God, as indeed you do not do. Be firm. (Ign., *Poly.* 4.1, emphasis added)

The church is to care for the true widows, ensuring their daily needs are met. In so doing widows are honored.

FAMILY TO CARE FOR WIDOWS (1TI 5:4–8)

But if any widow has children or grandchildren, they must learn to show profound respect for their own household first, and to pay back recompense to their parents, for this is pleasing in the sight of God. But the widow who is one truly, and is left alone, has put her hope in God and continues in her petitions and prayers night and day. But the one who lives for sensual pleasure is dead even though she lives. And command these things, in order that they may be irreproachable. But if someone does not provide for his own relatives, and especially the members of his household, he has denied the faith and is worse than an unbeliever. (1Ti 5:4–8)

VERSE 4

But if any widow has children or grandchildren

The Greek word translated "children" is τέκνον. Earlier, Paul used τέκνον to describe Timothy as his "genuine child" (cf. 1Ti 1:2). Here, the word is used in its common, literal sense of 'child,'[1] though the translation is "children" as the word is plural. The word translated as "grandchildren" is ἔκγονος, generically meaning 'descendant'[2].

they must learn

The phrase "they must learn" is translated from the Greek verb μανθάνω.[3] Here it is an imperative, used in much the same way earlier in the text:

> A woman *must learn* in quietness with all submission. (1Ti 2:11, emphasis added)

In 1Ti 2:11, the woman is the subject and is therefore the one who learns. Here in v. 4 the widow's progeny ("children and grandchildren") are the subject, they are the ones who are to learn. Specifically, they are to learn "first;" [4] before the church initiates care for the widow, family is to bear the responsibility (cf. Acts 6:1–7).

---

[1] BDAG, p. 994. Occurs 111x in NT, 11x in PE.

[2] BDAG, p. 300. *hapax.*

[3] BDAG, p. 615. Occurs 25x in NT, 7x in PE. See comment on 1Ti 2:11.

[4] In the LEB, "first" comes after "to show profound respect for their own household;" in the Greek it directly follows the verb "they must learn."

to show profound respect for their own household first, and to pay back recompense to their parents

The word translated "to show profound respect" is εὐσεβέω, a verb typically meaning to 'show respect' or 'show devotion.'[5] It is related to words such as εὐσέβεια[6] and εὐσεβῶς,[7] which are traditionally translated as "godly" or "godliness." Both εὐσέβεια and εὐσεβέω are used in the following excerpt from Philo:

> … but they who follow after virtue, placing it above all these things which are earthly and mortal, disregard their strength in their exceeding abundance, using God as the guide to conduct them in their ascent, who proffers to them the produce of the earth for their enjoyment and most profitable use, likening the virtues to fields, and the fruits of the virtues to the produce of the fields, according to the principles of their generation; for from prudence is derived prudent action, and from temperance temperate action, *and from piety pious conduct*, and from each of the other virtues is derived the energy in accordance with it. (Philo, *Worse* 114, emphasis added)

The word "piety" in the quotation from Philo is a translation of εὐσέβεια; "pious conduct" of εὐσεβέω. If εὐσέβεια has to do with piety, then εὐσεβέω has to do with pious action in general or toward others. Caring for one's widowed mother (or grandmother) is therefore one way of showing respect (acting piously); this action shows godliness toward the recipient.

This godliness is said to be shown "to their own household." The "household" is the common word for "house," οἶκος. As it did in 1Ti 3:4, οἶκος here indicates things (family, items, structures) having to do with the house; therefore the household. The family is honored through showing godliness by taking care of the widow's needs.

The phrase "to pay back recompense to their parents" carries similar meaning. The phrase "to pay back recompense" comes from the combination of the Greek words ἀποδίδωμι and ἀμοιβή. The word ἀποδίδωμι here has the sense of 'recompense' or 'render.'[8] It also occurs in Second Timothy:

> Alexander the metalworker did me much harm; may the Lord *pay back to him* according to his deeds, (2Ti 4:14, emphasis added)

---

[5] BDAG, p. 413. Occurs 2x in NT: Ac 17:23; 1Ti 5:4.

[6] Distinctive to the PE as 10 of 15 NT occurrences are in the PE (four of the remaining five are found in 2 Peter). See comment on 1Ti 2:2.

[7] An adverb meaning "godly," occurring only in the PE: 2Ti 3:12; Tt 2:12. Also occurs in Philo, *Eternity* 10.

[8] BDAG, p. 110. Occurs 48x in NT, 3x in PE: 1Ti 5:4; 2Ti 4:8, 14.

As in Second Timothy, the idea here is to give back. The word ἀμοιβή means 'a return' or 'a recompense.'[9] It only occurs here in the NT and represents what is being given back, thus "recompense" is being returned through the service of the child to his parents. These two words occur in close proximity in Josephus' *Antiquities of the Jews*:

> So these spies acknowledged that they owed her thanks for what she had done already, and withal swore *to requite her kindness*, not only in words, but in deeds; (Jos., *Ant.* 5.13, emphasis added)

In Josephus, the context is that of the spies in Canaan at the house of Rahab.[10] The spies, grateful for the assistance they have received, promise to repay Rahab on account of her kind action toward them. They offer to make a return, to pay her back for the goodness she has shown to them.

Paul makes a similar request. Children are to make return to their parents and grandparents; caring for them in their old age. The word translated "parents" comes from the Greek word πρόγονος. The word generally refers to 'ancestors,' 'parents,' or 'forbears,'[11] as it does in 2Ti 1:3:

> I am thankful to God, whom I have served with a clear conscience as my *ancestors* did, when I remember you constantly in my prayers night and day, (2Ti 1:3, emphasis added)

In 1Ti 5:4, πρόγονος refers specifically to living ancestors that require attention and care. Recall that verse 4 begins with the phrase, "If a widow has children or grandchildren ..." These children and grandchildren are to "make return" to the widow by caring for her in her need. The living descendants, not the church, have a primary responsibility to care for widows. If there are no such descendants, the church is to care for the widow if the widow qualifies for such care (cf. 1Ti 5:9–16).

for this is pleasing in the sight of God

Children and grandchildren are to care for their widowed mothers and grandmothers. This is pleasing and acceptable "in the sight of God." A phrase similar to this, "is ... acceptable in the sight of God our Savior," occurs in 1Ti 2:3.[12]

---

[9] BDAG, p. 54. *hapax*.

[10] cf. Joshua 2; 6.

[11] BDAG, p. 867. Occurs 2x in NT, both in PE: 1Ti 5:4; 2Ti 1:3.

[12] See comment on 1Ti 2:3.

VERSE 5

But the widow who is one truly

The word translated "truly" is the Greek adverb ὄντως. It qualifies the word χήρα. A similar phrase is found in 1Ti 5:3, "... who are *truly widows*." Verse 4 contained instructions for the children and grandchildren of widows; verse 5 marks further qualifications of widowhood.

and is left alone

This English phrase "is left alone" is translated from the Greek verb μονόω; here a perfect passive participle with the sense of 'make solitary.'[13] Thus the widow has been made solitary, and is alone. This word is used similarly in Josephus' *Life*:

> for John had chosen the most trusty of those armed men that were about him out of those thousand that he had with him, and had given them orders when he sent them to kill me, having learned that *I was alone*, excepting some of my domestics. (Jos., *Life* 195, emphasis added)

In this instance from Josephus, μονόω is used to show that the author was alone, by himself, with no defense. The qualification "excepting some of my domestics" is made to clarify, though the sense that Josephus was vulnerable without friend or peer is plain.

Josephus uses μονόω in a somewhat different context in his *Antiquities*:

> but she was desirous of having her husband's unreasonable sorrow taken away; accordingly she entreated God to send the angel again, that he might be seen by her husband. So the angel came again by the favor of God, while they were in the suburbs, and appeared to her *when she was alone,* without her husband. She desired the angel to stay so long till she might bring her husband; and that request being granted, she goes to call Manoah. (Jos., *Ant.* 5.280, emphasis added)[14]

Here, μονόω is used to convey that the woman is alone temporarily; the state is not permanent. The woman's husband is not physically present, but he is alive and will be in her presence again. In the interim, she is alone.

The situation with widows in First Timothy is different. These widows are alone; and they will continue to be alone. But the perpetuity of their state of aloneness is not determined from the Greek word; it is determined from the context: They are widows

---

[13] BDAG, p. 659. NT *hapax.*

[14] This is from Josephus' description of the story of Manoah; cf. Jdg 13.

with no surviving family. They are truly widows, left all alone, and thus require assistance and care.

has put her hope in God

A phrase similar to this is used earlier in 1Ti 4:10: "... because we have put our hope in the living God." In 4:10, the context is that of providing reason for the toil and struggle of the Christian. In 5:5, the context is similar, providing further qualification of the true widow. The true widow is one who has put her hope in God.[15]

and continues in her petitions and prayers night and day

This phrase is a continuation of the previous phrase. The true widow prays. The word translated "continues" is the Greek word προσμένω. Here the sense is that of 'remain/stay with.'[16] The word also occurs in 1Ti 1:3, but here the sense is slightly different as προσμένω is used with a thing (petitions and prayers) instead of a place (Ephesus). An instance of προσμένω in Acts has comparable usage:

> And after the synagogue had broken up, many of the Jews and the devout proselytes followed Paul and Barnabas, who were speaking to them and were persuading them *to continue* in the grace of God. (Ac 13:43, emphasis added)

In Acts, continuing "in grace" is urged. In First Timothy, widows are to continue in "petitions and prayers." The underlying words are δέησις and προσευχή. Similar language occurs in 1Ti 2:1[17] with Paul offering a general exhortation to pray:

> Therefore, I urge first of all that *petitions*, *prayers*, requests, and thanksgiving be made on behalf of all people, (1Ti 2:1, emphasis added)

In chapter 2, Paul uses four different words that describe types of prayer. Here in 1Ti 5:5, Paul, using only two words, does not ignore the other two types of prayer he earlier advocated. In both instances Paul uses very general language to cover the concept of prayer as a whole. Paul uses the terms "petition"[18] and "prayer" in conjunction with each other (and sometimes with other prayer terms) when speaking generally of prayer. Consider the following examples:

---

[15] See comment on 1Ti 4:10.

[16] BDAG, p. 883. Occurs 7x in NT; 2x in PE: 1Ti 1:3; 5:5.

[17] See note on 1Ti 2:1.

[18] An alternate translation could be "supplication."

> with all *prayer* and *supplication* praying at all times in the Spirit, and to this end being alert with all perseverance and supplication for all the saints, (Eph 6:18, emphasis added)

> Be anxious for nothing, but in everything by *prayer* and *supplication* with thanksgiving let your requests be made known to God. (Php 4:6, emphasis added)

Similar language occurs in the epistle to the Hebrews:

> who in the days of his flesh offered up both *prayers* and *supplications*, with loud crying and tears, to the one who was able to save him from death, and he was heard as a result of his reverence. (Heb 5:7, emphasis added)

In 1Ti 5:5, the general sense of praying is more evident due to the inclusion of "night and day." The underlying words are νύξ and ἡμέρα. This phrase is used in a general sense, not an absolute sense.[19] That is, it does not literally mean that through every moment of the night and every moment of the day the widow is making prayers and petitions. Rather, it means that the widow is devoted to prayer. Paul mentions or advocates prayer both "night and day" two other times:

> I am thankful to God, whom I have served with a clear conscience as my ancestors did, when I remember you *constantly in my prayers night and day*, (2Ti 1:3, emphasis added)

> For what thanks can we repay to God concerning you, because of all the joy with which we rejoice because of you before our God, *night and day praying beyond all measure* that we may see your face and complete what is lacking in your faith? (1Th 3:9–10, emphasis added)

Again, Paul does not literally mean that he is in prayer every waking moment of every night and day; he instead means that his prayers, which are frequent, are focused upon the issue at hand. He expects that widows should offer similar devotion in prayer.

Verse 6

But the one who lives for sensual pleasure is dead even though she lives.

In being devoted to prayer, widows should not be devoted to themselves, indulging in items or actions that serve to glorify themselves. The phrase "one who lives for

---

[19] The order may be "night and day" (Mark and the Paulines, generally) or "day and night" (Luke/Acts and Revelation, generally).

sensual pleasure" is translated from the Greek word σπαταλάω, which means 'live luxuriously/voluptuously.'[20] The only other NT instance of σπαταλάω is in James:

> You have lived self-indulgently on the earth and *have lived luxuriously*. You have fattened your hearts in the day of slaughter. (Jam 5:5, emphasis added)

An instance of σπαταλάω occurs in the *Epistle of Barnabas* in the context of explaining how Deuteronomic laws that prohibited certain meats were (in the mind of the author of that epistle) spiritual in nature and not literal:

> Therefore, he mentioned the pig for this reason: you will not be joined, he says, with people such as these, who are like pigs. That is, *when they live luxuriously* they forget the Lord, but when they have need, they acknowledge the Lord, as also the pig when it eats it does not know its owner, but when it is hungry it cries out, and after receiving food, it is silent again. (*Ep. Barn.* 10.3, emphasis added)

The concern here is similar to the concern expressed in 1 Timothy; when one has a lifestyle focused on indulging self, one cannot be devoted to the Lord. Paul's concern is for the widow to be focused on glorifying the Lord through focusing on prayer and supplication.

The widow who is self-indulgent "is dead even though she lives." The Greek word translated "is dead" is the word θνῄσκω; a verb meaning 'to die.'[21] While θνῄσκω is usually used in the context of physical death,[22] here the context is that of non-physical death. The word is used similarly in the *Shepherd of Hermas*:

> So then, you consider yourselves blessed but think you have done a great deed if any of you suffers on account of God. The Lord is graciously giving life to you, and you do not understand, for your sins have burdened you. And if you had not suffered on account of the name of the Lord, *you would have died* to God on account of your sins. (Hermas, *Similitudes* IX, xxviii, 6, emphasis added)

In this instance from Hermas, the death being discussed is the separation from God that comes as a result from sin; it is not death in the physical sense. The context implies that the death is otherwise.

As in Hermas, the context in 1Ti 5:6 requires that the death discussed not be physical because the one to whom death is applied to is said to be dead "even though she lives." This phrase is translated from the Greek word ζάω, here a participle meaning 'to live.'[23] The self-indulgent widow lives in a physical sense, but her soul is dead to

---

[20] BDAG, p. 936. Occurs 2x in NT: 1Ti 5:6; Jam 5:5.

[21] BDAG, p. 457. Occurs 9x in NT, only here in PE.

[22] In the NT, anyway. Cf. Mt 2:20; Mk 15:44; Lk 7:12; 8:49; Jn 11:44; 19:33; Ac 14:19; 25:19.

[23] BDAG p. 424. Occurs 140x in NT.

God. She is the opposite of the widow who offers prayers and supplications both night and day.

VERSE 7

And command these things

Similar phrasing is used earlier in 1Ti 4:11, "Command and teach these things." In 4:11, the content of the commands and teaching followed the phrase. In 5:7 the phrase follows the commands, reiterating their importance.[24] Widows are to be honored (3); surviving family are to provide primary support for widows (4); and widows are to focus their attention on God instead of on their own desires (5–6).

in order that they may be irreproachable

The result of obedience to the command is that they (the widows) will be "irreproachable." The Greek word used is ἀνεπίλημπτος. This same word is used in 1Ti 3:2 as one of the desired qualities for overseers, noting that an overseer "must be irreproachable."[25] The idea is similar here; if the widow follows the commands, she will be above reproach and therefore she qualifies as a true widow.

VERSE 8

But if someone does not provide for his own relatives

The verb is the Greek word προνοέω, here with the sense of 'care for' or 'provide for someone/something.'[26] The word is used in Philo's tractate *De Virtutibus*:

> … for which reason he is the first person who is said to have believed in God, since he was the first who had an unswerving and firm comprehension of him, apprehending that there is one supreme cause, and that he it is *which governs the world by his providence*, and all the things that are therein. (Philo, *Virtues* 216, emphasis added)

In this instance in Philo, προνοέω is used to portray how God cares and governs for the world. In First Timothy, Paul uses the word similarly to show how surviving family is to provide for the widow.

---

[24] See comment on 1Ti 4:11.

[25] See comment on 1Ti 3:2.

[26] BDAG p. 872. Occurs 3x in NT: Ro 12:17; 2Co 8:21; 1Ti 5:8.

The word translated "relatives" is the adjective ἴδιος.[27] Here the adjective has an article, which means it is substantive. The Gospel of John uses ἴδιος with an article a few times: [28]

> He came to *his own* things, and *his own* people did not receive him. (Jn 1:11, emphasis added)[29]
>
> Now before the feast of Passover, Jesus, knowing that his hour had come that he would depart from this world to the Father, and having loved *his own* in the world, loved them to the end. (Jn 13:1, emphasis added)

In John, ἴδιος as an articular substantive represents those who are associated with Jesus; his people. In First Timothy, the structure is used to represent those who are somehow related to or associated with the widow. These are the ones (male or female; the "his" is generic) who would consider the widow as a relative.

and especially the members of his household

While the command is for relatives to care for widowed relatives; the expectations are greater for those who would consider the widow in their own household. The word translated "members of his household" is οἰκεῖος. It is broadly defined as 'persons who are related by kinship or circumstances and form a closely knit group.'[30] The word occurs in the *Martyrdom of Polycarp*:

> And when those searching for him persisted, he moved to a different country house. And immediately upon his departure those searching for him arrived at the first country house and not finding him, they arrested two young slaves, one of whom being tortured confessed. For indeed it was impossible for him to remain hidden, because those who betrayed him *also belonged to his own household.* (*Mart. Poly.* 6.1–2a, emphasis added)

Polycarp's household included those who worked in the house. The primary intent in First Timothy, however, involves those in close relationship with the one widowed. The *Epistle of Barnabas* also uses οἰκεῖος:

---

[27] BDAG, p. 467. Occurs 114x in NT.

[28] Knight, *The Pastoral Epistles : A Commentary on the Greek Text*, 220.

[29] Note the LEB supplies the word "things," a translation I do not agree with. The phrase in question occurs twice in this verse.

[30] BDAG, p. 694. Occurs 3x in NT: Ga 6:10; Eph 2:19; 1Ti 5:8. Note that 1Ti 5:8 is the only NT instance where οἰκεῖος is used with a focus on family relations; Ga 6:10 and Eph 2:19 speak of the "household of God" and "household of faith" respectively.

> But he says to us, "'Behold, this is the fast which I have chosen,' says the Lord, 'loose every bond of unrighteousness, untie the knots of forced agreements, send away the downtrodden in forgiveness, and tear apart every unjust contract. Break your bread with those who hunger, and if you see a naked man, clothe him. Bring the homeless into your house, and if you see someone of low status, do not disregard him, neither your descendants from your *household*.' " (*Ep. Barn.* 3.3, emphasis added)[31]

Here the usage assumes a familial connection; the context of 1Ti 5:8 requires a similar connection.

he has denied the faith and is worse than an unbeliever

The word translated "denied" is the Greek word ἀρνέομαι. Here it has the sense of 'refuse,' 'reject,' or 'decline.'[32] The word is used similarly in Revelation:

> I know where you live, where the throne of Satan is. And you hold fast to my name and did not *deny* your faith in me, even in the days of Antipas my faithful witness, who was killed among you, where Satan lives. (Re 2:13, emphasis added)

In both Re 2:13 and 1Ti 5:8, the faith is what is denied. This speaks of "the faith" as the essential nature of Christianity. The word is used similarly in 1Ti 1:2:

> to Timothy, my true child *in the faith*. Grace, mercy, and peace from God the Father and Christ Jesus our Lord. (1Ti 1:2, emphasis added)

Not only has the faith — the essential nature of Christianity — been denied (the faithful would act to provide for a widowed relative) but the disobedience means that the one who disobeys is "worse than an unbeliever." This phrase is a combination of two words. The word translated "worse than" is χείρων; a comparative adjective.[33] When it occurs, it is typically used to compare two things, noting one thing as worse than the other. The word is also used in Second Timothy:

> And indeed, all those who want to live in a godly manner in Christ Jesus will be persecuted. But evil people and imposters will progress to the *worse*, deceiving and being deceived. (2Ti 3:12–13, emphasis added)

In First Timothy, the one who does not obey the command to honor widows is unfavorably compared to the unbeliever. The word translated "unbeliever" is ἄπιστος.[34] The unbeliever is the one without faith. The word also occurs in Titus:

---

[31] Quotation is based on Is 58:6–7.

[32] BDAG, p. 132. Occurs 33x in NT; 7x in PE.

[33] BDAG, p. 1083. Occurs 11x in NT; 2x in PE: 1Ti 5:8; 2Ti 3:13.

[34] BDAG, p. 103. Occurs 26x in NT, 2x in PE: 1Ti 5:8; Tt 1:15.

> To the pure all things are pure, but to those who are defiled and *unbelieving* nothing is pure, but both their mind and conscience are defiled. (Tt 1:15, emphasis added)

In Titus, as in First Timothy, the one who is ἄπιστος is one who is impure or unbelieving. Indeed, the word is used to indicate the opposite of faithful from early origins. BDAG notes parenthetically that the word is used

> ... in relation to a divine activity as early as SIG 1168, 32 [c. 320 B.C.], a patient sneers in disbelief at healings recorded in a shrine of Asclepius and subsequently receives the sobriquet Ἄπιστος[35]

The complete comparison is effective. Paul's command that widows be honored and that they are provided for by immediate family members leaves no question. The one who fails in this endeavor is in need of repentance.

[35] BDAG, p. 103.

Determining True Widows (1Ti 5:9–10)

Let a widow be put on the list if she is not less than sixty years old, the wife of one husband, being well-attested by good works, if she has brought up children, if she has shown hospitality, if she has washed the feet of the saints, if she has helped those who are oppressed, if she has devoted herself to every good work. (1Ti 5:9–10)

Verse 9

Let a widow be put on the list

The phrase "let … be put on the list" is a translation of the Greek word καταλέγω, which here means 'to make a selection for membership in a group.'[1] In this instance the context shows that the widow is to be enrolled if she meets the subsequently listed criteria. The widow does not petition for acceptance to a group; she is instead included into the group of widows cared for by the church if she is deemed as qualified.

The use of the language of being selected or enrolled implies the existence of a group or list of widows for which the church has taken primary responsibility. The word καταλέγω is used in similar contexts of selection outside of the New Testament:

> But the ruler of the whole nation, infusing into the ears of his people doctrines of piety, and charming the souls of his subjects with them, selected and *picked out* a thousand men of each tribe, choosing them with regard to their excellence, and he bade them to inflict upon the enemy punishment for the treachery which they had contrived by means of the women, when they hoped to destroy the whole multitude by casting them down from the heights of their pure and sublime piety, though, in effect, they were only able to delude those whom I have enumerated. (Philo, *Virtues* 42, emphasis added)

In the above, Philo uses several terms that have to do with selection or calling out, notably the two juxtaposed words "selected" and "picked out." The word translated "picked out" is καταλέγω, the term used in 1Ti 5:9 and translated "let be enrolled." The word translated "selected" is ἐπιλέγω, which has to do with being named or

[1] BDAG, p. 520. NT *hapax*.

counted.[2] In Philo's tractate, these two words combine to portray the whole process. The men from each tribe were distinguished from the others and then assembled into groups.

The First Timothy instance is similar. Qualified widows are assembled into a group that the church takes the responsibility of caring for.[3]

if she is not less than sixty years old

The fact that a woman has been widowed is the primary qualification for the group, but it is not the only qualification. An further qualification has to do with the age of the widow: she must be at least sixty years old in order to qualify for the group of widows. Thus a distinction of need is made between older widows and younger widows.

the wife of one husband

The widow has no one else to care for her; thus she has only had one husband. She is not to have been in a polygamous relationship; the context here demands that one woman and one man have been in a monogamous marriage relationship; the woman has been widowed and thus left alone.[4]

Verse 10

being well-attested by good works

The word translated "being well-attested" is the Greek verb μαρτυρέω. The sense used here is that of 'be well spoken of' or 'be approved.'[5] Deissmann reports:

> This word, especially the participle, is common in the Acts of the Apostles and other early Christian writings, as a designation of honour, *viz., to be well reported of*;[6]

The word is used in this manner in Acts:

---

[2] BDAG, p. 373.

[3] Knight, *The Pastoral Epistles : A Commentary on the Greek Text*, 222–223.

[4] See comment on 1Ti 3:2, "husband of one wife" for further discussion on the phrase in general.

[5] BDAG, p. 618. Occurs 76x in NT, 2x in PE: 1Ti 5:10; 6:13.

[6] Deissmann, *Bible Studies*, 265.

> So, brothers, select from among you seven men *of good reputation*, full of the Spirit and wisdom, whom we will put in charge of this need. (Ac 6:3, emphasis added)

The reputation of the widow must precede her. Her actions and the things that others say about her must be positive and must amount to a good testimony concerning her. This is similar to the qualification for overseers:

> But he must also have a good testimony from those outside, in order that he may not fall into disgrace and the trap of the devil. (1Ti 3:7)

The instance from chapter 3 uses the noun form of the word μαρτυρέω so the parallel is a weak one, but the underlying context and idea is the same: Widows who qualify for enrollment are well thought of by those inside and outside of the fellowship.

The reputation of widows is to be one of "good works." The context is general; some kinds of good works are enumerated next. These kinds of good works are not a specific and exhaustive list; they rather reflect the sorts of good works that widows who qualify for enrollment should find themselves doing.

if she has brought up children

One of the good works that would serve to provide a good reputation for the widow would be if she had raised up children in a proper manner. The Greek word translated "she has brought up children" is τεκνοτροφέω, meaning 'bring up children.'[7] The word is fairly uncommon[8] though its compound nature makes its meaning rather certain. It is a combination of one of the words used for child (τέκνον) and a word used for the rearing of children (τρέφω).

This is somewhat reminiscent of the qualifications for deacon mentioned earlier:

> Deacons must be husbands of one wife, managing their children and their own households well. (1Ti 3:12)

In such circumstances (with widows and with deacons, as well as overseers[9]) the proper upbringing of children is a witness or testimony to the general abilities and nature of the individual who does the upbringing.

---

[7] BDAG, p. 995. NT *hapax.*

[8] Apparently does not occur in LXX, Josephus, Philo, Greek OT Pseudepigrapha or the Apostolic Fathers.

[9] cf. 1Ti 3:4–5.

if she has shown hospitality

The Greek word translated "she has shown hospitality" is ξενοδοχέω. This is a compound word that only occurs here in the NT.[10] The basic meaning is plain, to 'show hospitality.'[11] Again, there are echoes of the qualifications of the overseer:

> Therefore the overseer must be irreproachable, the husband of one wife, temperate, self-controlled, respectable, *hospitable*, skillful in teaching, (1Ti 3:2, emphasis added)

While the same word is not used[12] the idea is similar. One factor in estimating the reputation of the widow (or the overseer, according to 1Ti 3:2) is to examine how she interacts with and treats others.

if she has washed the feet of saints

The Greek word translated "has washed" is νίπτω, meaning to 'wash'[13] in the sense of a partial washing.[14] This word is used several times in similar context in the Gospel of John:

> Then he poured water into the washbasin and began *to wash* the feet of the disciples, and to wipe them dry with the towel which he had tied around himself. Then he came to Simon Peter. He said to him, "Lord, are you going *to wash* my feet?" Jesus answered and said to him, "What I am doing you do not understand now, but you will understand after these things." Peter said to him, "You will never *wash* my feet forever!" Jesus replied to him, "Unless *I wash* you, you do not have a share with me." Simon Peter said to him, "Lord, not my feet only, but also my hands and my head!" Jesus said to him, "The one who has bathed only needs *to wash* his feet, but is completely clean. And you are clean, but not all of you." (Jn 13:5–10, emphasis added)

In John, νίπτω is used both of a literal washing and of a figurative or spiritual washing. The instance in First Timothy likely refers to a literal washing or a washing as figurative extension of hospitality. The context in John indicates that Jesus alone is able to cleanse ceremonially and purely.

---

[10] Like τεκνοτροφέω, it does not seem to occur in LXX, Josephus, Philo, Greek OT Pseudepigrapha or the Apostolic Fathers.

[11] BDAG, p. 684. NT *hapax*.

[12] 1Ti 3:2 uses φιλόξενος, see comments on 1Ti 3:2 for more information.

[13] BDAG, p. 674. Occurs 17x in NT; only here in PE.

[14] TDNT 4:947.

The concept of foot-washing is not unique to the New Testament. There are many references to foot-washing in the LXX (Ge 18:4; 19:2; 43:24; Ex 30:21; Jdg 19:21; 1Sa 25:41; 2Sa 11:8; Song 5:3); some literal and some ceremonial. Several of these instances have to do with extending hospitality. Travelers are lodged at some point on their journey; part of treating them well was to ensure they were able to wash the dirt of the road from their feet, allowing them rest and refreshment. At a minimum, the statement about widows providing good testimony through the washing of feet has to do with offering similar hospitality.

Good testimony is provided through washing the feet "of saints." The word translated "of saints" is the Greek word ἅγιος, here with the sense of 'holy ones,' 'believers,' 'loyal followers,' or 'saints.'[15] Paul uses the word in his letter to the Ephesians:

> Consequently, therefore, you are no longer strangers and foreigners, but you are fellow citizens of *the saints* and members of the household of God, built on the foundation of the apostles and prophets, Christ Jesus himself being the cornerstone, in whom the whole building, joined together, grows into a holy temple in the Lord, (Eph 2:19–21, emphasis added)

In Ephesians, the saints make up the household of God; which is the church. The word ἅγιος occurs with this sense in epistolary salutations as well, with Paul extending greetings to the saints.[16] Therefore, when widows extend hospitality to the saints, likely in lodging those passing through and perhaps even physically washing their feet or similarly providing restful and rejuvenating accommodation,[17] they provide good testimony for themselves.

if she has helped those who are oppressed

The Greek word translated "has helped" is ἐπαρκέω, meaning 'help' or 'aid.'[18] This word occurs twice in v. 16:

> If any believing woman has widows, *she must help* them, and the church must not be burdened, in order that *it may help* those who are truly widows. (1Ti 5:16, emphasis added)

The word has to do with one party extending help or aid to another party. It is used similarly by Josephus:

---

[15] BDAG p. 11; this sense applies particularly to the plural instances. Occurs 233x in NT.

[16] Cf. Ro 1:7; 1Co 1:2; 2Co 1:1; Col 1:4.

[17] As the qualified widows likely have empty houses and are able to lodge itinerant evangelists on short notice and without questions of purity or inappropriateness arising.

[18] BDAG, p. 359. Occurs 3x in NT, all in PE: 1Ti 5:10; 16 (twice).

> So king Herod, when he despaired of the battle, rode up to them to bring them assistance, yet did he not come time enough *to do them any service*, though he labored hard to do it; but the Jewish camp was taken, so that the Arabians had unexpectedly a most glorious success, having gained that victory which of themselves they were no way likely to have gained, and slaying a great part of the enemy's army; (Jos., *Ant.* 15.119, emphasis added)

In this instance, Herod intended to assist in some way but was precluded from so doing. The meaning of ἐπαρκέω is the same; the context shows that the desire was not able to be carried out.

Widows are to care for "those who are oppressed." The word in question is the Greek word θλίβω. In this context, the sense is that of 'oppress' or 'afflict.'[19] The word occurs a few times in the second epistle to the Thessalonians:

> a proof of the righteous judgment of God, so that you may be considered worthy of the kingdom of God, on behalf of which also you are suffering, since it is righteous in the sight of God to pay back those *who are afflicting* you with affliction, and to you *who are being afflicted*, rest with us at the revelation of the Lord Jesus from heaven with his powerful angels, with burning flame giving punishment to those who do not know God and who do not obey the gospel of our Lord Jesus, (2Th 1:5–8, emphasis added)

The word also occurs in Ignatius' *Letter to the Smyrneans*:

> But observe those who hold divisive opinions concerning the grace of Jesus Christ that came to us; how opposed they are to the mind of God. For love does not concern them, no concern for the widow, none for the orphan, none for *the afflicted*, none for the ones imprisoned or the ones set free, none for the hungry or the thirsty. (Ign., *Smyrn.* 6.2, emphasis added)

In Ignatius, the ones "opposed to the mind of God" have nothing to do with serving the needs of those who are afflicted or oppressed. The widow, as the recipient of such service (from either the church or from family members) should be sensitive to the needs of those in similar situations whom she can assist.

if she has devoted herself to every good work

The Greek word translated "has devoted herself" is ἐπακολουθέω, here with the sense of 'follow after' or 'devote oneself.'[20] The word occurs in a similar sense in the LXX of Joshua, here with the decree of the Lord as the object of devotion:

---

[19] BDAG, p. 457. Occurs 10x in NT; only here in PE.

[20] BDAG, p. 358. Occurs 4x in NT; 2x in PE: 1Ti 5:10, 24.

> Because of this, Hebron was Caleb's, the son of Jephunneh the Kenizzite as his share until this day because *he followed* the command of the Lord God of Israel. (Jos 14:14 [LXX], emphasis added).

In Joshua, ἐπακολουθέω is used to show that Caleb not only heard the decree, but had more than casual obedience. He responded and followed the decree.

Widows are called to similar devotion, though the object of the obedience is to do "good works" when the opportunity arises. As with other lists in the Pastoral Epistles, this last item is a catch-all to cover all of the options that would otherwise be impossible to enumerate. Paul does not stipulate that widows, in order to qualify as widows to be cared for by the church, must always do every good work at every opportunity; rather the qualified widow is one that has a life with evidence of good works done for others and a propensity to do good works in the future.

Recommendations for Younger Widows (1Ti 5:11–16)

> *But refuse younger widows, for whenever their physical desires lead them away from Christ, they want to marry, thus incurring condemnation because they have broken their former pledge. And at the same time also, going around from house to house, they learn to be idle, and not only idle, but also gossipy and busybodies, saying the things that are not necessary. Therefore I want younger widows to marry, to bear children, to manage a household, to give the adversary no opportunity for reproach. For already some have turned away and followed after Satan. If any believing woman has widows, she must help them, and the church must not be burdened, in order that it may help those who are truly widows. (1Ti 5:11–16)*

Verse 11

But refuse younger widows

The Greek word translated "refuse" is παραιτέομαι, which has the sense of 'decline,' 'refuse,' 'avoid,' or 'reject;'[1] much like it is used in 1Ti 4:7:

> But *reject* those worthless myths told by elderly women, and train yourself for godliness. (1Ti 4:7, emphasis added)

As Timothy is to refuse involvement with irreverent and silly myths; the church is to refuse enrollment of younger widows even though they may qualify for enrollment on grounds that are not based on age. Paul next lays out his reasons for disqualifying younger widows.

---

[1] BDAG, p. 764. Occurs 12x in NT; 4x in PE: 1Ti 4:7; 5:11; 2Ti 2:23; Tt 3:10. See comment on 1Ti 4:7.

for whenever their physical desires lead them away from Christ

The word translated by the phrase "their physical desires lead them away" is καταστρηνιάω, here having to do with 'be governed by strong physical desire.'[2] Of this compound verb, Knight notes:

> καταστρηνιάζω** (a biblical hapax) is a compound verb composed of στρηνιάζω[3] and κατά, in the sense of "against," which requires that the object be genitive. The meaning of the uncompounded form expresses the strong impulse of sexual desire, which naturally makes such young widows "want to marry."[4]

These intense desires will draw them away from Christ.

they want to marry

The phrase "they want" is a translation of the Greek word θέλω, meaning 'desire,' 'wish,' or 'want.'[5] A similar structure, θέλω with an infinitive verb, occurs earlier in First Timothy:

> *wanting* to be teachers of the law, although they do not understand either the things which they are saying or the things concerning which they are speaking confidently. (1Ti 1:7, emphasis added)

Another instance is in Galatians:

> Tell me, you who *are wanting* to be under the law, do you not understand the law? (Ga 4:21, emphasis added)

In the phrase introduced by θέλω, an infinitive verb signifies the action one desires to do. The infinitive verb, translated "to marry" is γαμέω.[6] For a widow to marry is not seen as a sin; marriage is exactly the recommendation Paul later makes (verse 14). However, it is not acceptable for a widow to make a vow to Christ and then the vow to marry another.

---

[2] BDAG, p. 528. NT *hapax*. BDF §181 glosses as 'become wanton against.'

[3] BDAG form of this word is στρηνιάω (p. 949).

[4] Knight, *The Pastoral Epistles : A Commentary on the Greek Text*, 226.

[5] BDAG, p. 447. Occurs 209x in NT.

[6] BDAG, p. 187. Occurs 28x in NT; 3x in PE: 1Ti 4:3; 5:11, 14.

Verse 12

thus incurring condemnation

The phrase "incur condemnation" is a translation of two Greek words. The first word is a common word, ἔχω, generally meaning 'have.'[7] The second word is κρίμα, here in the sense of 'verdict.'[8] As a result of being drawn away from Christ by intense physical desire and replacing the younger widows' commitment to Christ with a desire to marry, these younger widows become subject to judgment. The widows' actions have a consequence.

because they have broken their former pledge

The word translated "they have broken" is the Greek word ἀθετέω, here with the sense of 'declare invalid,' 'nullify,' or 'ignore.'[9] Polybius uses the word to mean "set at naught a treaty, promise."[10] The word is also used in Galatians:

> I do not *declare invalid* the grace of God, for if righteousness is through the law, then Christ died to no purpose. (Ga 2:21, emphasis added)
>
> Brothers, I am speaking according to a human perspective. Nevertheless, when the covenant of a man has been ratified, no one *declares it invalid* or adds additional provisions to it. (Ga 3:15, emphasis added)

The general idea is to nullify or set aside a previous agreement. The younger widows are in danger of nullifying or setting aside "their former pledge." The word translated "former" is πρῶτος, which has to do with 'first,' 'former,' or 'previous.'[11] The word translated "pledge" is πίστις, here with the sense of 'assurance' or 'oath.'[12] The younger widows have not necessarily committed apostasy and denied their faith and doctrine; they are instead guilty of breaking a pledge or vow they had previously made. They had made an agreement based on trust, and they broke that agreement.

---

[7] BDAG, p. 420. Occurs 626x in NT.

[8] BDAG, p. 567. Occurs 26x in NT, 2x in PE: 1Ti 3:6; 5:11. See comment on 1Ti 3:7.

[9] BDAG, p. 24. Occurs 16x in NT; only here in PE.

[10] Polybius Historicus, 8.36.5; quoted in LSJ, p. 31.

[11] BDAG, p. 892.

[12] BDAG, p. 818.

VERSE 13

And at the same time also, going around from house to house

The Greek word translated "going around" is περιέρχομαι, meaning 'go about.'[13] It is used similarly in Hebrews:

> They were stoned, they were sawed in two, they died by murder with a sword, *they wandered about* in sheepskins, in goatskins, impoverished, afflicted, mistreated, of whom the world was not worthy, wandering about on deserts and mountains and in caves and in holes in the ground. (Heb 11:37–38, emphasis added)

Here περιέρχομαι speaks of prophets and preachers wandering around. Josephus uses the word in his *Antiquities of the Jews*:

> Whereupon the king betook himself to thanksgivings and sacrifices to God; after which he presently *went over* all that country which he ruled round about, and taught the people, as well the laws which God gave them by Moses, as that religious worship was due to him. (Jos., *Ant.* 9.2, emphasis added)

The usage is similar; in the context περιέρχομαι speaks of wide travels. Generally, the scope of περιέρχομαι is not implied in the use of the word but by the context; it need not mean one "goes about" aimlessly or in wide and circuitous routes.

In First Timothy, the scope of travel is "from house to house." The words can be literally translated as "the houses,"[14] οἰκία. It is a common word and here simply means 'house.'[15]

they learn to be idle

The word translated "they learn" is the Greek word μανθάνω, here meaning to 'learn' or 'appropriate to oneself.'[16] In the LEB, "to be" is supplied to ease the translation. The word translated "idle" is ἀργός, here in the sense of 'unemployed' or 'idle.'[17] It occurs in this verse twice; it also occurs in the Gospel of Matthew:

---

[13] BDAG, p. 800. Occurs 3x in NT: Ac 19:13; 1Ti 5:13; Heb 11:37.

[14] As the widows were "going about the houses," a translation of "going around from house to house" is possible and even accurate. For the purposes of this discussion it is important to note that the word "house" (οἰκία) occurs once in the verse, not twice.

[15] BDAG, p. 695. Occurs 93x in NT; 3x in PE: 1Ti 5:13; 2Ti 2:20; 3:6.

[16] BDAG, p. 516. Occurs 25x in NT, 6x in PE. Cf. comments on 1Ti 2:11; 5:4.

[17] BDAG, p. 128. Occurs 8x in NT; 3x in PE: 1Ti 5:13 (2x); Tt 1:12.

> And going out about the third hour, he saw others standing *idle* in the marketplace. (Mt 20:3, emphasis added)

> And about the eleventh hour he went out and found others standing there and said to them, 'Why are you standing here the whole day *unemployed*?' (Mt 20:6, emphasis added)

In the context of Matthew, the ones standing idle were not working and therefore were available to do work. The word also occurs in the *Didache*, in the context of describing how to treat itinerant prophets/preachers who desire to stay among the community for more than a day or two:

> And if he desires to stay with you, being an artisan, let him work and let him earn his keep. And if he has no craft, take this into consideration according to your understanding how he shall live among you as a Christian without *being idle.* (*Did.* 12.3–4, emphasis added)

In the *Didache*, as in Matthew, the one who is idle is the one who is not occupied with work (labor) during the day. He has no vocation or trade and does nothing; he is idle. Similar meaning is used in First Timothy with widows as the ones who are idle.

and not only idle, but also gossipy and busybodies, saying the things that are not necessary

The younger widows, spending their time idly[18] wandering from house to house, engage in other needless pursuits. The Greek word translated "gossipy" is φλύαρος.[19] Josephus uses the word as well:

> but when I was informed of this, I instructed the multitude again, that those who fled to them for refuge ought not to be persecuted: I also laughed at *the allegation* about witchcraft; and told them that the Romans would not maintain so many ten thousand soldiers, if they could overcome their enemies by wizards. (Jos., *Life* 150, emphasis added)

In Josephus, φλύαρος is used to refer to the allegation itself, while in First Timothy, the word is used to describe the unfounded allegations, thus the translation "gossipy."

---

[18] See above on "idle."

[19] BDAG, p. 1060. NT *hapax*.

The younger widows are also described as "busybodies." The Greek word is περίεργος, here meaning 'meddlesome,' 'officious,' or 'curious.' The word is used in the *Testament of Issachar*:

> I was no *meddler* in my dealings, nor was I evil or slanderous to my neighbor. (*T. Iss.* 3.3, emphasis added)

The same word is used in the *Shepherd of Hermas*:

> I asked her about the four colors which the beast had on its head. And answering me she said, "Again you are *meddlesome* about such things?" "Yes," I said, "Lady, explain to me what these things are." (Hermas, *Visions* IV, iii, 1, emphasis added)

In Hermas, περίεργος takes on the meaning of being curious or probing regarding things that one is not directly involved in. The instance in the *Testament of Issachar* is similar, with Issachar protesting that in his actions he had not busied himself with the concern of minor and meaningless portions of the lives of others. In First Timothy, the younger widows are caught up in doing these exact things—busying themselves with minutiae and needless concerns.[20] They have filled their time with needless and harmful pursuits; proceeding from house to house spreading rumors through gossip. These are things that they should not be doing,

VERSE 14

Therefore I want younger widows

The word translated "I want" is the Greek word βούλομαι.[21] In the present context, βούλομαι is followed by an accusative noun ("younger widows") and an infinitive verb ("marry"). This same structure (βούλομαι + accusative noun + infinitive verb) occurs elsewhere in the Pastoral Epistles, notably in 1Ti 2:8:[22]

> Therefore *I want* the men in every place to pray, lifting up holy hands without anger and dispute. (1Ti 2:8, emphasis added)

As in 2:8, Paul expresses his desire, but here for younger widows. There are four things he would have them do; each involving an infinitive verb in the Greek: to

---

[20] A translation of this verse very well could be, "At the same time they learn to be lazy, going around to houses. They are not only lazy (ἀργός) but are also gossipy (φλύαρος) and nosey (περίεργος), talking about things that are not necessary."

[21] BDAG, p. 182. Occurs 37x in NT; 4x in PE: 1Ti 3:8; 5:14; 6:9; Tt 3:8.

[22] See discussion on 1Ti 2:8. The structure also occurs in Tt 3:8.

marry, to bear children, to manage a household, and to give the adversary no opportunity for reproach.

to marry

This is a simple and straightforward translation of the Greek verb γαμέω, 'to marry.'[23] Younger widows will likely want to marry (1Ti 5:11–12), so they should marry instead of make a vow they are likely to break.

to bear children

This is a translation of the Greek verb τεκνογονέω, a compound word meaning to 'bear children' or 'beget children.'[24] The noun form of τεκνογονέω is used in 1Ti 2:15 to mean "childbearing."[25]

to manage a household

This is a translation of the Greek verb οἰκοδεσποτέω.[26] This as well is a compound word, only occurring here in the New Testament. This word has less to do with the sort of household management described in 1Ti 3:4–5 as a responsibility of the overseer and more to do with the active management and doing of day-to-day household affairs. It is more along the lines of what is described in Tt 2:5 as "working at home."

to give the adversary no opportunity for reproach.

The infinitive verb in this phrase is "to give," which is the Greek word δίδωμι. When the younger widows are idlers going about from house to house, promulgating rumors and busying themselves with needless things; they provide ample fodder for accusation and criticism. But if they marry, have children, and concern themselves with the smooth running of the daily affairs of the house; they will provide less opportunity for slanderous accusations to be levied against them.

The word translated "adversary" is the Greek word ἀντίκειμαι. While a verb, here it is a substantive participle with an article and functions like a noun. The basic meaning is to 'be in opposition to;'[27] since this instance is substantive it means the

---

[23] BDAG, p. 187. Occurs 28x in NT; 3x in PE: 1Ti 4:3; 5:11, 14.

[24] BDAG, p. 994. NT *hapax*.

[25] See note on 1Ti 2:15.

[26] BDAG, p. 695. NT *hapax*.

[27] BDAG, p. 88. Occurs 8x in NT, 2x in PE: 1Ti 1:10; 5:14.

one who is acting in opposition, therefore "adversary." Similar use of ἀντίκειμαι occurs in *First Clement*:

> However, then, we have fallen away and whatever we have done through any insidious plots of *the opponent*, let us ask that we be forgiven. And those also who became leaders of the rebellion and dissension ought to pay careful attention to the common hope. (*1Cl* 51.1, emphasis added)

And in the Martyrdom of Polycarp:

> But the jealous and envious and evil one *who opposes* the family of the righteous, having seen both the greatness of his martyrdom and his irreproachable way of life from the beginning, both that he was now crowned with the crown of immortality and had won a prize nobody could deny, he took care that not even his poor body should be taken away by us, although many desired to do this and to have a share in his holy flesh. (*Mart. Poly.* 17.1, emphasis added)

Reading "the adversary" in 1Ti 5:14 as referring to Satan is appropriate as Satan is explicitly mentioned in v. 15.[28] This adversary is to be given "no occasion for slander." The word translated "slander" is the Greek word λοιδορία, meaning 'abuse,' 'reproach,' or 'reviling.'[29] The same word is used in First Peter:

> not repaying evil for evil or *insult* for *insult*, but on the other hand blessing others, because for this reason you were called, so that you could inherit a blessing. (1Pe 3:9, emphasis added)[30]

Similar usage occurs in Philo:

> On which account one of the ancients, when challenged to a contest *of abuse*, said, "I will never engage in such a contest as that in which he who wins is more dishonoured than he who is defeated." (Philo, *Agriculture* 110, emphasis added)

In Philo, the reference is to slander or invective; similar intent is found in 1Pe 3:9. Much as Christians are not to repay slander or abuse with the same; so actions should not invite slander or abuse. Paul's goal is that the younger widows, who likely are dabbling in the realm of false doctrine, no longer provide opportunity for opponents to heap slander upon the community of believers.

---

[28] In 1Ti 5:15, UBS5 and SBLGNT have τοῦ Σατανᾶ, assuming the proper name, "Satan." NA28 have τοῦ σατανᾶ, "the slanderer."

[29] BDAG, p.602. Occurs

[30] The same phrase, "insult for insult," occurs in Poly., *Phil.* 2.2.

Verse 15

For already some have turned away and followed after Satan

Some of the younger widows in question have already rejected the sound doctrine; they have "turned away and followed" Satan.[31] The Greek word translated "turned away" is ἐκτρέπω.[32] It is used earlier in First Timothy:[33]

> from which some have deviated, and *have turned away* into fruitless discussion, wanting to be teachers of the law, although they do not understand either the things which they are saying or the things concerning which they are speaking confidently. (1Ti 1:6–7, emphasis added)

The younger widows are akin to those who are desirous of being teachers of the law: they have turned away from the sound doctrine and embraced falsehood. Paul desires to stop the turning away and turn the focus of the younger widows from idle pursuits to pursuits worthy of their attention and worship.[34]

Verse 16

If any believing woman has widows, she must help them

Verse 16 reiterates the basic premise of 1Ti 5:4: Surviving relatives need to provide care for widows. The phrase "believing woman" is a translation of the feminine form of πιστός, here with an article, thus meaning 'faithful woman' or 'female believer.'

The phrase "she must help" is a translation of the Greek verb ἐπαρκέω. This same word was used earlier in 1Ti 5:10 regarding the widow "caring for" the afflicted.[35]

and the church must not be burdened

The phrase "must … be burdened" is from the Greek word βαρέω, generally meaning 'weigh down' or 'burden.'[36] The word can be used to describe a physical burden or

---

[31] Or, perhaps, they have strayed after "the slanderer." SBLGNT and UBS5 have τοῦ Σατανᾶ, assuming the proper name, "Satan." NA28 have τοῦ σατανᾶ, "the slanderer."

[32] BDAG, p. 311. Occurs 5x in NT, 4x in PE: 1Ti 1:6; 5:15; 6:20; 2Ti 4:4.

[33] See comment on 1Ti 1:6.

[34] On turning away to "Satan," see comment on 1Ti 1:20.

[35] See comment on 1Ti 5:10.

[36] BDAG, p. 166. Occurs 6x in NT; only here in PE.

load being carried or a figurative (intangible) weight or obligation. This instance is figuative; the burden of the church is that of caring for widows.

The word βαρέω is used in Second Corinthians:

> For we do not want you to be ignorant, brothers, concerning our affliction that happened in the province of Asia, that *we were burdened* to an extraordinary degree, beyond our strength, so that we were in despair even of living. (2Co 1:8, emphasis added)

> For indeed we who are in this tent groan, *being burdened* for this reason, that we do not want to be unclothed, but to be clothed, in order that what is mortal may be swallowed up by life. (2Co 5:4, emphasis added)

The concept of being burdened is similar in First Timothy; the burden is an obligation that must be carried out. Paul desires to keep the church from being unduly burdened by widows who have other means of provision—family members and other relatives who can provide for the needs of the widows.

in order that it may help those who are truly widows

This phrase restates many of the ideas previously examined. The pronoun "it" refers to the church (see above); the church is to "help" (ἐπαρκέω, cf. 1Ti 5:10, 15) those who are truly widows (cf. 1Ti 5:3). Paul wants the church to fulfill its obligations in caring for widows, but Paul also desires that surviving family provide for the needs of widows as they are able.

Honor Responsible Elders (1Ti 5:17–19)

The elders who lead well must be considered worthy of double honor, especially those who labor by speaking and teaching. For the scripture says, "You must not muzzle an ox while it is threshing," and "The worker is worthy of his wages." Do not accept an accusation against an elder except on the evidence of two or three witnesses. (1Ti 5:17–19)

Verse 17

The elders who lead well

The Greek word translated "elders" is πρεσβύτερος, seen previously in 1Ti 5:2 having the meaning of "older man." The present context, 15 verses removed from the previous instance, is somewhat different. Instead of generally denoting an older man deserving of respect, this instance points to a position of leadership worthy of honor. The usual meaning of this sense is 'elder' or 'presbyter.'[1] The word is used similarly in the epistle to Titus:

> On account of this, I left you behind in Crete, in order that what remains may be set in order and you may appoint *elders* in every town, as I ordered you. If anyone is blameless, the husband of one wife, having faithful children, not accused of dissipation or rebellious. (Tt 1:5–6, emphasis added)

In Titus, elders are those appointed to leadership of the church in a town.[2] These elders are likely owners of the house in which the church meets[3] and therefore are likely older, respected men in the community. However, the qualifications for elders, as listed in Titus, are similar to the qualifications listed for overseer in 1 Timothy 3.[4]

---

[1] BDAG, p. 862. Occurs 67x in NT.

[2] Likely held in a house; and likely one house church per town. Over one hundred towns were known on the island of Crete in the first century. See David W.J. Gill, "A Saviour for the Cities of Crete: The Roman Background to the Epistle to Titus" in P.J. Williams, et. al., *The New Testament in its First Century Setting* (Grand Rapids: Eerdmans, 2004), 220–230.

[3] R. Alastair Campbell, *The Elders: Seniority within Earliest Christianity* (London: T&T Clark, 2004), 173.

[4] See comment on 1Ti 3:1–7.

Is the overseer of chapter 3 an elder? Are the terms "elder" and "overseer" synonymous?

In the Ignatian church (early second century) the order of hierarchy seems to be that of overseer (bishop), followed by elders (presbyters), followed by deacons:

> Therefore, since I have by faith seen and loved, in the people mentioned above, the whole congregation. I urge you: be eager to do everything in the harmony of God, the bishop presiding in the place of God, and *the presbyters* in the place of the council of the apostles, and the deacons, who to me are especially dear, entrusted with the ministry of Jesus Christ, who before the ages was with the Father and has been revealed at the end. (Ign., *Magn.* 6.1, emphasis added)

The Ignatian ecclesiology is somewhat more developed when compared to the nascent ecclesial state encountered in the Pastoral Epistles. Ignatius, in his *Letter to the Trallians*, provides more detail:

> Likewise, let everyone respect the deacons as Jesus Christ, as also the bishop is an example of the Father, and *the presbyters* as the council of God and as the band of apostles. Without these things a group is not recognized as a church. (Ign., *Trall.* 3.1, emphasis added)

The order is evident in the picture Ignatius paints. The bishop is in analogous position to the Father—one of leadership and control. The presbyters (elders) are akin to the council of God. Deacons are compared to Jesus Christ, thus they are different from the presbyters, serving the interest of the bishop much like Jesus Christ is a model of obedience and complete submission to the Father.

Ignatius' description of ecclesial order, however insightful it is for understanding church order and terminology in the early second century, is a later snapshot that does not necessarily match the picture during the time in which the Pastoral Epistles were written. According to Campbell,[5] the elders (πρεσβύτερος) in the Pastoral Epistles are house-church leaders. They are well-to-do older men; natural leaders with houses and finances capable of supporting such an endeavor.[6] The overseer (ἐπίσκοπος) is an elder who oversees the house-churches in a particular locality (e.g. Ephesus or Crete). In this scheme, the deacons are attached to the overseer, serving as agents to support his ministry. Campbell holds that one function of the Pastoral Epistles is to spur migration from a loose house-church model (such as that in Acts and elsewhere in Paul) to something more formal. The Pastoral Epistles were written

---

[5] Campbell, *The Elders: Seniority within Earliest Christianity*, 194–205.

[6] Campbell argues that this is generally true of elders, that it is an ad hoc position of honor filled by people we would call "pillars of the church" whether or not they serve any official function or duty in the church community. Campbell, *Elders*, 96.

at the beginning of this shift; the Ignatian epistles represent ecclesiology after the shift was complete.

The elders, then, "rule well" over a house church. The Greek word translated "rule" is προΐστημι, which was used earlier in the description of qualifications for the overseers in 1Ti 3:

> *managing* his own household well, having children in submission with all dignity (but if someone does not know how to manage his own household, how will he take care of the church of God?), (1Ti 3:4–5, emphasis added)

The sense of προΐστημι in 1Ti 5 is roughly the same as that in 1Ti 3; the elders (πρεσβύτερος) are in a position of authority.

must be considered worthy of double honor

The Greek word translated "be considered worthy" is ἀξιόω, here in the sense of 'consider worthy' or 'deserving.'[7] The word is used similarly in Hebrews:

> For this one *is considered worthy* of greater glory than Moses, inasmuch as the one who builds it has greater honor than the house. (Heb 3:3, emphasis added)

> How much worse punishment do you think the person *will be considered* worthy of who treats with disdain the Son of God and who considers ordinary the blood of the covenant by which he was made holy and who insults the Spirit of grace? (Heb 10:29, emphasis added)

In Hebrews, ἀξιόω is used to show what one is worthy of receiving; be it honorable or dishonorable. Ignatius uses the word in the same way:

> Pray for the church in Syria, from where, being imprisoned, I am led away to Rome, being the least of the faithful there, even as I have been considered worthy to be found honorable to God. Farewell in God the Father and in Jesus Christ our common hope. (Ign., *Eph.* 21.2, emphasis added)

Ignatius claims to have been "considered worthy" to be "found honorable" to God. In 1Ti 5:17 Paul claims that elders who serve properly are worthy of "double honor." The word translated "honor" is τιμή, here having to do with 'honor' or 'esteem.'[8] The verb form of the word (τιμάω) was used earlier in 1Ti 5:3 ("honor widows who are truly widows") and the noun form (τιμή) is used later, at the start of chapter 6:

---

[7] BDAG, p. 94. Occurs 7x in NT, only here in PE.

[8] BDAG, p. 1005. Occurs 41x in NT; 6x in PE. Note that BDAG glosses 1Ti 5:17 as 'honorarium' or 'compensation,' but 1Ti 6:1 as 'honor' or 'reverence.'

> All those who are under the yoke as slaves must regard their own masters as worthy of all *honor*, lest the name of God and the teaching be slandered. (1Ti 6:1, emphasis added)

In 1Ti 6:1, Christian slaves are to treat their masters with honor; this serves to protect the name of God from slander.[9] Similarly, Christians are to treat the ones esteemed as elders with honor.

In this passage, though, Paul notes the elders are worthy of "double honor." The word translated "double" is διπλοῦς, meaning 'double' or 'two-fold.'[10] The same word is used twice in Revelation:

> Pay back to her as she herself also paid out, and *pay back double* according to her deeds; in the cup that she mixed, mix *double* for her. (Re 18:6, emphasis added)

The word has to do with doubling in quantity. A similar usage is found in Hermas' *Similitudes*:

> Therefore, among people the elm tree seems not to bear fruit, and they do not know or understand that when there is drought, the elm tree, having water, nourishes the vine, and the vine, continuously having water, gives *double* the fruit, both for itself and for the elm. So also the poor, interceding to the Lord for the rich, complement their wealth, and again the rich, providing to the poor what is necessary, complement their prayers. (Hermas, *Similitudes* II, 8)

In the case of First Timothy, the honor is what is doubled. There is question as to the nature of the "honor;" it may be some form of respect or it may involve monetary compensation to the elders. The word τιμή is used in the context of monetary compensation in Sirach:

> Honor a physician for his services with *honors*, for the Lord created him also. For healing is from the Most High, and he will receive a gift from the king. (Sir 38:1–2, emphasis added)

The following context in 1Ti 5:18 also indicates that monetary compensation may be intended.

especially those who labor by speaking and teaching

Those elders "who labor in preaching and teaching" are especially worthy of receiving honor. The Greek word translated "especially" is μάλιστα, here with the

---

[9] See comment on 1Ti 6:1.

[10] BDAG, p. 251. Occurs 4x in NT: Mt 23:15; 1Ti 5:17; Re 18:6 (2x).

sense of 'above all,' 'particularly,' or 'especially.'[11] Here it serves to project or further describe the role of the elders being honored; it is functioning epexegetically.[12]

The word translated "labor" is the Greek verb κοπιάω. Here (as in 1Ti 4:10) it has the sense of 'work hard,' 'toil,' 'strive,' or 'struggle.'[13] "Preaching and teaching" is not a formal responsibility list; it is rather an explanation of the tasks that the elders are expending energy and effort to accomplish. The *Epistle of Barnabas* uses κοπιάω similarly:

> You shall remember the day of judgment night and day, and you shall seek out every day the presence of the saints, either by *laboring* in word and going out to encourage and striving to save a soul by the word, or with your hands doing work as a ransom for your sins. (*Ep. Barn.* 19.10, emphasis added)

These elders labor in preaching and teaching. The word translated "preaching" is λόγος. It is a versatile word that takes on nuance depending on context. It this instance, it is not personified and therefore does not refer to Jesus Christ as λόγος.[14] Here, λόγος represents the communication that is the work of the elders; hence 'preaching' or 'speaking.'[15] The word λόγος is used similarly in First Corinthians:

> And I was with you in weakness and in fear and much trembling, and my *speech* and my message[16] were not in plausible words of wisdom, but in demonstration of the Spirit and of power, that your faith might not rest in the wisdom of men but in the power of God. (1Co 2:3–5, emphasis added)

The other word is "teaching," διδασκαλία. It is used in the Pastoral Epistles to refer to the sound doctrine, the proper representation of the Gospel.[17] The elders who exert themselves in speaking and teaching, working hard to properly proclaim the gospel and to teach and edify believers under their care, are deserving of honor.

---

[11] BDAG, p. 613. Occurs 12x in NT, 5x in PE: 1Ti 4:10; 5:8, 17; 2Ti 4:13; Tt 1:10. See discussion on 1Ti 4:10.

[12] Campbell, *The Elders: Seniority within Earliest Christianity*, 200–201.

[13] BDAG, p. 558. Occurs 23x in NT, 3x in PE: 1Ti 4:10; 5:17; 2Ti 2:6.

[14] e.g. Jn 1:1.

[15] BDAG, p. 599.

[16] The word 'message' is a translation of the Greek word κήρυγμά, typically translated 'preaching;' hence my preference for translating λόγος in 1Ti 5:17 as 'speaking' instead of 'preaching.'

[17] See comment on "sound doctrine" at 1Ti 1:10.

VERSE 18

Verse 18 appeals to scripture to provide justification for the double honor due to the hard-working elders who exert themselves in speaking and teaching.

For the scripture says

The Greek word γραφή is translated "scripture" in this instance, though it may more generally mean 'writing.'[18] Here it does refer to scripture as two passages of scripture are referenced in the balance of the verse. The word γραφή occurs similarly in Second Timothy, describing writings that were "breathed out by God":

> All *scripture* is inspired by God and profitable for teaching, for reproof, for correction, for training in righteousness, (2Ti 3:16, emphasis added)

The referred Scriptures, in this case, are two quotations.

"You must not muzzle an ox while it is threshing," and "The worker is worthy of his wages."

Both citations are found in Deuteronomy (cf. De 25:4 and 24:15). Paul uses De 25:4 in First Corinthians:

> For in the law of Moses it is written, "*You must not muzzle an ox while it is threshing.*" It is not about oxen God is concerned, is it? (1Co 9:9, emphasis added)

The quoted passage refers to threshing oxen; that they not be muzzled. If they hunger during their labor, then they are able to feed upon the grain that they are threshing. They are able to refresh themselves with the fruits of their labor. Paul goes on to explain his citation of Deuteronomy further:

> Or doubtless does [God] speak for our sake? For it is written for our sake, because the one who plows ought to plow in hope and the one who threshes ought to do so in hope of a share. If we have sown spiritual things among you, is it too great a thing if we reap material things from you? If others share this right over you, do we not do so even more? Yet we have not made use of this right, but we endure all things, in order that we may not cause any hindrance to the gospel of Christ. (1Co 9:10–12)

The second quotation, "the laborer deserves his wages" hearkens back to De 24:15 though something more like its present form is attributed to Jesus in Matthew:

---

[18] BDAG, p. 206. Occurs 50x in NT; 2x in PE: 1Ti 5:18; 2Ti 3:16.

> Do not procure gold or silver or copper for your belts. Do not take a traveler's bag for the road, or two tunics, or sandals, or a staff, for *the worker is deserving of his provisions.* (Mt 10:9–10, emphasis added)

The underlying principle can be traced back to several sources (Le 19:13; De 24:15) that affirm the principle that the one who works (slave or otherwise) is deserving of his agreed-upon wages.

Both of these citations show that the worker—in this case the elder—is worthy of receipt of the "double honor" mentioned in 1Ti 5:17.

Verse 19

Do not accept

The phrase "Do ... accept" is translated from the Greek word παραδέχομαι, here with the sense of 'accept.'[19] The word is used similarly in Acts:

> "And it happened that when I returned to Jerusalem and I was praying in the temple courts, I was in a trance, and saw him saying to me, 'Hurry and depart quickly from Jerusalem, because *they will* not *accept* your testimony about me.'" (Ac 22:17–18, emphasis added)

As Paul's testimony concerning Christ would not be received, so too unsubstantiated charges against an elder are to not be received. Ignatius records another instance:

> But I have learned that some from elsewhere have passed by, having evil doctrine. Your ear did not permit them to sow among you, your ears being plugged, so that *you might* not *receive* what was sown by them. (Ign., *Eph.* 9.1a, emphasis added)

The *Epistle to Diognetus* provides witness to this usage as well:

> For then, the things created by God for the use of people, some of which were created *to be received* as good, others of which to be rejected as useless and superfluous, how is this not forbidden? (*Ep. Diog.* 4.2, emphasis added)

Each of these instances has to do with acknowledging, receiving or accepting something as true. Ignatius used παραδέχομαι to describe the rejection[20] of "seeds" sown by false prophets. The author of *Diognetus* used it similarly to show an arbitrary distinction. The use here in First Timothy is much the same, accusations against

---

[19] BDAG, p. 761. Occurs 6x in NT, only here in PE.

[20] That is, not receiving where "not" comes from the negative particle.

elders are not acknowledged unless they are properly lodged, with corroborating witnesses.

an accusation against an elder

The Greek word κατηγορία is translated "an accusation."[21] It is also used in the epistle to Titus:

> If anyone is blameless, the husband of one wife, having faithful children, not *accused* of dissipation or rebellious. (Tt 1:6, emphasis added)

The word is used similarly in the gospel of John:

> So Pilate came outside to them and said, "What *accusation* do you bring against this man?" (Jn 18:29, emphasis added)

Josephus also uses κατηγορία:

> … so I returned as fast as ever I could, and found the whole council assembled, and the body of the people gotten together, and Jonathan and his colleagues bringing *vehement accusations* against me, as one who had no concern to ease them of the burdens of war, and as one that lived luxuriously. (Jos., *Life* 1.284, emphasis added)

That κατηγορία, in these cases and in First Timothy, has to do with an accusation or charge of some sort seems plain.

except on the evidence of two or three witnesses

The Greek word translated "except" is the adverb ἐκτός. Here it has the meaning of 'unless' or 'except,' though in general it has to do with being outside of something.[22] Similar usage is found in First Corinthians:

> Now I want you all to speak with tongues, but even more that you may prophesy. The one who prophesies is greater than the one who speaks with tongues, *unless* he interprets, in order that the church may receive edification. (1Co 14:5, emphasis added)

> by which you are also being saved, if you hold fast to the message I proclaimed to you, *unless* you believed to no purpose. (1Co 15:2, emphasis added)

The phrase "on the evidence of two or three witnesses" may be an allusion to the gospel of Matthew:

---

[21] BDAG, p. 533. Occurs 3x in NT: Jn 18:29; 1Ti 5:19; Tt 1:6.

[22] BDAG, p. 311. Occurs 8x in NT; only here in PE.

> "Now if your brother sins against you, go correct him between you and him alone. If he listens to you, you have gained your brother. But if he does not listen, take with you in addition one or two others, so that by the testimony *of two or three witnesses* every matter may be established. (Mt 18:15–16, emphasis added)

Or perhaps a recollection from Second Corinthians:

> This is the third time I am coming to you. By the testimony *of two or three witnesses* every word will be established. (2Co 13:1, emphasis added)

Or perhaps from the Torah:

> "One witness shall not stand to be a witness against a man as regards any injustice and as regards any offence and according to any sin that he may have sinned; *on the mouth of two witnesses and upon the mouth of three witnesses* any word shall stand. (De 19:15, emphasis added)

Whatever the source, the thought that charges must be substantiated by the testimony "of two or three witnesses" is not a foreign one, it is rooted in Torah, in the sayings of Jesus, and witnessed in earlier Pauline letters. Accusations hurled against elders that are unsubstantiated are to be ignored; charges testified to by two or more must be considered and dealt with.

Rebuke Irresponsible Elders (1 Ti 5:20–22)

> *Reprove those who sin in the presence of all, in order that the rest also may experience fear. I testify solemnly before God and Christ Jesus and the elect angels that you observe these things without prejudice, doing nothing according to partiality. Lay hands on no one hastily, and do not participate in the sins of others. Keep yourself pure. (1 Ti 5:20–22)*

Verse 20

Reprove those who sin in the presence of all

The Greek word translated "reprove" is ἐλέγχω, here with the sense of 'reprove' or 'correct.'[1] In this instance it is in the imperative mood. The word occurs in this same form two times in the epistle to Titus:

> holding fast to the faithful message according to the teaching, in order that he may be able both to exhort with sound instruction and *to reprove* those who speak against it. (Tt 1:9, emphasis added)

> Speak these things and exhort and *reprove* with all authority. Let no one disregard you. (Tt 2:15, emphasis added)

In the present context, ἐλέγχω has to do with addressing and correcting elders' sinful action that has been brought to light and corroborated. This is one of the tasks that was imparted to Timothy by Paul in his second epistle to Timothy:

> I solemnly charge you before God and Christ Jesus, who is going to judge the living and the dead, and by his appearing and his kingdom, preach the word, be ready in season and out of season, *reprove*, rebuke, exhort, with all patience and instruction. (2 Ti 4:1–2, emphasis added)

One of Timothy's responsibilities is to correct improper action. Correction is necessary to address the sin among (and perhaps even perpetuated by) the leaders of the community. When this sort of situation occurs—and it will as the problem of unsound doctrine is prevalent in the Ephesian church—Timothy must act decisively to rebuke and correct offenders.

---

[1] BDAG, p. 315. Occurs 17x in NT, 5x in PE: 1 Ti 5:20; 2 Ti 4:2; Tt 1:9, 13; 2:15.

The phrase "those who sin" comes from two Greek words. The first is the definite article, here in the plural accusative functioning as a relative pronoun, hence "those." The second word is the participial form of the verb ἁμαρτάνω, translated "who sin." The verb is the generic verb meaning 'to sin,'[2] here substantive and therefore relating to the ones who are sinning. Similar usage is found in First John:

> If anyone should see his brother sinning a sin not leading to death, he should ask, and he will grant life to him, *to those who sin* not leading to death. (There is a sin leading to death; I do not say that he should ask about that. (1Jn 5:16, emphasis added)

In classical literature (e.g. Homer, *Iliad* 5.287) ἁμαρτάνω is used much more generally in the sense of 'miss the mark,' particularly of thrown spears.[3] This came to be seen generally as failing or of doing wrong. An example of this can be seen in the fragments of Papias, as preserved by Eusebius:

> And this is what the elder used to say, 'when Mark was the interpreter of Peter, he wrote down accurately everything that he recalled of the Lord's words and deeds—but not in order. For he neither heard the Lord nor accompanied him; but later, as I indicated, he accompanied Peter, who used to adapt his teachings for the needs at hand, not arranging, as it were, an orderly composition of the Lord's sayings. And so Mark *did* nothing *wrong* by writing some of the matters as he remembered them. For he was intent on just one purpose: to leave out nothing that he heard or to include any falsehood among them.' [4] (*Papias* 3.15, emphasis added)

In the context of the fragment from Papias, Mark is not accused of sinning *per se*, though Papias defends Mark's actions as acceptable. While Papias and Homer reflect perfectly valid usage of ἁμαρτάνω, they are not typical NT usages of the word. In the NT, ἁμαρτάνω is less casual, involving transgression of a standard established by "divinity, custom or law."[5] This is the primary force of the word as used in the LXX.[6] In 1Ti 5 the context indicates rebuke is the proper action to pursue against those whose action is reflected by the word ἁμαρτάνω. Accusations of ἁμαρτάνω require substantiation, so the offense of ἁμαρτάνω must be a serious transgression. It

---

[2] BDAG, p. 49. Occurs 43x in NT; 2x in PE: 1Ti 5:20; Tt 3:11.

[3] LSJ, p. 77.

[4] Bart D. Ehrman, *Apostolic Fathers: Volume II. Epistle of Barnabas. Papias and Quadratus. Epistle to Diognetus. The Shepherd of Hermas*, New edition., Loeb Classical Library 25N (Cambridge, Mass: Harvard University Press, 2003).

[5] BDAG, p. 49.

[6] LEH ἁμαρτάνω.

contradicts the teaching and doctrine of Christ as presented by Paul and affirmed by Timothy. Thus it must be sin that elders persist in unrepentantly.

Reproof of sin is to be done "in the presence of all." The scope of "all" is at question here. In this context, does "all" refer to the whole of the group of elders, or does it refer to the community of believers at large? Knight discusses this question:

> The reproof is to be made "before" (ἐνώπιον), in the sense of "in the presence of," "all." The question is: "all" of whom? Some commentators think that since the frame of reference is elders, "all" means "all the elders" (Bernard, Hendriksen, Lock, Ridderbos). This is certainly possible. But since the level at which the sin of the elder is being dealt with is that of two or three witnesses, the analogy with Mt 18:15–18, particularly v. 17, "tell it to the church," would point to "all the church" as more likely (thus *TEV* and *NIV* render ἐνώπιον πάντων by "publicly;" cf. Bratcher, Calvin, Fee, Guthrie, Kelly).[7]

If the appeal in v. 19 to "two or three witnesses" refers to the teaching in Matthew 18, then "all" likely refers to the whole community or the church.

in order that the rest may also experience fear

The Greek word λοιπός is translated as "the rest." The sense is that of 'others' or 'rest of' where a group is concerned.[8] In this context, "the rest" are those elders who have not sinned. They will learn from the reproof of the elders found to be in sin; knowing there will be present and public consequence for sinful action. However, as with "all" above, the group represented by "the rest" is somewhat in dispute. Again, Knight:

> The purpose of such public rebuke is ἵνα καὶ οἱ λοιποὶ φόβον ἔχωσιν. καί, "also," indicates that the disciplinary action was not only for the individual but "also" that it might have its result in οἱ λοιποί, "the others," or "the rest." It may well be that with the latter Paul has in mind just the other elders (so Bernard, Dibelius-Conzelmann, Hanson, Huther, Kelly, Lock, Ridderbos, and Robertson) rather than the whole congregation (so Brox and Wilson); but if a public rebuke would have that effect on the elders it would have the same effect on other believers, since the discipline would be no different for them than for the elders.[9]

Knight's reasoning is generally sound; witnessing of public rebuke would generally remind one of the consequences of sinful action. However, for a leader of the community to witness public rebuke of a fellow leader may be of more import. The similarity of situation underscores the necessity of leaders to pursue proper teaching

---

[7] Knight, *The Pastoral Epistles : A Commentary on the Greek Text*, 236.

[8] BDAG, p. 602. Occurs 55x in NT; 2x in PE: 1Ti 5:20; 2Ti 4:8.

[9] Knight, *The Pastoral Epistles : A Commentary on the Greek Text*, 236.

and sound doctrine. Leaders, as Paul earlier reminded Timothy (cf. 1Ti 4:16), are in a unique position of responsibility. They must remain diligent and proper in what they teach as the substance of their teaching directly affects the community at large.

As the primary group under consideration in the larger context (vv. 17–20) is the group of elders, and as charges specifically against elders are under discussion (vv. 19–20), to view "the rest" as reflecting the remainder of the group of elders seems proper. The rebuke itself is to be public, before the church.

The remaining elders, then, are immediately reminded of the consequences of sin and the seriousness of their role in the instruction and leadership of the church.[10] These remaining elders "may also experience fear." This phrase is translated by two Greek words and could be more literally rendered "might have fear." The word translated "may also experience" is from the Greek word ἔχω, generally meaning 'to have' or 'possess.'[11] It is used similarly in 1Ti 1:12:

> *I give thanks* to the one who strengthens me, Christ Jesus our Lord, because he considered me faithful, placing me into ministry, (1Ti 1:12, emphasis added)

The emphasis above is somewhat misleading as ἔχω is not directly represented, but "I give thanks" is rather a rendering of two Greek words that could literally be translated as "I have thanks." Similar use of ἔχω plus a noun is encountered here in 1Ti 5:20 with "stand in fear."

The Greek word translated as "fear" is the Greek word φόβος, here in the sense of 'fear,' 'alarm,' or 'fright.'[12] An instance of ἔχω with φόβος occurs in the *Shepherd of Hermas*:

> But do not fear the devil, for by fearing the Lord, you will exercise dominion over the devil because power is not in him. And where there is no power, there is neither fear, but where there is glorious power, there is also fear. For everyone who has power *has fear*, but the one who does not have power is despised by all.[13] (Hermas, *Mandates* VII, 2)

Interesting in Hermas is the comparison between being feared and being despised—they are not the same. The fear is that of a trembling sense of being in awe of one with glorious power. In First Timothy, elders who have thus far concealed sin in their

---

[10] This is the view represented by the translator notes in the NET Bible.

[11] BDAG, p. 421.

[12] BDAG, p. 1062. Occurs 47x in NT; only here in PE.

[13] Of the times 'fear' occurs in the translation above, the first two are verbs (φοβέω), the third is an implied ἐστίν carried over from "is no power" plus φόβος, the fourth is the noun φόβος, the fifth is our instance (πᾶς γὰρ ὁ δύναμιν ἔχων φόβον ἔχει·).

lives are to view the rebuke of a fellow elder as a warning and an impetus to repent if they are guilty of similar sin. They are to be in fear, a sense of glorious awe, of God and therefore in awe of His glory and intolerance of sin. Understanding the consequence of sin serves as motive for other elders to be proactive in addressing sin in their own lives.

VERSE 21

I testify solemnly

The Greek word translated "I testify solemnly" is διαμαρτύρομαι, here in the sense of 'solemnly urge,' 'exhort,' or 'warn.'[14] This word occurs two other times in the Pastorals:

> Remind people of these things, *solemnly urging* them before the Lord not to dispute about words. This is in no way beneficial and leads to the ruin of the hearers. (2Ti 2:14, emphasis added)

> *I solemnly charge you* before God and Christ Jesus, who is going to judge the living and the dead, and by his appearing and his kingdom, (2Ti 4:1, emphasis added)

The use in 2Ti 4:1 is incredibly similar to the use here; the Greek word order is almost exactly the same. Use of διαμαρτύρομαι in 2Ti 2:14 is slightly different, though the appeal "before God" is worth noting. In all of these instances, the witnesses of the charge underscore seriousness of the charge.

before God and Christ Jesus and the elect angels

The Greek word translated "before" is the same word used in verse 20; ἐνώπιον.[15] Paul is setting the stage for the charge he will make. The assembled witnesses for the charge, in contrast to "the presence of all" in verse 20, include God, Christ Jesus and the elect angels.

The Pastoral Epistles use a phrase like "before God and Christ Jesus" two other times, both in similar invocations:[16]

> I command you, in the sight of God who gives life to all things and Christ Jesus who testified the good confession before Pontius Pilate, (1Ti 6:13)

---

[14] BDAG, p. 233. Occurs 15x in the NT; 3x in PE: 1Ti 5:21; 2Ti 2:14; 2Ti 4:1.

[15] See comment on 1Ti 2:3.

[16] Knight, *The Pastoral Epistles : A Commentary on the Greek Text*, p. 238.

> I solemnly charge you before God and Christ Jesus, who is going to judge the living and the dead, and by his appearing and his kingdom, (2Ti 4:1)

Both of these invocations occur near the ends of letters, introducing general exhortations such as to hold fast to the commands of God and to preach the Word along with correction, rebuking and encouragement. The seriousness of the following text is underscored by the seriousness of the witnesses of the exhortation.

The instance in 1Ti 5:21 includes a third witness to the charge, the "elect angels." The Greek word translated "elect" is ἐκλεκτός, which typically has to do with being "elect" in a salvific sense. In this case, the sense is that of 'pertaining to being especially distinguished.'[17] The word translated "angels" is simply ἄγγελος, here in the plural.[18]

The *Apocalypse of Moses* uses the term "elect angels" in a similar context:

> Then Eve rose and went out and fell on the ground and said, [2] "I have sinned, O God; I have sinned, O Father of all; I have sinned against you, I have sinned against your *chosen angels*, I have sinned against the cherubim, I have sinned against your steadfast throne; I have sinned, Lord, I have sinned much; I have sinned before you, and all sin in creation has come about through me." (*Apoc. Mos.* 32.1–2, emphasis added)

In the *Apocalypse of Moses*, the term "elect angels" is used in a veritable laundry list of divine beings and things that Eve has sinned against: God, the elect angels, the Cherubim, the throne of God; Eve then offers the realization that her sin is the cause of all subsequent sin "in the creation." Paul may be using the term "elect angels" in a similar way here; as reflective of the pantheon of heavenly witnesses of the charge he is laying before Timothy.[19]

that you observe these things without prejudice

The Greek word φυλάσσω is translated "observe these things." Here, φυλάσσω is used in the sense of 'observe' or 'follow.' The word is used similarly in the Gospels:

> And behold, someone came up to him and said, "Teacher, what good thing must I do so that I will have eternal life?" And he said to him, "Why are you asking me about what is good? There is one who is good. But if you want to enter into life, keep the commandments!" He said to him, "Which ones?" And Jesus said, "Do not commit murder, do not commit adultery, do not steal, do not give false testimony, honor your father and your mother, and love your neighbor as

---

[17] BDAG, p. 306. Occurs 22x in NT; 3x in PE: 1Ti 5:21; 2Ti 2:10; Tt 1:1.

[18] BDAG, p. 8. Occurs 175x in NT; 2x in PE: 1Ti 3:16; 5:21.

[19] See comment regarding angels as witnesses in 1Ti 3:16.

> yourself." The young man said to him, "All these *I have observed.* What do I still lack?" (Mt 19:16–20, emphasis added. Cf. parallel in Lk 18:18–21)

In this example, the text uses φυλάσσω to refer back to what the young man claims to keep: the commandments. Similar use is found in the *Shepherd of Hermas*:

> Therefore preserve purity and holiness, and you will live to God. These things, whatever I say and am about to say to you, *keep* them from now on, from the day which you were handed over to me, and I will dwell in your house. (Hermas, *Mandates* IV, iv, 3, emphasis added)

What has been given is to be kept or adhered to; guarded from misuse. Timothy is to keep in mind the rules about honoring and disciplining elders (cf. verses 17–20) and he is to do it "without prejudice." The Greek word translated "prejudice" is πρόκριμα, having to do with 'prejudgment' or 'discrimination.'[20] TDNT has discussion of this particular instance of πρόκριμα:

> In 1Ti 5:21 [πρόκριμα] cannot be used in a strict legal sense. It bears a more general moral sense, just as the word pre-judgment has passed from the legal sphere into the moral. The meaning here is a pre-judgment or preconceived opinion in favour of the accused or accuser which would hinder judges from exercising the justice required in Church discipline, v. 19f.[21]

Therefore Timothy is not to allow pre-formed opinions to guide him in either honoring or disciplining elders.

doing nothing according to partiality

The word "partiality" is a translation of the Greek word πρόσκλισις, here in the sense of 'inclination' or 'a relatively strong preference for something.'[22] Similar usage occurs in *First Clement*:

> Take up the letter of the blessed Paul the apostle. What first did he write to you at the beginning of his gospel? Truthfully he wrote to you in the Spirit about himself and Cephas and Apollos, because even then you had engaged in *partisan strife.* But that *partisanship* brought less sin to you, for you joined with[23] reputable apostles and with a man approved by them. (*1Cl* 47.1–4, emphasis added)

This excerpt from *First Clement* likely refers to 1Co 1:10–17:

---

[20] BDAG, p. 871. NT *hapax.*

[21] TDNT 3:953.

[22] BDAG, p. 881. NT *hapax.*

[23] The phrase "you joined with" is a translation of the verb form of πρόσκλισις.

> Now I exhort you, brothers, by the name of our Lord Jesus Christ, that you all say the same thing and there not be divisions among you, and that you be made complete in the same mind and with the same purpose. For it has been made clear to me concerning you, my brothers, by Chloe's people, that there are quarrels among you. But I say this, that each of you is saying, "I am with Paul," and "I am with Apollos," and "I am with Cephas," and "I am with Christ." Has Christ been divided? Paul was not crucified for you, was he? Or were you baptized in the name of Paul? ... For Christ did not send me to baptize, but to proclaim the gospel, not with clever speech, lest the cross of Christ be emptied. (1Co 1:10–13, 17)

The word πρόσκλισις, then, has to do with preferring one thing over and against another. In the Corinthian church there were divisions with some preferring (having partiality toward) one side. *First Clement* (also written to the Corinthians) uses this same thought and exhorts them to do away with partisanship (πρόσκλισις) of preferring one teacher over another when the message taught is the gospel of Jesus Christ.

Similarly in First Timothy, partisanship is not to be shown to elders. Preference should not dictate complementary or disciplinary action.

VERSE 22

Lay hands on no one hastily

The concept of "laying on of hands" was discussed earlier, in 1Ti 4:14.[24] In the present instance, the Greek verb translated "laying on" (ἐπιτίθημι) is in the imperative mood.[25] The act of laying on of hands is how "the council of elders" conferred gifts upon Timothy. Now, Timothy is warned of the dangers of being hasty in the laying of hands—bestowing gifts—upon others.

The Greek word translated "hastily" is the adverb ταχέως, here in the sense of 'too quickly' or 'too easily.'[26] The word is used to convey action pursued too swiftly in Galatians:

> I am astonished that you are turning away *so quickly* from the one who called you by the grace of Christ to a different gospel, not that there is a different gospel,

[24] See comment on 1Ti 4:14.

[25] This is important as the two subsequent verbs in this verse are also in the second person singular imperative.

[26] BDAG, p. 992. Occurs 15x in NT; 2x in PE: 1Ti 5:22; 2Ti 4:9.

> except there are some who are disturbing you and wanting to distort the gospel of Christ. (Ga 1:6–7, emphasis added)

Similar use occurs in Polycarp's *Letter to the Philippians*:

> And the presbyters also *must be* compassionate, merciful to all, turning back those who have gone astray, caring for all sick, neglecting neither widow or orphan or the poor, but always taking thought for the good before God and people, refraining from all anger, partiality, unjust judgment, being far removed from all love of money, not *quickly* believing against anyone, not relentless in judgment, understanding that we are all debtors in the matter of sin. (Poly., *Phil.* 6.1, emphasis added)

The sense in both of these instances is that action was pursued without diligence and thought; the action was hasty. Paul requires Timothy to be deliberate and to act with purpose in the laying on of hands.

and do not participate in the sins of others

The Greek word translated "do ... participate" is the verb κοινωνέω, here in the imperative mood as well. The sense has to do with 'share' or 'participate.'[27] The word carries a similar sense in Second John:

> If anyone comes to you and does not bring this teaching, do not receive him into your house and do not speak a greeting to him, because the one who speaks a greeting to him *shares in* his evil deeds. (2Jn 10–11, emphasis added)

In Second John, as here in First Timothy, the verb takes a dative object; this is the item or practice that one participates in. Paul exhorts Timothy to not lay hands on another hastily, and to not participate in the sins of others.

Keep yourself pure

The Greek word translated "keep" is the verb τηρέω.[28] As with ἐπιτίθημι and κοινωνέω before it, this instance is in the imperative mood. The word is used similarly in the next chapter:

> I command you, in the sight of God who gives life to all things and Christ Jesus who testified the good confession before Pontius Pilate, that *you observe* the commandment without fault, irreproachable until the appearing of our Lord Jesus Christ, (1Ti 6:13–14, emphasis added)

---

[27] BDAG, p. 552. Occurs 8x in NT, only here in PE.

[28] BDAG, p. 1002. Occurs 70x in NT; 3x in PE: 1Ti 5:22; 6:14; 2Ti 4:7.

In 6:14, τηρέω has to do with keeping or honoring or remaining in; protecting and keeping something undisturbed or unharmed.[29] Instead of taking part in the sins of others, or improperly administering gifts through the laying on of hands, Timothy is to keep himself pure, ensuring that his purity remains unchallenged and unassailable. This echoes previous material that focused on Timothy's personal ethic and manner of living (e.g. 1Ti 4:6–10).

Timothy is to keep himself "pure." The Greek word used here is ἁγνός, typically glossed as 'pure' or 'holy.'[30] The word used in the epistle to Titus, speaking of qualities that women are to hold:

> Older women likewise are to be reverent in their behavior, not slanderous, not enslaved to much wine, teaching what is good, in order that they may encourage the young women to love their husbands and to love their children, to be self-controlled, *pure*, busy at home, good, being subject to their own husbands, in order that the word of God may not be slandered. Likewise, exhort the young men to be self-controlled, (Tt 2:3–6, emphasis added)

The word is also used in *First Clement*:

> Let the strong care for the weak and let the weak respect the strong. Let the rich provide for the poor and let the poor give thanks to God, that he gave to him *one* through whom he might supply his need. Let the wise one demonstrate his wisdom not with words but with good works. Do not let the humble person testify about himself, but allow him to be testified about by another. Do not let *the pure* in the flesh boast, knowing that another is the one who provides for his self control. (*1Cl* 38.2, emphasis added)

The general idea behind all of these instances of ἁγνός is to keep oneself distant from acting sinfully, thus remaining pure. For Timothy, the proper alternative to hastily and improperly laying hands on others, or taking part in the sins of others is to keep himself pure.

---

[29] BDAG, p. 1002.

[30] BDAG, p. 13. Occurs 8x in NT; 2x in PE: 1Ti 5:22; Tt 2:5.

Parenthentical Note to Timothy (1Ti 5:23)

> *(No longer drink only water, but use a little wine for your stomach and your frequent illnesses.) (1Ti 5:23)*

Verse 23

(No longer drink only water, but use a little wine for your stomach and your frequent illnesses.)

This short aside noting concern for Timothy's health comes after an exhortation for Timothy to keep himself pure. Paul's instructions for purity are not to trump proper treatment of a weak stomach or delicate constitution.

The word translated "drink only water" is the Greek verb ὑδροποτέω.[1] The same word occurs in the LXX, in Daniel:

> "Indeed, test your servants for ten days, and let us be given some edible vegetables and seeds from the land so that we may eat them and *drink water*. (Da 1:12, emphasis added)

This portion of Daniel discusses a period of consuming only vegetables and water as a test, thus in Daniel ὑδροποτέω has to do with restraining one's intake of liquid to water alone. This is likely the case in First Timothy as well.

When necessary "for the sake of [his] stomach and [his] frequent ailments," Paul instructs Timothy to "use" wine. The word translated "use" is χράομαι, here with the sense of 'make use of' or 'employ.'[2] The same word was used earlier in First Timothy:

> But we know that the law is good, if anyone *makes use of it* lawfully, (1Ti 1:8, emphasis added)

The sense of χράομαι is also seen in an example from the *Epistle to Diognetus*:

---

[1] Though this is a parenthetical aside, Paul's tone using imperative verbs carries though the whole paragraph/pericope. This shows cohesion across the entire paragraph.

[2] BDAG, p. 1087. Occurs 11x in NT; 2x in PE: 1Ti 1:8; 5:23.

> For what is written is not insignificant, that from the beginning God planted the tree of knowledge and the tree of life in the middle of paradise, showing life through knowledge. Those who did not *use* it in purity, they were stripped naked from the beginning by deceit of the snake. (*Ep. Diog.* 12.3, emphasis added)

Paul urges Timothy to "use" wine when necessary to address issues of health. Timothy apparently has health issues concerning his stomach and other ailments. He is to address these issues as necessary, not forsaking his health and therefore jeopardizing the ministry.

Concluding Advice Regarding Elders (1Ti 5:24–25)

The sins of some people are evident, preceding them to judgment, but for some also they follow after them. Likewise also good works are evident, and those considered otherwise are not able to be hidden. (1Ti 5:24–25)

Verse 24

Paul's short aside addressing Timothy's health is complete; the dialogue returns to that of sin among elders. Verses 24–25 offer a short conclusion to the whole section.

The sins of some people are evident

The word translated "sins" is ἁμαρτία.[1] This is the general word for "sin" in the New Testament and was used earlier, in verse 22; the sense is similar here.[2] These sins are "evident." The Greek word translated "evident" is the adjective πρόδηλος, meaning 'clear,' 'evident,' or 'known (to all).'[3] The word is also used in Hebrews:

> For *it is evident* that our Lord is a descendant of Judah, a tribe with reference to which Moses said nothing concerning priests. (Heb 7:14, emphasis added)

First Clement uses πρόδηλος with some frequency:[4]

> For it is better for a person to confess concerning his sin than to harden his heart, just as the heart of those who rebelled was hardened against the servant of God, Moses, the condemnation of whom *became evident*. (*1Cl* 51.3, emphasis added)

The sense of πρόδηλος is that the thing it describes is plain and clear for all to see. In First Timothy, πρόδηλος agrees with ἁμαρτία in case, number and gender. The sins of some are obvious; they need no further description or confirmation.

---

[1] BDAG, p. 50. Occurs 173x in the NT; 3x in PE: 1Ti 5:22, 24; 2Ti 3:6.

[2] See earlier discussion on the verb form of this word (ἁμαρτάνω) in 1Ti 5:20.

[3] BDAG, p. 867. Occurs 3x in NT: 1Ti 5:24, 25; He 7:14.

[4] *1Cl* 11.1; 12.7; 40.1; 51.3.

preceding them to judgment

The Greek word translated "preceding them" is προάγω, here in the sense of 'go before,' 'lead the way,' 'precede.'[5] The same word is used earlier in First Timothy, describing prophecies:[6]

> I am setting before you this instruction, Timothy my child, in accordance with the prophecies *spoken long ago* about you, in order that by them you may fight the good fight, (1Ti 1:18, emphasis added)

In 1Ti 5:24 the conspicuous sins are the harbinger of judgment; they pave the path that leads to judgment.

but for some also they follow after them

The words translated "they follow after" are from the Greek word ἐπακολουθέω, here meaning 'following'[7] or perhaps even 'subsequent.' Polycarp's *Letter to the Philippians* uses ἐπακολουθέω in contrast with προάγω:

> [faith] is the mother of all of us, hope *follows after* and the love which is for God and Christ and for the neighbor *goes before*. For if anyone is in their company, he has fulfilled the commandment of righteousness, for he who has love is a long way from all sin. (Poly., *Phil.* 3.3, emphasis added)[8]

In Polycarp, hope follows faith. In First Timothy, the idea is that some commit sin conspicuously but the less obvious sin of others only becomes known later. Sin, conspicuous or not, is made known sooner or later.

VERSE 25

Likewise also good works are evident, and those considered otherwise are not able to be hidden.

The structure of this verse is similar to v. 24; the idea is the same. Good works are obvious; those that are not immediately evident will be made known at some point. Some are "evident," others are "hidden."

---

[5] BDAG, p. 864. Occurs 20x in NT; 2x in PE: 1Ti 1:18; 5:24.

[6] See comment on 1Ti 1.18.

[7] BDAG, p. 358. Occurs 4x in NT: Mk 16.20; 1Ti 5.10, 24; 1Pe 2.21.

[8] The first emphasized instance is ἐπακολουθέω, the second προάγω.

Verse 24	Verse 25
The sins of some people are evident, preceding them to judgment,	Likewise also good works are evident,
but for some also they follow after them.	and those considered otherwise are not able to be hidden.

The word translated "hidden" is the Greek verb κρύπτω, here in the sense of 'hide' or 'keep secret.'[9] Similar use of κρύπτω, describing hidden actions, occurs in Philo's tractate *On the Special Laws*:

> If you have not transgressed the laws of your marriage, and if no other man has been associated with you, so that you have not violated the rights of him who is joined to you by the law, you are blameless and innocent; but if you have neglected your husband and have followed empty appetites, either loving some one yourself or yielding to some lover, betraying your nearest and dearest connections, and adulterating them by a spurious mixture, then learn that you are deservedly liable to every kind of curse, the proofs of which you will exhibit on your body. Come then and drink the draught of conviction, which shall uncover and lay bare all thy *hidden* and secret actions. (Philo, *Spec. Laws* III 61, emphasis added)

In Philo, "hidden and secret" actions will be disclosed and made known. Similarly, in First Timothy, undisclosed sins and good works (things that are currently hidden) will eventually be made known. In the larger context of chapter 5 Paul is instructing Timothy to be cautious in promoting leaders. Some things (both sins and good works) are evident without further examination; but other things (again, both sins and good works) will not be kept hidden forever. They will eventually be made known.

---

[9] BDAG, p. 571. Occurs 18x in NT; only here in PE.

Slaves in the Fellowship (1Ti 6:1–2a)

> *All those who are under the yoke as slaves must regard their own masters as worthy of all honor, lest the name of God and the teaching be slandered. And those who have believing masters must not look down on them because they are brothers, but rather they must serve, because those who benefit by their service are believers and dearly loved. (1Ti 6:1–2a)*

Verse 1

All those who are under the yoke as slaves

The phrase "under the yoke" is a prepositional phrase created by the combination of ὑπὸ ('under') and its accusative object, ζυγός. In this context, ζυγός is a 'yoke'[1] which can be further described as "a frame used to control working animals or, in the case of humans, to expedite the bearing of burdens."[2] The NT always uses this second, figurative use.[3] Paul uses yoke imagery in Galatians:

> For freedom Christ has set us free. Stand firm, therefore, and do not be subject again to *a yoke* of slavery. (Ga 5:1, emphasis added)

In Galatians, the "yoke of slavery" is well described in Ga 4:1–30; it has to do with one being in slavery to sin. The yoke in 1Ti 6:1, while having to do with slaves, is different. It is the yoke of actual, physical slavery. Paul is addressing those who really are slaves.

Those under the yoke, the ones bearing a burden, are "slaves." The Greek word is δοῦλος, here occurring in its literal sense of 'slave' or 'bond servant.' Paul frequently uses δοῦλος in epistolary greetings, calling himself a "slave of Christ." In 1Ti 6:1, however, the sense is that of a slave, one who is bonded in servitude to his master.

---

[1] BDAG, p. 429. Occurs 6x in NT, only here in the PE.

[2] BDAG, p. 429.

[3] See De 21:3 [LXX] for an example of the literal usage.

must regard

As with previous sections (cf. 1Ti 5:9, 17) the verb in this instructional section is an imperative verb. The verb used here translated "must regard" is ἡγέομαι. The sense is that of 'think,' 'consider,' or 'regard'[4] and is similar to 1Ti 1:12:

> I give thanks to the one who strengthens me, Christ Jesus our Lord, because *he considered* me faithful, placing me into ministry, (1Ti 1:12, emphasis added)

In 1Ti 1:12, Paul notes that Christ Jesus has judged him, giving the sense that he or some aspect of his being has been sized up and considered. The outcome of the consideration is the appointing of Paul to service. The same verb, ἡγέομαι, is also used in the *Martyrdom of Polycarp*:

> The proconsul responded, "Persuade the people." But Polycarp said, "You, perhaps, I should have considered worthy of an account, for we have been taught to render honor, as is fitting, to rulers and authorities under God, if it does not hurt us. But to show it to them? *I do* not *consider* them worthy that a defense should be made before them." (*Mart. Poly.* 10.2, emphasis added)

Polycarp's estimation of the crowd is rather low; based on the crowd's actions and treatment of him they do not merit a defense. Another example of the verb is found in *Second Clement*:

> And you know, brothers, that the sojourn, the one in this world, of this flesh is small and of short duration, but the promise of Christ is great and wonderful: the rest of the coming kingdom and life eternal. Therefore, what are we to do to obtain them, except to conduct ourselves reverently and rightly, and *to consider* these worldly things as foreign and not to desire them? For when we desire to acquire these things, we fall away from the way of the righteous. (*2Cl* 5.5–7, emphasis added)

In Second Clement, the "worldly affairs" are to be considered foreign while the heavenly affairs (rest in the coming kingdom and eternal life) are to be considered normal. Doing this is equated with conducting one's self "in a holy and upright way."

In each of these examples, the considering (ἡγέομαι) is a re-evaluation of conceptions and conclusions based on new information. 1Ti 6:1 has similar meaning; slaves are to consider their own masters. For the slaves, the new information is their status as Christians. They are to size their masters up in light of their own confession as Christians and act accordingly.

---

[4] BDAG p. 434. Occurs 28x in NT, 2x in PE: 1Ti 1:12; 6:1.

their own masters as worthy of all honor

Slaves have masters. Paul here is careful to qualify the slaves' masters as "their own," leading to no confusion with other masters. Paul is not mixing metaphors here; there is no confusion between being a slave of Christ (being spiritually devoted to Christ) and being a slave of an earthly master.

The word translated "master" is δεσπότης, which can be glossed as 'lord' or 'master.'[5] The word is used similarly in Titus:

> Slaves must be subject *to their own masters* in everything, to be well-pleasing, not to talk back, not stealing, but demonstrating all good faith, in order that they may do credit to the teaching of God our Savior in everything. (Tt 2:9–10, emphasis added)

As implored in the above example from Titus, slaves are to hold their masters "as worthy of all honor." Tt 2:9–10 shows the practical side of doing so; in their actions slaves are submissive to their masters. In First Timothy, a larger rationale is given.

lest the name of God and the teaching be slandered

The reason that slaves who are also Christian should obey their masters has not to do, ultimately, with honoring their masters. It has to do with honoring God. Paul uses the phrase "name of God" with the concept of reviling (or 'blaspheming') in Romans:

> Who boast in the law, by the transgression of the law you dishonor God! For just as it is written, "*The name of God* is blasphemed among the Gentiles because of you." (Ro 2:23–24, emphasis added)

The name of God and the teaching (διδασκαλία)[6] are not to "be reviled." This reflects the Greek verb βλασφημέω,[7] meaning 'slander,' 'revile,' 'defame,'[8] or even 'blaspheme.' In addition to the example from Ro 2:23–24 above, Revelation offers examples of this word used in conjunction with the "name of God":

> And he opened his mouth for blasphemies toward God, to blaspheme his name and his dwelling, those who live in heaven. (Re 13:6, emphasis added)

Second Clement also carries the idea of the name of God being blasphemed.

---

[5] BDAG, p. 220. Occurs 11x in NT, 4x in PE: 1Ti 6:1, 2; 2Ti 2:21; Tt 2:9. Note that δεσπότης occurs frequently (over 40x) in *1Cl* and Hermas.

[6] See comment on 1Ti 1:10.

[7] See comment on 1Ti 1:20.

[8] BDAG p. 178. Occurs 34x in NT, 4x in PE: 1Ti 1:20; 6:1; Tt 2:5; 3:2.

> … And do not let us become people pleasers, nor let us wish to please ourselves alone, but also those people outside of us by righteousness, *that the name may not be blasphemed* because of us. For the Lord says, "My name is blasphemed continually among all the nations," (Is 52:5) and again "Woe to him on account of whom *my name is blasphemed.*" How is it *blasphemed*? By you who do not do what I desire. For when the nations hear from our mouth the sayings of God, they marvel at their beauty and greatness. Later, upon learning our works are not worthy of the words which we speak, they turn from wonder to blasphemy, saying it is some myth and deception. … but when they see that not only do we not love those who hate us, but that not even those who love us, they laugh at us and *the name is blasphemed.* (*2Cl* 13, emphasis added)

This extended reference from *Second Clement* is important because it defines that author's view of what it means to blaspheme the name of God: when the actions of those who confess Him are inconsistent with their professed faith. When they claim to love their enemies but don't even love those who love them (cf. 1Jn 2:9–11) then the name is reviled or blasphemed. The name is shown to be unimportant because the teaching associated with the name is not followed.

The idea is similar in First Timothy. Slaves who confess Christianity are to esteem their masters, not because their masters deserve it but because this properly reflects the teaching they profess.

Verse 2a

And those who have believing masters

A further clarification is added for slaves who have masters that are fellow confessors of Christ. The word translated 'masters' is the same as that in the previous verse. The word translated 'believing' is the phrase πιστοὺς ἔχοντες, a combination of the verb 'having' with the object 'faith;' thus 'believing.'

must not look down on them because they are brothers

The verb καταφρονέω is here an active imperative meaning 'look down on,' 'despise,' 'scorn,' or 'treat with contempt.'[9] The word was used earlier First Timothy:

> Let no one *look down on* your youth, but be an example for the believers in word, in conduct, in love, in faith, in purity. (1Ti 4:12, emphasis added)

---

[9] BDAG, p. 529. Occurs 9x in NT, twice in PE: 1Ti 4:12; 6:2.

In 4:12[10] Timothy is to let no one despise him. Here, in 6:2, even believing slaves are not to be disrespectful toward their masters. As with many words, καταφρονέω has a range of meaning with specific meaning understood in a specific context. The context in 1Ti 6:2 is not necessarily that of scorn or derision; slaves are to give their masters proper respect even if both master and slave are believers and therefore brothers in Christ.

The next phrase is "because they are brothers." Being brothers in Christ is no reason for disrespect between parties; indeed it is reason for even more respect. Paul's intent is clear: believing slaves who serve believing masters are still subject to their masters.

but rather they must serve

The word translated "but" is the conjunction ἀλλὰ. It draws a contrast between what happens before it and what happens after it. Here it is used to focus the proper practice of the slaves: they are not only to obey their believing masters, they must serve their believing masters even more so.

The Greek word translated "rather" is the adverb μᾶλλον. It is a commonly used word, commonly rendered 'rather,' 'instead,' or 'much more.'[11] The word is used similarly elsewhere:

> Therefore my dear friends, just as you have always obeyed, not as in my presence only but now *much more* in my absence, work out your own salvation with fear and trembling. (Php 2:12, emphasis added)
>
> Furthermore, we have had our earthly fathers who disciplined us, and we respected them. Will we not much *rather* subject ourselves to the Father of spirits and live? (Heb 12:9, emphasis added)

The above examples, particularly Heb 12:9, use contrast in much the same way. In First Timothy, the function of the contrast is to emphasize the relationship that believing slaves are to have with believing masters.

---

[10] See comment on 1Ti 4:12.

[11] BDAG, p. 613. Occurs 81x in NT, 3x in PE: 1Ti 1:4; 6:2; 2Ti 3:4.

because those who benefit by their service are believers and dearly loved

Next, a reason is given for the service of slaves to believing masters. The slaves are to render "service." This is the Greek word εὐεργεσία, here meaning 'doing of good.'[12] Acts has the only other NT occurrence of the word:

> if we are being examined today concerning *a good deed* done to a sick man—by what means this man was healed (Ac 4:9, emphasis added)

This idea is similar to what is going on in First Timothy, though First Timothy refers to the concept of service (a pattern of deeds) instead of an instance (a single deed). The use in First Timothy likely draws on its classical usage where the concept of good citizenship or civic-minded service is in mind. Plato *Leges* 850b notes "good service done" to the state[13] and Lysias uses the plural of the word to describe "public services."[14] In the same way that citizens are under the rulers of the state and are to render the state civic service and obeisance, so believing slaves, under believing masters, are to render their masters the best service they are able to muster.

The primary reason for the good service to believing masters is because the masters are also believers, and as a result the masters are to be beloved.[15]

---

[12] BDAG, p. 405. Occurs 2x in NT: Ac 4:9; 1Ti 6:2.

[13] LSJ, p. 712.

[14] LSJ, p. 712.

[15] The corollary is also true; believing masters should be kind to believing slaves because the slaves are also believers and beloved.

Transition (1Ti 6:2b)

Teach and encourage these things (1Ti 6:2b)

Verse 2b

Teach and encourage these things

Translations and commentaries differ as to whether this sentence ends the previous paragraph or begins the current paragraph. Its function is evident: it provides transition from Paul's previous emphasis on relationships within the church to his current emphasis on proper teaching of doctrine. Knight describes this:

> Paul adds the admonition ταῦτα δίδασκε καὶ παρακάλει, "these things teach and exhort," which is similar to the admonition added at 4:11. These two admonitions indicate a pattern in the letter, coming between sections of instruction for the church (here 5:1 [or 5:3] through 6:2) and more direct instruction of Timothy (here 6:3ff.; note σύ in v. 11). Before he turns to this more personal and direct instruction, just as at 4:11, Paul urges Timothy to be sure to teach and exhort the previously given truths.[1]

---

[1] Knight, *The Pastoral Epistles : A Commentary on the Greek Text*, 247.

Characteristics of False Teachers (1Ti 6:3–5)

If anyone teaches other doctrine and does not devote himself to the sound words of our Lord Jesus Christ and the teaching that is in accordance with godliness, he is conceited, understanding nothing, but having a morbid interest concerning controversies and disputes about words, from which come envy, strife, slanders, evil suspicions, constant wrangling by people of depraved mind and deprived of the truth, who consider godliness to be a means of gain. (1Ti 6:3–5)

Verse 3

If anyone teaches other doctrine

Paul opened the letter (1:3) exhorting Timothy "that you may charge certain persons not to teach any different doctrine." The Greek word translated "teaching different doctrine" in both 1:3 and 6:3 is ἑτεροδιδασκαλέω, glossed as 'give devisive instruction.'[1]

and does not devote himself to

The word translated "does … devote himself to" is προσέρχομαι; "not" comes from a negative particle functioning adverbially. In general the word means 'come toward,' 'go to' or 'approach'[2] but here the meaning is more heavily nuanced due to the context. In this instance it carries the sense of 'turn to' or 'occupy oneself with.'[3] The basic sense is that one (false teaching) is not the same as the other (the words of Jesus Christ). The word is used this way in *First Clement*:

> Let us consider that all the righteous have been adorned with good works; and even the Lord himself, having adorned himself with good works, rejoiced. Therefore, having this example, *let us unhesitatingly devote ourselves* to his will; let

---

[1] BDAG p. 399. Occurs 2x in NT: 1Ti 1:3; 6:3. See comment on 1Ti 1:3 for further discussion.

[2] BDAG p. 878.

[3] BDAG p. 878. Occurs 86x in the NT; only here in the PE.

> us work the work of righteousness with all of our strength. (*1Cl* 33.7–8, emphasis added)

The context and use of προσέρχομαι is much the same as that in First Timothy. In *First Clement*, the Lord is held as the standard; both Clement and his audience are urged to come toward or approach that standard. In First Timothy, the teachers of different doctrine are negatively contrasted (due to inclusion of the negative particle) with the standard of the words of Jesus Christ. Thus προσέρχομαι, in this type of context, has to do with one concept or practice "coming toward" or "approaching" another concept or practice. In these two examples, the concepts compared are in harmony (*First Clement*) or in dissonance (First Timothy).

the sound words of our Lord Jesus Christ and the teaching that is in accordance with godliness

The phrase "sound words" echoes the consistent theme of "sound doctrine" found within the Pastoral Epistles.[4] In all instances, the word for "sound" is the same, ὑγιαίνω.[5] The word translated "words" is a plural form of the Greek word λόγος. A similar phrase is used in Titus:

> concerning everything showing yourself to be an example of good deeds, in your teaching demonstrating soundness, dignity, *a sound message* beyond reproach, in order that an opponent may be put to shame, because he has nothing bad to say concerning us. (Tt 2:7–8, emphasis added)

Sound speech is associated with proper teaching; teaching which cannot be condemned. Philo uses this phrase as well:

> And I mean by this those virtues which are of common utility, for each one of these ten laws separately, and all of them together, train men and encourage them to prudence, and justice, and piety, towards God and all the rest of the company of virtues, connecting *sound words* with good intentions, and virtuous actions with wise language, that so the organ of the soul may be wholly and entirely held together in a good and harmonious manner so as to produce a well-regulated and faultless innocence and consistency of life. (Philo, *Spec. Laws* IV 134, emphasis added)[6]

In this instance from Philo, the "sound words" help form the basis of one's proper life. In First Timothy, the "sound words" come from the mouth of the Lord Jesus

---

[4] "Sound" words or doctrine or teaching is found 5x: 1Ti 1:10; 6:3; 2Ti 4:3; Tt 1:9; 2:1.

[5] See comment on 1Ti 1:10.

[6] See Philo, *Planting* 157; *Abraham* 223 for further instances of the phrase.

Christ. These words of Christ are further explained as "the teaching that accords with godliness."

The entire structure of the verse is a contrast that identifies the target of the condemnation to come in vv. 4–5. The first portion of the contrast is the different doctrine. The contrasting portion is twofold, involving the sound words of Christ and the teaching that accords with godliness. Thus "the teaching that accords with godliness" further explains "the sound words" of Christ. Both phrases relate to the same thing; one simply helps explain the other in greater detail.

The Greek word translated "teaching" is διδασκαλία, a common word in the Pastoral Epistles.[7] The word translated "godliness" (εὐσέβεια) is relatively common in the Pastorals as well.[8] These terms have been used within First Timothy to describe proper doctrine and proper action. Their combination in contrast with the "different doctrine" emphasizes what is right, and how the substance of the teaching purveyed by the false teachers in Ephesus is wrong.

Verse 4

He is conceited

The "he" in this verse is the one who teaches contrary to Christ;[9] his teaching does not accord with godliness. Because he is teaching wrongly, he is worthy of condemnation. So Paul gives the condemnation.

Paul's first charge is that the false teacher is "conceited." This is the Greek word τυφόω.[10] Paul earlier warned against this:

> not newly converted, lest *he become conceited* and fall into the condemnation of the devil. (1Ti 3:6, emphasis added)

In 1Ti 3:6, Paul advises that overseers must be mature; they must have a proper foundation. If they do not, they are likely to become conceited. The effect of this conceit is to succumb to the adversary's trap—which the false teachers of 1Ti 6:4 have already fallen done.

---

[7] BDAG, p. 240. Occurs 21x in NT, 15x in PE. See comment on 1Ti 1:10.

[8] BDAG, p. 412. Occurs 15x in NT, 10x in PE. See comment on 1Ti 2:2.

[9] Note that Paul has not set up himself as the source of the sound words and godliness. Paul, as Christ's representative, bears the sound words of Christ.

[10] BDAG, p. 1021. Occurs 3x in NT: 1Ti 3:6; 6:4; 2Ti 3:4. See comment on 1Ti 3:6.

understanding nothing

The word "understanding" is a translation of ἐπίσταμαι.[11] The usage here is similar to Mark's use of the word, describing Peter's denial:

> And while Peter was below in the courtyard, one of the female slaves of the high priest came up And when she saw Peter warming himself, she looked intently at him and said, "You also were with the Nazarene, Jesus." But he denied it, saying, "I neither know nor *understand* what you mean!" And he went out into the gateway, and a rooster crowed. (Mk 14:66–68, emphasis added)

Here "I neither know nor understand" uses ἐπίσταμαι in the explanation of Peter's denial. Peter, lying, says that not only was he not with Jesus but he doesn't even understand what the girl speaking to him is charging him with. He feigns innocence, and to support the innocence he acts as if he has no comprehension of the actions the servant girl attributes to him.

The indictment against the false teachers in First Timothy is similar. Paul contends that these teachers have more than an inflated view of themselves—they have no comprehension of what they are teaching. This again echoes First Timothy's opening:

> But the goal of our instruction is love from a pure heart and a good conscience and a faith without hypocrisy, from which some have deviated, and have turned away into fruitless discussion, wanting to be teachers of the law, although *they do not understand either the things which they are saying or the things concerning which they are speaking confidently*. (1Ti 1:5–7, emphasis added)

Though these false teachers confidently proclaim their heresy, in reality they understand nothing.

but having a morbid interest

The phrase "having a morbid interest" is a translation of the Greek verb νοσέω. The word has the sense of 'be sick' or 'ailing.'[12] The usage in First Timothy is figurative; this is easily determined because of the things the false teachers are sick for: controversy and word-quarrels.

---

[11] BDAG, p. 380. Occurs 14x in NT, only here in PE.

[12] BDAG, p. 678. NT *hapax*. The word is frequent in Philo (34x); BDAG cites Philo, *Alleg. Interp.* III 211 as an example of the figurative sense.

There are no other NT instances of νοσέω, though Plutarchus, writing in either the first or second century AD, uses it similarly: "to be full of unhealthy ambition."[13] The figurative use of νοσέω also occurs in the *Wisdom of Solomon*:

> For those who promised to drive away the fears and troubles of a sick soul *were themselves sick* with ridiculous fear. (Wis 17:8, emphasis added)

The same sort of usage is also found in Josephus' *Antiquities of the Jews*:

> Now it was Antipater who was the cause of all this; who when he knew what a *mad and licentious way of acting* his father was in, and had been a great while one of his counsellors, he hurried him on, and then thought he should bring him to do somewhat to purpose, when everyone that could oppose him was taken away. (Jos., *Ant.* 16.244, emphasis added)

Thus νοσέω, in its figurative sense, has to do with vehemently and improperly pursuing something, or pursuing something nonsensical. One's seeming obsession with an object or idea is seen as being "sick" because it is so obviously improper.

concerning controversies and disputes about words

This morbid interest or sick pursuit is after "controversy" and "disputes about words." The Greek word translated "controversy" is ζήτησις, having to do with 'discussion,' 'debate' or 'argument.'[14] The usage of ζήτησις in Acts provides insight:

> And some men came down from Judea and began teaching the brothers, "Unless you are circumcised according to the custom prescribed by Moses, you cannot be saved." And after there was no little strife and *debate* by Paul and Barnabas against them, they appointed Paul and Barnabas and some others from among them to go up to the apostles and elders in Jerusalem concerning this issue. (Ac 15:1–2, emphasis added)

The word ζήτησις is used to describe the dispute over the issue of circumcision. Here, the debate itself is not improper. In First Timothy, however, the debate or controversy is sought after. In that context, the question itself is not important, but the dispute is.

---

[13] Plut. Laud. s. Inv., 20 (II, 546 f.), quoted in TDNT 4:1091. Supplies the Greek: νοσεῖν περὶ δόξαν. Note also that LSJ p. 1181 contains the same citation, translating it "to have a morbid craving for fame."

[14] BDAG, p. 428. Occurs 7x in NT, 3x in PE: 1Ti 6:4; 2Ti 2:23; Tt 3:9. Three of the remaining four instances occur in Acts (Ac 15:2, 7; 25:20).

The same is true of the "disputes about words." The Greek word used is λογομαχία, meaning 'word-battle' or 'dispute about words.'[15] The word only occurs here in the NT. In its discussion on λογομαχία, TDNT notes:

> In profane use few examples of λογομαχία have been found: Porphyrius in Eus. Praep. Ev., XIV, 10, 2; the title of a Menippean satire of Varro in which he calls the debate between the Stoics and Epicureans a λογομαχία, Porphyrius on Horat. Sat., II, 4 (ed. A. Holder [1894], 308; cf. F. Buecheler, Petronii Saturae[5] [1912], 209).[16]

Teachers should not be focused on controversies and fighting over words and ideas; they should instead be focused on the sound doctrine.

from which come envy, strife, slanders, evil suspicions,

These controversies and word-fights that the false teachers invest themselves in have no fruit, instead they only produce evil offspring. The phrase translated "from which" is a prepositional phrase (ἐξ ὧν, or "out of which" or "from which"[17]) modifying the common verb γίνομαι here meaning 'arise,' 'come about,' or 'develop.'[18]

The things that come about as a result of these controversies include envy, dissension, slander and evil suspicions.

Envy is a translation of φθόνος, 'envy' or 'jealousy,'[19] and frequently occurs in lists of vices (Ro 1:29; Ga 5:21; 1Pe 2:1) as it does here. It is also used in the epistle to Titus:

> For we also were once foolish, disobedient, led astray, enslaved to various desires and pleasures, spending our lives in wickedness and *envy*, despicable, hating one another. (Tt 3:3, emphasis added)

Interestingly, φθόνος is elsewhere used in the NT as the reason Christ was "delivered up":

> And the crowd came up and began to ask him to do as he customarily did for them. So Pilate answered them, saying, "Do you want me to release for you the

[15] BDAG, p. 598. NT *hapax*, though BDAG notes a variant Tt 3:9 also uses the word.

[16] TDNT 4:143.

[17] The exact phrase ἐξ ὧν also appears in Ac 15:29; Ro 9:5; 1Co 15:6. Similar phrases (differing declensions of the pronoun) appear in Mt 1:16; 1Co 8:6; Eph 3:15; 4:16; Php 3:20; Col 2:19; Heb 13:10. The general sense of the phrase is "from which" or "from whom."

[18] BDAG, p. 197. Occurs 669x in NT.

[19] BDAG, p. 1054. Occurs 9x in NT, 2x in PE: 1Ti 6:4; Tt 3:3.

> king of the Jews?" (For he realized that the chief priests had handed him over because of *envy*.) (Mk 15:8–10, emphasis added)[20]

In other words, φθόνος is attributed as the primary reason the chief priests gave Jesus over to Pilate for trial. They were envious and wanted Jesus killed.

First Clement also uses φθόνος (envy) in conjunction with ζῆλος (jealousy) to establish the basis by which Cain murdered Abel (*1Cl* 4.1–6, cf. Ge 4:3–8), Jacob fled Esau (*1Cl* 4.8–10, cf. Ge 27:4ff), Joseph's brothers sold him into slavery (*1Cl* 4.9, cf. Ge 37), Moses fled Pharoah (*1Cl* 4.10, cf. Ex 2:14), Aaron and Miriam opposed Moses (*1Cl* 4.11, cf. Nu 12), Dathan and Abiram opposed Moses (*1Cl* 4.12, cf. Nu 16:13–40), and Saul's persecution of David (*1Cl* 4.13, cf. 1Sa 18). Further, *First Clement* posits envy and jealousy as the primary reason for current (i.e. first century) persecution:

> Because of jealousy and *envy*, the greatest and most righteous pillars of the church were persecuted and they competed until death. (*1Cl* 5.2, emphasis added)

Peter and Paul are then listed as the primary examples (*1Cl* 5.3–7). Envy leads to persecution and, frequently, to murder. This is the path the false teachers referenced in First Timothy had begun to chart for themselves (cf. also Php 1:15).

The path of the false teachers also included "strife." The Greek word is ἔρις, usually glossed as 'strife,' 'discord,' or 'contention.'[21] This word also occurs in the epistle to Titus:

> But avoid foolish controversies and genealogies and *contentions* and quarrels about the law, for they are useless and fruitless. (Tt 3:9, emphasis added)

These dissensions, where people take positions irreconcilably at odds with one another, are unhealthy and contrary to sound doctrine. This is underscored again in *First Clement*:

> Therefore it is right and holy, men and brothers, for us to be obedient to God rather than to follow those instigators of loathsome jealousy in arrogance and insurrection. For it is not common harm but rather great danger we will endure if we recklessly surrender ourselves to the purposes of the people who plunge into *strife* and rebellion in order to estrange us from what is good. (*1Cl* 14.1–2, emphasis added)

---

[20] cf. Mt 28:17–18.

[21] BDAG, p. 392. Occurs 9x in NT, 2x in PE: 1Ti 6:4; Tt 3:9. In the 10 AF occurrences, nine are in *1Cl* and one in Ign., *Eph.*

Slander is also associated with the false teachers. "Slanders" is a translation of βλασφημία, typically meaning 'reviling,' 'denigration,' 'disrespect,' 'slander,'[22] or even 'blasphemy.' The word is also used in Matthew:

> But the things that come out of the mouth come from the heart, and these defile the person. For from the heart come evil plans, murder, adultery, sexual immorality, theft, false witness, *abusive speech*. (Mt 15:18–19, emphasis added)

Thus slander is spoken, and it defiles the one who speaks it. Slander is spoken with evil intent; it is not intended for the benefit or building up of a person. The false teachers in First Timothy slander their opponents.

The false teachers are also guilty of "evil suspicions." The word translated "evil" is the Greek word πονηρός, a relatively common word meaning 'wicked,' 'evil,' 'bad,' 'base,' 'worthless,' 'vicious,' or 'degenerate.'[23] The word translated "suspicions" is ὑπόνοια, an NT *hapax* meaning 'suspicion' or 'conjecture.'[24] The word ὑπόνοια is used with some frequency (41 times) by Philo, the following from his tractate on the *Special Laws*:

> But if the charge which is made against her be contested, and if the evidence be doubtful, so as not to incline to either side, then let the two parties go up to the temple, and let the man stand in front of the altar, in the presence of the priest for the day, and then let him state his *suspicions* and his grounds for them, and let him produce and offer some barley flour, as a species of oblation on behalf of his wife, to prove that he accuses her, not out of insult, but with an honest intention, because he has a reasonable doubt. (Philo, *Spec. Laws* III 55, emphasis added)

In this instance, having to do with adultery, when a charge is brought up against a woman where the evidence is inconclusive, the man bringing the charge is to state "his suspicions and his grounds" for the charge before the woman and the priest. The man suspects but cannot conclusively prove his charge. In First Timothy, the false teachers craving for word-battles and debate are seen to seed "evil suspicions." This could also perhaps be "false conjectures;"[25] the false teachers crafting lies describing untrue actions of others.

---

[22] BDAG, p. 178. Occurs 18x in NT, only here in PE. See also comment on 1Ti 1:13

[23] BDAG, p. 851. Occurs 80x in NT, 3x in PE: 1Ti 6:4; 2Ti 3:13; 4:18.

[24] BDAG, p. 1040. NT *hapax*.

[25] BDAG, p. 1040.

VERSE 5

constant wrangling by people

In this verse "constant wrangling" is a translation of διαπαρατριβή, defined as "that which is characterized by constant argumentativeness and therefore irritating."[26] This word is virtually nonexistent in known sources. Luke Timothy Johnson writes:

> This is the only occurrence in ancient literature of the term *diaparatribai*. It appears to function as an intensified form of *paratribai* (friction/irritation, Polybius, *Histories* 2.36.5).[27]

This constant friction is "by people." Recall the entire statement that runs through verses 4–5 is:

> [The one teaching different doctrine] is conceited, understanding nothing, but having a morbid interest concerning controversies and disputes about words, from which come envy, strife, slanders, evil suspicions, constant wrangling *by people* of depraved mind and deprived of the truth, who consider godliness to be a means of gain. (1Ti 6:4–5, emphasis added).

This whole sentence shows a progression. First it establishes the problem of striving after debate and word-fights. The effect of that misplaced striving is then discussed: it leads to sin primarily evidenced in interpersonal enmity (slander, lies, rumor-mongering and the like). Those who persist in proclaiming the different doctrine, who chase unhealthily after controversy and quarrels, who snipe at those they disagree with; they will do nothing but entrench themselves in their untenable positions of false doctrine. These are the people (ἄνθρωπος)[28] referenced.

of depraved mind and deprived of the truth, who consider godliness to be a means of gain

This is a series of three participial phrases, all of which further describe the group of false teachers and their adherents. That the three participle clauses further describe the noun "people" (ἀνθρώπων) seems evident as the noun and participles agree in case, number and gender (genitive plural masculine). Further, the first two participles also agree in tense and voice (perfect passives) and are joined by καὶ, joining the first two participle clauses into a compound statement. The third

---

[26] BDAG, p. 235. NT *hapax*. Note also the gloss in BDF §116.4 of 'constant disputations.'

[27] Luke Timothy Johnson, *The First and Second Letters to Timothy: A New Translation with Introduction and Commentary* (New Haven; London: Yale University Press, 2008), 293.

[28] BDAG, p. 81.

participle clause (which has an embedded infinitival clause, "who consider godliness *to be* a means of gain") functions epexegetically, further explaining the frame of mind of these mentally-depraved and truthfully-deprived false teachers.

of depraved mind: The word translated "depraved" is διαφθείρω. The Greek word here has the sense of 'deprave' or 'ruin.'[29] It is also used in Revelation:

> And the nations were angry, and your wrath has come, and the time for the dead to be judged, and to give their reward to your slaves the prophets and to the saints and to the ones who fear your name, the small and the great, and *to destroy* those *who destroy* the earth." (Re 11:18, emphasis added)

In this example from Revelation, the word διαφθείρω occurs twice. The first occurrence is an infinitive verb, the second is a substantive participle functioning as the subject. Thus, in this participle clause in Revelation, the same word (διαφθείρω) functions as both the verb and the subject of the clause. The meaning is fairly clear; the ones who have destroyed/ruined the earth will themselves be thoroughly destroyed/ruined. What was pristine has been ruined; those who ruined it will themselves be similarly treated.

The word also occurs in Ignatius' *Epistle to the Romans*:

> The ruler of this age wants to abduct me and to *corrupt* my mind towards God. Therefore let none of you who are present help him. Instead be on my side, that is, God's side. Do not speak of Jesus Christ but desire the world. (Ign., *Rom.* 7.1, emphasis added)

Notably this instance of διαφθείρω is also in the context of corrupting/ruining the mind.[30] Ignatius is a prisoner, on his way to be martyred in Rome. Later in §7 he instructs the Roman believers so that they may know his mind before he arrives in Rome: He desires to serve God, to not betray Christ, and to die a martyr. He says this and urges them to know this is his goal, and if he says otherwise when in Rome they are not to believe him. In other words, if Ignatius' mind and thinking is *corrupted* along the way—corrupted so that he no longer desires to remain true to his testimony—the Romans are to hold him to his previous word and not intervene to save him.

In First Timothy, the minds of the false teachers have already been corrupted and destroyed. They no longer hold to the true teaching of Christ.

---

[29] BDAG, p. 239. Occurs 6x in NT, only here in PE.

[30] Though Ign., *Rom.* 7.1 uses a different word for "mind" (γνώμη; 1Ti 6:5 uses νοῦς).

deprived of the truth: The Greek word ἀποστερέω is the source of "deprived." It is usually glossed as 'rob,' 'steal,' 'despoil,' or 'defraud.'[31] First Corinthians uses the term:

> Therefore it is already completely a loss for you that you have lawsuits with one another. Why not rather be wronged? Why not rather *be defrauded*? But you wrong and *defraud*, and do this to brothers! (1Co 6:7–8, emphasis added)

The verb occurs twice in these two verses. The context is that of lawsuits among the brethren. The goal of the lawsuit—pursuing gain of something at the expense of another believer—is not a worthy goal for believers to aspire after. In attempting to rob or steal in such a way from a fellow believer (or anyone, for that manner), one only ends up defrauding one's self. Ignatius, in his *Letter to the Ephesians*, works this to the opposite extreme:

> Let us be found to be by gentleness their brothers and sisters, and let us be eager to be imitators of the Lord. Who was treated more unjustly? Who was more *cheated*? Who was more rejected? So that some weed of the devil may not be found in you, but with all purity and self-control you may remain outwardly and inwardly in Jesus Christ. (Ign., *Eph.* 10.3, emphasis added)[32]

Ignatius, noting that Christ was the most wronged as he had no sin yet bore all sin, implores the Ephesians to follow in Christ's steps and be mistreated, wronged and defrauded. In First Timothy, however, the false teachers are already defrauded, they have already been robbed of the truth.

who consider godliness to be a means of gain: The false teachers, depraved in mind and bankrupt in terms of the truth, consider godliness primarily to be a method of financial gain. The word translated "who consider" is νομίζω, occurring here in the sense of 'think,' 'believe,' 'hold,' or 'consider.'[33] Three instances in Acts provide assistance in understanding this word:

> And *he thought* his brothers would understand that God was granting deliverance to them by his hand, but they did not understand. (Ac 7:25, emphasis added)

> But Jews arrived from Antioch and Iconium, and when they had won over the crowds and stoned Paul, they dragged him outside the city, *thinking* he was dead. (Ac 14:19, emphasis added)

> And after the jailer was awake and saw the doors of the prison open, he drew his sword and was about to kill himself, because *he thought* the prisoners had escaped. (Ac 16:27, emphasis added)

---

[31] BDAG, p. 121. Occurs 6x in NT, only here in PE.

[32] Cf. Ign., *Eph.* 10.2 for clarification on what "do this" means in the context.

[33] BDAG, p. 675. Occurs 15x in NT, only here in PE.

Each of these instances, translating νομίζω as some form of "think," portrays the primary meaning of the word. In each example, someone makes a tentative judgment concerning the situation and then acts (or almost acts) upon it. The judgment, however, is in need of more evidence to be corroborated. The same is true in First Timothy; the false teachers have made an incorrect judgment that godliness[34] is a means of financial gain. They are wrong and are in need of correction.

The word translated "means of gain" is the Greek word πορισμός.[35] In the NT, it only occurs in 1Ti 6:5 and 6:6. An enlightening classical usage is that of Plutarch: "he had only two *means of gain*: farming and frugality."[36] As with First Timothy, πορισμός is used to describe some sort of occupation or means by which one finances one's daily living needs. These false teachers, relying on the practice of godliness to finance their needs, are Christmongers; trading on Christ to make a living. The warnings against such from *Didache* 12 may echo the same sentiment:

> And if [the traveler claiming Christianity] has no craft, take this into consideration according to your understanding how he shall live among you as a Christian without being idle. And if he does not want to act in this way, *he is a Christmonger. Beware of such as these.* (*Did.* 12.4–5, emphasis added)

In their depravity, the false teachers have perverted godliness. Christians are to stay away from such as these.

---

[34] On "godliness" (εὐσέβεια) see comment on 1Ti 2:2.

[35] BDAG, p. 854. Occurs 2x in NT, both in PE: 1Ti 6:5, 6.

[36] Plutarch, *Cato Maj.* 351 [25, 1], as cited and translated in BDAG p. 854. Plutarch is routinely dated in the 1st or 2nd century AD, so usage is roughly contemporary with that of the New Testament.

True Riches and Contentment (1Ti 6:6–10)

> *But godliness with contentment is a great means of gain. For we have brought nothing into the world, so that neither can we bring anything out. But if we have food and clothing, with these things we will be content. But those who want to be rich fall into temptation and a trap and many foolish and harmful desires, which plunge those people into ruin and destruction. For the love of money is a root of all evil, by which some, because they desire it, have gone astray from the faith and have pierced themselves with many pains. (1Ti 6:6–10)*

Verse 6

But godliness with contentment is a great means of gain.

The false teachers saw great gain in godliness (v. 5). Paul corrects this notion by qualifying it: godliness must be "with contentment" in order for gain to occur. The word translated "contentment" is αὐτάρκεια here having to do with 'contentment' or 'self-sufficiency.'[1] The word is used in the *Mandates* of the Shepherd of Hermas:

> Hear now," he said, "about faith. There are two angels with each person, one of righteousness and one of wickedness." [2] "How then," I said, "sir, will I know their workings, because both angels dwell with me?" [3] "Listen," he said, "and understand them. Indeed the angel of righteousness is delicate and modest and gentle and quiet. Therefore when this one enters into your heart, immediately he speaks with you about righteousness, about purity, about holiness, and about *contentment*, and about every righteous deed, and about all glorious virtue. When all these things enter into your heart, you know that the angel of righteousness is with you. Therefore these things are the works of the angel of righteousness. So believe in this one and in his works." (Hermas, *Mandates* VI, ii, 1–3, emphasis added)

In Hermas' *Mandates*, the qualities reinforced by the angel of righteousness include contentment; the list is rounded out with inclusions of "every righteous deed" and "all glorious virtue." BDAG confirms contentment's status as a classical virtue in

[1] BDAG, p. 152. Occurs 2x in NT: 2Co 9:8; 1Ti 6:6.

remarking it is "… a favorite virtue of the Cynics and the Stoics."[2] This is expanded in the TDNT:

> The word is both a central concept in ethical discussion from the time of Socrates and yet also a well-worn term in ordinary usage. In Cynic and Stoic philosophy it denotes one who exercises ἀρκεῖσθαι in relation to his own inner possibility and who thus becomes an independent man sufficient to himself and in need of none else.[3]

The idea in First Timothy is that if one is content, one need not strive after ill-gotten gain. Verses 7–8 further describe this contentment.

VERSE 7

For we have brought nothing into the world

The description of "contentment" is prefaced with the notion that "we have brought nothing into the world." The word translated "we brought" is εἰσφέρω, roughly meaning 'bring in.'[4] The word is also used in Hebrews:

> For the bodies of those animals whose blood *is brought into* the sanctuary by the high priest for sins are burned up outside the camp. (Heb 13:11, emphasis added)

This reinforces the basic idea of εἰσφέρω. It also appears that Polycarp referenced this exact portion of First Timothy in his *Letter to the Philippians*:

> But the beginning of all difficulty is the love of money. Knowing, therefore, *that we have brought nothing into the world, and neither are we able to take out anything*, let us arm ourselves with the weapons of righteousness and let us teach ourselves first to follow in the commandment of the Lord. (Poly., *Phil.* 4.1, emphasis added)[5]

Polycarp, following the teaching established here in First Timothy, notes that greed is a source of trouble and contrasts that trouble against the notion that one cannot take anything, including money, with him upon exit from this world. The view of the long run, then, should be focused upon things transcendent.

---

[2] BDAG p. 152.

[3] TDNT 1:466; the entire article merits examination.

[4] BDAG, p. 295. Occurs 8x in NT, only here in PE.

[5] Note also the use of 1Ti 6:10 (on which see comment). 2Co 6:7 and Ro 6:13 are also related to this portion of Polycarp's letter to the Philippians.

so that neither can we bring anything out

The verb translated "take ... out" is ἐκφέρω. The contrast between "bring in" (εἰσ + φέρω) and "take out" (ἐκ + φέρω) is obvious in the Greek; both verbs are formed by adding a preposition to the verb φέρω.

Verse 7 puts contentment into perspective. If one is motivated by godliness, his perspective is properly adjusted and not bound to life in the world. Because godly contentment is not reliant upon things of the world, material means cannot influence it. Instead, one has greater gain because hope in Christ will eventually be realized.

Verse 8

But if we have food and clothing, with these things we will be content

The word translated "food" is διατροφή, meaning 'support' or 'sustenance.'[6] Josephus also uses διατροφή:

> Let not those that reap and gather in the corn that is reaped, gather in the gleanings also, but let them rather leave some handfuls for those that are in want of the necessaries of life, that it may be a support and a supply to them, in order to their *subsistence*. (Jos., *Ant.* 4.231, emphasis added)

Josephus uses διατροφή in reference to the corn gleaned from the field by those in need. The fields were not completely harvested; some corn was left for those in need to gather up for their own sustenance. The word διατροφή is also attested in P.Oxy III. 494[16], a will from 156 AD: "my said wife shall supply to my son Dius for his *sustenance* and other expenses."[7]

In both cases, διατροφή refers to the necessaries of life, the food one needs to live. It does not refer to overabundance or extravagance.

The word translated "clothing" is another NT *hapax*, σκέπασμα, here defined as "that which serves as a cover and hence as a protection, *covering*."[8] Philo uses the term in his tractate *On the Decalogue*:

> The bull, as a plougher, draws furrows for the reception of the seed, and is again the most powerful of all animals to thresh the corn out when it is necessary to purify it of the chaff; the ram gives us the most beautiful garments for *the coverings of our persons*; for if our bodies were naked, they would easily be

---

[6] BDAG, p. 238. NT *hapax*.

[7] M-M, p. 156, emphasis added.

[8] BDAG, p. 927. NT *hapax*.

> destroyed either through heat, or though intense cold, caused at one time by the blaze of the sun, and at another by the cooling of the air. (Philo, *Decalogue* 77, emphasis added)

Philo uses and adequately defines the literal sense of σκέπασμα:[9] they are garments that cover the nakedness of the body, protecting the body from the harshness of the elements.

The phrase "we will be content" is a translation of ἀρκέω. In this context, ἀρκέω means to 'be satisfied' or 'content' with something.[10] The word is also used in Hebrews:

> Your lifestyle must be free from the love of money, *being content* with what you have. For he himself has said, "I will never desert you, and I will never abandon you." (Heb 13:5, emphasis added)

The context in Hebrews is much the same as that of First Timothy, with an emphasis on contentment as an alternative to seeking unhealthy gain. *First Clement* also uses ἀρκέω:

> And you were all humble-minded, in no way being boastful, being submissive rather than forcing submission, giving more gladly than receiving, *being satisfied* with the provisions of Christ, and paying attention to his words you have carefully stored away in your innermost being, and his sufferings were before your eyes. (*1Cl* 2.1, emphasis added)

First Clement, like Hebrews and First Timothy, focuses on contentment springing from what has already been supplied instead of setting sights on gaining more.

VERSE 9

But those who want to be rich

The word translated "want" is βούλομαι.[11] Here it is paired with the infinitive verb πλουτέω, translated "to be rich."[12] In its primary usage, the verb πλουτέω has to do with material wealth, an overabundance of financial means. Consider this excerpt from the *Shepherd of Hermas*:

---

[9] M-M (p. 577) cover the metaphorical use of σκέπασμα, that of protection. The instance in 1Ti 6:8 may or may not have metaphorical connotations.

[10] BDAG, p. 131. Occurs 8x in NT, only here in PE.

[11] BDAG, p. 182. Occurs 37x in NT, 4x in PE: 1Ti 2:8; 5:14; 6:9; Tt 3:8. See comment on 1Ti 2:8.

[12] BDAG, p. 831. Occurs 12x in NT, 2x in PE: 1Ti 6:9, 18.

> And answering her, I said, "Lady, then when will they be useful for the building?" "Whenever," she said, "the riches that beguile them may be cut away from them, then they will be useful to God. For just as the round stone, unless it is hewn and the rubble is thrown away from it, is not able to become square, so also *those who are rich* in this world, unless their riches are hewn away, they are not able to be useful to the Lord. Understand first from yourself: when you were rich you were useless, but now you are useful and beneficial for life. Be useful to God, for you yourself also are taken from the same stones." (Hermas, *Visions* III, vi, 6–7, emphasis added)

In Hermas, the focus on riches highlights how being wealthy can hinder one's service. In First Timothy, the focus is on the desire to be wealthy and its potential corrupting influence.

fall into temptation

The word translated "fall" is ἐμπίπτω[13] with "into" coming from the preposition εἰς. The notion of "falling into" something was introduced earlier, in 1Ti 3:6 and 7:

> not newly converted, lest he become conceited and *fall into* the condemnation of the devil. But he must also have a good testimony from those outside, in order that he may not *fall into* disgrace and the trap of the devil. (1Ti 3:6–7, emphasis added)

Much like the potential overseer is warned from falling into various negative states (condemnation of the devil, disgrace, snare of the devil), in 1Ti 6 chasing after the desire to be rich is strongly warned against.

One problem with desiring wealth is that of "temptation." This is a translation of the Greek word πειρασμός, here having to do with 'temptation' or 'enticement' toward sin.[14] The word is used (along with the preposition εἰς) in the Lord's Prayer: "And do not bring us *into temptation*, but deliver us from evil." (Mt 6:13, emphasis added). In that sentence, temptation and evil are associated.

Second Clement uses πειρασμός as well:

> For even I am utterly sinful and have not yet escaped *temptation*, but am still in the midst of the tools of the devil. I am eager to pursue righteousness so that I may even be able to be near it, being in fear of the coming judgment. (*2Cl* 18.2, emphasis added)

---

[13] BDAG, p. 324. Occurs 7x in NT, 3x in PE: 1Ti 3:6, 7; 6:9. See comment on 1Ti 3:6.

[14] BDAG, p. 793. Occurs 21x in NT, only here in PE.

In *Second Clement*, the author provides a threefold description of himself. He is "completely sinful," he has "not yet fled temptation" and he is "still surrounded by the instruments of the Devil." In such contexts, the sense of being tempted toward sin is plainly evident.

and a trap

The underlying Greek relies on context and grammatical structure to provide the idea of "falling into a trap." The Greek word translated "trap" is παγίς, 'trap' or 'snare.'[15] This also occurs in 1Ti 3:7, describing potential overseers:

> But he must also have a good testimony from those outside, in order that he may not fall into disgrace and the *trap* of the devil. (1Ti 3:7, emphasis added)

and many foolish and harmful desires

The word translated "foolish" is the Greek word ἀνόητος. The word has the sense of 'unintelligent,' 'foolish' or 'dull-witted.'[16] The epistle to Titus also uses ἀνόητος:

> For we also were once *foolish*, disobedient, led astray, enslaved to various desires and pleasures, spending our lives in wickedness and envy, despicable, hating one another. (Tt 3:3, emphasis added)

In Titus, the label "foolish" (ἀνόητος) is used to describe people. Romans uses ἀνόητος in contrast with "wise":

> I am under obligation both to Greeks and to barbarians, both to the wise and to *the foolish*. (Ro 1:14, emphasis added)

The contrasting nature is evident because multiple comparisons are made in this one verse. As "Greeks" are to "barbarians" (civilized to uncivilized) so are the "wise" to the "foolish."

More along the lines of the First Timothy instance which uses "foolish" adjectivally to describe "desires," the *Corpus Hermeticum* uses ἀνόητος to describe thoughts:

> In God alone, is, therefore, Good, or rather Good is God Himself. So then, Asclepius, the name alone of Good is found in men, the thing itself nowhere [in them], for this can never be. For no material body doth contain It—a thing bound on all sides by bad, by labors, pains, desires and passions, by error and by *foolish* thoughts. (*Corpus Hermeticum* 6.3b, emphasis added)

---

[15] BDAG, p. 747. Occurs 5x in NT: Lk 21:35; Ro 11:9; 1Ti 3:7; 6:9; 2Ti 2:26. See comment on 1Ti 3:7 for further discussion.

[16] BDAG, p. 84. Occurs 8x in NT, 2x in PE: 1Ti 6:9; Tt 3:3.

In the *Corpus Hermeticum*, the thoughts are not wise, they are foolish and unthinking. First Timothy uses ἀνόητος similarly; the desire for wealth plunges one into ever more foolish (senseless) desires.

These desires are also "harmful." The Greek word is βλαβερός, only occurring here in the New Testament.[17] The word is also used in the *Shepherd of Hermas*:

> "What sort," I said, "of luxuries, sir, are *harmful*?" He said, "Every deed is a luxury to the person whoever does *it* with pleasure. For even the irritable one, giving satisfaction to his own temper, lives luxuriously. And the adulterer and the drunkard and the slanderer and the liar and the greedy person and the defrauder and the one who does similar to these things gives satisfaction to his own sickness, so he lives in luxury from his deed. (Hermas, *Similitudes* VI, v, 5, emphasis added)

In Hermas, luxuries have a "harmful" effect on the believer. In First Timothy, the same can be said of the desire to be rich; it spurs further desires that will be harmful.

The Greek word translated "desires" is ἐπιθυμία, meaning 'craving' or 'lust.'[18] The word is also used in Second Timothy:

> For there will be a time when they will not put up with sound teaching, but in accordance with their own *desires*, they will accumulate for themselves teachers, because they have an insatiable curiosity, and they will turn away from the hearing of the truth, but will turn to myths. (2Ti 4:3–4, emphasis added)

As seen above, the word ἐπιθυμία does not have to do specifically with sexual lust; it has to do with strong desire after anything. Polycarp's *Letter to the Philippians* uses ἐπιθυμία with the sense of non-sexual desire or lust:

> For everyone who does not confess that Jesus Christ has come in the flesh is an antichrist, and whoever does not confess the testimony of the cross is from the devil, and whoever twists the sayings of the Lord for one's own sinful *passions*, and says that there is neither resurrection nor judgment, this one is the firstborn of Satan. (Poly., *Phil.* 7.1, emphasis added)

These desires spurred on by the desire for riches are "foolish" and "harmful" and avoided when the desire for riches is properly dealt with.

which plunge those people into ruin and destruction

Chasing after these "foolish and harmful desires" has the effect of plunging "people into ruin and destruction." The Greek word βυθίζω, here translated "plunge," is

---

[17] BDAG, p. 177. NT *hapax*.

[18] BDAG, p. 372. Occurs 38x in NT, 6x in PE.

glossed as 'plunge' or 'expose to.'[19] This use in First Timothy is in a figurative sense. The only other instance of βυθίζω in the NT uses the word literally:

> And they signaled to their partners in the other boat to come and help them, and they came and filled both the boats so that *they began to sink*. (Lk 5:7, emphasis added)

The word is also used literally in Second Maccabees:

> And the people of Joppa accomplished so great an impiety as inviting those Judeans who dwelt among themselves to embark with their women and children in boats that were equipped by them as if there were no ill will toward them. And this was after the public decree of the city. And when the Judeans accepted, as desiring to live in peace and having no suspicion, they were brought and *drowned*, being no fewer than two hundred people. (2Ma 12:3–4, emphasis added)

In these examples, βυθίζω has to do with the sinking of a ship or the drowning of a person. When used figuratively, βυθίζω has to do with something external having a detrimental impact on someone, either physically or otherwise. In 1Ti 6:9, desires for riches are plunging people (ἄνθρωπος) toward ruin and destruction.

The word "ruin" is a translation of the Greek word ὄλεθρος, having to do with 'destruction,' 'ruin' or 'death.'[20] The same word is used in First Thessalonians:

> Whenever they say "Peace and security," then sudden *destruction* will overtake them like the birth pains of a pregnant woman, and they will not possibly escape. (1Th 5:3, emphasis added).

The word is also used by Ignatius in his *Letter to the Ephesians*:

> Therefore make every effort to come together as often as possible to give thanks and to glory to God. For when you gather together frequently, the powers of Satan are destroyed and his *destruction* is brought to an end by the unanimity of your faith. (Ign., *Eph.* 13.1, emphasis added)

In First Timothy, ruin (ὄλεθρος) is complemented with "destruction," a translation of the Greek word ἀπώλεια. This word has to do with 'ruin' or 'annihilation.'[21] This word is also used in Second Peter:

> And regard the patience of our Lord as salvation, just as also our dear brother Paul wrote to you, according to the wisdom that was given to him, as he does also in all his letters, speaking in them about these things, in which there are some things hard to understand, which the ignorant and unstable distort to their own

---

[19] BDAG, p. 185. Occurs 2x in NT: Lk 5:7; 1Ti 6:9.

[20] BDAG, p. 702. Occurs 4x in NT: 1Co 5:5; 1Th 5:3; 2Th 1:9; 1Ti 6:9.

[21] BDAG, p. 127. Occurs 18x in the NT, only here in the PE.

> *destruction*, as they also do the rest of the scriptures. (2Pe 3:15–16, emphasis added)

Both words (ὄλεθρος and ἀπώλεια) carry the same basic semantic connotation, but when used together they draw attention to the nature, depth and breadth of the ruin/destruction. Consider *First Clement*:

> Since I called and you did not obey and I extended words and you did not pay attention but disregarded my counsel and disobeyed my correction, therefore I also will laugh at your *destruction* and will rejoice whenever *destruction* comes to you and whenever turmoil suddenly reaches you and destruction arrives like a sudden blast of wind or when tribulation and siege come upon you. (*1Cl* 57.4, emphasis added)[22]

In *First Clement*, the different pictures of destruction are not each separate instances, it is a consecutive picture, image building upon image, of the totality of destruction the unrepentant one will be subject to.[23] The idea is similar in First Timothy. Those who fall prey to the desire of riches are not destined both for "ruin" and "destruction;" these are two words describing the same bitter end.

Verse 10

For the love of money is a root of all evil

The phrase "love of money" is a translation of the Greek word φιλαργυρία. It is a compound word, only occurring here in the NT.[24] In the context of First Timothy 6, the "love of money" (φιλαργυρία) corresponds with the "desire to be rich" in 1Ti 6:9. The word also occurs twice in the pseudepigraphal *Testament of Judah*:

> Guard yourselves therefore, my children, against sexual promiscuity and love of money; (*T. Judah* 18.2, emphasis added)[25]

> My children, love of money leads to idolatry, because once they are led astray by money, they designate as gods those who are not gods. It makes anyone who has it go out of his mind. (*T. Judah* 19.1, emphasis added)

---

[22] The first emphasized word is ἀπώλεια, the second ὄλεθρος.

[23] cf. 1Cl 57.1–2.

[24] BDAG, p. 1056. NT *hapax*.

[25] Notable also are *T. Judah* 18.3-6 which describe the effect that fornication and love of money will have on the individual.

The second instance, from *T. Judah* 19.1, summarizes the thrust of *T. Judah* 18.2–6: chasing after sin—such as the love of money—widens the chasm between man and God.

In First Timothy, the love of money is described as "a root of all evil." The word translated "root" is ῥίζα.[26] While ῥίζα can literally mean the root of a physical plant, here the sense is "that which constitutes a basic source or reason for an event or state—'source, cause, reason.' "[27] The *Wisdom of Solomon* uses ῥίζα in this sense:

> For to know you is complete righteousness, and to know your might is *the root* of immortality. (Wis 15:3, emphasis added)

The *Sibylline Oracles* use the word similarly:

> But they care for righteousness and virtue and not *love of money*, which *begets* innumerable evils for mortal men, war, and limitless famine. (*Sib. Or.* 3.234–236, emphasis added)

In the *Sibylline Oracles*, an idiomatic translation is used to show that the love of money "begets (ῥίζα) of innumerable ills to mortal men." Polycarp, in his *Letter to the Philippians*, uses ῥίζα in the thanksgiving section of his letter:

> and because of *the secure root* of your faith, being proclaimed from ancient times, still continues and bears fruit to our Lord Jesus Christ, who endured because of our sins, to reach even death, whom God raised up having loosed the birth pains of Hades. (Poly., *Phil.* 1.2, emphasis added)

In Polycarp, ῥίζα is used of things good—the "secure root" of faith. He furthers the analogy with references to growing and bearing fruit.

All three of these sources—*Wisdom of Solomon*, Polycarp and the *Oracles*—use ῥίζα similarly to this instance in First Timothy, indicating the commonality of the illustration. In First Timothy, the use of ῥίζα to indicate that the love of money lurks deeply as a source of evils, would have been understood as easily as we understand it today.

On the phrase "all evil," there are two Greek words at play. The first is κακός, here with the article and also in the plural. This word is typically translated as 'evil' or 'bad.'[28] The second is πᾶς, typically translated 'each,' 'every,' or 'all.'[29] A woodenly literal translation of the phrase could be "of all the evils." In English, this is typically

---

[26] BDAG, p. 905. Occurs 17x in NT, only here in PE.

[27] LN 89.17

[28] BDAG, p. 501. Occurs 50x in NT, 3x in PE: 1Ti 6:10; 2Ti 4:14; Tt 1:12.

[29] BDAG, p. 782. Occurs 1243x in NT.

rendered idiomatically as "of evil" or "of all kinds of evil." Similar "of all the [plural]" statements occur elsewhere in the NT,[30] below are a few examples:

> Mk 4:32: "but when it is sown it grows up and becomes the largest of *all the garden herbs* ..."
> Lk 11:50: "so that the blood *of all of the prophets* ..."
> 2Co 11:28: "... there is the pressure on me every day of the anxiety *about all the churches.*"

This sort of language appears to be used in comparisons, as in Mk 4:32 where the mustard seed develops into a plant that "becomes the largest of all the garden plants;" or in statements that appear to be stating something comprehensive as background for the current discussion, as in Lk 11:50 and 2Co 11:38. This is the same usage in First Timothy; "all evil" is the comprehensive item; "love of money" is then used as an example of a "root;" an initial or primary cause that in this case leads into the further broad category of "all kinds of evil."

by which some, because they desire it

The word translated "they desire" is ὀρέγω, here meaning 'aspire to,' 'strive for,' or 'desire.' The same word is used earlier in 1Ti 3:1:[31]

> The saying is trustworthy: if anyone *aspires* to supervision, he desires a good work. (1Ti 3:1, emphasis added)

The usage here in chapter six is similar.

have gone astray from the faith

The phrase "have gone astray" is a translation of the Greek word ἀποπλανάω. The word has the basic sense of 'mislead.'[32] The only other NT occurrence of ἀποπλανάω is in Mark 13:22:

> For false messiahs and false prophets will appear, and will produce signs and wonders in order *to mislead*, if possible, the elect. (Mk 13:22, emphasis added)

In Polycarp's *Letter to the Philippians*, a substantive participle of ἀποπλανάω is used:

> And the presbyters also *must be* compassionate, merciful to all, turning back *those who have gone astray*, caring for all sick, neglecting neither widow or orphan or

---

[30] Eight times in addition to the instance in 1Ti 6:10: Mt 13:32; Mk 4:32; 12:33; Lk 2:31; Ac 3:18; 2Co 11:28; Re 8:3.

[31] See comment on 1Ti 3:1.

[32] BDAG, p. 118. Occurs 2x in NT: Mk 13:22; 1Ti 6:10.

> the poor, but always taking thought for the good before God and people, refraining from all anger, partiality, unjust judgment, being far removed from all love of money, not quickly believing against anyone, not relentless in judgment, understanding that we are all debtors in the matter of sin. (Poly., *Phil.* 6.1, emphasis added)

Here one of the responsibilities of the elders is to address those who have gone astray; those who have strayed from the path of faith. In First Timothy, the "love of money" is a pressure that has enticed some to wander away from the faith.

The structure in 1Ti 6:10 involves the verb ἀποπλανάω modified by a prepositional phrase using the preposition ἀπὸ ("from"). This does not describe what the people are being led astray *by*—that is done earlier in the verse—this describes the good thing that the people are forsaking. This same structure (ἀποπλανάω + ἀπὸ) is used in the *Shepherd of Hermas*:

> Just as the good vineyards, when they experience neglect, become barren by the thorns and various weeds, so too people who have believed and who have fallen into these many deeds which have been previously mentioned *are misled by their way of thinking* and they really understand nothing about righteousness, but even when they hear about deity and truth, their understanding has been busied with their deed and they really understand nothing. (Hermas, *Mandates* X, i, 5, emphasis added)

> Therefore he takes those who have strayed from God and walked in the lusts and deceptions of this world and he punishes them, just as is proper, with severe and various kinds of punishments. (Hermas, *Similitudes* VI, iii, 3, emphasis added)

The use of this structure in First Timothy is similar; the craving after material wealth may draw some away from the faith.

and have pierced themselves with many pains

The word "pierced" is a translation of the Greek verb περιπείρω, glossed as 'pierce through' or 'impale.'[33] Here the usage is figurative, describing how those who wander from the faith in pursuit of the love of money have injured themselves. The literal usage of περιπείρω is found in Josephus' *Wars of the Jews*:

> so they were enclosed between two walls, and were slain in great numbers together; many of them *were run through* by swords of their own men, and many by their own swords, besides an immense number that were slain by the Romans;—nor had they any courage to revenge themselves; for there was added

[33] BDAG, p. 803. NT *hapax*.

> to the consternation they were in from the enemy, their being betrayed by their own friends, which quite broke their spirits: (Jos., *Wars* 3.296, emphasis added)

Philo uses περιπείρω as well, perhaps more in line with the usage in First Timothy:

> Flaccus Avillius succeeded Sejanus in his hatred of and hostile designs against the Jewish nation. He was not, indeed, able to injure the whole people by open and direct means as he had been, inasmuch as he had less power for such a purpose, but *he inflicted* the most intolerable evils on all who came within his reach. (Philo, *Flaccus* 1, emphasis added)

In Philo, the sense is not of a physical impaling with a sword but reflective of the general idea of inflicting evil. The sense in First Timothy is similar; the pursuit of material gain inflicts harm in that it separates one from God.

The piercing is "with many pains." The Greek word translated "pains" is ὀδύνη, here used in the sense of 'distress.'[34] The only other NT occurrence is in Romans:

> I am telling the truth in Christ—I am not lying; my conscience bears witness to me in the Holy Spirit—that my grief is great and there is *constant distress* in my heart. (Ro 9:1–2, emphasis added)

In Romans, ὀδύνη is translated as "unceasing anguish;" the non-physical sense further clarified with "in my heart." This is in accordance with LSJ's glosses of ὀδύνη, 'pain of mind,' 'grief.'[35]

Though ὀδύνη does not occur frequently in the New Testament, it is used with some frequency in the LXX. One example is found in Proverbs:

> Give strong drink to those in pain, and wine to drink for those in *grief*, (Pr 31:6 [LXX 24:74])

The *Letter of Aristeas* also uses ὀδύνη.

> The king commended him (for his answer) and said to the guest after him, "How might one be a friend of man?" He replied, "By observing that the human race increases and is created over many years and in painful suffering, so that it is your duty neither to inflict punishments easily nor to submit men to torments, knowing that the life of mankind is constituted in *pain* and punishment. If you bear in mind each set of facts, you will be inclined to mercy, even as God is merciful." (*Let. Arist.* 208, emphasis added)

In *Letter of Aristeas*, as in Proverbs, the sense of ὀδύνη is that of mental grief or anguish. The same can be said of the use of ὀδύνη in First Timothy; the "piercing" of

---

[34] Having to do with "mental pain." BDAG, p. 692. Occurs 2x in NT: Ro 9:2; 1Ti 6:10.

[35] LSJ, p. 1199.

1Ti 6:10 is not a physical impalement. The grief and anguish is within the soul as a result of pursuing the love of money instead of pursuing the faith.

Characteristics of True Teachers (1Ti 6:11–12)

> *But you, O man of God, flee from these things, and pursue righteousness, godliness, faith, love, patient endurance, gentleness. Fight the good fight of the faith; take hold of the eternal life to which you were called, and confessed the good confession in the presence of many witnesses. (1Ti 6:11–12)*

Verse 11

But you, O man of God, flee from these things,

This transition from the previous section on false teachers contrasts them with Timothy, Paul's agent and the "man of God." The pronoun "you" is in the second person singular and refers to the addressee of the letter. The phrase "man of God" is in the vocative, suggesting "deep emotion on the part of the speaker."[1] Paul desires Timothy to hear what he has to say next; he gets his attention with the vocative construction.

The man of God (here Timothy) is to flee from the influence of materialism. The word translated "flee" is φεύγω, with the sense of 'flee from,' 'avoid,' or 'shun.'[2] Here it is in the imperative, matching well with the vocative "O man of God." Similar use of φεύγω is found in Second Timothy:

> But *flee* from youthful desires, and pursue righteousness, faith, love, and peace, in company with those who call upon the Lord from a pure heart. (2Ti 2:22, emphasis added)

In Second Timothy, as in First Timothy, Paul's advice is to flee whatever leads to sin and instead pursue righteousness.

---

[1] Maximilian Zerwick, *Biblical Greek, Illustrated by Examples*, English Edition, Adapted from the Fourth Latin Edition, trans. Joseph Smith (Rome: Pontifical Biblical Institute, 1963), 12.

[2] BDAG, p. 1052. Occurs 29x in NT; 2x in PE: 1Ti 6:11; 2Ti 2:22.

and pursue righteousness, godliness, faith, love, patient endurance, gentleness.

Materialism and its pursuit has corrupted many; Paul wants Timothy to pursue righteousness instead of money. The word translated "pursue" is the verb διώκω, here in the imperative. It carries the sense of 'pursue,' 'strive for,' 'seek after,' or 'aspire to.'[3] As noted above, this pair of imperative verbs (φεύγω and διώκω) also occurs in 2Ti 2:22. In both instances Paul urges Timothy to run from things that lead to sin (materialism and youthful passions) and to run toward righteousness (as well as 'faith' and 'love,' amongst other qualities).

righteousness: This is a translation of the Greek word δικαιοσύνη.[4] The same concept of pursuit of righteousness is found in *Second Clement*:

> For even I am utterly sinful and have not yet escaped temptation, but am still in the midst of the tools of the devil. I am eager *to pursue righteousness* so that I may even be able to be near it, being in fear of the coming judgment. (*2Cl* 18.2, emphasis added)

In First Timothy, the pursuit of righteousness (and other things) is what one does instead of pursuing material gain. *Second Clement* is a bit more general; pursuing righteousness is a method for combating sin and temptation of all kinds.

godliness, faith, love: These terms are all discussed earlier.[5]

patient endurance: The Greek word is ὑπομονή, meaning 'patience,' 'endurance,' 'fortitude,' 'steadfastness,' or 'perseverance.'[6] The word is used in a list of similar qualities in Second Timothy:

> But you have faithfully followed my teaching, way of life, purpose, faith, patience, love, *endurance*, persecutions, and sufferings that happened to me in Antioch, in Iconium, and in Lystra, what sort of persecutions I endured, and the Lord delivered me from all of them. (2Ti 3:10–11, emphasis added)

According to Second Timothy, Timothy followed Paul's model of endurance. In First Timothy, Paul was reminding and encouraging Timothy to pursue endurance as part of his effort to resist the call of materialism.

---

[3] BDAG, p. 254. Occurs 45x in NT; 3x in PE: 1Ti 6:11; 2Ti 2:22; 3:12.

[4] BDAG, p. 247. Occurs 92x in NT, 5x in PE: 1Ti 6:11; 2Ti 2:22; 3:16; 4:8; Tt 3:5.

[5] On godliness, see comment on 1Ti 2:2. On faith and love, see comment on 1Ti 1:5.

[6] BDAG, p. 1039. Occurs 32x in NT; 3x in PE: 1Ti 6:11; 2Ti 3:10; Tt 2:2.

gentleness: The Greek word translated "gentleness" is πραϋπαθία.[7] A comment from BDAG is helpful: "Hesychius explains it by using the words ἡσυχία and πραΰτης as synonyms, hence the opposite of an overbearing attitude."[8] The word is also found in Ignatius' *Letter to the Trallians*:

> Since I do not know of anything of such a kind among you, but I am protecting you, being my beloved, anticipating the snares of the devil. Therefore you, adopting *gentleness*, regain your strength in faith which is the flesh of the Lord and in love which is the blood of Jesus Christ. (Ign., *Trall.* 8.1, emphasis added)

Again, gentleness is seen as a response to "the snares of the devil." It is a response to sin and temptation; pursuing gentleness is one way to combat such things.

VERSE 12

Fight the good fight of the faith

The Greek word translated "Fight" is the verb ἀγωνίζομαι.[9] Consider Josephus' use of the word:

> [Trypho] also sent soldiers against those two thousand that were left in Galilee, in order to destroy them: but those men having heard the report of what had happened to Jonathan, they prevented the execution, and before those that were sent by Trypho came, they covered themselves with their armor, and went away out of the country. Now when those that were sent against them saw that *they were ready to fight* for their lives, they gave them no disturbance, but returned back to Trypho. (Jos., *Ant.* 13.192b–193, emphasis added)

However, ἀγωνίζομαι need not take on a military aura. The same word occurs in *First Clement*:

> Therefore what, then, are the things being prepared for those who wait? The Creator and Father of the ages, the All-holy one himself, knows their magnitude and beauty. Therefore *let us strive* to be found among the number of those who wait, so that we may have a share in the gifts which were promised. (*1Cl* 35.3–4, emphasis added)[10]

---

[7] BDAG, p. 861. NT *hapax*.

[8] BDAG, p. 861.

[9] BDAG, p. 17. Occurs 7x in NT, 2x in PE: 1Ti 6:12; 2Ti 4:7. Note that the noun "fight" is the nominal form of this verb.

[10] See also *2Cl* 7.

The basic idea involved is to expend effort to reach a goal. In Josephus, the opponents of Trypho were ready to fight for their very lives as that is what was at stake. Their goal was to live; they would strive (fight) for that goal with whatever effort was necessary. Likewise, in *First Clement*, the author exhorts his readers to strive to be included within those who are God's. They are to expend whatever effort necessary (discussed in *1Cl* 35.5–12) to meet this exhortation.

In First Timothy, Paul exhorts Timothy to enjoin and continue the fight. Paul uses this same language at the close of Second Timothy:

> For I am already being poured out as a drink offering, and the time of my departure is imminent. *I have fought the good fight*, I have completed the race, I have kept the faith. Finally, the crown of righteousness is reserved for me, that the Lord, the righteous Judge, will award to me on that day, and not only to me, but also to all who have loved his appearing. (2Ti 4:6–8, emphasis added)

Paul used a similar metaphor earlier in First Timothy:

> I am setting before you this instruction, Timothy my child, in accordance with the prophecies spoken long ago about you, in order that by them *you may fight the good fight*, having faith and a good conscience, which some, because they have rejected these, have suffered shipwreck concerning their faith, among whom are Hymenaeus and Alexander, whom I have handed over to Satan, in order that they may be taught not to blaspheme. (1Ti 1:18–20, emphasis added)

In 1Ti 1:18, however, "you may fight the good fight" is stated differently in the underlying Greek with terms perhaps better translated "wage the good warfare" as it uses military terminology; [11] "fight the good fight" is more generic. In 6:12, the "good fight" is "of the faith." In 2Ti 4:7, the "good fight" is equated with finishing the race and keeping the faith. And in 1Ti 1:18, the "good warfare" is waged by "holding faith and a good conscience." The struggle is properly enjoined when motivated and fueled by faith.

It is significant that First Timothy opens (1:18) and closes (6:12) with usage of similar alliterative metaphor. Paul is closing the discussion he opened earlier, and preparing to conclude his letter.

Take hold of the eternal life

"Take hold" is a translation of the Greek word ἐπιλαμβάνομαι.[12] The same word is used later in this chapter:

---

[11] See comment on 1Ti 1:18.

[12] BDAG, p. 373. Occurs 19x in NT; 2x in PE: 1Ti 6:12, 19.

> to do good, to be rich in good works, to be generous, sharing freely, storing up for themselves a good foundation for the future, in order that *they may take hold of what is truly life.* (1Ti 6:18–19, emphasis added)

In both instances, "life" (ζωή)[13] is what is taken hold of. In verse 12 Paul exhorts Timothy; in verse 19 he describes a goal to Timothy for the Ephesians to strive toward. In both cases, this is "eternal life."

The word translated "eternal" is αἰώνιος. The sense of αἰώνιος is typically either 'eternal' (without beginning or end) or 'without end.'[14] The word is an adjective, and it usually modifies "life" (ζωή) as it does here.[15] The meaning is "life without end."

to which you were called

This is a prepositional phrase that uses a relative pronoun ("which") to refer back to "eternal life." Paul specifically notes that Timothy was "called" into eternal life. The word translated "you were called" is the verb καλέω. Here it means 'choose for receipt of a special benefit or experience;' or simply 'call.'[16] The word is used in this particular sense throughout the New Testament and other early Christian literature. It is used in Second Timothy:

> Therefore, do not be ashamed of the testimony about our Lord, nor me his prisoner, but suffer along with me for the gospel, according to the power of God, who saved us and *called* us with a holy calling, not according to our works but according to his own purpose and grace that was given to us in Christ Jesus before time began, (2Ti 1:8–9, emphasis added)

In Second Timothy, the special experience is being called "to a holy calling." In other uses, though, the calling from eternal death and into eternal life is highlighted:

> But you are a chosen race, a royal priesthood, a holy nation, a people for God's possession, so that you may proclaim the virtues of the one who *called* you out of darkness into his marvelous light, who once were not a people, but now are the people of God, the ones who were not shown mercy, but now are shown mercy. (1Pe 2:9–10, emphasis added)

Similar use is found in *First Clement*:

---

[13] See comment on 1Ti 1:16.

[14] BDAG, p. 33. Occurs 71x in NT; 8x in PE. See comment on 1Ti 1:16.

[15] In Pauline literature, αἰώνιος modifies another concept 18x: 'life' (10x); 'times' (3x); 'God' (1x); 'house' (1x); 'destruction' (1x); 'comfort' (1x); 'glory' (1x).

[16] BDAG, p. 503. Occurs 148x in NT; 2x in PE: 1Ti 6:12; 2Ti 1:9.

> But we will be innocent of this sin and will ask, making earnest prayer and supplication, that the number of those who are counted among his elect throughout the whole world, the Creator of everything may guard unharmed through his beloved child Jesus Christ, through whom *he called* us from darkness into light, from ignorance into the knowledge of the glory of his name. (*1Cl* 59.2, emphasis added)

In *First Clement*, not only is the calling from darkness (eternal death) into light (eternal life) evident, but the status of those in the light as "counted among his elect ... through his beloved child Jesus Christ" is also made plain.

According to Paul, this is the sort of calling that Timothy has been called into.

and confessed the good confession

Paul reminds Timothy that he has "confessed the good confession" about eternal life.[17] The verb is ὁμολογέω, here in the sense of 'acknowledge,' 'claim,' 'profess,' or 'praise;'[18] the accusative noun translated "confession" is ὁμολογία.[19] This combination of words[20] is also found in Philo's tractate *On the Change of Names*:

> Therefore admiring this same disposition when thus taking to flight, and submitting to a voluntary fall by reason of *the confession which it had made* respecting the living God, namely, that he stands in truth and is one only, while all other things beneath him are subject to all kinds of motions and alterations, he speaks to it, and allows it to enter into conversation with him, saying, "And I, behold my covenant is with thee." (Philo, *Names* 57, emphasis added)[21]

In Philo, confessing the confession involves adherence to a statement concerning the "living God," who, among other things, "stands in truth and is one only." The one who confesses this confession believes it is the truth. Similarly, Timothy "confessed the good confession" regarding eternal life in the presence of many others. At a particular point in time, Timothy stated adherence to a particular truth concerning eternal life; the same truth about eternal life that Paul professed earlier in the letter:

> The saying is trustworthy and worthy of all acceptance: Christ Jesus came into the world to save sinners, of whom I am the foremost. But because of this I was shown

---

[17] Note that "confessed the good confession" is similar in structure to "fight the good fight" which starts the verse.

[18] BDAG, p. 708. Occurs 26x in NT; 2x in PE: 1Ti 6:12; Tt 1:16.

[19] BDAG, p. 709. Occurs 6x in NT, 2x in PE: 1Ti 6:12, 13. Notably three of the remaining four instances occur in Hebrews: 3:1; 4:14; 10:23. The final instance is found in 2Co 9:13.

[20] ὁμολογέω as verb with accusative ὁμολογία

[21] See also Philo, *Abraham* 203.

> mercy, in order that in me foremost, Christ Jesus might demonstrate his total patience, for an example for those who are going to believe in him for *eternal life*. (1Ti 1:15–16, emphasis added)

Making the confession about eternal life means one has confessed his belief that Jesus Christ is the Messiah; that eternal life is found only through Him, the one who saves sinners.

in the presence of many witnesses

This confession is not made in isolation; it is made "in the presence of many witnesses." The phrase "in the presence" is a translation of the Greek preposition ἐνώπιον, which is used similarly throughout First Timothy.[22][23]

---

[22] See comment on 1Ti 2:3 and 5:21 for more discussion. Also: 1Ti 5:4, 20, 21; 6:12, 13. The preposition occurs twice in 2Ti: 2:14; 4:1.

[23] On "witnesses," see comment on 1Ti 5:19.

Exhortation to Proper Teaching (1Ti 6:13–16)

I command you, in the sight of God who gives life to all things and Christ Jesus who testified the good confession before Pontius Pilate, that you observe the commandment without fault, irreproachable until the appearing of our Lord Jesus Christ, which he will make known in his own time, the blessed and only Sovereign, the King of those who reign as kings and Lord of those who rule as lords, the one who alone possesses immortality, who lives in unapproachable light, whom no human being has seen nor is able to see, to whom be honor and eternal power. Amen. (1Ti 6:13–16)

Verse 13

I command you, in the sight of God who gives life to all things

Again, the preposition ἐνώπιον ("in the sight") is used;[1] here combined with παραγγέλλω.[2] Paul here implores Timothy; to underscore the seriousness he formally commands Timothy "in the presence of God … and Christ Jesus."

The structure here is similar to the charge in 1Ti 5:21.[3] A charge verb is used, followed by ἐνώπιον, followed by a list of witnesses. Compare the two verses:

> I command you, in the sight of God who gives life to all things and Christ Jesus who testified the good confession before Pontius Pilate, (1Ti 6:13)

> I testify solemnly before God and Christ Jesus and the elect angels that you observe these things without prejudice, doing nothing according to partiality. (1Ti 5:21)

In 1Ti 5:21, there are three witnesses (God, Christ Jesus, and the "elect angels"). In 1Ti 6:13 there are only two witnesses, each further modified by a clarifying statement. In the first portion of the verse, God is further described as the one "who

---

[1] See comment on 1Ti 5:21.

[2] See comment on 1Ti 1:3 and 4:11.

[3] It is also very similar to the charge in 2Ti 4:1–5.

gives life to all things." The word translated "who gives life" is ζωογονέω, here meaning 'give life to' or 'make alive.'[4] The word is used similarly in the Septuagint:

> The Lord puts to death and *brings to life*; he leads down to the grave and leads up. (1Sa 2:6 [LXX 1Kgdms 2:6], emphasis added)

Paul uses the word with similar meaning in First Timothy. Paul not only charges Timothy in God's presence; he reminds Timothy that the eternal life in which Timothy partakes has God as its ultimate source. This points back to 1Ti 6:12 and possibly 1Ti 1:17.

and Christ Jesus who testified the good confession before Pontius Pilate

Additionally, Paul charges Timothy in the presence of Christ Jesus. Paul further describes Christ Jesus as the one who "testified the good confession before Pontius Pilate." Compare this to 1Ti 6:12:

> Fight the good fight of the faith; take hold of the eternal life to which you were called, and *confessed the good confession* in the presence of many witnesses. (1Ti 6:12, emphasis added)

Christ Jesus "confessed the good confession" before Pontius Pilate; the result was his crucifixion. Timothy has "confessed the good confession" before many witnesses. Paul is implicitly stating that Timothy is following the sound doctrine, he is enacting the words of Christ.[5]

Verse 14

that you observe the commandment without fault, irreproachable

Verse 13 described the ones whom Paul made the charge before; now the content of the charge is made explicit. This is translated similarly to the earlier charge of 1Ti 5:21:

> I testify solemnly before God and Christ Jesus and the elect angels that you *observe* these things without prejudice, doing nothing according to partiality. (1Ti 5:21, emphasis added)

---

[4] BDAG, p. 431. Occurs 3x in NT: Lk 17:33; Ac 7:19; 1Ti 6:13.

[5] See comment on 1Ti 6:3 where "sound doctrine" is essentially equated with following the words of Jesus.

The similarity of the translation of these two charges, however, is not because the underlying Greek text is the same. 1Ti 5:21 uses a different charge verb (διαμαρτύρομαι instead of 6:13's παραγγέλλω)[6] and a different verb translated "observe" (φυλάσσω instead of 6:14's τηρέω).[7]

One of Timothy's responsibilities is to keep the commandment "unstained." The Greek word is ἄσπιλος, here meaning 'pure' or 'without fault.'[8] The word is used similarly in James:

> Pure and undefiled religion in the sight of our God and Father is this: to look after orphans and widows in their affliction, and to keep oneself *unstained* by the world. (Jam 1:27, emphasis added)

In James, the goal is to keep oneself unstained; in First Timothy it is to keep the commandment unstained. *Second Clement* uses ἄσπιλος as well:

> For after we depart from the world, we are no longer able to confess or even repent in that place. So then, brothers, having done the will of the Father and having kept the flesh pure and having obeyed the commandments of the Lord, we will receive eternal life. For the Lord says in the gospel, "If you did not guard the small things, who will give you the big things? For I say to you that whoever is faithful with the least important is also faithful with the very important." Therefore he means this: keep the flesh pure and the seal *unstained*, in order that we may receive eternal life. (*2Cl* 8.3–6, emphasis added)

In *Second Clement*, the "seal" is unstained. Remaining unstained involves ensuring that one keeps himself from things that taint. The stain ruins purity; thus anything that stains is to be avoided. For Timothy, who is to keep the commandment unstained, this is a call to adhere to and promote the sound doctrine.

In addition to being unstained, the commandment is to be "irreproachable." These two phrases—"unstained" and "irreproachable" are appositional; they both state the same basic idea, albeit in two different ways. The Greek word is ἀνεπίλημπτος, here used in the sense of 'free from reproach.'[9] This is very similar to use of the word earlier, both in 1Ti 3:2 and 5:7.

---

[6] On παραγγέλλω, see comment on 1Ti 1:3.

[7] See comment on 1Ti 5:21; also note τηρέω is discussed in 1Ti 5:22.

[8] BDAG, p. 144. Occurs 4x in NT: 1Ti 6:14; Jam 1:27; 1Pe 1:19; 2Pe 3:14.

[9] BDAG, p. 77. Occurs 3x in NT: 1Ti 3:2; 5:7; 6:14. See comment on 1Ti 3:2.

until the appearing of our Lord Jesus Christ

A temporal restraint is placed on Timothy's charge. He is to keep the commandment "unstained and irreproachable"—proclaim the sound doctrine properly—until Christ's appearing. The word translated "appearing" is ἐπιφάνεια, here in the sense of 'appearance.'[10] The word occurs in similar context (a charge to Timothy) in Second Timothy:

> I solemnly charge you before God and Christ Jesus, who is going to judge the living and the dead, and by his *appearing* and his kingdom, (2Ti 4:1, emphasis added)

In Second Timothy, ἐπιφάνεια the reference does not specify a temporal boundary (as it does in 1Ti 6:14), but it does refer to the same chronological time, the return of Christ; or, when he appears again.

VERSE 15

which he will make known in his own time

The Greek word translated "he will make known" is δείκνυμι. Here the sense is 'point out,' 'show,' or 'make known.'[11] Similar use occurs in the *Epistle of Barnabas*:

> But when he chose his own apostles (who were going to preach his gospel, who were wicked above all sin) in order that *he might demonstrate* that "he came not to call the righteous, but sinners." Then he revealed himself to be the Son of God. (*Ep. Barn.* 5.9, emphasis added)

What will be made known? This is in reference to Christ's appearing, mentioned in v. 14. This appearing will happen "in his own time." This phrase is used earlier in the letter (1Ti 2:6) and also in the salutation to the epistle to Titus:

> Paul, a slave of God and an apostle of Jesus Christ for the faith of the chosen of God and the knowledge of the truth that is according to godliness, in the hope of eternal life which God, who does not lie, promised before eternal ages, but *at the proper time* has disclosed his message in the proclamation with which I was entrusted according to the command of God our Savior, (Tt 1:1–3, emphasis added)

This same phrase also occurs in *First Clement*:

---

[10] BDAG, p. 385. Occurs 6x in the NT, 5x in PE: 1Ti 6:14; 2Ti 1:10; 4:1, 8; Tt 2:13. The other NT instance is 2Th 2:8.

[11] BDAG, p. 214. Occurs 30x in NT, only here in PE.

> The earth, bearing fruit according to his purpose, *at the proper season*, in full abundance, both for humans and beasts and all the living beings that exist upon it, puts forth food without dissent and without changing any of the things decreed by him. (*1Cl* 20.4, emphasis added)

Again, this is a temporal reference referring to the timing of the appearance of the Lord Jesus Christ. Timothy knows not when Christ will appear; he only knows that Christ will appear, and that he is to continue preaching the sound doctrine until then.

the blessed and only Sovereign

Next is a description of the returning Christ, which sounds very much like a benediction,[12] that runs through verse 16. Much of the vocabulary of this section is familiar, having been used earlier in chapter 1. The word translated "blessed" is μακάριος;[13] here an adjective modifying "Sovereign." The same word was used earlier in 1Ti 1:11:

> according to the glorious gospel of the *blessed* God that I was entrusted with. (1Ti 1:11, emphasis added)

In both cases, μακάριος modifies a noun referring to deity. In 6:15, not only is the Sovereign blessed, he is the "only" Sovereign. The word translated "only" is μόνος.[14] Similar use also occurs in 1Ti 1:17:

> Now to the King of the ages, immortal, invisible, to the *only* God, be honor and glory forever and ever. Amen. (1Ti 1:17, emphasis added)

In 1Ti 1:17, μόνος is used as an adjective modifying a noun of deity, just as it is in 1Ti 6:15. Both adjectives in 6:15, μακάριος and μόνος, modify the Greek word δυνάστης. This word is typically translated as 'ruler' or 'sovereign.'[15] The word is used similarly (of God) in Second Maccabees:

> Then he also fell upon a certain city, bridging over that which was enclosed with fortifications and walls and inhabited by a variety of Gentile peoples. And its name was Caspin. But those within, trusting in the strength of its walls and in their store of food, began treating those with Judas rudely, reviling them and, even more, blaspheming and saying what is not lawful to say. But those with Judas, after calling upon the great *ruler* of the universe who, without battering rams and devices serving as instruments of war, threw down Jericho in the times of Joshua,

---

[12] Note also the benediction in 1Ti 1:17.

[13] BDAG, p. 610. Occurs 50x in NT; 3x in PE: 1Ti 1:11; 6:15; Tt 2:13.

[14] BDAG, p. 658. Occurs 114x in NT; 7x in PE.

[15] BDAG, p. 264. Occurs 3x in NT: Lk 1:52; Ac 8:27; 1Ti 6:15.

> savagely attacked the wall. And overtaking the city by the will of God, they carried out a massive slaughter, so that the adjacent lake, which had a width of two stadia, appeared to be filled, running with blood. (2Ma 12:13–16, emphasis added)

In Second Maccabbees, the word δυνάστης refers to the one who delivered Judas Maccabeus and his men. In First Timothy it likewise refers to the "blessed and only" sovereign, God, who is further described in following lines (running through the end of verse 16).

the King of those who reign as kings and Lord of those who rule as lords

Both of these phrases are somewhat curious in the Greek. They are not simply combinations of nouns ([*singular*] of [*plural*]) but a combination of noun and substantive participle. The end is the same as if only nouns were used[16] ("King of kings and Lord of lords") but the path is slightly different. In both cases it is clear the God is exalted above all other kings and lords, be they earthly or heavenly.

VERSE 16

the one who alone possesses immortality

The word translated "alone" is the Greek word μόνος, just used in v. 15. God alone has "immortality." This is a translation of ἀθανασία.[17] The only other NT occurrences of the word are in First Corinthians:

> For it is necessary for this perishable body to put on incorruptibility, and this mortal body to put on *immortality*. But whenever this perishable body puts on incorruptibility and this mortal body puts on *immortality*, then the saying that is written will take place: "Death is swallowed up in victory." (1Co 15:53–54, emphasis added)

This passage makes clear that immortality (the inability to die) is the opposite of mortality (being able and even destined to die).

---

[16] Note that the phrase "King of kings and Lord of lords," using nouns only, appears in Re 19:16.

[17] BDAG, p. 23. Occurs 3x in NT: 1Co 15:53, 54; 1Ti 6:16.

who lives in unapproachable light

The word translated "lives" is the Greek verb οἰκέω.[18] The same word is used in the *Epistle to Diognetus*:

> *They live* in their own countries, but as aliens. They share in everything as citizens and endure everything as foreigners. Every foreign country is their country, and every country is foreign. (*Ep. Diog.* 5.5, emphasis added)

In First Timothy, God dwells not in a physical location (a country) but in "unapproachable light." The word translated "unapproachable" is ἀπρόσιτος. Josephus uses the word in *Antiquities of the Jews*:

> When he had said this, he ascended up to Mount Sinai, which is the highest of all the mountains that are in that country, and is not only very difficult to be ascended by men, on account of its vast altitude, but because of the sharpness of its precipices also; nay, indeed, it cannot be looked at without pain of the eyes; and besides this, it was terrible and *inaccessible*, on account of the rumor that passed about, that God dwelt there. (Jos., *Ant.* 3.76, emphasis added)

The example from Josephus is relevant because it describes the inaccessibility of Mount Sinai almost to the point of absurdity and also because it uses the concept of inaccessibility (or unapproachability) in conjunction with God dwelling in the unapproachable place.

whom no human being has seen nor is able to see

The Greek word εἶδον occurs twice in this verse, translated "has … seen" and "see." God is not seen, he is invisible—which matches the benediction given earlier, in 1Ti 1:17:

> Now to the King of the ages, immortal, invisible, to the only God, be honor and glory forever and ever. Amen. (1Ti 1:17)

to whom be honor and eternal power. Amen.

The only and blessed Sovereign who is immortal and unapproachable, who cannot be seen; this one deserves "honor" and "eternal power." The Greek word translated "honor" is τιμή, which also occurs in the previous benediction found in 1Ti 1:17, where it has similar meaning.

---

[18] BDAG, p. 694. Occurs 9x in NT, only here in PE.

The word translated "power" is κράτος, meaning 'power,' 'rule,' or 'sovereignty.'[19] It occurs in a benediction in First Peter (along with the concept of eternity) as well:

> Just as each one has received a gift, use it for serving one another, as good stewards of the varied grace of God. If anyone speaks, let it be as the oracles of God; if anyone serves, let it be as by the strength that God provides, so that in all things God will be glorified through Jesus Christ, to whom is the glory and the *power* forever and ever. Amen. (1Pe 4:10–11, emphasis added)

It is also used in a benediction, again with the concept of an eternal reign, in *First Clement*:

> The grace of our Lord Jesus Christ be with you and with everyone everywhere who have been called by God through him, through whom to him be the glory, honor, *power* and majesty, and an eternal throne from eternity into eternity, amen. (*1Cl* 65.2, emphasis added)

Thus associating the notion of power or rule in the context of God's eternal reign is not unknown or uncommon. The picture would be as easily understood then as it is now: God reigns, and as such He deserves all honor and subservience that can be given Him.

[19] BDAG, p. 565. Occurs 12x in NT, only here in PE.

Wealthy Believers in the Fellowship (1Ti 6:17–19)

> *Command those who are rich in this present age not to be proud and not to put their hope in the uncertainty of riches, but in God, who provides us all things richly for enjoyment, to do good, to be rich in good works, to be generous, sharing freely, storing up for themselves a good foundation for the future, in order that they may take hold of what is truly life. (1Ti 6:17–19)*

Verse 17

Command those who are rich in this present age not to be proud

The word translated "command" is παραγγέλλω, used earlier in 1Ti 4:11 and 5:7.[1] The word translated "rich" is the Greek word πλούσιος, here with the sense of 'rich' or 'wealthy.'[2] These are further qualified via prepositional phrase as being rich "in this present age." This same prepositional phrase is used in the epistle to Titus:

> For the grace of God has appeared, bringing salvation to all people, training us in order that, denying impiety and worldly desires, we may live self-controlled and righteously and godly *in the present age*, looking forward to the blessed hope and the glorious appearing of our great God and Savior Jesus Christ, who gave himself for us, in order that he might redeem us from all lawlessness and purify for himself a people for his own possession, zealous for good deeds. (Tt 2:11–14, emphasis added)

In both instances (First Timothy and Titus) it is clear that the present age is the one currently being experienced; it will pass when Jesus Christ returns. From here, Paul launches into a five-fold charge for Timothy to deliver to the Ephesians.

The first command is to "not be proud." Here, Paul is not charging Timothy; he is instead instructing Timothy to first charge those "rich in this age" to not be proud. This is a translation of ὑψηλοφρονέω, meaning 'be proud,' 'be haughty,'[3] or perhaps

---

[1] See comment on 1Ti 4:11.

[2] BDAG, p. 831. Occurs 28x in NT, only here in PE.

[3] BDAG, p. 1045. NT *hapax*, though note Byzantine/TR editions of Ro 11:20 use ὑψηλοφρονέω.

'be high-minded.'[4] The "not" comes from a negator. A more colloquial translation might be 'to not be snooty.'

and not to put their hope in the uncertainty of riches

The second portion of the charge is also negative. The phrase 'to put their hopes' is a translation of the Greek word ἐλπίζω, meaning 'to put confidence in something or someone.'[5] Here the confidence is being put on "the uncertainty of riches." The word translated "uncertainty" is the Greek word ἀδηλότης,[6] witnessed only here in the NT. While an NT hapax, the meaning is relatively certain; it is the negative form of the well-attested word δῆλος, meaning 'clear,' 'plain,' or 'evident.'[7]

In this context, "riches" are uncertain. This is a translation of πλοῦτος, meaning 'wealth.'[8] The problems with riches were tackled previously, in 1Ti 6:3–10; thus wealth is not a foundation upon which one should set his hope.

but in God, who provides us all things richly for enjoyment,

In contrast with the two negative portions of the charge comes a positive portion. Do not be proud, do not put hope in the uncertainty of riches, but put your hope on God. The positive portion uses the same verb, ἐλπίζω, to show that instead of hoping on riches (which are uncertain) one should hope on God (who is very certain).

Paul further describes the God upon whom he wants the Ephesians to set their hope. God is the one "who richly provides us with everything to enjoy." The word translated "richly" is the adverb πλουσίως, meaning 'richly' or 'abundantly.'[9] The repetition of "riches" (πλοῦτος /πλουσίως) is important. Instead of hoping on the uncertainty of riches; one should hope on the certainty of God, who will provide richly.

The word "provides" is a translation of the Greek word παρέχω, typically meaning 'grant' or 'show.'[10] Here the word is a substantive participle, with definite article, leading to the translation "who provides." The word is used similarly, in the context of God giving benefit, in the *Epistle to Diognetus*:

---

[4] LSJ, p. 1909.

[5] BDAG, p. 319. Occurs 31x in NT; 4x in PE: 1Ti 3:14; 4:10; 5:5; 6:14. See comment on 1Ti 3:14.

[6] BDAG, p. 19. NT *hapax*.

[7] BDAG, p. 222.

[8] BDAG, p. 832. Occurs 22x in NT; only here in PE.

[9] BDAG, p. 831. Occurs 4x in NT; 2x in PE: 1Ti 6:17; Tt 3:6.

[10] BDAG, p. 776. Occurs 16x in NT; 3x in PE: 1Ti 1:4; 6:17; Tt 2:7.

> But since he was revealed through his beloved child and made known all the things prepared from the beginning, at the same time *he gave* everything to us, both to have a share in his benefits and to see and understand, who of us would ever have expected these things? (*Ep. Diog.* 8.11, emphasis added)

In First Timothy, the benefit given is "everything to enjoy." "Everything" is a translation of πᾶς, which generally means 'all' or 'every.'[11] The word "enjoy" is a translation of the Greek word ἀπόλαυσις, with the sense of 'enjoyment.'[12] Hebrews uses this word:

> By faith Moses, when he was grown up, refused to be called the son of Pharaoh's daughter, choosing instead to be mistreated with the people of God rather than to *experience* the transitory enjoyment of sin, (Heb 11:24–25, emphasis added)

Usage similar to First Timothy is found in *First Clement*:

> The stations of the winds complete their service without stumbling according to their own season. And the ever-flowing springs created *for enjoyment* and health supply sustenance for human life without fail. And the smallest of the animals accomplish their intercourse[9] in harmony and peace. (*1Cl* 20.10, emphasis added)

Here, Clement speaks of things created "for enjoyment." The *Didache* uses similar language, noting things given for men "to enjoy":

> You, All-Powerful Master, you have created all things for the sake of your name. Both food and drink you have given to the people *for enjoyment*, so that they might give thanks to you. But to us you have graciously given spiritual food and drink and life eternal through your son. (*Did.* 10.3, emphasis added)

The sense is the same in First Timothy. God abundantly provides all that is needed for enjoyment. Fixing one's hope on God, then, is better than hoping on riches.

Verse 18

to do good

After the short digression on God's abundant provision, Paul returns to his charge. The third item in the charge is "to do good." This is a translation of the verb ἀγαθοεργέω, here meaning 'do good' or 'confer benefits.'[13] The word is also used in Acts:

---

[11] BDAG, p. 782. Occurs 1243x in NT.

[12] BDAG, p. 115. Occurs 2x in NT: Heb 11:25; 1Ti 6:17.

[13] BDAG, p. 2. Occurs 2x in NT: Ac 14:17; 1Ti 6:18.

> And yet he did not leave himself without witness by *doing good*, giving you rain from heaven and fruitful seasons, satisfying you with food and your hearts with gladness." (Ac 14:17, emphasis added)

TDNT provides a summary of the use of the word in First Timothy:

> In the admonition to the rich in 1 Tm. 6:18, it signifies a demand for good action consisting in the demonstration of love to others.[14]

to be rich in good works

The fourth portion of the charge continues with the idea of being rich. The word translated "to be rich" is the verb πλουτέω, 'be rich.' This is the same underlying root that was seen earlier in verse 17, the "*rich* in this present age," "uncertainty of *riches*," and "who *richly* provides."

In this portion of the charge, richness is redirected from material wealth to the area of good works. This brings to recollection 1Ti 2:10:

> Likewise also the women should adorn themselves in appropriate clothing, with modesty and self-control, not with braided hair and gold jewelry or pearls or expensive clothing, but with *good deeds* which are fitting for women who profess godliness. (1Ti 2:9–10, emphasis added)

While 1Ti 2:10 was directed specifically to women in the fellowship, 6:18 is directed toward all those who are "rich in this present age," both women and men. They are all to be rich in good works.

to be generous, sharing freely

The fifth portion of the charge to those who are rich in the present age is to be generous and ready to share. The phrase "to be generous" is a translation of the infinitive form of εἰμί ('to be') and the word εὐμετάδοτος, meaning 'generous'[15] or even 'readily imparting.'[16] This is combined with "ready to share," a translation of κοινωνικός, which has the sense of 'liberal' or 'generous.'[17] This word is also used in Josephus' *Wars of the Jews*:

> These men are despisers of riches, and so very communicative as raises our admiration. Nor is there any one to be found among them who hath more than another; for it is a law among them, that those who come to them *must let what*

[14] TDNT, 1:17

[15] BDAG, p. 409. NT *hapax.*

[16] LSJ, p. 722.

[17] BDAG, p. 553. NT *hapax.*

> *they have be common to the whole order*,—insomuch, that among them all there is no appearance of poverty or excess of riches, but every one's possessions are intermingled with every other's possessions: and so there is, as it were, one patrimony among all the brethren.(Jos., *Wars* 2.122, emphasis added)

In First Timothy, Paul's emphasis is to ensure that those who are wealthy put their trust in the Lord, not in their wealth. If one's hope is in the Lord, then one's material goods will be used with that end in sight. If one's hope is in wealth, then their hope will be revealed by their actions.

Verse 19

storing up for themselves a good foundation for the future,

The phrase "storing up" is a translation of ἀποθησαυρίζω, meaning 'store up' or 'lay up.'[18] The same word is used in Sirach:

> The one who honors his father will make atonement for sins, and the one who glorifies his mother is like one who *stores up treasure*. (Sir 3:3–4, emphasis added)

Josephus uses the word as well:

> There was also found here a large quantity of all sorts of weapons of war, which *had been treasured up* by that king, and were sufficient for ten thousand men; there was cast iron, and brass, and tin, which show that he had taken much pains to have all things here ready for the greatest occasions; (Jos., *Wars* 7.299, emphasis added)

The idea is of storing something valued for later use. Here Paul advocates the content of his charge—setting hope on God and using material wealth in the service of God instead of relying upon it for future certainty—as a method of storing up what really matters.

A "good foundation" is what is being stored up. The word translated "good" is καλός, a very common word with the general sense of 'good.'[19] The word translated "foundation" is θεμέλιος, here meaning 'a stable foundation.'[20] Philo uses θεμέλιος similarly:

> "And he is accursed beyond all the beasts of the field." And I mean by this, beyond all the passions of the soul, for it is only there that the mind is wounded and

---

[18] BDAG, p. 110. NT *hapax*.

[19] BDAG, p. 504. Occurs 101x in NT.

[20] BDAG, p. 449. Occurs 12x in NT, 2x in PE: 1Ti 6:19; 2Ti 2:19.

> destroyed. Why then does this one appear to be worse than all the other passions? Because it is almost at the bottom of them all, as a sort of base or foundation for them, for desire originates in the love of pleasure, and pain consists in the removal of pleasure; and fear again is caused by a desire to guard against its absence. So it is plain that all the passions are anchored on pleasure; and perhaps one might say that they would absolutely have had no existence at all if pleasure had not been previously laid down as *a foundation* to support them. (Philo, *Alleg. Interp.* III 113, emphasis added)

The foundation (θεμέλιος) is the thing laid down that supports and perhaps even directs future action.

This foundation is "for the future." The word "future" is a translation of the Greek word μέλλω, meaning 'in the future' or 'to come.'[21] The word is used similarly in *First Clement*:

> Isaac, knowing *what was about to happen* with confidence, gladly was brought as a sacrifice. (*1Cl* 31.3, emphasis added)

The foundation is for the time which is about to come, the future.

in order that they may take hold of what is truly life.

This is a subordinate clause, providing the reason for the charge of verses 17–18. Paul wants these wealthy members of the Ephesian fellowship to set their hope on God, to focus on good works, and be generous with their resources. In this, he echoes a phrase from verse 12, "Take hold of the eternal life"[22] by imploring the wealthy members to take hold of "that which is truly life." The word translated "truly" is the adverb ὄντως,[23] used similarly in 1Ti 5:3:

> Honor widows who are *truly* widows. (1Ti 5:3, emphasis added)

In following Paul's charge, the wealthy will set their hopes on God, and therefore take hold of that which is truly life.

---

[21] BDAG, p. 628. Occurs 109x in NT.

[22] See comment on 1Ti 6:12.

[23] BDAG, p. 715. Occurs 10x in NT; 4x in PE: 1Ti 5:3, 5, 16; 6:19. See comment on 1Ti 5:3.

FINAL WORDS TO TIMOTHY (1TI 6:20–21A)

O Timothy, guard what has been entrusted to you. Turn away from pointless empty talk and contradictions of what is falsely called knowledge, which some, by professing it, have deviated concerning the faith. (1Ti 6:20–21a)

VERSE 20

O Timothy, guard what has been entrusted to you.

In this last portion of the letter, Paul addresses Timothy by name. The information that follows is important.

Paul instructs Timothy to "guard what has been entrusted." The word "guard" is a translation of the Greek verb φυλάσσω. Here, in the imperative, it means 'guard' or 'protect.'[1] Similar language is used in Second Timothy:

> *Guard* the good deposit through the Holy Spirit who lives in us. (2Ti 1:14, emphasis added).

Similar language is found in the *Didache*:

> Do not ever forsake the commandments of the Lord, but guard what you have received, neither adding to nor taking away from. (*Did.* 4.13, emphasis added)[2]

Paul wants Timothy to protect what he has received. In this case, Timothy has received "what has been entrusted" to him. This is a translation of παραθήκη, meaning 'deposit' or 'property entrusted to another.'[3] In this case, it likely refers to the teaching of Paul. This same language is used in Second Timothy, in 1:14 (cited above) and in 1:12:

> for which reason also I suffer these things. But I am not ashamed, because I know in whom I have believed, and I am convinced that he is able to guard *what I have entrusted* until that day. (2Ti 1:12, emphasis added)

In 2Ti 1:12, Paul notes that Jesus Christ is "able to guard what I have entrusted until that day;" in 2Ti 1:14 notes that the indwelling Holy Spirit is the agent Timothy

---

[1] BDAG, p. 1068. Occurs 31x in NT; 5x in PE: 1Ti 5:21; 6:20; 2Ti 1:12, 14, 2Ti 4:15.

[2] See also *Ep. Barn.* 19.11.

[3] BDAG, p. 764. Occurs 3x in NT: 1Ti 6:20; 2Ti 1:12, 14.

should use to guard what was entrusted to him. The deposit (παραθήκη) is "the spiritual heritage entrusted to the orthodox Christian."[4] Paul has railed against false doctrine and encouraged sound, true doctrine throughout the letter. This sound, true doctrine has been entrusted to Timothy; he is to guard it and teach it, that it may be known.

This also brings to mind 1Ti 1:18, "I am setting before you this instruction, Timothy, my child."[5] The verb "setting before you" is cognate with the noun in 1Ti 6:20, "what has been entrusted." Thus it may be that the content of the letter (so, from chapter 2 through chapter 6) is the teaching entrusted to Timothy.

Turn away from pointless empty talk and contradictions of what is falsely called knowledge,

Paul next notes some things that Timothy is to avoid. The Greek word is ἐκτρέπω; a word used previously in 1Ti 1:6 and 5:15.[6] He is to turn away from "pointless empty talk." The word translated "pointless" is βέβηλος, meaning 'pointless' or 'worthless.'[7] It describes "empty talk," a translation of κενοφωνία. Here it means 'chatter' or 'empty talk.'[8] The two words are also used together in Second Timothy:

> But avoid *pointless chatter*, for it will progress to greater ungodliness, (2Ti 2:16, emphasis added)

This is vain talk; chatter that has no value whatsoever in the context of teaching the sound doctrine.

Timothy is also to avoid the "contradictions of what is falsely called 'knowledge.' " The word translated "contradictions" is ἀντίθεσις, here representing a 'statement that involves contradiction or inconsistency.'[9] This same word is used in Philo's tractate *On Drunkenness*:

> Nor indeed is any one ignorant that scarcely anything whatever of existing things, if you consider it in itself and by itself, is accurately understood; but by comparing it with its opposite, then we arrive at a knowledge of its true nature. ... In the same way also, in whatever is referred to virtue or to vice, what is advantageous is recognised by a comparison with what is injurious, what is beautiful by a

---

[4] BDAG, p. 764.

[5] See comment on 1Ti 1:18.

[6] See comment on 1Ti 1:6.

[7] See comment on 1Ti 4:7; see also the alternate sense used in 1Ti 1:9. BDAG, p. 173. Occurs 5x in NT: 1Ti 1:9; 4:7; 6:20; 2Ti 2:16; Heb 12:16.

[8] BDAG, p. 539. Occurs 2x in NT: 1Ti 6:20; 2Ti 2:16.

[9] BDAG, p. 88. NT *hapax*.

> comparison with what is unseemly, what is just and generally good, *by placing it in juxta-position* with what is unjust and bad. And, indeed, if any one considers everything that there is in the world, he will be able to arrive at a proper estimate of its character, by taking it in the same manner; for each separate thing is by itself incomprehensible, but by a comparison with another thing, is easy to understand it. (Philo, *Drunkenness* 186–187, emphasis added)[10]

The first sentence is important; it explains what is meant to be accomplished with the comparisons. That which is good is seen and known by comparing it with its opposite, that which is bad. In this way, good is the *antithesis* (ἀντίθεσις) of bad. In First Timothy, Paul is setting up a similar juxtaposition: That thing which "is falsely called 'knowledge'" is the exact opposite. The doctrine being preached is false, it is the antithesis of the sound doctrine espoused by Paul.

The word translated "falsely called" is ψευδώνυμος, meaning 'falsely bearing a name' or 'falsely called.'[11] Philo uses the word in his tractate *On the Embassy to Gaius*:

> But when our pleadings on behalf of justice were thus broken up, and cut short, and interrupted, and crushed as one may almost say, we, being wearied and exhausted, and having no strength left in us, but being in continual expectation of nothing else than death, could not longer keep our hearts as they had been, but in our agony we took refuge in supplications to the one true God, praying him to check the wrath of this *falsely called* god. (Philo, *Embassy* 366, emphasis added)

Here, Philo uses ψευδώνυμος to distinguish between the true God (to whom he prays) and the falsely-called god. Paul uses ψευδώνυμος similarly, to distinguish between the true knowledge and the false knowledge of the opponents in Ephesus.

The word translated "knowledge" is the Greek word γνῶσις. The word generally means 'knowledge,'[12] and here it is best translated in its general sense.[13] This false knowledge may be contrasted with the "knowledge of the truth" in 1Ti 2:4:

> This is good and acceptable before God our Savior, who wants all people to be saved and to come to a *knowledge of the truth.* (1Ti 2:3–4, emphasis added)

God, the one who saves, desires all to come to "knowledge of the truth." False knowledge, therefore, is dangerous and must be avoided.

---

[10] See also Philo, *Providence II* 2

[11] BDAG, p. 1097. NT *hapax.*

[12] BDAG, p. 204. Occurs 29x in NT; only here in PE.

[13] "The lack of knowledge about any clearly definable 'Gnostic' system as object of attack in 1 Ti suggests that the definition of γ. be left sufficiently general for this passage." BDAG, p. 204.

Verse 21a

which some, by professing it,

The word translated "professing" is ἐπαγγέλλομαι, here meaning 'profess' or 'lay claim to.'[14] The word is used similarly in 1Ti 2:10:[15]

> Likewise also the women should adorn themselves in appropriate clothing, with modesty and self-control, not with braided hair and gold jewelry or pearls or expensive clothing, but with good deeds which are fitting for women who *profess* godliness. (1Ti 2:9–10, emphasis added)

Here, in 1Ti 6:21, the falsely-called knowledge is being professed, and such profession has consequences.

have deviated concerning the faith

The consequence of professing the falsely-called knowledge is deviating from the faith. The word translated "have deviated" is the verb ἀστοχέω, meaning 'miss,' 'fail,' 'deviate,' or 'depart.'[16] This word was used near the beginning of First Timothy:[17]

> But the goal of our instruction is love from a pure heart and a good conscience and a faith without hypocrisy, from which some *have deviated*, and have turned away into fruitless discussion, wanting to be teachers of the law, although they do not understand either the things which they are saying or the things concerning which they are speaking confidently. (1Ti 1:5–7, emphasis added)

The use of ἀστοχέω in 1Ti 1:6 is similar to that of 6:21.

	1:6	6:21
Who swerved:	Certain persons	some
What they swerved from:	love from pure heart, good conscience, sincere faith	the faith
What they swerved into:	vain discussion	irreverent babble and contradictions

---

[14] BDAG, p. 356. Occurs 15x in NT, 3x in PE: 1Ti 2:10; 6:21; Tt 1:2.

[15] See comment on 1Ti 2:10.

[16] BDAG, p. 146. Occurs 3x in NT, all in PE: 1Ti 1:6; 6:21; 2Ti 2:18.

[17] For further information on ἀστοχέω, see comment on 1Ti 1:6.

BENEDICTION (1TI 6:21B)

Grace be with you all. (1Ti 6:21b)

VERSE 21B

Grace be with you all.

This benediction is standard for the Pastoral Epistles (cf. 2Ti 4:22; Tt 3:15) and is similar to most Pauline letter closings that offer grace to the letter's readers. Its distinctive feature is the plural "you," rendered as "you all," which almost seems out of place in a personal letter such as First Timothy (and the balance of the Pastorals). It is possible to read this final sentence as evidence that the letter was intended to be read aloud to the Ephesian believers instead; it is also possible that Paul (or, in this case, his amanuensis) closed all letters in the plural.

INDEXES

INDEX OF GREEK WORDS

Index of Scripture References

Hebrew Bible

Deuterocanonical and Apocryphal Literature

New Testament

Index of Ancient Sources

Apostolic Fathers

Clement of Rome

Ignatius of Antioch

Polycarp of Smyrna

Didache

Epistle of Barnabas

Shepherd of Hermas

Epistle to Diognetus, Papias

WORKS OF JOSEPHUS

Works of Philo

Old Testament Pseudepigrapha

Other Material

About Appian Way Press

The *Appian Way Press* is a new venture. An experiment. An outlet to publish useful resources with a focus on exegesis and teaching that might not otherwise be published.

The name *Appian Way Press* refers to one of the earliest roads established in Ancient Rome, the *Via Appia*. For centuries — and even now — if you were going to Rome or leaving Rome, you would likely spend some time on this road. In the same way, the *Appian Way Press* hopes to establish an easily traversed conduit into and out of scholarship as it relates to Biblical Studies.

For more information about *Appian Way Press*:

- **Web:** http://appianwaypress.com
- **Email:** info@appianwaypress.com
- **Twitter:** @AppianWayPress
- **Facebook:** https://www.facebook.com/AppianWayPress
- **Faithlife:** https://faithlife.com/appian-way-press

13075059R00199

Made in the USA
San Bernardino, CA
13 December 2018